LOUISA MAY ALCOTT

LOUISA
MAY
ALCOTT

Madeleine B. Stern

RANDOM HOUSE
NEW YORK

Library of Congress Cataloging-in-Publication Data

Stern, Madeleine B., 1912–
Louisa May Alcott / by Madeleine B. Stern.
p.   cm.
Includes bibliographical references (p.   ) and index.
ISBN 0-679-76949-8 (acid-free paper)
1. Alcott, Louisa May, 1832–1888—Bibliography.   2. Women
authors, American—19th century—Biography.   I. Title.
PS1018.S75   1996
813'.4—dc20
[B]   95-30242

Manufactured in the United States of America on
acid-free paper
2 4 6 8 9 7 5 3
First Random House Edition

To

LEONA ROSTENBERG

A faithful friend is a strong defense;
And he that hath found him hath found a treasure.

When the family history, out of which this remarkable authorship grew, shall be told to the public, it will be apparent that few New England homes have ever had closer converse with the great things of human destiny than that of the Alcotts.

— *The Boston Herald*, MARCH 7, 1888

She unlatches the door to one house, and . . . all find it is their own house which they enter.

— CYRUS BARTOL

She is a natural source of stories. . . . She is and is to be, the poet of children. She knows their angels.

— RALPH WALDO EMERSON

ACKNOWLEDGMENTS

For their invaluable aid in the preparation of this biography, I wish to thank my mother, Mrs. Lillie M. Stern, and my friend Miss Leona Rostenberg, who, by their constructive criticism and ceaseless encouragement, lightened the task at every step.

I wish to thank Mr. Van Wyck Brooks for his generous criticism of the manuscript.

I wish also to thank the John Simon Guggenheim Memorial Foundation for the grant that expedited the preparation of this biography.

To the curators and librarians of the following institutions, as well as to the owners of private collections of significant Alcott material, I should like to express my gratitude for the privilege of examining manuscripts, letters, and documents: The Louisa May Alcott Association, for the use of important source material in the Orchard House; Miss Sarah R. Bartlett, for some of the material in the Concord Public Library; Mr. Charles B. Blanchard, for material at Little, Brown and Company; Mr. Percy Whiting Brown, for his collection of the Alcott-Hosmer correspondence; Mr. Zoltán Haraszti, for material at the Boston Public Library; Mr. William A. Jackson, for the important collection at The Houghton Library; The New York Historical Society, for the Alcott-Redpath correspondence; Mr. F. W. Pratt, for some of the material at the Concord Public Library; Mr. Paul North Rice, for material at the New

York Public Library or in the Berg Collection; Miss Clara Endicott Sears, for the important sources at Fruitlands; and the late Mr. Carroll A. Wilson, for his Alcott letters and documents.

To the following individuals or libraries I wish to express my thanks for information, letters, pictures, and photostats: Mrs. Margaret L. S. Adamson; Dr. M. May Allen; American Antiquarian Society; the late Mrs. Larz Anderson; Miss Katharine Anthony; Miss Mary R. Botsford; Mrs. Dorothy K. Brintnall; Mr. James L. Bruce of The Bostonian Society; Miss Mary H. Buckingham; Mrs. Herman Burr; Mr. Frank H. Burt; Mr. T. P. Carter; the Hon. Charles A. Chandler; Mrs. Meriel Whitman Chapman; Rev. Mr. Hugh Clark; Columbia University; Concord Antiquarian Society; Mr. Frederic W. Cook; Mr. Henry H. Crapo; Mr. J. Dembinski; Miss Annie A. Dunne; Mr. P. D. Fallon; Miss Minnie Farnsworth; Mr. William M. Fitzgerald; Mr. Allyn B. Forbes; Mrs. George M. Forbes; Miss Lillian Gilson; Mr. Henry Halladay; Dr. P. M. Hamer; Mrs. Jessie M. Haynes; Miss Josephine Hewins; Historical Society of Pennsylvania; Mr. Cyrus Hosmer; Miss Mary Hovey; Mrs. Clara M. Howe; Mr. M. A. de W. Howe; Mr. Jerome C. Hunsaker; Huntington Library; Mrs. M. H. S. Jenney; Mrs. George Johnson; Miss Elizabeth Almy Jones; Mr. Loring P. Jordan; Miss Rosabelle Kelp; Mrs. George S. Keyes; Mr. J. B. Kincer; Miss Leva Lash; Mrs. Lucretia Little; Miss Margaret Lothrop; Mr. Albert Edgar Lownes; Miss Elizabeth Lowrie; Miss Grace McClary; Mrs. M. A. McDowell; Dr. Archibald Malloch; Mr. Horace Mann; Mrs. Marie de Mare; Mrs. Mary Vaughan Marvin; Mrs. K. D. Metcalf; Miss Genevieve Miller; Mrs. Harris P. Mosher; Mr. Jack Neiburg; Mr. G. H. Noyes; Mr. E. H. O'Neill; Mr. Michael Papantonio; Mrs. Herbert Payson; the late Mr. Arthur Pforzheimer; Mrs. B. Alcott Pratt; *Publishers Weekly*; Mrs. A. M. Pugh; Miss Cornelia Raymond; Mr. E. H. Redstone; Prof. William Howell Reed; Registry Department of Boston; Mrs. Bert Roller; George Routledge and Sons; Miss Marian B. Rowe; Mrs. S. P. Rugg; Mr. F. Savage; Mr. R. B. Shipley; Mrs. Vida Croly Sidney; Mr. Rollo G. Silver; Dr. William M. Siskind; Mrs. S. Stern; Mrs. Anna M. Stevens; Mr. M. Storey; Mr. Robert

L. Straker; Mr. Arthur Sullivan; Syracuse Public Library; Miss Marion Talbot; Mr. Mayo Tolman; Mr. William N. Tolman; Mrs. S. Alice Trickey; Miss Joan Trumbull; University of Pennsylvania; Mr. Samuel Vaughan; Dr. Burnham S. Walker; Mrs. J. Y. G. Walker; Mr. Robert A. Ware; Mrs. Abraham E. Weigel; Miss Frederika Wendté; Miss Charlotte West; Mrs. Caleb Wheeler; Miss Mary Wheeler; Miss Viola C. White; Mr. Edmund A. Whitman; Mr. and Mrs. John Pratt Whitman; Miss Katharine May Wilkinson; Mr. H. W. Winkley; Yale University; Mr. Malcolm Young.

Finally, I wish to thank the editors of *Americana, American Notes & Queries, More Books,* and *The New England Quarterly,* for permission to use or reprint material originally published in those periodicals.

MADELEINE B. STERN

New York City

CONTENTS

Almost half a century after its first appearance, Random House now reintroduces my biography of Louisa May Alcott to the public. It is an occasion not only to rejoice at longevity but to reflect upon causes and effects, episodes and their influences.

Researching that biography involved many pivotal incidents, but perhaps the most consequential was a visit to a book collector who lived on Horatio Street in New York City, where he had amassed extensive Alcott holdings. I was accompanied, those many decades ago, by my lifelong friend and future partner in the rare-book business, Leona Rostenberg. Carroll Atwood Wilson turned out to be a charming, generous, and most helpful source of information. The evening spent in his home was—for Leona Rostenberg, for myself, and for Louisa May Alcott— epochal.

Having shown us his treasures—his first editions of Alcott, his collection of her letters and related materials—Mr. Wilson made two landmark suggestions. To Leona he said: "Miss Rostenberg, we all suspect, from Miss Alcott's remarks in her journals as well as from Jo March's clandestine literary ventures in *Little Women,* that Louisa May Alcott had some sort of pseudonym and wrote sensational stories over that pseudonym. I know," he continued, "that you have done quite some work in printing history. Why don't you set out to discover the Alcott pseudonym and the thrillers she wrote?" Then Carroll Wilson turned to me and said: "Go on and complete this biography, Miss Stern, and be sure to apply for a Guggenheim so you can complete it more quickly."

Carroll Wilson's two injunctions proceeded to make history of a sort. I did apply for a Guggenheim Fellowship, and described my plans for a biography in the following somewhat pretentious but certainly sincere terms:

> I shall endeavor not only to re-create Louisa Alcott, making her, as she was, a living, breathing, extremely *human* being—with all her moods and dissatisfactions, her humor and courage, her love of family and her growing slavery to her pen—but also to make the world in which she moved come alive again. It is my belief that no biography is really a written life, a *bios*, unless the reader is made to see the streets along which the subject walked, the clothes she wore, the food she ate, the whole rich background against which she lived.... Louisa Alcott's "stockings with a profusion of toe, but no heel" are, in themselves, trivial, but when they appear on feet that marched three times around the Common, they help to round out and complete the picture.

I added that I also planned to trace Alcott's literary development "from the witch's cauldron to the family hearth."

The tracing of that evolution, from the gruesome plots and violent villains of the early comic tragedies, to the serenity of her domestic novels, was made possible by the fulfillment of Carroll Wilson's other injunction. Leona Rostenberg, who had accompanied me to Horatio Street on that portentous night, also accompanied me to Harvard's Houghton Library, where we both worked through the masses of Alcott family papers and manuscripts brought to our desk. Seated side by side, we took notes on a journal entry or a phrase in a letter, a comment by Bronson Alcott, a reference to sister Anna or May. Nothing was heard but the scraping of a pencil or the turn of a page. Suddenly the profound stillness of the decorous library room was shattered by a war whoop from my seatmate. Leona had come upon a small clutch of papers, five letters from a Boston publisher to dear Miss

Alcott. The letterhead listed the periodicals published by his firm. And he himself—Mr. James R. Elliott of Elliott, Thomes and Talbot—disclosed to the discoverer Rostenberg and the biographer Stern a secret that had been kept for more than three-quarters of a century. "We would like more stories from you," he wrote, "like 'Behind a Mask' or 'V.V.' or 'A Marble Woman.' And if you prefer, you may use the pseudonym of A. M. Barnard or any other man's name if you will. And, if we like them, we will publish them."

Louisa Alcott late in life confessed to an interviewer that her "natural ambition" was for the "lurid style. I indulge in gorgeous fancies and wish that I dared inscribe them upon my pages and set them before the public." Now we knew that she had indeed yielded to that style, those fancies, and set them before the public. At least three of her sensation stories could be traced, read, savored, placed in the context of her life. The evolutionary path from witch's cauldron to family hearth could be illuminated.

In a diary kept during the period of my Guggenheim Fellowship I recorded my readings, my visits to Alcott relatives and friends, clues followed, and Leona's publication of her discovery in the *Papers of the Bibliographical Society of America*. While I sought to integrate Louisa Alcott's background with her life, my own insinuated itself in mine. World War II had forced most libraries to place their treasures in safekeeping "for the duration," and as a result very few issues of the nineteenth-century story periodicals that had emblazoned Alcott's thrillers in their columns were available. I could read enough of them, however, to analyze their plots and characterizations, and appreciate the fervor with which the author of *Flower Fables* released her own emotions in imagined tales of violence and revenge. All this I sought to intertwine in my account of Alcott's life.

In the fullness of time, the biography was finished. I believed I had conciliated background with character and conveyed a sense of the extraordinary literary professional who could experiment successfully with so many different genres. One of the most curious of the many episodes connected with my Alcott biography is that it was published thanks to a footnote. An annotation about me in an article published by a scholarly periodical stated that I had just completed a biography of Louisa May Alcott. The University of Oklahoma Press was just releasing a book by an Oklahoma professor, Sandford Salyer, entitled *Marmee: The Mother of Little Women*. The Press's director, the astute, delightful and learned Savoie Lottinville, noted the footnote, realized the benefit of publishing a companion piece, and sent me a contract for *Louisa May Alcott*. It was published in April, 1950, and reviews were in general appreciative.

The consensus was that, from a "mass of published and unpublished material" Alcott's life had been reconstructed "as she lived it, integrated with the period in which she lived." Since that had been my purpose, as presented to the Guggenheim Foundation, I was satisfied. Even more satisfying is the 1995 statement by an Alcott scholar, Barbara Sicherman, that "the classic biography is still Madeleine B. Stern's *Louisa May Alcott*." It is interesting that, although only a few of the sensation stories had been analyzed in the biography, critics at the time saw fit to mention them. The new biography, one pundit remarked, traced Alcott's "rise from the author of potboilers in lean days to an influential position in the literary world." According to another, the biography explained "how a writer of sensational potboilers . . . became the author of one of America's best-loved classics."

It is of course this last transposition that has fascinated readers and challenged critics. Both the Rostenberg article, "Some Anonymous and Pseudonymous Thrillers of Louisa M. Alcott," and my own biography had made the fact of that transposition known. At that time, however, no one except Rostenberg and myself had actually read the so-called sensational potboilers concocted by a needy Louisa May Alcott before *Little Women* turned her words into gold nuggets. They had never been excavated from the now-crumbling pages of nineteenth-century weekly story periodicals and presented in reprint to the public.

There was good reason for this apparently inexplicable omission. Between 1950, when the Alcott biography appeared, and

1975, when I published the first collection of her thrillers, I was otherwise engaged. Besides serving as partner in the rare-book business founded by Leona Rostenberg, I was searching out other lives and writing other biographies. One of them was curiously linked with my work on the author of *Little Women*. As the University of Oklahoma Press put it in a catalogue: "Miss Stern's current plan is to follow the Alcott biography with a biography of [another] American woman."

That other "American woman" who attracted my attention was Miriam Florence Squier Leslie, generally known as Mrs. Frank Leslie. She had been head of a mammoth New York publishing house founded by one of her husbands, Frank Leslie. Her private life included four husbands (the last of them Oscar Wilde's brother Willie) as well as a number of lovers. Her public life had been punctuated with drama and melodrama. Her career could have provided Alcott with a succession of sensation stories by A. M. Barnard. And, as it turned out, she had actually published some of Alcott's "potboilers." This biography of Mrs. Frank Leslie, *Purple Passage*, occupied the period after publication of the Alcott life. Other books, rare and otherwise, consumed the years that followed.

It was not until 1974 that I conceived the idea of tracing as many of the Alcott sensation stories as possible to their ephemeral newspaper sources, compiling and reprinting a volume of them. The result was *Behind a Mask: The Unknown Thrillers of Louisa May Alcott*, published in 1975 and including four stories: "Behind a Mask: or, A Woman's Power," a forceful feminist tale; "Pauline's Passion and Punishment," a story that won a $100 prize from *Frank Leslie's Illustrated Newspaper*; and two other narratives originally issued by Alcott's Boston publisher, Elliott, Thomes and Talbot: "The Mysterious Key" and "The Abbot's Ghost."

Reaction to *Behind a Mask* was gratifying. Critics were intrigued; the paperback rights were sold; a stage adaptation of one of the stories was performed off Broadway; and Barbara Walters interviewed me on the *Today* show. Ms. Walters, interested as she was in the dichotomy between the Alcott who had written

"Pauline's Passion" and the Alcott who had written *Little Women*, was perhaps more concerned with the question of why Alcott had never married. At all events, interest in Louisa Alcott's other life was intense enough to allow for a second volume a year later. *Plots and Counterplots: More Unknown Thrillers of Louisa May Alcott* presented five stories for public enchantment, including the two that James R. Elliott had bought from dear Miss Alcott in 1865: "V.V.: or, Plots and Counterplots" by A Well Known Author, and "A Marble Woman: or, The Mysterious Model" by A. M. Barnard. Those stories had been discussed in my biography of Alcott, but not until now had they become available to readers.

The results were inevitable. The building blocks for reconstruction were at hand, and revisionist critics were eager to start work. One reviewer astutely commented after publication of the Alcott page-turners, "Never again will you have quite the same image of this particular 'little woman.'" The first new image of "this particular 'little woman'" was sculpted by Martha Saxton in a book entitled *Louisa May: A Modern Biography of Louisa May Alcott*. There Alcott was envisioned as an undesirable character from one of her own thrillers. Saxton saw her subject as a "withdrawn, hostile introvert," who suffered from both a "deep fear of men" and her own "devils of guilt." According to Saxton, the portrait of Pauline in "Pauline's Passion" as a "wicked and grotesque" member of her sex was in reality a self-portrait.

The reassessment continued, as more of the anonymous and pseudonymous Alcott effusions were traced and reprinted. The Alcott persona was revised to reflect the darker aspects of the woman who had come to be revered as the "Children's Friend," but who was now becoming a character in her own sensation fiction. At the same time, all the Alcott oeuvre was reevaluated in light of her thrillers. Even *Little Women* and its successors, *Little Men* and *Jo's Boys*, were not immune from critics in hot pursuit of gender relations, power struggles, and sexual politics.

The tendency to search out hidden meanings is perhaps too much with us today. Revisionists are upon occasion guilty of manufacturing motives, prying out deviations, reshaping the causes and consequences of events to their own purposes, revising for the sake of revision. In the case of Louisa May Alcott, such reinterpretations are very tempting, since she herself provided such an intriguing arsenal of ammunition. Although she kept her role in sensational literature secret, she continued to be fascinated by it. When the need or the desire arose, she used and re-used her melodramatic inventions. In 1873, when she wrote her autobiographical novel *Work: A Story of Experience*, she incorporated in it much of her thriller "A Nurse's Story," a sensation tale woven about the theme of inherited insanity, published originally in *Frank Leslie's Chimney Corner.* A few years later, when she was asked to contribute a full-length novel to her publisher's "No Name Series" of anonymous books, she turned back to a sensation novel she had written a decade earlier. Originally entitled "A Modern Mephistopheles or The Long, Fatal Love Chase," it had been refused by James R. Elliott on the grounds that it was too long and too sensational. A century later nothing can be too long or too sensational. Random House has recently issued the novel as *A Long Fatal Love Chase*, as well as a Modern Library edition of selected Alcott thrillers. In 1877, eager to comply with the request for an anonymous novel, Alcott bethought herself of the story that had been turned down. As a professional writer engaged in the revision process, she culled from her rejected effort a variety of Satanic allusions, a Mephistophelian character, and a title: *A Modern Mephistopheles.*

The fact that Louisa May Alcott was throughout her life a professional author skilled in creation and the re-creation implicit in revision must never be overlooked. To obscure that power she possessed and exercised in a mist of artificial interpretations and manipulated reconstructions is factitious. It reminds me of another recent Alcott misinterpretation. This biography of Louisa May Alcott is dedicated to Leona Rostenberg over words quoted from the Bible: "A faithful friend is a strong defense; And he that hath found him hath found a treasure." *Wit and Wisdom of Women*, an anthology published in 1993, includes that biblical quotation— and attributes it to Louisa May Alcott!

Louisa May Alcott was the author neither of Hell nor of Heaven, but of a multitude of stories in a variety of literary genres, ranging from fairy tales to realistic war sketches, from sensation thrillers to domestic sagas. For all of them she used as source material episodes from her life, her observations, her travels, her experiences, her reading. Even the thrillers that have triggered so much revisionist criticism are based in large measure upon the life she lived. That life included depths and heights, in the course of which she went through a humiliating period as a domestic servant and became the recipient of nationwide paeans of praise as *the* Miss Alcott. It included poverty and opiates for pain, and it included riches from within and from without. It included especially a loving but atypical father, a loving but overworked mother, and sisters who made a warm and loving home in spite of the extremes of poverty. Throughout Alcott's life, her devotion to that family was the motivation for most of her action, the spur that led to overwork and perhaps to premature death.

This is the Alcott portrayed in my biography, marching around Boston Common in her heelless stockings, concocting stories, living out her very human life. And this is the enduring image of Alcott, an image that revision cannot change.

LOUISA MAY ALCOTT

🕸🕸

CHAPTER I

The South End

Mrs. Meribah Beach was strangely puzzled by the noise that issued from the upstairs room of her sedate boardinghouse at 3 Somerset Court. As far as she knew, November 28, 1835, was no holiday. Surely Mr. Bronson Alcott, for all his idiosyncrasies, was too much the gentleman to make such a disturbance, though his wife was not above occasional outbursts. Anna was so docile and obedient that she could not possibly be the source of the commotion. Could little Louy Alcott make all that noise by herself? That, sighed Mrs. Beach, was all too possible.

Bronson Alcott's blue eyes opened wide with a wonder that was not entirely serene and his wife's darker eyes danced with a sympathetic sparkle as their daughters' antiphonal chorus speedily worked itself into a mighty crescendo:

"Today is more exciting than personating Hannah Lee in the Snow Storm."

"Or seeing the Circus at the Lion Tavern."

"Or watching Signor Blitz at the Concert Hall."

Above such heights neither of the little girls could be transported. The celebration of Louy's birthday, and Father's, too, by the pupils of the Temple School was more exciting than the jugglery of Signor Blitz.

It required as much skill and patience as Mrs. Alcott could muster to brush little Louy's long dark hair back from her high forehead, for the child persisted in running to the window to make sure that the snow was still on the ground. As she tied the strings of her velvet bonnet, Mother tried to explain to Louy that actually tomorrow was her birthday, but since that was Sunday, the celebration would take place today. As far as Louy was concerned, there was no distinction whatsoever; to all intents and purposes she had already reached the heights of three years of age, and in anticipation of the coming celebration danced about the room so wildly that the legerdemain of Signor Blitz himself was needed before her gaiters could be properly adjusted. Even the little ceremony of kissing baby Lizzie good-bye was a trying delay, but at last shawls and gaiters and bonnets were approximately where they belonged, and the family was ready to walk to the Temple School.

The red brick of Somerset Court was redder because it was Louy's birthday. The gilded letters on the signboards were more golden than ever before, as hand in hand with Mother and Anna, Louy skipped along the cobblestones of Bowdoin Street. The sign of the blue ball on the Hancock House was never so blue, and as they caught a glimpse of the old stone mansion on the Hill, Father came springing along to tell for the twentieth time the wonderful stories of Louy's Great-Aunt Hancock, into whose august presence Mr. and Mrs. Alcott had once been received to partake of a roast carved by the great lady herself. For once Louy was too excited to listen to the account of Great-Aunt's acquaintance with Martha Washington and Lafayette, and was glad that Father's story ended just as the towers of the Masonic Temple loomed into view.

Louy's bright eyes widened as Anna led her little sister round rooms 7 and 8 at the very top of the Temple. There was too much to see all at once—the large Gothic window lighting up the carpets, Father's arclike desk facing it, the busts of learned men in the four corners, the figure of Silence with raised finger on the table, the globes, the slates, and the blocks. Proudly Anna pointed out the books, while Father took occasion to murmur once again his deep regret that there were so very few suitable to the wants of the young. He had in mind, he went on quietly, a tale embodying the simple facts and persons and scenery of the family, for there was no class of writing more happy in its influence upon children than that which embodied the lives of children. At the moment, however, Louy was far more interested in examining Father's pupils than in hearing him dilate upon the deficiencies of Mrs. Plumtree's *Stories for Children.* There were many girls and boys, all seated in a semicircle around Father's desk, intent upon their slates, while Miss Peabody bustled about, her petticoats peeping where they should not be peeping. From nine to ten, while the children wrote in their journals, Louy tiptoed round the room, looking over Samuel Tuckerman's shoulder or peering into Lemuel Shaw's pensive face as he scribbled away.

At last the clock pealed the hour of ten, and the great moment had begun. With excitement not to be subdued even by Mr. Alcott's gentle remonstrances, the pupils marched to the desk to crown their teacher and his little daughter with wreaths of laurel. Her crown tilted on the side of her head, Louy listened gravely to an address given in the name of the school by one of the pupils, at the close of which the boys offered a beautiful book called *Paradise Lost* to Father. Then, having taken their seats once more, the children looked up at their teacher, at the fair face with the corn-colored silken hair and the blue eyes that gazed serenely down upon the group. Speaking in quiet, slow tones, Mr. Alcott explained that instead of conversing as usual on Saturdays at ten o'clock upon the Gospels of the life of Christ, he would today take another child for his text and speak about himself, showing his pupils the milestones in another Pilgrim's Picture Progress. In broad strokes he painted the scenes of his early life, telling the pupils that he had been born on November 29, 1799, at Spindle Hill, in the Connecticut village of Wolcott with its tiny common and sandy roads. How well he recalled the evenings in the south room, when his father wove baskets while his mother examined her spinning wheel, and his brothers and sisters pared apples or sewed. As for himself, he had learned to write with charcoal on the planks of the kitchen floor, while his mother churned butter and baked bread. Later on he had thawed his ink to write a diary, for with whom, after all, should one become better acquainted than with one's most familiar companion, oneself?

Louy could not help wishing that he would soon become better acquainted with her own self and get on with the story so that she would be included. But Father was still telling about his own school days, when mending pens, setting copies, and pointing the alphabet had been considered more important than reading Miss Edgeworth's *Moral Tales*. He had found books, however, *The Dignity of Human Nature*, and, best of all, *Pilgrim's Progress*.

Father was showing another picture now, in his own Pilgrim's Progress, the picture of Miss Abigail May, a tall lady with flashing dark eyes and masses of chestnut hair, whom he had met at her brother's home. One of her ancestors had been Judge Samuel Sewall, who had condemned the witches to be hanged, but he had atoned for his misdeeds, and her father had been warden of King's Chapel. What a pretty picture he painted now, of Miss May in her plaid silk walking dress with the puff sleeves and her black beaver hat, joining his hand in marriage on May 23, 1830.

Just before she could pinch Samuel Tuckerman in her excitement, Louy caught her father glancing toward the figure of Silence and turned to hear of the removal to Germantown, where four years ago Anna had been born, and of the school where, with William Russell, Father had taught as agent of the Great Instructor Himself. And then, at last, she heard with bubbling enjoyment of the double white house with its row of pines in the front, its garden and orchard, of the Rookery Cottage where, shortly after Friend Haines had died, little Louy had been born, on November 29, three years ago. She had been named for her aunt, Louisa May Greele, who had been known for her charming voice and her gentle nature, and Father ardently hoped that the present possessor of the name would deserve a place in the estimation of society.

At this Louy could not restrain a perceptible puffing-up and would have pulled Lucia Peabody's hair had not Lucia been so deeply interested in hearing how the school in the Masonic Temple had been opened the year before, so that Mr. Alcott could read at close hand those illuminated textbooks, those breviaries of doctrine, that all children were to him. And then he turned the pictures quickly, telling of Lizzie's birth last June, and of how she had been named after Miss Peabody, their distinguished teacher. To bring the pictures up to date, he told his audience of three recent events in his life, of his abandonment of animal food, at which pronouncement Mrs. Alcott could not restrain a brief sigh; of his first encounter last month with a Mr. "Emison," in the village of Concord, a very great man indeed; and finally of his visit, three days later, to see Mr. Garrison behind a grated window in the Leverett Street Jail. The last two pictures, he thought, were symbols of the times—a lean, angular man in a white cottage at the fork of the roads in Concord, writing down his thoughts, and another, behind the grated windows of a Boston jail, living out his thoughts.

Setting her laurel wreath in place, Louy forgot the gravity of the moment, and listened eagerly to one of the girls recite an ode in honor of the double birthday:

A time for joy,—for joy!
  Let joy then swell around;
From every girl and boy
  Let joy's full tones resound.

This hour in love we come,
  With hearts of happy mirth;
We've sallied forth from home
  To celebrate a birth.

A time for joy,—for joy!
  Let joy then swell around;
From every girl and boy
  Let joy's full tones resound.

Finally, the crowning moment when refreshments were to be served arrived, and Father lifted his little daughter to a table to dispense the cakes. To each child she handed a cake as the pro-

cession marched past. But Lucia Peabody was left, besides herself, and in solitary splendor on the plate there reposed one last
cake. Glancing toward her mother, Louy clutched it tightly.
Then Mrs. Alcott whispered quietly, "It is always better to give
away than to keep the nice things. I know my Louy will not let
the little friend go without." It was hard to watch the plummy
cake go into Lucia Peabody's eager hand, especially after such a
day, but a kiss stopped the tears from flowing. No kiss, however,
could make Louy understand why the day had just fallen short of
being perfect.

Winter was not winter to Louy without a race along the paths, a
race as swift as the whistling of the sharp winds through the bare
boughs of the ginkgo tree and the English elms. Right outside the
Common there was the thrilling slide down the Long Coast,
where she daringly imitated the boys who pitched down the coast
headforemost. Her own shrill cry of "Lullah" mingled with the
shouts of the coasters as "South End" sleds vied with "West End"
sleds for the honor of the race.

The only delight of winter that equaled the joys of coasting
for Louy was 'Lection Day on the Common. Her 'Lection money
in her pocket, she wandered about with Mother and Anna along
the malls with their rows of tents, trying to decide just how to
spend the precious pennies. Should she buy a seedcake, or would
it be wiser to peep through the telescope for a view of astronomi-
cal wonders? Faced by such endless rows of oysters and tamarinds
and gingernuts, how could one little girl decide?

Yet there was a quieter joy that could sometimes vie with the
splendors of the Common. It was pleasant to watch Father as he
sat in his study, stroking his knee or drawing diagrams on the
table. It would not do to interrupt him while he read about Mr.
Coleridge's thoughts or wrote about baby Lizzie in an endless pile
of papers called "Psyche." Soon, however, he would turn from his
books to teach Louy how to trace letters and to copy his beauti-
fully printed words so that later on she would learn "scrip" hand.
If she became too restless or made too many blots on the paper, he

would let her build towers and bridges out of his huge dictionaries, or look at the pictures in *The Story Without an End*, to which he was writing a preface. And if the pictures were simply too enticing, he would read the story aloud, while Anna listened in wonder and Louy gradually left off building London Bridge. "There was once a Child who lived in a little hut, and in the hut there was nothing but a little bed and a looking-glass which hung in a dark corner." Surely Louy was the child who shook dewdrops from the cowslip and set a little breakfast upon a lime leaf. It was she who spoke to the dragonfly and the waves, or the rose and the larkspur, learning that "nothing returned inwards, but rather that all strove outwards into the free air." And after *The Story Without an End* that ended all too soon, Father would speak to Anna and Louy about the state of their consciences, telling them gravely to follow the star of promise first seen in their early morning, to act out their genius, for nothing else availed.

If Father forgot occasionally that Louy was not yet four and therefore grew a little weary when he went on to read Krummacher's parable on the "Progress of Sin," then her new little rocking chair would creak ominously, and her small hand would be instinctively tempted to pinch Anna or even Father, right in the spot where those two deep wrinkles swept down to the corners of his mouth. "You don't wish to do that," he would suggest gently. But she did wish to do just that. Why would she never be so well behaved as little Ariadne Bliss, whose exemplary conduct she should follow? Father went on to murmur that her fiery temper was inherited from those peppery Mays, that her temperament was bilious and demonic, unlike his own sanguine nature, and that no doubt was left in his mind that his daughter was not a child of light.

It was Mother who tried to explain to Louy that Father was preoccupied at present, that there were not so many pupils at his school as there had been last year, and that therefore there would not be so many pennies for Artillery Election in June, for example, as there had been for Election proper in January. That was also the reason why, on April 1, the family moved away from Mrs.

Beach's excellent boardinghouse to number 26 Front Street, a little farther away from the Common and a little nearer to the wharves.

Front Street or Somerset Court made no difference to Louy, except that she ran into the Common through a different gate. Then "commerce," "slap everlasting," "cup and ball," and "coronella" were forgotten, for the elm trees were in leaf and the time for examining last year's hoops had come round. The boys might have their marbles and their kites to fly in the air over Park Street; Louy would drive her hoop until she had at last sent it all around the Common without a stop. And if that great day had not yet arrived, and if she had to pause at the Wishing Stone near Joy Street, what better wish was there to make than that one fine spring day she would drive her hoop around the Common so that the boys would forget their kites and their marbles and watch its perfect progress? Meantime, there were always buns to share with the baker's boy, and one-ring circuses to watch in the big tent near Beacon Street. Meantime, the elephants would wade in the Frog Pond to the end of their chains while the great willow wept to keep the waters from drying up.

Once, in her zeal to make the Wishing Stone grant her wish, Louy drove not only her hoop into that very Frog Pond, but her own self after it. Wet and bedraggled but clutching the hoop, she reached out for help and found herself lifted speedily out of the water by a pair of black arms, while a pair of black eyes twinkled beneath as black a brow, and Louy thanked her new friend and ran home to tell Mother about the Negro boy who had saved her life.

As summer unfolded, Louy found pleasures that almost equaled those of falling into the Frog Pond. Grandfather May was always ready to receive the children in his home on Washington Street at the corner of Oak. It was far more exciting than a lesson in Peale's *Graphics* at the Temple School, or even than being rescued from the Frog Pond, to sit watching Grandfather May in his smallclothes, with knee buckles set with brilliants, looking exactly like George Washington's portrait in Faneuil Hall. In his armchair by the hearth he sat, his head forward and inclined to one side, the snuffbox in one hand as he tapped it with the other, his eyes as mirthful as Louy's while he told stories of his adventures in the distant wilds of New Hampshire. And, at the end of the visit, the snuffbox would disappear, and in its place were held forth cakes and prunes and even little frocks for the girls to take home from Washington Street. Along with the prunes and the cakes Louy carried another gift, an unforgettable midsummer image of an aged man near a hearthstone, his knee buckles shining with brilliants, his fingers tapping a snuffbox.

Other images glowed before the bright eyes as the season turned to fall and then again to winter. There was the picture of the tall Concord man with the kindly eyes and stooping shoulders who came to sit and talk with a great many others at one of Father's meetings, while the children tiptoed on cat feet round the house so that the gentlemen would not be interrupted when they discussed American Genius. Better still, there was the shining, ever-changing picture of the wharves near Front Street.

Louy could not resist the temptation to wander down to Russia Wharf or Liverpool Wharf, where she saw the barrels and fig drums and crates and hogsheads, and sniffed the fragrance of mingled spices from the Indies. Once, when Mother had bought her a pair of new green shoes, Louy skipped around, past the sign of the Wharfinger, hoping that at least one fisherman would stop to gaze at the splendor of her feet. On she wandered to Rowe's Wharf and India Wharf, and the old salt stores of Long Wharf, inhaling the odor of ginger and nutmeg and dusty palm leaf. When no one at the water front would stop lifting bales of oranges or look out of the windows of the brick warehouses to see the new green shoes, Louy suddenly realized with some slight despair that not only were her feet no attraction to the West Indiamen, but that she herself was quite lost. The sun was going down and the warehouses and packet ships were shrouded in the oncoming twilight, but Louy had forgotten the way back to Front Street. She knew, of course, that Mother would find her, and until then there was nothing to do but sit on a doorstep where a curly Newfoundland dog seemed also to have found a home. A sympathetic Irish child stopped by for a moment to share his bit of salt fish with her, and then, after the picnic, she curled up on the breast of the dog and waited for Mother to come.

It was not Mother, but Mr. Wilson, the city crier, who, recollecting that he had a lost child on his list of pronouncements, shouted out his message. "Lost! A Little Girl. Curly Brown Hair. Had on a White Frock and Green Shoes." Green shoes! Why, that's me! And Mr. Wilson struck an item off his list, shouldered the little girl, green shoes and all, while the Newfoundland dog stared mournfully into the distance.

There was adventure of a different sort for Louy closer home than the Boston wharves after the new year of 1837 had begun its course. Brisk and determined, Miss Peabody had bustled away from the Temple School, her petticoats as low and her head as high as ever, and in her place the immaculately dressed Miss Fuller had arrived, a lady who seemed to know more even than Father about Greek mythology. After Father had written a book to tell everybody how well the children discussed the Gospels, some dreadful things began to happen. Louy and Anna heard him read aloud to Mother the words that wicked men had written about his book in the newspapers, the strange words they did not quite understand—"absurd," "blasphemous," "obscene." Instead of the forty pupils who had once filled the rooms on the top of the Masonic Temple, ten were left. Somehow hoop rolling had lost its delights, for in April, Father came home to say that the little desks and the figure of Silence, the bright carpets, and all the books had been sold under the auctioneer's hammer.

In April, too, the family moved again, down to the South End at 1 Cottage Place, near Mother's distant relatives, the Reeds. It was some consolation for being so far from the Common to be able to fly around the corner and play with the tiny Reed baby named William Howell, and although Faneuil Hall Market was quite distant, Louy could run off to Washington Street and press her nose against the shop windows where ivory chessmen stared back at her and a cow spouted burning gas. Always there came the desire to run back home or to walk with Father down to the small, dark basement room in the Temple where he was holding school for six pupils.

For an hour every morning, in the new home on Beach Street to which they moved in October, the little sisters sat with Father, writing, reading, drawing, spelling, defining, or talking. They read about Jesus walking on the water and Peter sinking beneath it; they discussed temperance with Father at breakfast, or heard him read for the twentieth time the story of Joseph and his Brethren. And after their unnamed little brother had been born and had died on the same April day, the sisters heard with deeper understanding than ever before the story of Christian's trials in his Pilgrim's Progress. The Granary Burying Ground became for them one kind of Slough of Despond. They saw another right in their own schoolroom when Father began to teach a little Negro girl named Susan Robinson. Lizzie and Anna and Louy, Susan, and Mr. Russell's son were all that were left now after the other children had been taken away from a school where a Negress was taught. Father looked so sad and his face was so deeply furrowed that Louy did not dare to interrupt his steady reading. At last even little Susan was dismissed, and one could hardly say there was any school at all, except that three small girls sat together while Mother taught them to sew and Father read aloud Krummacher's parable of the "Moss Rose."

South Scituate, where Uncle Sam May lived, was a pleasant place for the family to visit in the summer. It was interesting to hear Uncle Sam tell cheerfully how he had been mobbed five times in one month in Vermont. Louy loved to see his merry brown eyes light up with a twinkle of genial good nature as he sat eating boiled rice and drinking tea, declaring himself a "*tea*-totaller.*" Even more delightful than racing all the way to the Indian Spring or lording it over the boys of the village school, was the Cold Water Army that Uncle Sam had mustered. How exciting it was to march with all the children through the streets, following Uncle Sam, reciting in concert,

So here we pledge perpetual hate
To all that can intoxicate.

There were picnics, too, in the groves near North River or on the "Field of Waterloo" close to the parsonage, and rides with Father to Hingham. Louy's dark eyes grew brighter, her hair more unkempt, her limbs longer, and her ways more hoydenish than ever.

In the fall the family was back in Boston, Louy back to the Common with her hoop, Father back to his Conversations, and Mother back to her stove and her needle. At length birthday time came round again, and Mother, Lizzie, and Anna watched Father open his new portfolio and receive his pocket pincushion, while Louy read aloud his letter to her. "You are Seven years old to-day. . . . You have learned a great many things, since you have lived in a Body, about things going on around you and within you. . . . You feel your Conscience, and have no real pleasure unless you obey it. . . . It is GOD trying in your soul to keep you always Good." Louy could scarcely find the patience to read so many sentences about obedience to conscience, for way down at the bottom of the note she had spied in large, beautiful print the word "BOX." And how she rummaged through the box for the wonderful doll within, presented with a little note from Mother saying that dolly would be a quiet playmate for active Louisa, and that she should be a kind mamma. For the moment Louy could think of no wish left to make on the Wishing Stone.

Soon, she knew, she would be able to wish no more on the Wishing Stone, for Father had decided to leave Boston for the village of Concord, where Mr. "Emison" lived. There was a little cottage there, she was told, with an acre of ground, and Father would garden and give Conversations. Father, especially, had much to say about the venture, not all of which Louy understood. Time, after all, he said, was the best critic. Time was one's friend, who taught the wisdom of silence. But Father was not silent, for he went on to say that the best apples fell latest and kept longest. Besides, there was always, and there would always be, Providence.

On a spring afternoon in 1840 the Alcott trunks and the Alcott family waited at Earl's Tavern on Hanover Street for the Concord accommodation stage. Mr. Alcott was still murmuring about the beneficence of time and of Providence, Anna and Lizzie were chatting like magpies, but Louy was for once so silent and her eyes were so wide with the marvel of new events that Mrs. Alcott suddenly found herself wondering whether, of all the strange gifts of Providence, the strangest might not be this child who was among them taking notes.

🌸🌸

CHAPTER 2

The Hosmer Cottage

After its three-hour journey the stage lumbered into Concord; and while the driver tied up at the hitching post, three tired little girls climbed down from their perch to spend the night at the Middlesex Hotel.

The next day the family entered the small brown cottage behind the elm and across the river beyond Main Street. How many little rooms there were for Louy to run through, how many sheds invited her inspection, while a race after Lizzie to a nearby hilltop rewarded her with a sight of Monadnock and Wachusett looming beyond in the spring sky. Next door, there was Major Hosmer's great homestead, which Louy promptly began to investigate. Mother seemed to share her joy also, for she went singing round the house, every song a paean of thanks to Mr. Emerson, who had paid the rent, while Father calmly surveyed the little cottage and garden, remarking that though they lay low in the landscape, there was the broad sky overhead and something still of its depth of azure in his hopes.

When neighborly calls had been paid, the trunks emptied, and the new home thoroughly explored, the children settled down to the routine that Father had inaugurated. They were up with the crowing cockerels. After a breakfast of unleavened bread, water, and porridge, Louy, Anna, and Lizzie assembled with Father for an hour's study. Sometimes they would take turns reading from the New Testament about unclean appetites and evil passions. Then Father taught gymnastic spelling, showing his girls how to represent "I" by walking primly across the room, "X" by crossing his arms, "S" by contorting himself into a figure that resembled a goose's neck. After Father had finished making compasses of his legs, he would reward them with a story from Mrs. Barbauld, or better still the passage from *Pilgrim's Progress* about the pictures at the Interpreter's house. Sometimes he would simply speak with them, telling why he had come to Concord and why his children must now give up a good many things that they cherished.

Besides the bread and water of breakfast time, dinner boasted squash and potatoes, boiled rice, or graham meal, making what Father called a Pythagorean banquet where wine was water and flesh, bread. If, however, the children had not done their lessons well, Father let them go without dinner, or, if they deserved a more cruel punishment, he himself would leave the table without having touched a thing.

In the afternoon, Louy, Anna, and Lizzie went out to play with their neighbors in the homestead. Lydia Hosmer became Lizzie's special playmate in the art of feeding or spanking rag dolls; Anna took as her property the person of Henry Joseph Hosmer, and promptly fell to adoring the gentle boy, who did not completely return her affections. For Louy the choice had been obvious from the first moment she walked into the Major's homestead. Cyrus Hosmer was just a year younger than she, and so she could compete successfully when he dared her to climb the elm or leap the fence or jump from the highest beam in the barn. Occasionally it was even possible for a Boston girl to lord it a bit over her country friend by driving a hoop higher than her head to Lee's Hill.

It was satisfying, too, to put on an exhibition in the corn barn in the manner of Signor Blitz. Arrayed in Grandfather May's military suit, Louy strutted the boards in "Jack and the Beanstalk" or "Cinderella," or depicted the foolish woman who wasted her three wishes and was punished by having to wear a black-pudding nose. As stage manager, Louy assigned to Anna the role of servant girl in all domestic tragedies, and to Lizzie and Lydia the less dramatic characters of "audience," who applauded when the giant came tumbling off the loft and accommodatingly screamed when Cinderella rolled away in a vast pumpkin. At the end of such performances, when Louy's voice was hoarse and even Cy was weary of jumping from the barn loft, Mrs. Hosmer would give the Alcott girls milk to take home to Mother. Then three children, whose eyes sparkled with the glow of magic footlights, sat down for their supper of bread, apples, brown sugar, and pudding, and went to bed to dream of pudding noses, barn lofts, and Jack and the Beanstalk.

Sometimes, after a tussle with Anna over the proprietorship of a particularly desirable rocking chair, or after too daring a challenge from Cy Hosmer, Louy liked to take a ramble by herself. Once, with amazement, she saw Mr. Emerson concealing a half-smoked cigar under the railing of a fence before he walked into his house. It was always good to meet him on the roadway, gleaming and shining and smiling at Louy as if there were nothing in the world so interesting as a little girl abroad on a journey of discovery. There were many people she befriended on her excursions—Mr. Minott building a fence or feeding a cow, Mr. Bowers marshaling a Cold Water Army, Nancy Barron, the madwoman, screaming hoarsely about her visions, or Miss Mary Emerson passing briskly along, a scarlet shawl thrown over her dimity shroud. All of them walked, new figures parading before Louy's eyes; all of them welcomed the little girl with a nod or a pat or a "good day."

There was as much to hear, really, as to see, and how different the sounds were from those of Beach Street! Loring's great wagon rumbled by with its six handsome horses, while the crickets chirped and the cocks crowed as they stalked among the chips in the sun. Sometimes she heard the bleating of a woodcock, the clink of the smith's hammer, or the baying of a dog.

On the Fourth of July, she heard a martial air when twenty-six guns fired a national salute at sunrise and every bell in Concord rang merrily. Despite the red-hot weather, the bugle, drums, and fifes of the Townsend Light Infantry had already struck up energetic airs, and never had Concord Center been more abustle and astir. How lively the street was, with the long lines of teams galloping in, the baggage wagons rumbling, the stages changing horses, and carriages from each of the three great roads lumbering into Concord. Old John Wesson's fiddle had never scraped livelier tunes, and Sam Staples's smile had never been readier, his oaths never rounder, and his laugh never heartier than today. Louy's feet had never danced more lightly along the paths than now, when arm in arm with Anna and Lizzie she skipped by the crowds at the Center to wait for the Great Ball to come rolling through Concord.

Louy shouted along with all the villagers as the great parade began. She saw the Log Cabin drawn by oxen and a wheeled barrel of hard cider on tap come rolling along the Milldam. Banners and flags waved "Tippecanoe and Tyler too" in the air. To the tune of "The Old Oaken Bucket" she, with all the others, sang "Old Tip," and sported her Tippecanoe badge as proudly as if she had been an ardent Whig.

Not long after the celebration there was occasion for still greater rejoicing at home, for a new baby arrived with the dawn of July 26. Providence, Father said, was sending successive daughters of love to quicken the sons of life, but Louy could not help wishing that Providence had sent just one little boy in place of a fourth little girl.

Later, when word came that Grandfather was ill, Mother took Baby with her to Boston, and Louy and Anna enjoyed several new dishes that Father made for them. One night they had a supper of toasted bread cut into little slices and dipped into warm water. Then Father read a fable to the children and told them of a dream of flying cherubs which he had imagined. Best of all, Louy sat down to send her first real letter to dearest Mother, writing straight across the page without a single blot. "I hope you will come home soon. I am glad Grandpa is better. I want to see you and baby."

Louy's first letter was quite as important to her as Baby's birth had been, and she raced down to the Cambridge Turnpike to report the great event to Miss Russell. During the summer Louy had begun to take lessons from the lady who was visiting the Emersons, and after Mother's return from Boston she continued her daily walk to the square clapboard house where Mr. Emerson lived. Especially now that Mother was preoccupied with Baby and Father was busy with the gentlemen who were arranging the end of the world at Groton, Louy found more to interest her at Mr. Emerson's house than at home.

Miss Russell had shown her the pretty bluebird box on the barn, the pear trees in the orchard, the tulips and roses in Mrs. Emerson's garden, the chickens, the dog, the black kitten, and the gray kitten. Sometimes Louy was allowed to go inside the house, where she gazed with the same admiration at the leather fire buckets as at Mr. Emerson himself, whose tall, spare figure with the stooping shoulders was to be seen in the study. Louy stood watching him dip his pen into ink and copy musty papers until red-faced Mrs. Mumford sent her back to the barn or the teacher called her pupils to school. There lessons in reading and writing were combined with spirited games of "I spy," "three-old-cat," and "thread-the-needle," until Louy marshaled her own company of redcoats and Indians and with the kindly guidance of Miss Russell projected a series of inspired military maneuvers.

Louy found still another teacher as summer gave way to autumn, who opened the door to a fairyland in Concord more marvelous than the "Cornwallis" and the cattle show rolled into one. Mr. Henry Thoreau and his brother John held a school in the Academy, which was very much like Father's Temple School, but an airing on the Common had never yielded such delights in larks and finches, and prunella and cardinal flowers, as burst forth in the Concord woods from the pointer of Mr. Henry Thoreau's magic finger.

There was, Louy sensed, a magic about Mr. Thoreau himself. She had never seen eyes that were bluer or deeper set than those under his overhanging brows. To her there was something warm and friendly about his large Roman nose, his soft brown hair, and his handclasp. Along with all the other children, Louy followed him as he swung by with his long Indian stride, his eyes on the ground. From Fairhaven he pointed out the expanse of Conantum, the slopes of Blue Hill and of Nobscot, or led them to the scraggy tracks where the scrub oak grew. Sometimes it was an excursion to "Heaven" he planned, along the old Marlborough Road through deep woods, or to Becky Stow's swampy hole, or to Bear Garden Hill and Nut Meadow Brook and Hubbard's Grove. As he walked he would strip a piece of birch bark from a tree and make a box to hold a lichen while the children crowded round to see it cut and folded.

Sometimes, and to Louy those were the best times of all, the birch-bark box was made to hold berries. Mr. Thoreau knew the best places to find huckleberries and blackberries, as he knew the best places to find Indian spearheads and otters' tracks. Sometimes he would start the children off in the hay cart, Louy sprawled with Anna and the others on the buffalo robe over the floor, Mr. Thoreau seated on a board across the front, driving to "Heaven" for sweet everlasting, driving to blue Monadnock for sweeter berries, or to swamps where the high bush blueberries grew.

While they walked or rode in search of berries, Mr. Thoreau spoke to the children, telling them, with that burr in his speech, of the "washing" days he loved when the wind came from the west and fogs were blown in from the sea, of a long soaking rain when drops trickled down on the stubble, of a majestic bird at the Cliff, or of the flowers by which he dated every day of the month. Louy had never seen a tanager before he told her that it set the woods on fire, or goldenrod until he said that it waved its yellow banners to march eastward to the Crusade. Never had she seen a cobweb until Mr. Thoreau reminded her that it was a handkerchief dropped by a fairy, or a squirrel until he remarked that it had the key to the pitch-pine cone. Father might not have agreed that the wood thrush was a more modern philosopher than Plato, but Louy did, solemnly. With her new teacher she heard in joy the note of the lark leaking up through the meadows as if its bill had been thawed by the sun. She rejoiced when he made for her a pipe of grass, a flageolet of an onion top, and peopled every leaf-stalk and willow shoot with Concord fairies.

Occasionally Mr. Thoreau took his friends out on the river, in his boat *Musketaquid*. Then Louy found, gliding quietly over the sluggish, grass-ground water, another magic fairyland. At Egg Rock, where hemlocks swept down and the boats met from up and down river, or in secluded places, where vines tangled among the trees, or in elfland, where cardinal flowers lit spiral flames along the banks, Mr. Thoreau rowed his boat, painted green for the grass and blue for the water. He showed her the bloom of the witch hazel; he brought down a swarm of titlarks with a call instead of a gun; in words, he opened for her the blossoms of the fragrant white pond lily.

Anna agreed with Louy that there were so many flowers and birds in Concord that the lack of a turkey for Thanksgiving was no great hardship. At least they did have bread for Louy's eighth birthday. In the morning Louy read Father's letter to her, with its two contrasting pictures: the first of an angel playing a harp, who represented Love, Music, and Concord; and the second of a bad angel with an arrow, symbolizing Anger and Discord. In the afternoon Lizzie and Anna flew round to help in the celebration, while even Baby, fitted up at last with a name, Abby May, and a broad new smile, prepared to receive the guests. The Hosmers and Priscilla Rice played out-of-doors until half-past five, when Mother told Louy to ask her little friends in to supper. They were solemnly conducted to the sitting room, where they were seated in a semicircle. Then Mother came in, placing a colored napkin on each lap. Next she brought in a plate of the bread that had been sliced into thin, square pieces, one for each guest. A plate of sliced apple was also passed, and again there was one portion for each. Finally everybody folded his napkin, and Mother said that the children might play for half an hour more, and then Louy must do her lessons.

Between lessons and games the winter passed uneventfully for her. Yet, Louy overheard much whispered discussion: whether Father should embark upon another peddling trip, or whether the family should accept Mr. Emerson's invitation to live at his house. Once in desperation Mother had said, "If I ask Mr. Alcott to bring home a quart of milk, he is quite likely to lead home a cow." But she did not wish to live with the Emersons, and she did not wish Father to live against his principles. And Father, sitting near the fireside, raised his pen from his journal long enough to remark that the family was, of all institutions, the most sacred, the primeval fact, the alpha of the social state.

In the midst of all, just when the ice was beginning to crack in the pond and signs of thaw were everywhere in evidence, news came that Grandfather May had died. Louy did not quite understand the meaning of death, although she knew that never again would she sit by the fire with the aged man in knee buckles and smallclothes, who gave her cakes and prunes. In his death also he had given, for there would be money now to pay some of the debts, and Mother liked to read the psalm and hymn book that came from his library. In spite of a snowstorm even in April, Louy found that her feet would dance as the lark soared up, and all the birds of spring sang a song that echoed in her heart.

When Louy spied the first robin that hopped boldly into the garden when the snow was melting, the song that rose in her heart came bubbling forth in words, and she raced into the cottage for a pen to write down her thoughts, her own first rhymes "To the First Robin."

Welcome, welcome, little stranger,
Fear no harm, and fear no danger;
We are glad to see you here,
For you sing "Sweet Spring is near."

Now the white snow melts away;
Now the flowers blossom gay:
Come dear bird and build your nest,
For we love our robin best.

"You will grow up a Shakespeare!" Mother cried delightedly, and carefully preserved the little paper, encouraging Louy to go on with her rhymes. Dead butterflies, lost kittens, and Baby's eyes were promptly trapped in a net of verse as spring gave way to summer.

Though not precisely an inspiration for a poem, the visit of Miss Fuller, who brought the latest in Boston finery and the earliest in Greek philosophy to her friends, Mr. Emerson and Mr. Alcott, was interesting to Louy. She had come to the cottage, she explained, to see Mr. Alcott's model children, and just as she arrived at the doorstep, Louy thundered along, champing and bridling, a very proper horse to pull the wheelbarrow Anna was driving, until her foot tripped, and down came the chariot in a laughing heap. Waving her hand dramatically, Mother announced, "Here are the model children, Miss Fuller."

For the "model children" there was soon exciting news at home, and there were exciting preparations to make. Father was going to England to visit a school that had been named after him. Mr. Greaves, who had written many letters to Father asking whether he could act with more effect upon strange children than upon his own, had established Alcott House near Richmond, and now a gentleman named Mr. Lane wrote, inviting Mr. Alcott to see another Temple School in England. Mr. Emerson was raising subscriptions for what he called the "Alcott-Voyage fund," while Mother was preparing Father's wardrobe so that he would shine before the transatlantic worthies. Finally his red pocketbook was filled with sovereigns, and his trunks were loaded with books and a basket of apples. Before he left, Uncle Junius arrived from Oriskany Falls to take his place at the cottage. At last, on May 8, armed with his apples, Mr. Emerson's *Essays*, and Mr. Emerson's encouraging words, Father embarked upon the ship *Rosalind* for London.

Although he was missed, the days were enlivened for Louy by excursions with Uncle Junius, and July brought another interesting gift to Concord in the shape of a gentleman named Mr. Hawthorne, who had come to stay at the Old Manse. To her there was something mysterious and somber about the two high granite posts and the gray house that stood back of the line of black ash trees. Veiled by a willow, the square wooden dwelling was almost hidden from her eyes, showing just enough of its weather-beaten clapboards and gambrel roof to suggest dark secrets behind the tiny panes of glass. She often stood there looking at the wheel track that led to the door, overgrown with grass that an old white horse was grazing. The lilac shrubs under the windows exhaled their perfume on the air; the gate, fallen from its hinges, creaked ominously in the stillness.

Sometimes Louy spied Mr. Hawthorne himself, who looked at her keenly with his great hazel eyes or smiled softly and sadly before he moved on in a rolling gait, his blue smock waving in the air. To her, he seemed a dark figure as he glided through the entry, his hat low over his eyes, a fitting shadow to inhabit a house of shadows.

Between the ghostly Manse and Father's letters about God's garden, Louy found new thoughts to people her mind. The garden, it appeared, was to be planted not in Old but in New England, where fruit was to be matured for the sustenance of the swarming nations. The world's hope, Father declared, was in "us." Louy did not know exactly how she could help mature fruit to sustain swarming nations, but Father seemed to think that his four little girls would be included in the plan, that Anna with her beauty-loving eyes and sweet visions, Louisa with her boundless curiosity and agile limbs, Elizabeth with her serene thoughts and happy gentleness, and even little Abby with her sagacious eyes and fair locks would each help to plant God's acre in New England. Mother explained to the children that it would be their task to help Father in his great work, and so she put on her hood and went forth to search for a farm at Stow or at Lincoln, where the "New Eden" might be planted.

To reap the harvest of Father's "Well done, good and faithful," the children began to prepare the cottage to receive him and his companions. At last, after Father's miniature was decorated with everlasting flowers, the happy evening of October 20, 1842, arrived, and with it came Father and his English friends. Louy's joy overflowed until she burst out with "Mother, what makes me so happy?" Reaching up to kiss Father's serene face—was that what made her so happy? Or was it William Lane, Mr. Lane's son, with whom she could compare English and American versions of "I spy" and "snap-the-whip"? Or was it Mr. Lane, with his violin and umbrella and the clipped speech about universal union that streamed from his thin lips? Or was it Mr. Wright in his fur cap and collar? Or was it all the boxes that stood about the little cottage?

When the cases and cowhide trunks were opened, she found herself walking on books, breathing the dust of books, and sitting on books. Along with all the cases and trunks, Louy soon discovered that Father's friends had brought something else with them, a phrase she had never heard before, "The Newness."

"The Newness," she was quick to perceive, was more than a phrase, for it was not long before the cottage routine that Father had inaugurated was altered to fit its purposes. Louy rose now at six in the morning, and after the wood fires were lighted, she and her sisters had a cold-water sponge and a rub with coarse crash linen towels. At a little after seven the family settled round the fireplace with their new companions for the breakfast which Father had prepared. It was a waste of energy to use plates; so Louy had only a napkin on her lap, and took the water, unleavened bread, apples, and potatoes that were handed around by the Ganymede of the day. Mr. Lane led Pythagorean conversation during breakfast, so that it would mingle, as he said, with the children's physical increment. There was less to eat than before, and there were scarcely any dishes to be washed; so Mother slipped upstairs about eight o'clock to arrange Mr. Lane's room. Then Louy and her sisters were ready for the singing lesson which Mr. Lane supervised, accompanying the pupils on the violin. Sometimes, if she found time, Mother added her own voice to the chorus, but usually she was too busy sewing and mending and teaching Father to bake bread. From ten until twelve-thirty, studies proceeded, diary-writing, reading, spelling, conversation, grammar, and arithmetic, which Father supervised until they were called to prepare for dinner.

It was dinner that made Louy understand more thoroughly than anything else what was meant by "The Newness." Although the meal was, this time, set upon the table by Father, it consisted entirely of coarse bread, water, and the apples that Uncle Junius had sent. In order to hold together in unity, Mr. Lane remarked, it was necessary for all to give up milk and cheese and sugar. Even so, an eighth of the food still went to poor neighbor Adams as his portion, and Mother tried to believe, as she glanced around the table, that the girls would grow strong on conversation if not on food. She looked lovingly at the four heads about her, Anna's so dark, Louy's the color of chestnut, Lizzie's lighter brown, Abby's fair, and tried to agree with Mr. Lane that certain issues were above cold potatoes and the absence of milk.

At least the dinner did not last long. At one o'clock, when Mr. Lane returned to his room, Louy could race with William to the barn until his Latin lesson began an hour later. At three she joined William and Anna in Mr. Lane's bedroom-study, where a fire burned cheerfully, and sat down to a "developing" lesson in geography, drawing, and geometry. Mr. Lane's face was sometimes so stubborn, and his mouth puckered so wryly, that Louy longed for Father's readings in place of her new teacher's lengthy expositions and geometric drawings. Four o'clock brought release from arithmetical problems, and then Louy sewed with Mother or went out to play. Supper was, like breakfast, taken around the fireplace, but now the Pythagorean conversation was more prolonged. In the evening Mr. Lane conducted another singing lesson, when Louy was permitted to dance with Anna to the music of his fiddle. It grew dark early, for there were not many candles to light the little parlor, and at eight o'clock the children were sent to bed to dream of "The Newness" in Concord.

Somehow Louy no longer raced up to Mother, bubbling over with "What makes me so happy?" Nor did Mother seem to enjoy her meals at the fireside while Mr. Lane spouted about the barbarism of family union and the peculiarity of maternal love that blinded one to all else. Louy and Anna both sensed the atmosphere of restriction that had come in the wake of "The

Newness"; the heavy silences, the averted eyes made them aware
of Mother's obscure struggle with Mr. Lane, and her despair.
Soon Mr. Wright decided to move to the Graham House in
Boston because of what he called the iron despotic order at the
cottage.

One bright spot there was amid "The Newness," the Household Post Office that Mother established in January. She said that
the children were to deposit their little notes and parcels in the
budget-basket over the entry, and the letters would be distributed
every evening after supper. Later, Mother had another plan, a
"Bon-Box," that stood inside the front door, the symbol of an
honor system. At the end of each day, if Louy had been good, a little slip bearing her name and the code word "Bon" with three
crosses after it was dropped into the box.

Under the new regime she found it very hard to earn a "Bon"
for it was tiresome for a ten-year-old to hear Father dictate the
story of his life so that Mr. Lane could send an article about it to
The Dial, or discuss the New Eden with him. Just as the books
spilled out of their cases on the floor, so the talk wreathed endlessly around the house, words about the fountains of happiness
that were opened as men were consociated with the Universal
Spirit, phrases about the dawn of Universal Truth and the virtues
of the Communitorium. Talk rose in billowy clouds in the parlor,
until Louy's despairing "Mamma, they have begun again" became
a reminder that chores would have to wait until Mr. Lane's eloquence had established tranquil households and redeemed every
farm from human ownership.

Sometimes they were joined in their talk by Mr. Ellery Channing, who had come to live in the little red cottage on the Cambridge Turnpike. Louy liked to watch the gaunt man with the
sunburned hair, who smoked a briar and puffed out pretty phrases
along with the blue smoke. His attitude toward the girls alternated capriciously between tenderness and roughness. There was
no doubt that if the discussions had been confusing before, they
were even more confusing when the unpredictable Mr. Channing
sat in the cottage parlor.

There were so many strange people now seated on the flowered sofa—Mr. Chace and Mr. Greene from Providence, Mr. Palmer and Mr. Everett—that Mother said she had better hang out a shingle reading "Come-outers' Haunt." While spring came on, Father and Mr. Lane went searching for the New Eden. They did not find it at the Codman Farm in Lincoln, nor at the Cliffs in Concord, nor at Milton or Roxbury or Brookline or Stow. They did find converts, however, gathering the planters before Paradise had been purchased. Mr. Larned, who had lived for one year on crackers and for another on apples, and Mr. Everett, who had been imprisoned in an insane asylum by his relatives, would both, they thought, make fine gardeners in the New Eden, members of a brotherhood whom God had designed to dwell together in His Paradise.

On May 20, Mr. Lane came home, announcing that he had purchased the New Eden in the shape of the Wyman Farm at Harvard. The barn and house were poor, he agreed with Father, but the prospect over the Nashua was sublime, and nuts, berries, and water were plentiful. While Father crated the books and packed the bust of Socrates, and Mr. Lane paid the family debts to the villagers, Louy, sensing something of her mother's hesitancy about the enterprise, wrote a poem under a picture that Mother had given her. There was another picture in the poem itself, of an Eden where Mother's garden would be sowed.

> *I hope that soon, dear mother,*
> *You and I may be*
> *In the quiet room my fancy*
> *Has so often made for thee,—*
>
> *The pleasant, sunny chamber,*
> *The cushioned easy-chair,*
> *The book laid for your reading,*
> *The vase of flowers fair;*
>
> *The desk beside the window*
> *Where the sun shines warm and bright:*

And there in ease and quiet
The promised book you write;

While I sit close beside you,
Content at last to see
That you can rest, dear mother,
And I can cherish thee.

William, Mr. Everett, and Mr. Larned had gone in advance to Harvard; and early on the morning of June 1, a day sharp and cold for the season, the Alcotts and Mr. Lane climbed into the carriage that was to take them to Eden. As they rode along the village street, Louy could not help thinking that she would no longer see Mr. Emerson walking out under the stars, or Mr. Hawthorne lurking darkly in the entry of the Old Manse. The village parades and celebrations were over, and on the Nashua there would be no Mr. Thoreau to pilot a little girl into fairyland. But surely the New Eden would be planted, and its gardens would flower in a place more enchanting even than Concord.

🐦🐦

CHAPTER 3

The New Eden

At her first glimpse of the old red house on the slope of Prospect Hill, Louy wondered why Father and Mr. Lane insisted on naming it "Fruitlands." No road led to the dilapidated dwelling on the hillside; and when Mother saw the kitchen in ruins, she could not help remarking that the seven-room house resembled a refined kind of pigsty. There was a huge chimney in the middle, however, which would soon send forth smoke, and there was a granary which would be filled with the produce of the Consociate Family.

The house dwindled into insignificance when the children walked forth with Mother to gather flowers while she collected an apron full of chips. Louy was sure that never before had she seen so much of the sky. The great bowl of heaven overturned around her, and from the eminence Escutney, Wachusett, and Monad-nock loomed in all their grandeur. To the west wound the stream of the Nashua among upland meadows and groves of nut trees, maples, and pines. In such a region, Mother thought, the soul expanded. But to the children the isolation and remoteness and the vistas, broken only by the mountains and the shadows of mountains, were frightening.

Mr. Lane and Father were already eloquent with plans for Fruitlands. On that nearest little copse, cottages might be built, and from their granite sources on the hillside, fountains would be made to descend. At their words the vision of a New Eden rose before Louy, and she saw its flowers bloom before its seeds were planted. Without work visions were visions still. Again the bust of Socrates must be moved in place, the settle, and all the furnishings that Mr. Palmer had brought from the homestead at No Town. At last the rooms were furnished and assigned to the members of the Consociate Family. The large room at the right of the entry would be used for community dining. Up the steep stairs leading to the garret the girls would march each night, for there seemed to be no other place for their beds. Although the ceiling sloped low, there was one small window on each side, and if they could not see Wachusett from the garret, at least they could hear the pines sing and the rain drip on the roof. Everything was in readiness now; the colored prints of John Wesley and "Searching the Scriptures" looked down from the walls; and the carpenter was busy sawing and hammering one hundred feet of shelves so that the library would at last stand upright.

It was harder, Louy decided, to sow the garden of Eden than it was to establish a dwelling place for its planters. The noise of plowing and chopping rivaled that of sawing and hammering, for now the Consociate Family gathered outside to sow the seeds of maize and rye, oats and barley, and potatoes and beans that would be reaped at harvest time. Mr. Wyman's mare was as busy as the Universal Brothers, plowing the land for melons and squash, clover, or buckwheat. Soon, Mr. Lane said, they would dispense with the plow and work the land by hand with spade and pruning knife, but in the meantime the yoke of oxen that Mr. Palmer had brought was most useful.

Now that Eden had been planted inside and outside, it remained for the Consociate Brotherhood to enter the kingdom of peace, as Father said, through the gates of self-denial and abandonment. As far as Louy could see, however, the gates of the kingdom did not differ greatly from the gates of the cottage at Concord. The girls did dress a little differently from the way they had done at home, for linen tunics were the only permissible raiment for Consociate Brothers. Mr. Lane designed the garments for the girls, along with broad-brimmed linen hats, since cotton would encourage slavery and wool would deprive the sheep of its natural clothing. Music was followed by the same bowls of sunrise for breakfast that had formed the fare at Concord, and when the sun cast its shadow upon the noon mark on the floor, the girls seated themselves around the community table to enjoy what Father called a solar diet of fountain waters and fruits that refreshed the spirit.

While Father and Mr. Lane in their linen raiment discussed the virtues of a pure and bloodless diet, Louy enjoyed watching the Consociate Brethren. Young Mr. Larned had already cast off the horrors of the countinghouse to bear turf to Fruitlands after he had been converted from the grosser life at Brook Farm. Louy wondered what he planned to eat this year, since he had spent two years alternating between apples and crackers and refused to drink milk that rightly belonged to the cow. Mr. Everett was older, but just as interesting, for the experience of having been confined in a madhouse had made him most serious. As she ate the cottage bread that Father had baked in the shape of animals, or went out to perform the labor that Mr. Lane said was "attractive," Louy liked to discuss the new Brethren with Anna.

The cold baths, the linen tunics, and the solar diet itself were joy in June. Even Mother enthusiastically agreed that the true life ought to be lived here if anywhere on earth, and added that although they might fail, it would be something that they had ventured what so few had dared. In her own way Louy also led the true life, rising at five, bathing, singing "When the day with rosy light," washing the dishes, and running up the hill to gaze upon the distant prospect. After lessons, which Anna supervised now, Louy enjoyed conversing with Father and the girls about the Universal Brotherhood of which she was a part. The evening songs crowned with joy a day of joy, for who could despair while the hill sloped down to the Nashua and Monadnock pierced the cloudless sky of June?

Of all the happy June days the happiest was Lizzie's eighth birthday on the twenty-fourth. Before five in the morning Louy was awake, ready to go to the woods with Anna, William, and Mother to prepare a bower and decorate a small pine with gifts and notes. Carefully they set upon the branches Anna's fan, Abby's little pitcher, and Louy's pincushion. Anna made an oak-leaf wreath for everyone, and after breakfast the Consociate Family escorted the queen of the day to the grove. To the accompaniment of Mr. Lane's violin, songs were sung in Lizzie's honor, and Father read a parable and an ode that he had composed for the occasion.

> *Here in the grove*
> *With those we love, . . .*
> *Father's here*
> *And Mother dear*
> *And sisters all,*
> *The short and tall.*

It was good to be one happy family in the bower on such a day.

Meanwhile, in bower and grove, on hillside and valley, Louy saw new faces, gardeners who had come to help Father water the soil of Eden. Another Englishman, Mr. Samuel Bower, zealously entered into all of the works and speculations of Fruitlands, agreeing fervently with Mr. Lane that the sin of eating forbidden substances was to be crushed. Besides Mr. Bower there was Mr. Wood, or Mr. Abram, for this newcomer liked to invert his name and be called "Wood Abram"; and there was Christopher Greene, who regaled the girls with stories of West Point and wished to be called "Uncle Christy."

The newcomers joined on Sundays to listen to Father's readings or to watch while he illustrated on the blackboard the subjection of the body to the soul, showing the cross upon which the lusts of the flesh were to be sacrificed. Louy sometimes found more inspiration in the woods than in Father's lessons, although Mr. Bower and Mr. Greene and all the gardeners of Eden continued to feast upon his thought and devour the crumbs of his reflection.

To share in the contemplative banquet, Mr. Emerson and Mr. Channing visited Fruitlands early in July. Louy was glad to see her Concord friends again, Mr. Emerson smiling kindly, shining as ever, Mr. Channing moodily uttering his whimsies in enigmatical phrases. The visitors were shown the newly plowed fields, the house, and the prospect over the Nashua; and although Mr. Emerson thought that if a man would accept a gold eagle, he might as readily accept the molasses and rice that the eagle would buy, still he considered the attainment of the Fruitlanders high and held that there was as much merit in beautiful manners as in hard work. In July they looked well. He would, he cautioned himself, see them in December.

Louy's joy in summer with its celebrations in the bower and its visitors from home was diminished a little when Mr. Lane resumed supervision of the children's lessons. As he questioned Louy on the virtues she wished more of and the vices she wished less of, she could not help feeling that her passion for study was not always excited, as it should have been, in "Harmony." Just as he had recorded the price of grain in London, Mr. Lane recorded now the long line of Louy's vices, listing with detached objectivity her impatience, her willfulness, her impudence, and her love of cats.

When Miss Page arrived to instruct the children, Louy's joy diminished further, and after a music lesson she confided frankly to her diary that she hated Miss P. Perhaps it was because Miss Page was so preoccupied with her own poems that she could not find much poetry in the children. At any rate, she insisted upon telling them how her verses, "The World," had been suggested by the statement that the world was a many-headed monster.

Mr. Lane's remarks were equally disturbing, for after he had contemplated the cornbins and haylofts of the Shakers, he began to suggest that Mother might do well to pattern herself after Ann Lee, their divine representative. Although marriage and children did not generate selfishness, he remarked, selfishness generated them. Louy did not understand everything Mr. Lane said about family good and universal good, but she did understand that there was a tension in the garden of Eden that had not been there in June. Mother's eyes darkened and her face clouded as Mr. Lane spoke, and the clouds did not lift when Father sat down with him to send a letter to *The Herald of Freedom* that expressed his ideal of *being* in preference to *doing*.

After the gardeners had set forth from Eden early in September to act out their ideal at Brook Farm, Providence, or New York, visitors came, bringing unpleasant stories with them. People, they hinted, were spreading all manner of rumors about the Consociate Family. Father, they reported, was said to admit to his table only those vegetables that aspired above the ground, spurning the baser products that grew downward. The gossips at Harvard were smirking over Mr. Alcott's maintenance of the rights of canker worms to apples. One of the Fruitlanders crowed like a cock at midnight if a happy thought struck him, while Mr. Bower danced naked under the moon upon the Nashua hills. Miss Page had cheese secreted in her trunk, and the Fruitlanders, when they did any plowing at all, did it by hand.

Louy knew the stories were not true, for they did have a team at the New Eden, though one of the "oxen" was a cow, and they most definitely ate potatoes, which as definitely grew downward; but the rumors, together with Mr. Lane's peculiar opinions about family life, created a tension at Fruitlands more frightening than any story that the gossips could invent. Sometimes Louy felt so cross that not even *The Vicar of Wakefield* could comfort her, and she cried when she went to bed. If only "Father . . . and Mother dear and sisters all, the short and tall" could be close together as they had been on Lizzie's happy birthday.

Especially on Mother's birthday Louy wished that they were all one happy family. After breakfast she presented her birthday poem to Mother, and the girls played in the woods, gathering red leaves and singing "Hail, all hail, thou merry month of May." They sang the song of May very often now that the fall of the year had come. Mother thanked the poet for her verses in a sweet note, but when Louy turned to her diary, all her eager longings surged up again as she wrote, "I wish I was rich, I was good, and we were all a happy family this day."

How could they be one happy family when Mother did not come to the table? Anna was right when she said that if Mother prepared the food, she ought to eat it with them. Louy missed Mother at mealtime, and although husking corn was fun, ironing was not, and there were gaps in her life at Fruitlands that not even a poem to the sunset could fill.

Miss Page had left, to benefit with her poetry youth of a more appreciative nature, but Mr. Lane continued to probe the girls for answers to his searching questions. After a long talk with him on the subject "What is man?" Louy climbed wearily to the garret, filled with confused notions of the body, the soul, and the mind. In her diary she copied his vegetarian principles: "Pluck your body from the orchard; do not snatch it from the shamble. Apollo eats no flesh and has no beard; his voice is melody itself. Without flesh diet there could be no blood-shedding war." Without flesh diet, however, there could be, Louy perceived, a kind of bloodless war.

November itself conspired to wage the bloodless war. It was almost impossible now to race down the slopes against the raging winds. The sweet bowl of heaven had turned into a cavernous whirlpool, and the bluish haze of Monadnock was a grim warning in the gray distance. Wind or no wind, Louy could not have raced down the hills, for she had a racking cough, headache, and a pain in her side. She was more alone than ever, for Anna was in Boston, and Louy wrote verses to her sister, bidding her

> *Think how we two have together*
> *Journeyed onward day by day,*
> *Joys and sorrows ever sharing,*
> *While the swift years roll away.*
> *Then may all the sunny hours*
> *Of our youth rise up to thee,*
> *And when your heart is light and happy,*
> *Anna, dear, then think of me.*

Anna did think of her sister, sending her a picture of Jenny Lind, which Louisa treasured, longing to be as famous as the great singer.

William could not fill Anna's place, for he was so ill that he could not even sit up in bed and Mr. Lane nursed him, complaining of the inclement weather and his own chapped hands. Mother thought Mr. Lane's weakness pitiable, reminding herself that no man was great to his valet, or to his housemaid either. When he denied the family the privilege of cutting wood or grinding any more grain, however, Mother thought his weakness more contemptible than pitiable, and was glad that Mr. Hecker had sent a barrel of wheat meal for the kitchen. Now instead of conversing on The Highest Aim, the members of the Consociate Family took to discussing the possibility of selling back thirty acres to Mr. Wyman and building a cottage on the lowland. Mother bravely fortified herself for all storms, for come what might, she would see that the peace of her children would be no more disturbed by discussions and doubts. But their peace was disturbed and their doubts rose high, for after a talk with Mr. Lane, Father asked them if they saw any reason for the Consociate Family to separate.

There were reasons. Mother, Mr. Lane complained, had no spontaneous inclination toward a larger family than her own natural one. Father had begun to consider that maternal instinct opposed the establishment of a community which stood on universal love, and Mother cried out against those who had devoured the substance of Fruitlands and turned around to scoff at the efforts of its gardeners. If wood and apples were not to be had, the children would freeze or starve in a bitter wilderness. Of the Consociate Family only faithful Mr. Palmer remained, while Mr. Lane became more moody and more enigmatical than ever. They could not live at Fruitlands. So much of the question was answered.

The other, more ominous question of whether the family should separate remained to be answered. It hung, insoluble, when Louy played in the snow on her eleventh birthday, and

Mother wrote a note encouraging her to make observations about her thoughts and transcribe in her diary an epitome of her life. The question remained, though it was forgotten momentarily when Louy sat and heard the pines sing in the winter wind. Momentary forgetfulness was good, for then Louy could write in her Imagination Book, and have a pleasant time with her mind, and awaken from happy dreams to watch the moon.

When Mr. Lane was in Boston, Father and Mother and Anna and Louy had a long talk, trying to find an answer. Uncle Sam May had invited Mother and the girls to take rooms near him in Lexington. As they discussed the offer, the unhappiness rose in Louy's heart until she could not force back the tears. Everyone cried, even after Mother said she would not accept the invitation.

Even Father seemed to have lost his hope, and would have reproached the gods had he found any in whom to trust. Now he, too, was outcast, driven from the gate, sick with the sickness of forlorn despair. Yet, despite his languor, he murmured in sepulchral tones, "Thy faith shall heal thee." Mother answered that her common sense was stronger than her faith, and insisted that he take some spearmint tea until his faith restored him. The question was answered. Mother could not live her neighbor's principle. Her own she must live, and her own was her family. They could not separate.

Uncle Sam May helped provide a refuge in Still River, a mile away, and there, in the three rooms and kitchen rented from neighbor Lovejoy, they would brave the remainder of the winter. At least they would be together. Fruitlands was no more. On January 14, Mr. Lane and William left for the Shakers. The books were catalogued and packed. A load of goods was sent on to Mr. Lovejoy's. On the sixteenth the Alcotts set forth to their new home in Still River.

There were other Edens, Father thought, to plant in the East. Though driven from one gate, they would be led to another threshold. Louy, turning back to glance at the dreary house outlined against the winter sky, thought of the verse that Christian had sung, "This place has been our second stage." Monadnock still loomed in the distance, and the long range of lofty hills shouldered the clouds. But now there were hands to hold; together they were a fortress strong to stand against a darkening world.

For three rooms and the use of the kitchen on Hog Street, Mr. Lovejoy charged fifty cents a week. As soon as the family was settled, Father proceeded to chop wood and write an account of the Fruitlands enterprise, while Mother varied her winter tasks by a visit to the communities at Hopedale and Northampton.

In the spring, after Mother had decided that the communities offered no advance on the old world, the family moved again, taking half of a house nearby at Still River. Mr. Lovejoy had named this dwelling "Brick Ends" because, although the building itself was wooden, its ends were made of brick. A door cut into the woodhouse and one into an adjoining chamber would place the family in a distinct range of rooms. For twenty-five dollars a year the Alcotts could have five rooms instead of three, and for an additional ten dollars, a three-quarter-acre garden. On the back piazza Father devised a shower bath in a canvas-walled enclosure, and Louy was allotted the little room at the head of the stairs. When Father was not wielding his spade, he was writing "Sighs for Paradise," but Mother seemed to believe that they were closer now to Paradise than they had ever been in Eden. A small income was due her from her father's estate, which, together with the vegetable garden, would produce Pythagorean diets for the children. There was a home in which they could be together. The year, she considered, had been less filled with events than signs, and the signs seemed at last to point the way in which Paradise would lie.

For Louy, however, events were more significant than signs, and delightful events seemed to be in store for her. In May she began to attend Miss Chase's district school with Anna, walking up the hill each morning to the brick schoolhouse, seating herself with the children on the plank bench, and listening attentively to the teachings of young Miss Maria Louisa Chase, who was as deeply interested in rides and picnics as in spelling and arithmetic.

Sometimes, after the parents of several children had complained to the selectmen about the diet of the Alcott girls, which seemed to them less Pythagorean than pitiable, Anna and Louy found "extras" for themselves in the dinner pails of their playmates. When the "extra" appeared in the form of the first banana ever seen in Still River, the "breadfruit" provided quite a sensation.

It was Annie Maria Lawrence who boasted the honor of tasting the first "breadfruit." Annie had selected Lizzie as her special playmate, while Louy found a friend in Sophia Gardner, whom Abby promptly dubbed "Fire." There were so many Gardners that several were left over after Louy had paired off with "Fire" and Anna with Margaret. Here was a proper community to join in the rites of spring.

To Louy it seemed as if May must last forever. The haycarts were trimmed with evergreen, the picnic baskets were stowed away, and the children perched on their seats, singing and laughing all the way to Leominster. Whether it was a matter of eating pickles and doughnuts, or jumping rope, or racing downhill, Louy was the ringleader of Still River. Anna might read stories aloud, Abby might captivate her friends with her round, rosy face, but when hoop rolling or ball tossing began, it was Louy's turn to reduce the Gardners and Lawrences to a state of open-mouthed admiration.

Now, for the celebration of Lizzie's birthday, there was a goodly audience. All day long the children worked, decorating the kitchen with evergreens, ornamenting the sitting room with a small tree from which hung gifts for every guest. The table was laden with cakes and cherries, a huge birthday cake in the center. Annie Lawrence and the Gardner children came, and Helen Lovejoy—all the boys and girls of Still River entering the dimly lighted room to sit opposite an open door over which a curtain had been hung. Soon a bell tinkled, the curtain was drawn from the doorway, and an overture of songs introduced the evening's entertainment. Again the bell tinkled, and Anna stepped forth, dressed like a Highlander in bonnet and plaid to recite a short ballad about Scotland. The next time the bell tinkled for the star of the evening, for Louy, whose face and arms had been stained red to impersonate an Indian girl. The feathers nodded violently from her head as she sang with gusto, "Wild roved an Indian girl, bright Alfarata." The star appeared a second time, charging forward with a shield to utter in bloodcurdling accents Ossian's lines, "O thou that rollest above, round as the shield of my fathers." Finally Louy topped the festivities with the recitation of "Geehale—An Indian Lament," and the enthusiastic audience retired for the more commonplace delights of fruit and cake.

Even when no such occasion as a birthday offered itself, Louy continued her duties as author-director, converting the floor of the barn into a stage. For the benefit of the children who stood in anticipation beneath the elm tree, the barn door was rolled back and the Louy Alcott troupe proceeded to tread the boards. The director announced with authoritative pomp her ruling that those who in her judgment did well would be invited to "make" another play.

One of the children who eagerly vied for the privilege of collaborating with Louy was Llewellyn Willis, whom Mother had met on the Boston coach. He planned to board at Still River for the summer, and immediately went to call on the Alcott girls. Four pairs of bright, mischievous eyes looked from the newcomer's black hair down to his large ears, his wing collar, and his bow tie, until they agreed that he was sufficiently dashing to join the Still River brigade. Within a week Llewellyn left his boardinghouse to live with the Alcotts, and when they were not performing in the barn or listening to Louy recite "Geehale," they allowed their new friend to tell the story of his life. It was a sad story, for Llewellyn's father had been imprisoned for debt and his mother had died three days after he was born. Llewellyn had been brought up by his grandmother, who had prepared him somewhat better for the life hereafter than for the life that was. He had found books, however, and eagerly confided to Louy the delights of *Robinson Crusoe* and *Alonzo and Melissa*, which he had read by candlelight. He had had a checkered career, though he was only fourteen, having been already apprenticed to a Cambridge apothecary and expelled from the church as a heretic. Frederick Llewellyn Hovey Willis, Louy decided, was a worthy candidate for her barnyard troupe.

Often during the happy summer Louy donned her broad-brimmed hat and loaded the little cart with books and wraps and cakes for a picnic at Bare Hill Pond. With Anna and Llewellyn she wandered over the rocky, mossy glen that opened upon the water's edge, christening the favorite spot "Spiderland." Llewellyn, it was decided, was king of the realm, Anna queen, and Louy the princess royal. If a spider were accidentally killed, the princess royal must build a monument to the unfortunate victim and write an epitaph appropriate for a demise in the royal realm.

Yet for every royal realm in Still River, Louy thought, there were twenty such in Concord, and Bare Hill Pond, for all its chestnut trees, could not compare with Egg Rock. When Mr. Emerson offered to buy a few acres for Father in Concord, she felt that no one could resist the temptation. Although there were more Gardners than Hosmers, when Louy returned after her unusual experiences, she would surely be accorded the position of queen instead of princess royal.

In October, rooms were engaged for the winter at Mr. Edmund Hosmer's home in Concord. Mother was tired of moving about, she said, and hoped the great Idea would be realized before a thousand years when they should all be transfixed in eternal marble. But she, too, was glad to leave Still River after the Millerite excitement of the fall. Although the neighbors worked feverishly to finish their canning and preserving and leave everything shipshape for God's approval, the world did not end on October 22. In fact, as far as Louy was concerned, a few weeks later it was reborn, for on November 12 she was perched on the top of the stage to Littleton, and from there the family continued their journey to Concord by the new and wonderful Fitchburg Railroad. The queen of the realm was returning, after her sojourn in Eden, to the royal kingdom that was home.

CHAPTER 4

The White Village

It was good to be back in Concord. It was good to be back where skating on the icy meadows would happily fill the season before picnics could be resumed on Dakin Hill, and the year would revolve to the cattle show and turn once again to the annual apple picking.

Until they found a house of their own, Edmund Hosmer's farm on Sandy Pond Road, beyond the Cambridge Turnpike, was a pleasant refuge for the Alcotts. Mrs. Hosmer hospitably crowded her large family together, giving up three rooms for her guests, along with permission to cut as much wood as they needed from the wood lot. Farmer Hosmer welcomed Father, although the school committeeman declined his services and Mother feared they should all contemplate into starvation. If Father found no avenues open to the sympathies of his towns-people, he could at least teach Mr. Hosmer's children along with his own. While Anna attended Mr. Bradford's school in the vil-lage, Louy followed Father's Plato as guide, learning as much about the Hosmer children as she did about Greek philosophy.

Jane and Abby Hosmer followed Louy's latest game with delight, running with her to the wood lot and riding "hobby-horse home" on the largest branch. When Louy was not invent-ing games, she argued with Jane about the relative merits of the two Abbys, composing verses that would prove authoritatively Abby Alcott's superiority over Abby Hosmer.

Yet climbing trees and munching brown bread with the Hosmers in the pantry did not satisfy her entirely. Unaccountably, as she listened to Mother read *Kenilworth* while the girls sewed, a fury seemed to rise in her heart. Her moods varied with the sun, or with the books she read. When the ice snapped and sparkled on the trees, she must write a poem to stormy winter. When she read *Philothea*, she must act out the part of Aspasia, the elegant and voluptuous Ionian. Yet there was not always a light within the Grecian temple, and poetry did not always sparkle from her soul like moonlight on the waters.

Perhaps after the family had moved to their own home Louy would find Plato's everlasting harmony. In January, with the money that had come to Mother from Grandfather May, and with help from Mr. Emerson, a very old house on the Lexington Road, the former home of Horatio Cogswell, was bought. While Mother prepared to leave Sandy Pond Road, Father and the Hosmers helped Mr. Thoreau raise the timbers of a hut at Walden, where he proposed to establish a community of one. Louy looked forward more eagerly to the community of six who would find a home in the house that Father had named "Hillside."

Horatio Cogswell had, it was obvious, raised hogs in the front yard, but the ancient house in Concord's East Quarter was redeemed by the legend that at one time it had been inhabited by a man who believed himself immortal. Father yielded to the necessity of settling near the roadside, for though it echoed now with the rumble of anxious wheels and raised the dust of the market, it was the same road along which the British had retreated seventy years before. The house had been old then. Its two peaked gables, its gambrel roof, its brick chimney, and its low ceilings with the heavy beams coming through attested the antiquity of the four-room dwelling, but there was a wheelwright's shop on one side which could be added to the house, and the sandy, graveled grounds would soon sprout trees.

On April 1 the family moved in, Louy and her sisters taking the second-story room with the old fireplace and four corner gunstock posts. Soon the curtains and the matting were in place, a bust of Pestalozzi looked approvingly down, and one small chair was reserved for the exclusive use of all stray cats. Louy wished more than ever for a room of her own, and perhaps with Father's carpentry the room would one day be hers.

All through the spring Father worked with carpenter Hosmer, cutting the wheelwright's shop in two and adding one part to each end of Hillside. Arrangements were made for a shower bath fixed with weights and pulleys; new stairs were built to the children's room; the barn was moved from the opposite side of the road, and the sound of hammers echoed ceaselessly in the East Quarter until a central peak and front porch had been added to Hillside, which glistened with a coat of rusty olive paint. When he was not working at carpentry, Father was forming the ridges into terraces, setting out his apple trees, or planting squash and lettuce, peas and beans, and buckwheat and rye. Louy weeded with him diligently as he discussed the properties of sage, Anna kept steadily at her books, Abby pranced around the new garden, and Lizzie smiled upon everything. Mother was busy and happy in her new home, and Louy knew that here they could stand together at last.

Another name was added to Louy's long list of Concord friends as summer came on, the name of Miss Sophia Foord. Father had wished to establish a small school in the village and had engaged the services of the estimable lady from Milton. Although the plan itself had failed, and Louy had begun to sense her father's unpopularity when he was dismissed as a talker at the gates of Concord, Miss Foord remained to teach the children. There was a warmth and vigor about her that appealed to Louy, who devotedly followed Miss Foord's efforts at high thinking and holy living. She knew as much about plants as about books, and told the Alcott girls of the parts of the strawberry and the grapes at Flint's Pond. In the woods she gathered the girls around her—Abby rosy-cheeked and wide-eyed, Lizzie gentle and smiling, Anna quiet and dignified, Louy dashing and boisterous—to give a botany lesson based on dwarf primroses or Venus's-looking-glass. After Louy had climbed an apple tree, tearing the clothes from her back and nearly breaking her bones, Miss Foord took the occasion to explain to the girls the bones in their bodies, and cautioned Louy in particular to be careful of hers. Together they walked to Flint's Pond, wading and splashing all the way across until the fish scurried away in the waters around Reed Island. Through the woods they ran singing aloud, to return home wet, muddy, and completely happy.

All summer long Louy found pleasure in the joys of Concord, forgetting the moods along with the frosts of winter. Often during the summer four pairs of feet marched up the ridge behind Hillside, climbing from Christian's Slough of Despond to his Celestial City. For an audience of the Hosmers and Llewellyn Willis, who had come to board for the summer, the episodes from *Pilgrim's Progress* were dramatized, from Goodwill at the Gate to Christian at the Interpreter's House, from the Iron Cage of Despair to the Wall of Salvation. Up the Hill Difficulty the little company trooped, seeing the Delectable Mountains in the distance, wandering through the Valley of Humiliation to come at last to the beautiful gate of the city in the land of Beulah. For the tableaux Mother joined the audience, her hearty laugh applauding four little girls in old laces and shawls who trod the boards of an enclosed piazza. When no entertainments were scheduled in the village, Louy planned her own, a happy player storming the barn of Hillside, finding in Concord a stage for all her exhibitions. In her heart summer ripened as if a midsummer night's dream would last forever.

The dream was not so long-lived. When the Hillside repairs were nearly complete and the garden yielded an abundance of melons and corn and tomatoes and turnips, Mr. Lane reappeared. He had brought his books to Hillside to be placed in Father's care, but when he saw the garden, declaring it the best piece of preaching that had emanated from Mr. Alcott, he readily accepted Mother's invitation to remain for the summer.

With Mr. Lane came the establishment of a rigid "Day's Order of Indoor Duties for Children," from which gypsying excursions seemed to be excluded. Now there were hours for rising, bathing, sewing, reading, housewifery, and conversation; and Hillside seemed, like Concord, bent upon keeping railroad time. Although Miss Foord was still in charge of recreations and chores, Mr. Lane supervised the schoolroom, proclaiming himself Socrates to Louy's

Alcibiades. The summer shadows lengthened as the catechism proceeded, and Socrates taught the virtue of self-denial or the distinction between wishing and hoping to little Alcibiades. In September, when Uncle Junius became ill and Father left for Spindle Hill, Mr. Lane stayed on, the Socrates of the schoolroom. Socrates did not seem to understand farming very well, however, for the garden looked shabby. Louy began to despair again as she went through the round of "Indoor Duties." Out of her despondency she wove a poem, asking

> *Oh, why these tears,*
> *And these idle fears*
> *For what may come tomorrow?*
> *The birds find food*
> *From God so good,*
> *And the flowers know no sorrow.*

Yet Louy knew sorrow, though she could forget it when she wrote to Sophia Gardner, recalling the happy days at Still River, or when she wrote "My Kingdom," praying

> *Dear Father, help me with the love*
> *That casteth out my fear;*
> *Teach me to lean on thee, and feel*
> *That thou art very near,*
> *That no temptation is unseen,*
> *No childish grief too small,*
> *Since thou, with patience infinite,*
> *Doth soothe and comfort all.*

> *I do not ask for any crown*
> *But that which all may win,*
> *Nor seek to conquer any world*
> *Except the one within.*

Toward the end of October, after Mr. Lane had left and Father had returned, Louy ran through the woods where the dew still sparkled on the velvet moss. Under the arches of red and yellow leaves she ran, singing for joy in a world so beautiful. Suddenly she saw the autumn sun rise over the wide Virginia meadows, flooding the leaves with the beneficence of early morning light. Everything Mr. Thoreau had ever said about fairyland came to her now as she stood near the house where he had been born on the winding Virginia Road. Every hope that Mother had cherished, every lesson that Father had taught, thronged her mind as she stood alone under the newborn sun. She, too, was newborn that morning.

Although the chores remained unchanged and the Alcott girls continued to sew and cook, scrub and fetch wood, winter brought a new experience to Louy and Anna. Every morning they walked together to the small East Quarter schoolroom to follow Mr. John Hosmer's teachings in physiology and English grammar. Father generously donated two large maps to the school, and Louy felt quite at home with her thirty new classmates, all of whom were speedily supplied with nicknames from "Mr. Smack" to "Mr. Mitten." Louy was proud that she was the fleetest runner in the school and could walk as far and climb as high as any boy in District Number Two. Leonard's *Arithmetic* might present insoluble problems, but the game of "Catapult" did not. After school there was whist to be played of an evening, or the game of dolls' dressmaker. There was the post office in the apple tree, where Clara Gowing and the Hosmer girls found notes and rhymes and bouquets. There were new books to read, and there was even new food to eat, for Mother and the girls enjoyed milk and cheese.

Father, too, had hopes for the new year of 1846, hopes that he would again in God's own time have the happiness of teaching a school and that there would be some relation between himself and his time. Meanwhile, he taught his own children, trying to rise from the Dismal Swamp of his townsmen's distrust. Louy also lived for a time in her own Dismal Swamp until Father found as diabolic traits in her quick temper as in her dark complexion.

One great desire was fulfilled, however, when in March she was given the little room she had wanted so long. The workbasket and desk were by the window, the closet was filled with sweet-smelling herbs, and the door opened into the garden. Mother liked to stop for a moment to admire the "poet's corner," while the poet decided to make a new plan for her life to match the new room in which she gloried.

Often during the late winter Lizzie would come to Louy's room with Abby, to read aloud the story of *Oliver Twist*. Together they wept over Oliver in the workhouse, raged over the false Noah Claypole and the practices of the Artful Dodger, and rejoiced when the hero at last came into his own. Lizzie was a good companion with whom to watch a rainbow from the hill, and many were the talks she had with Louy about drawing Mrs. Richardson's baby in the wagon or solving problems in division.

For them all the "Day's Order" continued, from singing and bedmaking to journal-writing and spelling, from dishwashing and sweeping to reading and playing. There was time during the spring for delightful "Outdoor Duties" also, when the girls walked to Ponkatasset Hill, or watched Father set out apple trees and make a path up the hillside from the kitchen door.

As summer came on, the stove was removed from Father's study, the bean rows stretched trim as an air line, and the birds seemed not to have heard of the war with Mexico. At home Father was building a summerhouse of willow wands, and Miss Foord was teaching in Mr. Emerson's barn. Quiet though it was, the time now was marked for Louy with signs if not with great events. It was Lizzie with whom she played "Vegetables and Fruit," or "Travel," "Going to Boston," or "School"; and as summer passed into autumn and autumn chilled into winter, all the seasons bore gifts to Louy, touches of beauty that she trapped in the net of her verses and stored forever in her mind. How proud she was, on her fourteenth birthday, to receive a new pen from Mother; prouder still to read the verses that accompanied it:

> *Oh, may this pen your muse inspire,*
> *When wrapt in pure poetic fire,*
> *To write some sweet, some thrilling verse. . . .*

Would she ever be able to write lines as noble as Whittier's "Branded Hand"? Surely there was inspiration for such a poem when, in February, a fugitive slave on his way to Canada took refuge at Hillside. Louy watched him saw and pile the wood and, hearing his stories of slavery in Maryland, learned an impressive lesson from the black man who savored the new taste of freedom. To her, he was a heroic figure, harassed by memories, fearful of the future, a fugitive sitting at the fireside, himself an unforgettable image of slavery.

It was little wonder that Father thought Louy "possessed" during the winter. She was indeed "possessed" by thoughts that even the new pen could not transcribe, by emotions that coasting on Ponkatasset Hill could not dispel. She was herself a fugitive, pursued by longings for she knew not what, for an uncertain glory that had never come to Concord, for an inner peace that the white village could not give. Perhaps the summer, and a visit to the magic man of Walden, would restore the fairyland that a child had found and lost again.

On a beautiful July day Mother and Father, Llewellyn Willis, and the Alcott girls walked to Mr. Thoreau's hut in the blackberry pasture on the bank of Walden water. They found him seated there, a man in shirt sleeves and cowhide boots, full of glad sounds of squirrel and of woodchuck, full of the secrets of maidenhair and climbing fern. His eyes were still the bright blue that the sky had lent. The birds admitted his whistle to their colloquies. The muskrat lost his caution at his door. The sachem was sachem still. Louy's magician was unchanged.

Gayly he led them to his rooftree, showing the children his cane bed and table, his desk and chairs—for none was so poor that he need sit upon a pumpkin. A corn broom would fathom the depth of the cellar. There was no lock to the door, no curtain to the window.

Mr. Thoreau took the five children out in his boat, so that they might see how the pond, lying between earth and heaven, partook of the color of both. A little distance from shore he raised his oars into the boat and piped the flute he had brought with him. The reedy notes echoed over the still, transparent water till even the perch were charmed and the frogs bewitched. As suddenly as he had begun, he stopped, laying down his flute, telling in grave, measured tones of the Indians and the woods they had inhabited. Blessed were the young, he laughed, for they did not read the President's message. Blessed was Louy, who had twice entered fairyland, and found the domain untouched by time.

When Mr. Emerson decided to sail for Europe, Mr. Thoreau moved from Walden in September to become "Mr. Rough-and-Tumble" in the little room at the head of the Emerson stairs, tightening the loose bolts and helping Father build a summerhouse for the wanderer. Often Louy watched Father as he returned home with gnarled and curving branches from the forests, or climbed gravely from the finite to the infinite upon a ridgepole. He cared not at all if the townspeople dubbed the arbor a whirligig or log cabin. He had found how to satisfy his genius, and was content now to sit down for the winter with Plato.

Louy's genius burned, too, with a brighter flame than ever before, as with Anna she wrote her scripts for the troupe in the Hillside barn. In a flowing hand she penned the love scenes between Zara and Ernest L'Estrange, and with a defiant backhand inscribed direful lines for the villain Rodolpho. More exciting than the tableaux of "William Tell" or "Taking the Veil" were the full-length plays complete with title, subtitle, and fourteen scenes. With much discussion and debate the preparations for the gala performances continued, the girls making green doublets with plush puffs for Count Antonio and a crimson robe with a brocaded waist for Lady Inez. Maenads and sentinels were properly garbed and noblemen practiced unsheathing their daggers, while draperies were converted into doublets and red curtains into Greek tunics.

The audience gathered—the Emersons, the Channings, the Hosmers—waiting for the little bell that would herald the drawing of the curtains. A Spanish peasant girl disguised as a page tripped onto the boards, ready to pursue her beloved Count Antonio until, after one desertion, one suicide, and several elaborate speeches, he returned the affection of "The Mysterious Page." On other occasions the curtain rose upon a witch concocting magic brews in a cave made of bureaus and tables. The Alcott troupe might offer "Norna; or, The Witch's Curse," or "The Captive of Castile," "The Unloved Wife," or "The Prince and the Peasant." What did the name matter when Louy appeared in doublet and hose, stamping her yellow boots, declaiming: "I am no coward, Ione; but there is a spell upon me. 'Tis a holy one, and the chain that holds me here I cannot break,—for it is *love.*"

Surely there was a spell upon them all when the Hillside barn was converted into Spain or Greece or some uncharted spot never to be found on land or sea. How the tones rang out as Louy stalked across the stage, playing in turn the haughty noble, the lover, the witch, and the bandit. For Anna, the quieter roles of Leonore or Zara; Louy would play the hero, tall and magnificent, tossing roses from balconies, gathering magic herbs in dark forests, unsheathing a dagger to encounter the spirits of the dead, or drinking love potions or death phials. Nothing could clip the wings of the dramatist-actor-manager, who with her sister had indeed gone barnstorming.

Little could compare with the delights of chilling the neighbors' blood or hearing their enthusiastic applause, except perhaps a session with Mr. Dickens. Louy sat for hours in her room, devouring *The Life and Adventures of Martin Chuzzlewit*, taking up quarters at Todgers's boardinghouse, delighting in Mark Tapley, reading aloud with Anna the dialogue of Sairey Gamp and Betsey Prig. Mrs. Gamp, with her husky voice and moist eye and red nose, was an even more interesting figure to dramatize than Zara, and Louy gladly offered Anna the role of the bearded Mrs. Prig so that she herself could play Sairey, bidding her dear friend, "Try the cowcumbers, God bless you!" Often she called at High Holborn to hear Sairey discourse upon the mythical Mrs. Harris, or to watch the nurse invest herself with the pattens, black shawl, and umbrella that were indispensable for a lying-in or a laying-out.

Sometimes Louy turned to *Barnaby Rudge* and, before the roaring fire of the Maypole, gathered with Solomon Daisy and

Phil Parkes to hear the tale of Reuben Haredale's murder. Best of all, she dipped into the *Pickwick Papers*, encountering the Fat Boy at Dingley Dell, witnessing the trial of Bardell *v*. Pickwick, and following Sam Weller and his master to prison. The Pickwick Club might have been dissolved in the Dickens version; it was reinaugurated at Hillside, where four sisters were ready to assume the roles of Pickwick, Tupman, Winkle, and Snodgrass. Adorned with cardboards marked "P C," dressed in tights and gaiters, shooting coat, or white cravat, the Pickwickians of Concord convened in the barn for Dickensian philosophy and good cheer.

In April the youngest Pickwickian left with Mother to spend the summer in Maine. The eldest was off to a Dingley Dell of her own in the form of Walpole, New Hampshire. Llewellyn Willis and Lizzie were excellent companions for Mr. Pickwick, but two followers did not make a club, and what was Sairey Gamp without Betsey to share a pint of porter? Louy would have been lonely indeed had it not been for the friend who returned in July to the white frame house on the Cambridge Turnpike.

Within Mr. Emerson's doors it was always morning. He sat in his rocking chair, one leg crossed over the other, his portfolio on his knee. In melodious, measured tones he welcomed his visitor, as if he had noticed for the first time that little Louy Alcott was growing very tall and slender, that in her clear, bright eyes a touch of softness had appeared, and that in her fifteen years of wisdom she had learned to love a poem as well as a race down Hardy's Hill. Louy understood the wise sweetness of Mr. Emerson's face, glowed at the welcome of his hand, and met the searching look of his sun-accustomed eyes. She glanced about her, at the large mahogany table in the middle of the room, with its morocco writing pad, at the mantel with its statuette of Psyche and the little bronze Goethe. Most of all she looked at the books that lined the wall, at the Plato, the Coleridge, and the Dante.

Much Mr. Emerson said to her, the sunrise smile lighting up his face as Louy's eyes wandered from Goethe to Shakespeare. Fiction, even the mighty Dickens, he could not enjoy. One day, he hoped, the novel would find the way to men's interiors. Round the book-lined room he led her, till she had found "the new and very interesting" volume, suggesting quietly, "Wait a little for that. Meantime try this." He would lend her *Wilhelm Meister* now, and she would go on to mine the treasures of Shakespeare, Dante, and Carlyle.

He spoke of other matters also to his new disciple, of the law of one's nature, above which no other law was sacred. Of words he spoke, too, and of writing. "He that writes to himself writes to an eternal public. That which is done at home must be the history of the times and the spirit of the age to us." What was genius but veracity? "With Genius there is always youth."

He listened as intently as he spoke, paying deference to the freedom of Louy's mind, leaning toward her with an unforgettable look as she groped to give utterance to some new thought. At times he read aloud when the children trooped into the study, his low tones sonorous and penetrating.

At charades in the drawing room, at apple-and-gingerbread receptions, on Sunday afternoon walks, Louy was there to follow, whether Mr. Emerson led the way to Walden picnics or to Plato's banquet. And as she followed, she worshiped, finding at last the subject for her poem, the doorstep for her garland of wild flowers. She was the "Bettina" to Mr. Emerson's Goethe, but her letters, though written, were never sent. In a cherry tree she sat at midnight, singing her love to the moon, and under his window she repeated the song of Mignon:

> *Kennst du das Land, wo die*
> *Citronen blühn?*
> *Im dunkeln Laub die Gold—*
> *Orangen glühn, . . .*
> *Kennst du es wohl!*
> *Dahin! Dahin!*
> *Mögt ich mit dir, o mein*
> *Geliebter, ziehn.*

It was not simply to earn a livelihood, but to return the kindness of the good friend who left money for the Alcotts on the mantel against which he had leaned, that Louy opened a school in the Hillside barn. With the Emerson children the new teacher shared the knowledge of arithmetic that Mr. Lane had given her, the reading skill she had learned from Father, the botanical information that Miss Foord had imparted, the games Miss Russell and Miss Chase had taught her, and the physiology she remembered from John Hosmer's lessons. Louy was proud to hold court in the barn, where her neighbors' eager faces looked up to her, and she gave without stint from the stores of her learning.

It was Ellen Emerson, who always loved a fairy story, whom the teacher singled out for her finest lessons. Often Louy ran to the old cartwheel half hidden in grass under the locusts to scribble a fairy tale for her scholar. Sitting in the barn or walking along the paths, she unfolded the fables of flowers scented with the sweetness Mr. Thoreau had given her, the tales of cobwebs dropped by fairies upon Concord meadows, of dewy roses gathered from *The Story Without an End.*

> Once upon a time, two little Fairies went out into the world to seek their fortune. Thistledown was as gay and gallant a little Elf as ever spread a wing. His purple mantle, and doublet of green, were embroidered with the brightest threads, and the plume in his cap came always from the wing of the gayest butterfly.

Ellen listened wide-eyed as Louy spun the tale of Thistledown, who was redeemed through his love of Lily-Bell. As Louy spoke, Ellen wandered through a fairyland where the only villains were droning bees, where glowworms and dew-elves plied their peaceful way, where Concord fairies feasted upon cakes of flower-dust with cream from the yellow milkweed. Dr. Dewdrop, the Water Cure physician, ministered to the village elves. The love of the tender Violet conquered the Frost King. A magic needle designed broad-brimmed cowslip hats for fairies who sipped dew from acorn cups and waved their fans of rose leaves. "The Frost King" was offered to Ellen in a green notebook, and "The Fairie Dell" appeared between gray marbled covers tied with pink ribbons. In the fairyland where she had wandered with Mr. Thoreau, Louy led Ellen now, spinning a magic tapestry with a thread that had no end.

Her scrapbook, too, was filled with lines from Goethe and from Wordsworth, as she read on and on in the books that lined the wall of Mr. Emerson's study. As she read, she perceived her own limitations, finding her flower fables freighted with far less sweetness than Wordsworth's primrose or than Goethe's green meadows far extending. Then the pages of Louy's journal were blank, her mind was a room in confusion, and it was only Mother who could encourage her to go on writing, to go on spinning tales. Louy read her mother's note so full of confidence and trust:

> I am sure your life has many fine passages well worth recording, and to me they are always precious. . . . Do write a little each day, dear, if but a line, to show me how bravely you begin the battle, how patiently you wait for the rewards sure to come when the victory is nobly won.

At her desk in the little room off the garden, Louy sat ready to write her first story. She wrote of Guido, the Florentine painter, who fell in love with Madeline, and of Count Ferdinand, his rival. Madeline's father would give his daughter to the one who "hath painted a picture the most perfect in grace, and beauty of form, design and coloring." The Count in his lesser love painted Madeline, but Guido sketched a portrait of his mother that won the prize. Louy had written her first story, "The Rival Painters. A Tale of Rome."

As the winter of 1848 came on, the author had less time to sit in her "poet's corner," less freedom of mind to weave her tales of flowers or of Rome. In winter the village fairies seemed to wander off to warmer regions, and another tale was spinning in Concord, whose end seemed less beneficent than Guido's. No prizes were offered there for Louy or for Father either, but in Boston Mother's friends were ready to give her a salary as their missionary to the poor, and Father might hold his Conversations before more eager audiences. Anna, back from Walpole, could teach in the city, and perhaps Louy also could earn money after her experiences in the Concord barn.

On a gloomy November day the family held their anxious council. For Mr. Emerson, Father could make solid the Platonic cloudland where he dwelt, but others saw in him merely the answer to a savage conundrum. "What is the difference between Emerson and Alcott? One is a seer, the other a seersucker." From the jeers of his townspeople at least he would escape. It was not Concord, after all, that had been beautiful, nor Hillside either, but, as Father said, the pure and happy, the kind and loving family, the home where peace and gentle quiet abode.

Louy ran out over the hill to the old cartwheel, not to scribble a fairy tale, but to think through to the end a living story. It would be good-bye to the Concord where she had grown up and tasted happiness, good-bye to cattle show and apple harvest. To Baker Farm and Fairhaven she would walk no longer. The slowly winding river would wind no more, nor cattle graze upon the low hills, nor bushes redden in the fall in the white village of Concord.

On Dedham Street a house was rented, and Father took rooms at 12 West Street, where he might give his Conversations. On the seventeenth of the coldest November they had known, the family left for Boston. Father would ever continue to take the farthest star into his scheme. Louy would look to a nearer planet for her plans and inventions. Under her old red shawl a hopeful heart beat warmly, and she shook her fist at fate, strong in the determination to do something, teach or sew, act or write, anything to help this family that was again uprooted. She would be rich and famous and happy before she died. She would make no bargain with fate. Father said that thoughts were the parents of deeds, and he wished to beget an illustrious family. He had already done so. Who was more patient than Anna, more serene than Lizzie, more sensitive than Abby? As for herself, whose strength was stronger to make all dreams come true? There was another farewell to be spoken at Hillside, a farewell to little Louy, who would live there always. It was Louisa Alcott now who walked through the gate, leaving a child behind, save for the memories of that child which she would ever treasure, save for the strength that child had given her to stand against the world and fling a gage at fortune.

CHAPTER 5

Greenrooms and City Missions

There was a sparkle, a glitter, a heady excitement in Boston that exhilarated Louisa as she walked about the crowded city. Boston, too, seemed to have gone forward to seek its fortune, and Louisa found in its ebullience a mood that answered her own. There was nothing that the city could not offer, from Chief Objewa at Faneuil Hall to the Booths at the Museum—nothing, Louisa reflected, provided she had the money for such delights.

As she kept house in Dedham Street, washing the dishes and cooking in the basement kitchen, Louisa saw a different Boston from the one she had glimpsed in the bright streets. Her only view of the city was a procession of muddy boots; her only prospect of fortune was screened by a brick wall that nothing but her concentrated devotion could vault. With her mother and Anna she went three evenings every week to teach a class of adult Negroes how to read and write and make out their washing bills. There, and in the Relief Room that Mother had established on Washington Street, was another Boston, whose sparkle had been dulled, whose gaiety had been wiped out.

Mrs. Samuel May, Mrs. Henry Lee, and Mrs. Tuckerman had joined with others to provide a fund that was placed in Cousin Hannah Robie's hands, out of which Mother was given thirty dollars a month for investigating the wants and merits of the poor. Besides visiting the destitute of the city, Mother collected bundles of clothing and parcels of medicines in her Relief Room. Louisa watched often when Boston's poverty-stricken women came to find employment or shoes, bonnets or shawls, needles or omnibus tickets. The scenes in that room, she agreed with Mother, rivaled those of Dickens. Here came the Temple Place beggars, the dregs of a teeming city. Even Father, hearing the stories of the Relief Room, was beginning to admit that philosophy appeared to be subsistence minus bread and butter.

At least no money was needed for the plays in the Dedham Street kitchen, where Louisa took five parts to Anna's four and delighted Mother with lightning changes of costume and characters ranging from a Greek prince in silver armor to a murderer in chains. Harps could be invented without benefit of heaven, and fairies' spangled wings sewed without reference to the marble fronts of Washington Street. Hamlet could intone his soliloquies with gloomy glare and tragic stalk though he lacked a ticket to the Boston Museum.

In the summer, when cholera spread through the congested courts of Boston, the Alcotts were glad to accept Uncle Samuel May's invitation to live at his large, comfortable home on Atkinson Street. For the delight of the family Louisa organized a little paper, "The Olive Leaf," to which the Pickwickians might offer their contributions. The editor completed her first issue on July 19, presenting a "Poet's Corner," in which Augustus Snodgrass warbled a lay to his kitty, Chapter One of a narrative entitled "Little Trot," hints on dirty nails, and announcements of a meeting at the George and Vulture. It was amusing to write notices about the Olympian in her three-columned newspaper, but Louisa found it difficult at times not to long for printer's ink and a larger circulation.

There were more immediate needs to long for after the family moved to Groton Street. Father started the new year with a Parliament on the Times; Mother, with a report on her work among the poor. Louisa, too, began work with the new year, assisting Anna in her school on Canton Street, but finding it difficult to be patient with children who were less interested in fairy tales than in mischief.

In spite of the constant labor of many days, the family's poverty, Louisa realized, had never been more extreme than now in the mid-century. At least, through the kindness of Uncle May, they were spared house rent. But it was hard to see Mother so dejected, weeping from anxiety until she could not be comforted. How could she help bewailing the low state of moral discrimination which drove into the regions of starvation an exalted spirit whose efforts for the twenty best years of his life had been to elevate the intellectual condition of mankind? Louisa understood that her father's defects were the defects of genius, that if he could not fortify the bodies of his children, he could fortify their souls. There would be recompense some day for his wrongs, and compensation for his long neglect. Yet now the day of redemption seemed to vanish to a far point in the future.

Wherever she turned, Louisa found disappointment. It was hard not to covet the fine things she saw, the bonnets that would have set off her long hair and well-shaped head, the grenadine veils, and the black velvet spencers. It was harder still to pass by the Howard Athenaeum, where Max Maretzek's opera company was performing, to linger outside the Museum and know that wax statuary and the Feejee Mermaid were exhibited for those who had the price of tickets. Yet her own poverty and disappointment paled into insignificance when Louisa heard the regret of good men everywhere over the passage of the Fugitive Slave Law and Daniel Webster's ignominious speech in its support, and she vowed to turn even despair into the substance of what she would one day write.

During the summer a more severe hardship arose after Mother had fed some immigrants in the garden. Now disease was coupled with poverty, for the family was stricken with smallpox, first Louisa and her sisters, then Mother and Father. No nurse or physician came to the Alcott house, but the pages of Hahnemann's *Organon of the Healing Art* were studied for homeopathic remedies that would bring relief. Often, now, when Louisa heard her parents discuss the mundane question of ways and means, or the gossip about Father's permitting Mother to work for the family, she longed for a quiet, lovely home unburdened by debts or troubles.

When their health was restored, the family moved again, to 50 High Street; but Louisa did not believe that the quiet, lovely home would be found there, where boardinghouses mingled with grocery stores, and a mason's signboard creaked in the wind next to an undertaker's establishment. Still, it was better to be earning a living in dirty High Street than to be starving in a country paradise. With Anna, Louisa continued her school, while Mother opened an intelligence office that grew out of her city missionary work, and Lizzie kept house in the cellar kitchen. There were moments to snatch for reading *The Scarlet Letter*, for discussing with sorrow Margaret Fuller's tragic death, and for writing "The Inheritance," a novel about Lord Percy's fast character and Amy's visit to England. With morbid delight Louisa and Anna followed the details of Professor Webster's hanging for the murder of George Parkman, and were inspired to more melodramatic plays than ever. Louisa confided to her journal that she would be a Siddons if she could, for surely the life of a tragedienne must be gayer than that of a schoolmarm. It was hard not to covet the Jenny Lind bandeaux and plaids that paraded in Boston, hard to see a lump of gold in a Washington Street window and think that she would never share it, hard to know that paradise was not quite fixed at 50 High Street.

It was from Mr. Lamson's parish in Dedham that Mother had received two barrels of clothing for the poor. When a gentleman from that village appeared in the intelligence office in search of a companion for his sister, Louisa suddenly stopped dreaming splendid dreams over the red petticoats she was piecing together from odds and ends, and decided to take the position herself. The visitor was tall and ministerial, and spoke in a fine flow of language as he waved his black-gloved hands about. There would be books, pictures, flowers, a piano, and the best of society. The companion would be one of the family, required to help only in the lighter work that his neuralgic sister could not do. Surely, Louisa thought, this would be more interesting than teaching and would pay better than sewing; she would have time to enjoy the books, and Dedham was not far from home. When Mother turned to her, asking if she could suggest anyone for the situation, Louisa answered briefly, "Only myself."

Why, after all, thought Louisa, should she not try the experiment? It could but fail like the others. She was too proud to be idle and dependent. She would scrub floors and take in washing first. When Mother cautioned her that, although she might be called a companion, she would actually be going out to service, Louisa recalled what Mr. Emerson had written: "Let the great soul incarnated in some woman's form, . . . go out to service, and sweep chambers and scour floors, and its effulgent daybeams cannot be muffled or hid, but to sweep and scour will instantly appear supreme and beautiful actions." Let the highly respectable relatives be horrified and foretell the disgrace that headstrong Louisa would bring upon the family; her aristocratic ancestors did not feed or clothe her.

Hiding her disappointment in descending from the part of Siddons to the role of Bel-cinder, Louisa packed the dresses she had made for herself, the two calicoes, the one delaine, along with several aprons and sweeping-caps, and set forth with her trunk, a stout heart, and a five-dollar bill. The Dedham family, she found, consisted of a nervous little woman enveloped in shawls and afflicted with neuralgia, her ancient and courteous father, and her brother, the Hon. James Richardson, whom Louisa had met in the intelligence office. She was shown to her tiny room, where she felt more like a giantess than ever, and proceeded to don her blue apron and prepare for work.

Louisa worked with a will, putting to rights the dilapidated furniture, sweeping away the cobwebs, kindling the fires, and making the beds. After the drudgery of the morning, she was invited into the study to hear her employer read aloud or discuss metaphysical philosophy. He began to ply her with poems while she washed the dishes and took to placing reproachful little notes under her door. Finally, Louisa could bear his maudlin attentions no longer and, stranded on a small island of water in a sea of soap-suds in the kitchen, she delivered an ultimatum with a flourish of her scrubbing brush. She had come, she reminded him, not to act as his companion, but his sister's.

It became apparent, however, that, as a result of her remarks, all the work of the household would fall into her hands. It was her duty now to dig paths through the snow, bring water from the well, split kindling, and sift ashes. All day long she cleaned the rusty knives, turned the sheets, mended the stockings, and balked only when she was commanded to polish muddy boots with the blacking hose. Every evening there was a bucketful of hard russets to pare, every morning the beds to make and the floors to scrub.

At last, after seven long weeks had ended, Louisa announced her decision to leave. The disappointed employer shut himself up in sulky retirement, while his sister tucked into Louisa's hand a sixpenny pocketbook. She trudged gaily away to the station, knowing how the fugitive Shadrach must have felt when he had escaped. Along the lonely road she walked, the dismal old house behind her, before her the wheelbarrow with her trunk, and in her pocket the return for the hardest labor she had ever done. Perhaps she could increase the rewards for her work by writing a story on domestic service in Dedham. Planning all the delightful things she would buy with her money, she opened the purse to find four dollars inside it. She stood there, the sixpenny pocketbook open in her chapped, grimy, chilblained hands, and grappled with her despair alone on the windy Dedham road.

When she reached home, Louisa's outraged family returned the four dollars to Dedham, and she herself resumed teaching. There was enough excitement in Boston for Louisa to forget the pain and bitterness of Dedham, except perhaps as the basis of a story she might one day be able to write. The fugitive Sims was returned to slavery after Cousin Samuel Sewall had defended him, and Louisa listened to Mother's account of the trial of a man guilty of no crime but the love of liberty. Everywhere she heard talk of Webster, who knew the heroes of 1776 but could not see those of 1851 when he met them on the street.

In her own family Louisa was a heroine, for in September she thrilled to the joy of seeing her first published work. The poem "Sunlight" was signed by "Flora Fairfield," but Louisa, gazing at the lines in *Peterson's Magazine*, knew that the flowery pseudonym was hers and that she had at last appeared in print.

Llewellyn Willis, who, while he was preparing to enter Harvard Divinity School, boarded with the Alcotts, was almost as pleased with Louisa's success as her sisters. It was Llewellyn who carried Louisa's first story, "The Rival Painters," to the office of the *Olive Branch*, a paper published by Thomas Norris and devoted to Christianity, polite literature, general intelligence, agriculture, and the arts. Besides the joy of receiving five dollars for her contribution, there was the delight of seeing her initials in print and her story published on the first page of the May 8, 1852, issue, which also carried C. S. Campbell's "British Queen," "Fanny Fern's" "Elise de Vaux," and advertisements for Wistar's Balsam of Wild Cherry and Carhart's Improved Melodeons. In her pleasure at having been welcomed into the realms of polite literature, the author immediately vowed to read no more novels except those of Dickens and Miss Bremer, and to devote herself to such substantial works as Carlyle's *French Revolution* and Eckermann's *Conversations*.

After Mr. Hawthorne's purchase of Hillside, the family was able to move to 20 Pinckney Street in the fall, and there the newly discovered author could write stories and rehearse Sairey Gamp's remarks upon the imaginary Mrs. Harris. She and Anna opened a school in the parlor, and Mother took lodgers. In the evenings the family gathered in the second-floor parlor to play proverbs or whist, to give plays or hem pillowcases as Louisa read aloud.

Louisa found pleasures that lifted her above the humdrum world of teaching and sewing. In November, Cousin Hamilton Willis sent tickets for Madame Sontag's concert at the new Music Hall. Louisa forgot the shabbiness of the dress she had made over from the Goddard ragbag when she entered the hall and walked through the wide corridors, looking up at the tiers of galleries brilliantly illuminated with a flood of gaslight. What a setting the hall would make for a story or a play; what a narrative could be worked around the career of a prima donna!

Louisa watched expectantly while Madame Henriette Sontag walked on the stage and Mr. Eckert raised his baton. Was it the prima donna or Louisa Alcott who stood there before thousands of admirers, a lithe, slender figure with braided hair, raising her perfect soprano in "I Know that My Redeemer Liveth"? Throughout Rossini's "Grand Oratorio of Stabat Mater" Louisa gloried in the brilliant colors and superb sounds of the Music Hall, thrilled to the applause from thousands of gloved hands, and longed to sip the cup of fame from which Madame Sontag had so deeply drunk.

Louisa returned to the Music Hall in December to hear the Sunday discourse of Theodore Parker. In low tones he began, speaking about laborious young women, grimly casting their adversaries into the amphitheater. Louisa felt the rugged, solemn earnestness of his benignant face and was greatly moved as he drove the deep plow of his sound righteousness under the roots of a false morality. As she listened, she marveled how this plain man with his low voice, reading a manuscript through his spectacles or standing motionless as a block, could so pour the fiery blood of his passion into her own soul. He seemed to have designed his sermon just for her, demanding that woman choose her own place of action, have her vote, and be eligible for office. With granite integrity he carried off the prison doors as Samson had borne away the gates of Gaza, until for Louisa the world became an unexplored domain where all things yet were possible.

Filled with the determination that the preacher's words had given her, Louisa taught school in the Pinckney Street parlor, where Mr. Whipple, Mr. Sargent, and Mr. Apthorp sent their children. It seemed less discouraging not to have money for Mr. Forrest's *Othello* at the National. She needed no money to hear Mr. Parker's sermon on "The Public Function of Woman." She needed no gloves to applaud Mother's signing of the woman's rights petition. Mr. Parker had given her the courage to take a position as second girl after school closed and do the wash for two dollars a week. The "second girl" would be "first lady" yet, and the queen of the tub would sing a song from the suds until the day came when out of her despair or her joy she could give voice to richer music.

The ceaseless round of work continued in the fall, when Louisa returned to her school, Abby to her lessons, and Mother to her boarders. Through the Mays, Anna was given a position as teacher in Syracuse, and Louisa found life lonely without the comfort of her presence. The family was less together now than before, and Louisa missed the strong union that had sweetened her days at Hillside. In October, Father started on a tour of the West, where he proposed to give Conversations on the representative minds of New England. His return in February was less propitious than his setting forth, and Louisa rushed down with Mother, Lizzie, and Abby to embrace the wanderer, who looked cold and thin as an icicle but still as serene as God. Louisa longed to ask whether he had had good fortune, but refrained, and it was Abby who finally demanded, "Well, did people pay you?" They looked on while Father opened his pocketbook and flourished a single dollar bill, saying, "Only that! My overcoat was stolen, and I had to buy a shawl. Many promises were not kept, and traveling is costly; but I have opened the way, and another year shall do better." The beaming smile never faded from Mother's face as she kissed him, assuring him that she called that doing very well since Father was once again safely home. Tears were close on the heels of laughter as Louisa looked at her mother in her big nightcap and old jacket, and she knew that the domestic scene she had witnessed was drama that needed no footlights.

She determined to work at her writing, preparing her old flower fables for print, and recounting the story of her experience at Dedham in hopes that it might be considered worthy of publication. With the manuscript in her hand she ventured into Mr. Fields's little room at the back of the Old Corner Bookstore, and waited in the hub of the hub where the littérateurs of Boston chatted with the publisher. Mr. Fields beckoned to her from his green-curtained desk while young Mr. Thomas Niles examined piles of manuscript, and Louisa handed the tale of her experience in domestic service to the ruler of the Old Corner. At last he looked up at her, his eyes twinkling keenly above his russet-red cheeks. "Stick to your teaching, Miss Alcott. You can't write."

Louisa walked slowly out of the office, the rejected manuscript in her hand. Over and over as she turned from Washington Street to Pinckney Street, the words echoed and re-echoed in her mind: "Stick to your teaching. You can't write." Here was a blow more difficult to sustain than any sixpenny pocketbook on a Dedham road. But Mr. Fields must be wrong. She would write. What was more, she would write a story that James T. Fields would pay for.

In June, Louisa saw Boston stricken with a more direful woe than even her own had been. Father had courageously joined with the members of the Vigilance Committee to rescue the fugitive Anthony Burns from the courthouse, but the attempt had failed, and on the second of June the slave was returned to his owner. Standing on Court Square, Louisa saw the houses draped in black, the sidewalks a seething mass of people hissing and hooting the troops who passed back and forth. All flags hung Union down. As the procession moved on, Louisa caught a glimpse of the fugitive's face, scarred by a burn or a brand. There was no martial music in this parade, only the rumble of angry throngs, only the clank of scabbards and the dull tramp of marching feet. Surely this rendition would one day be redeemed. Remembering another fugitive at Hillside, Louisa hoped that she would have a part in the redemption, when pistols would be cocked not at the slave but at his owner.

There was little hope in her own heart or in Boston in times like these. Louisa was glad to leave the ignominies of the city to spend a month with Anna in Syracuse. In her restlessness and uncertainty, it was a pleasant interim to be with Anna and Uncle Sam May, good to know that here were people who had found themselves and learned their way of life. Observing Uncle Sam May as he prepared sermons, visited parishioners, and helped fugitives to escape, Louisa desired to share his accomplishments and find her own niche in the eternal order of things. Yet she would not imitate. She would insist always on herself.

Louisa did more than teach when she returned to Pinckney Street. With renewed determination she scanned the pages of the *Saturday Evening Gazette* to learn the type of story that Mr. Clapp found sufficiently amusing for publication, and decided to try her hand at writing for that weekly. In the garret above the third floor she sat after her class was dismissed, writing a narrative about Beatrice and Theresa, rivals on the stage and in love. From her memories of the Music Hall she described the gay opera house of her story, while Madame Sontag's superb soprano and Jenny Lind's voice were borrowed for her own prima donnas. No other hint was needed for Louisa to embroider upon that frame a tale of vengeance in which one singer crushed her competitor to death by means of an iron ring placed upon her head. The story, she decided, ended quite suitably with the remorse of the gentleman who had caused the tragedy and the sudden insanity of the perpetrator of the crime. Mr. Clapp seemed to agree with the author, for he paid ten dollars for the privilege of filling over three columns of his paper with "The Rival Prima Donnas." On November 11, 1854, the story was published, again by "Flora Fairfield," but it was Louisa Alcott who raised her heart in gratitude. Thanks to "Flora Fairfield," Louisa's twenty-second birthday was happy indeed.

The author delighted also in the greater joy of correcting the proof sheets of her first book, for after Father had consulted with Mr. Briggs, the publisher decided to print 1,600 copies of *Flower Fables*. To Ellen Emerson, for whom they had been created, the author dedicated her book on December 9; and ten days later it was published by George Briggs, who advertised it as the most beautiful fairy book that had appeared for a long time, a work destined to be the most popular juvenile of the season. Now "Flora Fairfield" and "L.M.A." were erased; in their place the full signature of Louisa May Alcott appeared below *Flower Fables* on December 19. The next day Louisa read with joy the brief paragraph in the *Transcript* that recommended *Flower Fables* as "agreeable sketches . . . adapted to the capacity of intelligent young persons." Although the *Gazette* called her book *Flower Tables*, it characterized the "little legends of faery land" as "very sweet." A copy arrived in time for the author to place it as a Christmas gift in Mother's stocking. With the book she added a little note, asking Mother to look upon her firstborn as an earnest of what she might yet do. If Mr. Thoreau had planted the seed from which these flowers had sprung, and Madame Sontag had unconsciously given the hint for "The Rival Prima Donnas," surely no experience was too unimportant to serve as grist for the author's mill. Everywhere she looked she would find a character or a scene; she needed but to open her eyes to find the source of stories.

In the garret with her papers around her and a pile of apples nearby, Louisa wrote down from memory the plots that she had designed. Ideas bubbled and boiled in her mind until she could not wait to fix them on paper. In two or three days she could complete a story that would bring five dollars from Mr. Clapp, and every experience she had had, every book she had read, went into the cauldron to appear transmuted in her manuscripts. Had Dickens's Little Nell brightened her grandfather's life? Louisa would write a poem to the heroine and a story in which she endowed Alice with the magic that would bring "A New Year's Blessing" into John Owen's cheerless home. Had Florence at last softened the heart of her father, Mr. Dombey? Louisa would embroider a tale about "Little Genevieve," who brought atonement to her erring parents. Through rose-colored glasses she saw a world where human beings simply took the place of the fairies of *Flower Fables*, where white doves cooed softly, and where virtue was always rewarded. In her own home she found the source of still another story, in which four sisters earned their living, Agnes following the stage, Ella working as governess, Amy studying art in Europe, and Nora remaining at home to write. "The Sisters' Trial" would succeed, all but Agnes finding their year's work crowned with love or achievement, and the author wondered if the Alcott girls would fare as well as their literary representatives.

In the garret she went on, filling her scrapbook, writing in her journal, and deciding at last that she could resist the lure of the footlights no longer and would convert "The Rival Prima Donnas" into a play. Louisa remembered enough of the technique she had employed in the Hillside barn to turn her prose into dialogue, and with satisfaction she listed her dramatis personae, from the painter, Claude, to Corilla, Beatrice's maid. Perhaps one day she would see her characters tread the boards of the Boston Theatre. Once having turned to playwriting, she could not stop, but must go on to write a farce for William Warren, whose bright, penetrating eyes would surely twinkle over "Nat Bachelor's Pleasure Trip."

Louisa knew that her cousin, Dr. Charles May Windship, was as interested in the theater as in his Roxbury practice. When she showed him her farce, he was set upon its coming out, and decided, since William Warren was too busy with *Poor Pillicoddy* to play Nat, to approach Mrs. William H. Smith with the request that she produce it at her benefit. Otherwise, he thought that Mr. Joseph M. Field, the prolific dramatist of the Mobile Theater Company, might be a likely candidate. At any rate, he would not give up hope that some day "Nat Bachelor, or The Trials of a Good-Natured Man" would find its place upon a billboard.

While she waited, dashing off stories for the *Gazette* or lines for her rival prima donnas, Louisa enjoyed her greatest pleasure in going to the theater with Hamilton Willis. Cousin Hamilton piloted her to the Boston Museum for a glimpse of wax figures, and nightly performances executed by Mr. Keach. Over a table at Mrs. Mayer's ice cream saloon opposite the Museum, they compared the dialogue of "The Rival Prima Donnas" with that of the professional stock company. One rival only was there to the Museum, the Boston Theatre, where Louisa could see herself in turn as actress, prima donna, manager, or playwright. At such moments the money she had earned from writing a story or sewing pillowcases had unlimited possibilities in shawls for Mother, crimson ribbons for Abby's shabby bonnet, and frocks for Lizzie; and the Alcott Fund that Mr. Emerson was planning seemed absurdly unnecessary.

It was at the suggestion of Cousin Hamilton Willis's sister, Lizzie Wells, that Louisa left her work along with the theater galleries of Boston to spend the summer at Walpole, New Hampshire. In July the family followed her there to live rent-free in Uncle Benjamin Willis's small house in the lane near the ravine. While Father farmed and conversed with his new neighbors, Louisa found herself busy among the young people who had organized the Amateur Dramatic Company of Walpole. Though they lacked the saloon promenade of the Boston Theatre, there was a cast at hand to play any comic drama—the Haywards, the Kittredges, and the troupe's scenic artist, Alfred Howland. When Abby consented to taking the lesser role of prompter and Anna agreed to play Patty, Louisa set herself to learning the lines of the Widow Pottle for the forthcoming production of *The Jacobite*.

While costumes were sewed and the backdrop was painted, Louisa rehearsed the role of the crass, ignorant, comical innkeeper, mouthing a "Ragamuffin" or an "Impudent varlet" or a "Pack up thee duds" with a fine gusto. She had never played to a better audience even at Hillside, for Howard Ticknor loved elocution as well as his own verses, and when Fanny Kemble appeared at Walpole, Louisa's cup of joy was filled to overflowing.

At seven o'clock on Tuesday, September 11, the fathers and mothers and sisters and brothers of the Amateur Dramatic Company began crowding into the hall, while the cast donned their eighteenth-century costumes, repeated their cues, and prepared for their entrances. At eight the curtain rose on the parlor of *The Crooked Billet*, and Louisa watched from the wings while sister Anna and Louisa Hayward walked on stage to explain Major Murray's difficulties. At last, from the cellar behind scenes, Louisa roared her first line: "I've told thee so a hundred times, fool; art thee deaf!" And from that moment she established her character, mouthed her dialect, and prepared to take her place upon the stage. Following her cue, she stalked the boards with a will, cuffed John Duck, "deary-me'd" his honor Sir Richard, and with a keen gusto provided all the comic relief that author Planché could have desired.

Throughout the second act Louisa had time to listen behind scenes as she exchanged her costume for the scarlet dress and white bonnet of Mrs. Bonnycastle, whose role she had been assigned in the second play of the evening. While the Walpole Serenade Band struck up, she gave herself a last-minute rehearsal to assume the character of a none-too-attractive woman "in a dreadful state of agitation" after the disappearance of her husband, last seen "rushing frantically down Holborn Hill with a carpetbag under his arm." At last, in a zealous desire to discover whether she was wife or widow, Louisa rushed on the stage, well supplied with asides and significant looks, and did not leave it until the comedy of errors had been straightened out. After the final line, Louisa, Anna, and the gentlemen of the troupe formed a semicircle to take their bows, and the curtain fell upon *The Two Bonnycastles*.

Louisa had finally listened to the applause she coveted and seen her name on a playbill. Throughout the summer she enjoyed her role of heavy comedian in plays that concerned a lady and gentleman in "a peculiarly perplexing predicament," and even rose to the heights of acting Mrs. Malaprop in a performance of *The Rivals*. Nothing could equal the joys of private theatricals; if she could never aspire to appearing at the Boston Theatre, she would at least interweave in her stories her recollections of the Walpole Amateur Dramatic Company. Besides, Louisa knew now that it was better to play a superior Widow Pottle than an inferior Lady Macbeth.

Between rehearsals and performances Louisa had time at Walpole to work on another book, "The Christmas Elves," which Abby illustrated. When Anna left to accept a position offered to her by Dr. Wilbur of the Syracuse Asylum, Louisa was determined to return to Boston. It was time for her to stop acting behind footlights and to start working so that Mother would not again be encumbered with debts. Packing the mousseline and batiste dresses she had made over from the finery in Lizzie Wells's ragbag, Louisa set out on a rainy November day, armed with her mother's blessing, her manuscripts, and the twenty dollars she had earned from her stories, to seek her fortune alone in Boston.

At Cousin Samuel Sewall's home in Melrose, or at his brother Thomas's house in Boston, Louisa found a welcome refuge where she could continue her writing. Her stories appeared quite regularly in the pages of the *Gazette*, and when readers began to speculate about the identity of "L.M.A.," author of "A New Year's Blessing" and "The Sisters' Trial," prices went up until "Bertha" and "Little Genevieve" brought ten dollars each instead of five. Learning that Joseph Field had taken her farce to Mobile and that Thomas Barry was considering the script of "The Rival Prima Donnas," Louisa set to work again with renewed determination, beginning a series of poems called "Beach Bubbles" and writing verses suggested by the death of Paul Dombey. When she saw a great yellow placard on the street announcing the publication of "Bertha" by the author of "The Rival Prima Donnas," Louisa expanded in the sunshine of her fame and proceeded to calculate the fortune that her pen would earn. Although Mr. Field's death prevented the theatergoers of Mobile from seeing "Nat Bachelor's Pleasure Trip," Louisa was asked to alter "The Rival Prima Donnas" for Mrs. Julia Barrow's next season. Mr. Clapp accepted "Beach Bubbles" for serial publication in the *Gazette*, and the author continued to send him the new stories that flowed from her pen.

Her head still spinning with plots about strong-minded women and poor lost creatures, the mainstay of the *Gazette* returned to Walpole for the summer only to find that Lizzie and Abby had been stricken with scarlet fever after Mother had tried to help a neighbor's sick children. Hahnemann's *Organon of the Healing Art* had restored Abby to health, but Louisa was pained to see Lizzie's round cheeks sunken, her bright eyes dull, and her firm mouth listless. While the family took turns nursing Lizzie, Father watered his little garden plot or discussed spiritualism at Dr. Bellows's, and Mother recorded recipes for tea cake or squash pudding that might appeal to the patient.

None of the diversions of Walpole could subdue Louisa's anxiety at Lizzie's bedside. Now more than ever before it would be necessary for her to help the family, and in October, after Father had gone to New York to visit Walt Whitman, she decided to go again to Boston, not merely to face, but to force the world.

This time, Louisa decided, she would not accept the easy refuge of the Sewalls. Mrs. David Reed had opened a boarding-house at 34 Chauncy Street next to the church, and from the room she rented for three dollars a week in the sky parlor Louisa could see a patch of the blue heavens and the gray church tower. She enjoyed living with the family, hearing Mr. Reed discuss the trials and rewards of publishing *The Christian Register,* and watching his small but prepossessing wife conduct a boardinghouse and work for the church.

With Cousin Hamilton Willis, Louisa visited Mr. Barry at the Boston Theatre to discuss "The Rival Prima Donnas." The manager escorted her all over the great theater on Washington Street, telling her that a dancing floor could be fitted over the orchestra chairs and the house converted into a ballroom. Without waiting for the necessary alterations of carpentry, Louisa executed a jig on the huge stage and received, besides a pass to the theater, the assurance that "The Rival Prima Donnas" would be brought out soon. Mr. Barry himself would take the part of Claude, and doubtless Mrs. Wood and Mrs. Barrow would share the honors of the rivals. That evening Louisa joyfully saw Lagrange as Norma and herself as an established playwright.

The next day, after the author had sewed a dozen bedsheets for Cousin Hamilton, she walked to Roxbury to tell Dr. Windship the fine news about the play. They chatted together about the relative merits of Mrs. Barrow and Mrs. Wood, and, feeling herself one day nearer to the Boston Theatre, Louisa climbed into the new horse railroad, scooped the hay over her cold feet, and settled back to dream of the ten dramatic passions.

She saw drama of a different nature and heard dialogue of a higher order when she attended Theodore Parker's Sunday evening receptions. Every week now Louisa donned the new cloak Cousin Lizzie Wells had given her and walked to 1 Exeter Place. The dramatis personae had always been more significant than the setting to the author of "The Rival Prima Donnas," and here a host of characters took their cues and spoke their lines for the silent dramatist who sat staring from her corner.

To the author of "Nat Bachelor" the parlor of 1 Exeter Place became a stage where the blond and slight Wendell Phillips modulated his silvery voice to honor mankind and speak for the oppressed, where Charles Sumner, grand and imposing, adjusted his pince-nez and coined phrases on the barbarism of slavery, and where Garrison raised his phrenological head illuminated to champion the cause of liberty. Of all the cast, however, none was more fascinating to Louisa than the host, who methodized, as he breathed, the profound philosophy that coursed through his veins, yet who comforted his young guest with a "Well, child, how goes it? God bless you, Louisa; come again."

Louisa needed Mr. Parker's encouragement, for Lizzie Wells's tickets and Mr. Barry's pass added no money to the Alcott sinking fund. For that the playwright spun a tale, "The Cross on the Church Tower," suggested by the view from her window, hemmed handkerchiefs for Mrs. Reed, and taught Mrs. Lovering's invalid daughter, Alice, in her home at Beacon Street, reading stories, teaching the multiplication table, and guiding her charge's hand through a maze of pothooks.

The new year moved on propitiously, and Louisa appeared often in her first new silk dress from Lizzie Wells to hear Mr. Parker's sermon on the Dangers and Duties of Young Women, to attend Fanny Kemble's reading or young Booth's princely and magnetic performance of Brutus. The silk was laid aside for sterner fabric when she sat at her window, writing or sewing, or packing a bundle to send to Walpole.

As she read *The Life of Charlotte Brontë*, the author of *Flower Fables* wondered whether she would ever be famous enough for people to care what her struggles had been. The years in Boston had, for all those struggles, been successful. She had seen her name in print. She had been paid for her writings in the *Saturday Evening Gazette* and had made thirty-two dollars through the sale of *Flower Fables*. "Nat Bachelor" was in the hands of Mrs. W. H. Smith, and though "The Rival Prima Donnas" might never be produced, she had had the practice of transposing a narrative into dramatic form. What was perhaps more important, she had learned how to embroider an elaborate plot from a hint of actuality; she had found people instead of fairies to throng her stories; she had heard enough dialogue in the Walpole Dramatic Company to enliven her tales with conversation. If she still viewed the world through rose-colored glasses, perhaps one day she would remove those spectacles and gain a closer insight into truth. A child had come to Boston, taking notes and watching silently from the corners of the world. She had heard enough also of the nation's good causes to long to share in them, to pray that some day she would help avenge the Fugitive Slave Law and by her writings or her work redeem in some measure the oppressed.

There were nearer troubles, however, that engrossed her. Since Lizzie had not yet recovered from the effects of scarlet fever, Louisa left for Walpole. There, Grandma Alcott paid the family a visit, telling Louisa the story of Father's boyhood, which she immediately planned to incorporate into a book on the trials and triumphs of the Pathetic Family. It was a pathetic family indeed who lived through the sad, anxious month of August, when Mother took the invalid to the seashore and Father came to the decision that he could never be happy far from Mr. Emerson. The kind friend helped again, so that John Moore's old house and orchard could be purchased and Father might live once more in Concord. With Anna, Louisa broke up the Walpole home and prepared for another removal of the pathetic family. In this way, too, she served an apprenticeship, to life as well as to literature.

CHAPTER 6

The Orchard House

Walking again beneath the scarlet maples of Main Street, Louisa felt that she could not live in Concord. The quiet village had slumbered on for nine years, during which she had changed from the girl who had stamped her boots in the Hillside barn and woven fairy tales for Ellen Emerson into a young woman who had gone forth to seek her fortune. Concord had not kept pace with her own metamorphosis. Below the Red Bridge there would be skating on the river, and skating would give way as always to the Carnival of Boats. There would be a nutting expedition to Estabrook Farm, and in the autumn the annual cattle show. Every day there would be the walk to the post office, where the good folk would gather round the stove for gossip. All of Concord seemed at first glance to have indulged in a nine-years' sleep, and Louisa was impatient with the sameness, the complacent serenity of the quiet village.

Yet there had been changes, slight alterations that gave sign of a decade passed. Along the Milldam were crowded flourishing businesses—Stacy's, Walcott and Holden's grocery, Jonas Hastings's boot shop, and Reynolds's apothecary. There was a new cemetery also, Sleepy Hollow. Mr. Emerson, Louisa saw, had enlarged his house so that there was a den where, perhaps, fugitive slaves might rest on their way to the North. No home in

Concord was complete without such a hiding place, for the village had become a station on the Underground Railroad.

Some Louisa had known had died, but others had grown up to fill the vacant places. George Bartlett was as interested as she was in dramatizing scenes from Dickens or organizing games and charades. There was a fine new flock of boys in Concord, with turned-up noses, spindle legs, and eyes that searched for birds' eggs. Surely in the slight newness that had come to Concord Louisa would find a source for stories, and the Milldam would become her Rialto.

Of all the changes in the village the one that promised the greatest interest for Louisa was Frank Sanborn's school. The young student had left Harvard to live at Mr. Channing's home on Main Street and, at Mr. Emerson's suggestion, to teach the young worthies of Concord. Often during her walks to the Milldam, Louisa met the tall, long-haired, book-laden instructor, who looked like a combination of Daniel Webster and d'Artagnan. She was delighted with his remarks about dances and picnics, declamations and fencing, troublesome boys and blooming girls, and enjoyed many a visit to the gray schoolhouse. In her deep sympathy with boys she was entertained by the antics of Bob Higginson, Faulkner, and young Sam Hoar, who would chew tobacco in spite of the law and the birch. Of all the boys who had come from the Sandwich Islands, Springfield, Boston, or Concord, to attend Frank Sanborn's school, Louisa found a yellow-haired lad named Alfred Whitman the most delightful. He was boarding at Pickle Roost, the Pratt home, and John Pratt often visited the Alcotts with his fifteen-year-old friend, who bubbled on about huskings at the farm, popcorn and pumpkin pies, and the Concord Dramatic Union that Mr. Sanborn was organizing.

After boarding for a week with Dr. Peabody at Mr. Hawthorne's Wayside—once their own Hillside—the family had settled in half of a yellow clapboard house on Bedford Street behind the Town Hall, while repairs went on at the Orchard House on the Lexington Road. Between Lizzie's room and the Concord school Louisa vibrated, leading two lives, one sorrowful, darkened by the shadow of fear, the other gay and light with plays in the church vestry and dances at Frank Sanborn's Friday evening parties.

To the music provided by the former turnkey of the jail, who played by ear and called the figures smartly, Louisa joined in the "Portland Fancy" or "Steamboat Quickstep," while Mr. Sanborn's more frivolous guests danced the waltz to the tune of "Buy a Broom." No one enjoyed the romping contradances more than she, but the acme of Louisa's delight was reached when "Old Poz" was produced, the part of the magpie taken by a parrot that bit everyone who approached its cage, or when "The Lady of the Lake" had a successful run until the dying Highlander brought down the house by rolling over the back curtain and exposing the dressing room.

Louisa agreed that the stock company of the Concord Dramatic Union rivaled Walpole's amateur troupe. As Abby listed the members of the 1857–58 season in the back of her diary, Louisa considered their histrionic abilities and anticipated the pleasures of barnstorming in Concord. Close upon the heels of Manager Sanborn came George Bartlett, the village doctor's son. Edith and Edward Emerson were duly entered in the company, and another name was inscribed, that of John Pratt, the twenty-four-year-old son of Minot Pratt, who had served during Association days at Brook Farm. Behind his mild eyes and bookkeeper's manner John harbored a lively wit as well as a gentle kindliness, and was ready to take any part assigned to him, especially, Louisa noticed, that of Darby to Anna's Joan. John's younger sister Carrie; Carrie Cheney, the lawyer's daughter; Joseph Wall, destined from birth to play the Wall in *A Midsummer Night's Dream;* and one or two other strolling players completed the list, except, of course, for Alfred Whitman.

As he had found his way to Louisa's home, the yellow-haired boy soon found his way to her heart, and many were the talks they had while he made the scenery for *Kill or Cure* or *A Morning Call.* He had worked for a year in the office of *The Boston Traveller,* but in spite of his business experience thought very little of himself or his abilities. He was the kind of boy Louisa would have wanted to be had she been born one of the lords of creation, and it was not long before she claimed him as "her boy." In his sober confidences to Louisa as he sat on the couch, he was fascinating without knowing it, and she thoroughly enjoyed her sessions with the keen-eyed, round-cheeked, flaxen-haired boy who was as full of good nature as of blunt truth, and who climaxed his good qualities by being as indolent at school as he was diligent at play. To Louisa he was a glorious, soaring, human boy, who would blister his hands rowing her about, or plan a moonlight skating party when the ice formed on the river, or sit till three in the morning staring at the dancers who bobbed around in Frank Sanborn's reels and cotillions.

It was time once again to assemble the theatrical properties for the opening season, and Louisa gathered together her white paste beads and silver buckles, her red scarf and long cloak, her plumed hat and sarcenet, and prepared to study the new roles that dominie Sanborn assigned to her. Draping her shawl over her tall figure and catching back her chestnut hair in a velvet band, she conned the repartee of Mrs. Chillingtone in *A Morning Call*, and picked up a green umbrella and carpetbag to play Mrs. O'Scuttle in *Poor Pillicoddy*. As "first old woman" she was a vigorous figure in the Town Hall or the church vestry, gladly relinquishing to Anna the role of ingénue.

For the triple performance of December 1, 1857, permissions were obtained from authors and cambric curtains converted into costumes. In the vestry of the Unitarian church a portable stage was erected, and Abby accepted the role of musical director for the production of *Naval Engagements*. Louisa donned her puce satin pelisse to take the part of Mrs. Pontifex, a charming young widow of forty. George Bartlett was her "Kingston dear" until he found a younger bride and until Louisa brought down the house in a storm of laughter while she looked on, unmoved. Alf made a smart young waiter at the Fountain Inn, and again Mrs. Alcott was roused to such enthusiasm that she clapped her dress gloves to rags, assuring her daughter that she made an irresistible Mrs. Pontifex.

Louisa carried the theater with her wherever she went, reciting the "Hoots of a Distracted Soul in the Wilderness," offering a travesty on the works of Rolf Walden Emerboy, or consulting with Frank Sanborn about the Dickens scenes that had been planned for Christmas. The prologue of Old Yule and Young Christmas ushered out the old year in lively fashion. After *The Cricket on the Hearth*, *The Haunted Man* was offered, Louisa playing Sophia Tetterby to Alf Whitman's Dolphus. Small, yellow-haired Tetterby sat with his "wife" Sophia, who would indeed have made two editions of himself, and together they learned that "but for some trouble and sorrow" they "should never know half the good" there was about them. Together they prayed that the Lord would keep their memory green.

Surely the sorrow that had come to Louisa's own life would never be forgotten. No brisk portrayals of noisy character parts could dull more than momentarily her memory of the nights in Lizzie's room. The scripts might pile up on her desk; Anna and John Pratt might perform most realistically in *The Loan of a Lover*—the Lord had kept Louisa's memory green. Mother might try to forget in her Johnson or her Fénelon, in her recipes for pea soup or squash pie, but her memory, too, was green. No one could forget that in Lizzie's room a quieter, more tragic drama was in progress than any that had been acted in the Town Hall.

In February, Lizzie began to fail rapidly from what Dr. Geist labeled consumption. With aching heart Louisa watched while her sister sewed or read or lay looking at the fire, all her pretty hair gone, an old woman, tired and worn, at twenty-three. Father had come home from the West to hear from Dr. Geist that there was no hope. All the plays were given up and Anna did the housekeeping so that Mother and Louisa could devote themselves to Lizzie. The sad, quiet days stretched on in her room, and during endless nights Louisa kindled the fire and watched her sister. Mr. Thoreau had said that nothing was so much to be feared as fear, and Louisa determined to cast fear from her heart and treasure the precious hours that were left. One night as she was watching, she loosed her pain in words.

Sitting patient in the shadow
    Till the blessed light shall come,
A serene and saintly presence
    Sanctifies our troubled home.
Earthly joys and hopes and sorrows
    Break like ripples on the strand
Of the deep and solemn river,
    Where her willing feet now stand.

O my sister, passing from me
    Out of human care and strife,
Leave me as a gift those virtues
    Which have beautified your life.
Dear, bequeath me that great patience
    Which has power to sustain
A cheerful, uncomplaining spirit
    In its prison-house of pain. . . .

Henceforth safe across the river
    I shall see forevermore
A beloved household spirit
    Waiting for me on the shore;
Hope and faith, born of my sorrow,
    Guardian angels shall become;
And the sister gone before me
    By their hands shall lead me home.

The farewells were spoken. To Anna, Lizzie gave her desk; her copy of *Undine*, her letters, all were given away; and for the Hosmers she sewed little keepsakes, a penwiper, a pin block, and a needlebook. At last, when the river opened in March, Lizzie became unconscious, quietly breathing her life away. The morning of March 14 was clear and calm, a fit time for so early a translation.

With her mother, Louisa dressed Lizzie for the last time. On Monday, Mr. Emerson, Mr. Thoreau, Frank Sanborn, and John Pratt carried her across the threshold and placed her in the carriage. Dr. Huntington read the King's Chapel Burial Service.

Lizzie's favorite hymn was sung, and all her friends—Ellen Emerson, Carrie Pratt, Dr. Bartlett, and Mr. Thoreau—joined their prayers with Dr. Huntington's. The first break had come. But had not Mr. Emerson said that immortality was not length of life, but depth of life, that the vault of the sky was only a Sleepy Hollow?

For the loneliness that came after, for the emptiness of Lizzie's room, it was harder to find solace. In April, while repairs were in progress at the Orchard House, the family moved to a wing of the Wayside, as Mr. Hawthorne was abroad. It was lonely for Louisa, with Abby in Boston and Anna at Pratt Farm. It was strange to be back in the home where she had grown up, but somehow Lizzie seemed closer now in the house where her footfall still echoed on the stairs, where her shadow still climbed the ridge to the Celestial City.

Another loss came to Louisa when, on the seventh of April, Anna and John Pratt walked in to announce their engagement. Apparently they had decided to make *The Loan of a Lover* permanent, and Louisa rejoiced for them, although she mourned in private at the thought of another empty place at home. To forget her lesser sorrow, she dashed off an acrostic to Alf Whitman, planned rowing excursions with her yellow-haired Dolphus, and walked all the way to Boston to join Abby, John, and Anna for an evening at the Howard. Louisa needed no more to be aroused once again to a desire to act, not merely in private but in public. Mr. Barry acquiesced to Dr. Windship's suggestion that she portray the Widow Pottle at the Boston. The arrangements were conducted in the strictest secrecy; the dress would make an excellent disguise. But alas, Mr. Barry broke his leg, and Louisa quite temporarily broke her heart.

Back at Concord there was much to take her mind from the lure of the greenroom. In July the family began to settle in the new home for which Cousin Sam Sewall had drawn up the papers. Father took ceaseless delight in viewing the Orchard House from every perspective, rejoicing in its brown porches and gables and its overshadowing elms. It was so near to the dwelling that had once been called Hillside that the family might well feel they had, after many wanderings, returned home at last. Before Father's serene eyes visions of terraces, arbors, rustic fences, and carved closets arose, while Abby cast appraising glances at every panel that might improve under a stroke of decorative paint. Louisa immediately befriended the owl that came visiting in the great elm, and saw that the gray cat was as comfortable as the red squirrels that lived in the pitch pine behind the house.

The furniture was moved once more: Father's books, his globe, and his manuscripts placed in his study, while on the walls of the parlor opposite hung an engraving of Murillo's *Virgin* with the moon under her feet. On the north side Abby found room for a tiny studio, where she might work on a portrait of Endymion. The family chose their rooms on the second floor, Abby deciding upon the little chamber over the back porch where the grapevine climbed across the window. There she moved her mirror, before which she might primp her blond curls undisturbed, and made artistic plans for gray-flowered wallpaper, panels of knights and ladies, and a gray-and-blue frame for her washstand. Louisa claimed the room next to Abby's and immediately moved all her possessions in place, the writing desk between the two windows that overlooked the Lexington Road, the marble paperweight, the leather portfolio, and on the mantel her few treasures.

Father took to converting old ash-holes and ovens into arched alcoves, and studied the history of the Orchard House. With his faggots and keg of nails he repaired the old shell of a house from cellar to garret and found deep happiness as he tinkered with his tools in the woodshed. While the trees and shrubs from Mr. Watson's nursery were set out, Abby lost no time painting birds and flowers and faces on every available panel, even perpetuating the countenance of the visiting owl upon Louisa's mantel.

Despite the renovations, Louisa insisted that the Orchard House would more appropriately be dubbed "Apple Slump." At least, she agreed, it was well that the wandering family was anchored. Her parents needed a mooring, and now that death and love had taken two away, she hoped she would soon be able to care for those who were left. While she dusted and swept and washed the dishpans, stories and novels simmered in her mind, and Louisa began to feed upon thoughts of the future instead of the past.

The Orchard House was ready now to receive on Monday evenings, and whether the guests brought their own refreshments in big baskets or partook of Father's apples and Mother's ginger cakes, the weekly affairs were jolly ones. Louisa liked to sit by the fireplace, knitting, with an open book in her lap, while the favored boys of Mr. Sanborn's school played whist, made hot-poker sketches, and talked with the ladies. Mother sat in a corner enjoying a chess game, and Abby, draped in blue, openly flirted with the liveliest of the scholars or seated herself at the piano to play "Rolling Home" or "Juanita." Then Louisa dropped her book to join in the songs and soon yielded to the unanimous demand for a ghost story. Whether she was drawn into a table of whist or played "Borrow the Bundle," whether she dropped phrases from Dickens or danced, Louisa was the gayest of all, making the old roof ring with the laughter of George Bartlett and Alf Whitman. After a drink of Father's cider she was inspired to play "High, Low, Jack" or "Literati," "Dumb Crambo" or charades, until apples and ginger cakes rounded off the Alcott Monday evening.

Yet, for all the joys that Concord offered, Louisa felt that she must leave the Orchard House and challenge her fate once again in Boston. Where was the wishing stone now that would grant her deep desires to write a good book, to be famous, to go abroad, and to make money? Cousin Thomas Sewall's red-brick house at 98 Chestnut Street was open to her, and there she laid her plans for work. She decided first to offer her services in teaching Alice Lovering. The Loverings, however, sent no answer. Louisa rushed across the Common to Mrs. Reed, but she had no sewing for her. She tried Mrs. Sargent, but there, too, there was no opening. Louisa's courage almost gave out, and when she looked at the water of the Mill Dam she was, for a moment, tempted to find the solution to her problems there. It would be contemptible, however, to turn and run away before the battle was over. She set her

teeth and vowed to force the world to her will. After a tempestuous night she walked, muddy and shabby, pale and red-eyed, to
Mr. Parker's home. Surely he would be able to advise her, to suggest a place where she was needed.

Mr. Parker was not at home, but his wife listened gravely to her
words. Grim one moment, choking the next, Louisa said simply
that her family was poor, that she must support herself, and that
she was willing to sew or write, to teach or nurse. Mrs. Parker was
kind and would confer with her husband and Miss Stevenson. Not
long after, Miss Stevenson called at Chestnut Street to offer Louisa
a place as seamstress at the Winchester Reform School. She would
be required to sew for ten hours a day for thirty girls, and although
the pay would be small at first, it would be a beginning. Louisa was
grateful, but she dreaded the thought of patching and darning day
after day with a dozen stories bubbling in her brain.

Immediately after she had determined to accept Miss Stevenson's offer, Louisa found a note from the Loverings saying that
they had decided to employ her as Alice's governess for the winter. Skipping for joy all the way to Exeter Place, she told Miss
Stevenson of her good fortune, and glowed with pride when Mr.
Parker remarked, "The little girl has got true grit; and we were all
pleased with you." The ten hours would dwindle to four, with
walking, play, and lessons to vary the time, and fair wages for her
work. It had been a hard week, but all was well now, for her
despair had found her friends, and the tragedy had turned, after
all, into tragicomedy.

Alice was a dyspeptic cherub who did not always yield to the
softening influences of her teacher. But for $250 a year Louisa
would make even a demonic little girl happy and instill into her
youthful mind as much knowledge as her dyspepsia would permit.
Mrs. Lovering was a kind and sympathetic woman, who provided
liberal funds for Alice's amusement, and Louisa found herself riding about the country in the family carriage and worshiping with
her invalid charge before the shrine of nature and of art.

There was time in the evenings for Louisa to incorporate her
temptation at the Mill Dam into a story about Basil Ventnor, an

elderly gentleman who married Little Effie to provide her with a home. The author gave to her tale a respectable and happy ending, but she found greater pleasure in dilating upon incompatibility and attempted suicide, and decided that she would allow Father to offer "Love and Self-Love" to *The Atlantic Monthly.*

While she waited for the editor's decision, there were other demands upon her pen in the form of letters if not of stories. In November, Alf Whitman left Concord to work on his father's farm in Lawrence, Kansas, and "Sophia Tetterby" sent long letters to her "Dolphus," telling all the news of Apple Slump and Pickle Roost, Beacon Street and Chestnut Street.

There was no doubt that the joy and the sorrow of the last year had changed her life. The experiences of Lizzie's death and Anna's betrothal had taken a deep hold, developing and maturing her. She must indeed be self-reliant, seeking in work salvation for weariness or disappointment. She felt as if she could write better now, more truly of the things she had felt and known. She hoped that one day she would write a great book, for writing seemed to be her work and she knew that she was growing up to it. Meanwhile, she could try her hand at another story for Mr. Clapp, developing in Mark Field a more realistic character than any she had produced for the readers of the *Gazette.*

Louisa had time between *Gazette* stories and bulletins to Alf to spend her salary on a carpet for the parlor, a bonnet for Anna, and some shoes and stockings for herself, for after three turns around the Common in stockings that boasted a profusion of toe but no heel and shoes that suffered from a paucity of toe, her feet cried aloud to be shod. Whatever fortune was left would be invested in the Alcott sinking fund, the Micawber Railroad, and the Skimpole percents. In December, Abby joined Louisa in Boston to study under Mr. Salisbury Tuckerman at the School of Design and fill her sister's free hours with remarks on the delights of skating or dancing and drawing at Temple Place.

At Christmas, Louisa was glad to leave the Loverings for home, joining in private theatricals at Pickle Roost. To provide a merry end to the season she acted, not Widow Pottle, but Major Murray in *The Jacobite*. They played in the Pratt parlor and had no stage or properties, simply rambling about among the audience in the vaguest manner. Louisa could never get through the first long speech, and utterly routed Carrie Pratt's ideas by informing her that her false name was Charles "Antwerp," a merchant of "Vardeck," instead of Charles Vardeck, a merchant of Antwerp. That seemed to set the tone of the entire performance. When John Duck hid under the table, the Major pried up the cloth with a wooden sword to drag him out. Mr. Pratt read the part of the villainous Sir Richard with angelic meekness, while Carrie darted in and out of Mrs. Pottle's and Lady Somerford's clothes with amazing rapidity. The only realistic presentations were offered by Anna and John, who, of course, did the lovers to the life.

Between Boston and Concord, Louisa went, participating in an exciting whirl of plays at the Sargents' or dancing the lancers at the Town Hall. When she was not dancing or acting, she was teaching Alice Lovering or rejoicing over the appearance of "Mark Field" in the March 12 issue of the *Gazette*. Whatever she did was done with the ardent desire that she would one day become the mainstay of her family and that Mr. Emerson's Alcott Fund would need no further subscriptions. She longed to face the world with the deep intent of Mr. Thoreau, who walked in the March rains setting his traps in solitude to catch light and life. She, too, was setting traps, but of a different kind, for prey that was as yet in darkness.

When in April, on behalf of the committee, Mr. Sanborn invited Father to accept the office of superintendent of the Concord schools, Louisa rejoiced for him and for the recognition that seemed at last to have come to one who had met failure so often and so serenely. There were other causes for pleasure, too—in the spring, plays before the Parker Fraternity, and at last the termination of her work with Alice Lovering. Then there was time to set forth with Abby upon "aquatic" shopping expeditions in India-rubber boots through the mud of Washington Street. No detail of Boston in the spring was lost upon Louisa as she observed the gentlemen looking like dandified buccaneers, and the ladies promenading like a flock of ostriches under old-fashioned fire buckets. None of the wishes had come true, not fame, not money, not the great book, not Europe. In a letter to Alf Whitman she confessed: "I still pine for a 'furrin' trip as I have done for the last ten years—Lets you & I go as sailors & work our passage over, then travel on foot like 'Consuelo' & 'Joseph Hayden.' " For the Concord Consuelo, however, there had at least been experience of a different nature.

Still another experience came to Louisa in May, when, as Frank Sanborn's guest, Captain John Brown spoke on Kansas affairs at the Concord Town Hall. As he discussed his invasion of Missouri, he seemed a dauntless figure, tall and imposing, his square shoulders ready to bear all burdens, his deep gray eyes prepared to face the world.

Concord slumbered on during the summer, quietly dreaming the lengthening days, forgetting Osawatomie Brown, unmindful that he had been there, and careless of where he had gone. In September, Concord remembered for a time, when the Great State Encampment mustered near the village. The maneuvers and the roar of cannon thrilled Louisa, and she could hardly wait to see the doubtful questions of the day come to an open war. She could not fight, but she could nurse, and she hoped for more stirring actions than a cattle show or a regatta on the Concord River.

On the October day when Frank Sanborn had arranged for the annual nutting expedition, news arrived in Concord that John Brown had entered Harpers Ferry, liberated the slaves, and with his small force held the town for thirty hours. A bold stroke had been made for justice, an impulse given to freedom and humanity, whatever might become of the victim. Louisa was glad to have lived to see this last heroic act in the antislavery movement and wished she could do her part in it. Mother boiled with excitement and Father was ready to leave, if necessary, for Virginia to aid in the rescue of the prisoner. Although some of the neighbors remarked that the captain was undoubtedly insane, Mr. Thoreau insisted upon speaking in the vestry to offer a plea for John

Brown. He rejoiced, he declared, that he lived in this age and was John Brown's contemporary, for he preferred the philanthropy of the captain to that philanthropy which neither shot nor liberated. In Louisa's own life, as in Concord's, November marked a milestone, when Mr. Lowell accepted "Love and Self-Love" for inclusion in *The Atlantic Monthly*. Besides the pleasure of knowing that her story would appear in the same magazine with the products of Boston's littérateurs, there was the delight of receiving fifty dollars and of feeling that she could write the flat kind of tale that the *Atlantic* critics endorsed. While Father harvested his apple crop and sorted his Baldwins for customers, Louisa's hallelujahs echoed to the roof top, for despite Mr. Fields's advice that she stick to her teaching, she had launched a ship upon the *Atlantic* that had not foundered.

Still there was no forgetting the tragedy of John Brown's martyrdom. On the mild December day when he was to be executed for his deed, Concord conducted a martyr service in the Town Hall. From his commonplace book of poetry Mr. Thoreau read his version of Tacitus upon Agricola: "You, Agricola, are fortunate, not only because your life was glorious, but because your death was timely." The villagers listened to Father as he read the service for the death of a martyr, and then the congregation, standing, sang the dirge that Frank Sanborn had written. Captain John Brown at the moment of his execution was more alive than he had ever been. He was not confined to North Elba or to Kansas. He was no longer working in secret.

Seeing a rose blossom before its season on the warm, springlike December day when John Brown died, Louisa accepted the token, weaving it into a poem for *The Liberator*.

> *In the long silence of the night,*
> *Nature's benignant power*
> *Woke aspirations for the light*
> *Within the folded flower. . . .*
>
> *Then blossomed forth a grander flower,*
> *In the wilderness of wrong,*

Untouched by Slavery's bitter frost,
A soul devout and strong. . . .

No monument of quarried stone,
No eloquence of speech,
Can grave the lessons on the land
His martyrdom will teach. . . .

After Mr. Redpath had come to Concord, gathering information for his life of John Brown, Louisa's poem was published in *The Liberator* on January 20.

Now, if ever, the time had come to write a story to advance the cause; and recalling the tales about Jonathan Walker, whose hand had been branded with the letters "S.S." for "Slave Stealer," remembering the scar she had seen on the face of Anthony Burns, and the fugitive who had once come to Hillside, Louisa evolved a tale about a mulatto, whose hand was branded with the mysterious initials, "M.L.," and whom a white woman loved. It was exciting to sit at her desk, weaving a weird and sinister plot about a hero who pleaded for abolition. Although the tale was rejected, she had her fifty dollars from *The Atlantic* to purchase a carpet, and on February 17 Father brought home the March issue of the monthly, where Louisa saw to her delight her story, "Love and Self-Love." Perhaps "M.L." had been too sensational in theme, too pointed in doctrine. She would plan another story for *The Atlantic* on a subject closer to home.

Whether she sewed costumes for the masquerade ball given by Frank Sanborn and his scholars or, draped in the crimson and white brocade of Lady Teazle, danced the lancers with Richard the Third and Figaro, Louisa searched everywhere for a theme, watched sharply for a character. Boys still interested her more than girls, and when she wrote to Alf Whitman she frankly declared her kinship with them:

There was always something very brave & beautiful to me in the sight of a boy when he first "wakes up" & seeing the worth of life takes it up with a stout heart & resolves to carry it nobly to the

end through all . . . seeming defeats. I was born with a boys
nature & . . . have fought my fight . . . with a boys spirit under
my "bib & tucker."

Yet, despite her "boys spirit," she found that there were a few girls
of whom she could write with an intimate knowledge. Recalling
the story she had written years before for the *Gazette*, "The Sisters' Trial," in which she had described one year in the lives of
four sisters, Louisa decided that she would begin with Anna for
the heroine and John for the hero. She found it impossible, however, to write a story about Anna's romance without incorporating
in it something of Abby's life and her own. It would be fine to
include in "A Modern Cinderella" a character who looked picturesque before her easel, and what greater pleasure could the
author find than in writing of herself? Under the alias of "Di" she
raced through the pages, losing herself in the delights of *Wilhelm
Meister*, corking her inkstand to plunge at housework as if it were
a five-barred gate, but determined to uncork it when the divine
afflatus chose to descend upon her. The course of Anna's love ran
so smoothly that Louisa found herself forced to expand her characters, since her plot consisted of nothing more involved than a
hardware clerk's wooing of her own sister. Did not Mr. Emerson
believe that the people, not the college, should be the writer's
home? Louisa was on the watch for characters now as well as incidents, and after she had completed "A Modern Cinderella," tried
her hand at describing Debby, a young crusader against established absurdities, a wholesome girl placed in an atmosphere of
affectation in her first season at the beach. "Debby's Début"
would follow "A Modern Cinderella" to Mr. Lowell's office. With
pride, Louisa reported her progress to Alf: ". . . my 'works of art'
are in such demand that I shall be one great blot soon. . . . your
topsy turvy friend has got into the 'Atlantic' & receives fifty dollars a story." While Debby awaited her debut, the author bided
her time by writing a song for Father's school festival.

Even in peaceful Concord, however, there were interruptions
that distracted the *Atlantic* contributor from her work. Early in

April, Horace Mann came to the Orchard House, informing the family that Mr. Sanborn had been arrested and handcuffed the night before and would have been carried off but for the heroic conduct of his sister and Anna Whiting. As soon as Louisa heard the news, she dashed off with Abby, through mud and rain, to Miss Whiting's home. There they listened to the amazing story of how eleven officers had rushed into Frank Sanborn's house on the Sudbury Road, collared him, handcuffed him, and dragged him out into the street. His crime, apparently, had been his friendship with John Brown, and the government wished to have him testify in regard to Harpers Ferry.

After the case was tried and decided in Frank Sanborn's favor, the villagers greeted the hero of the hour with cheers and shouts, while all the bells in town were rung, cannon was fired, and the Town Hall was crowded for an indignation meeting. There Louisa and Miss Whiting were chosen as members of a vigilance committee and Sarah Sanborn was presented with a handsome revolver. Harpers Ferry drew nearer than ever before. The smell of gunpowder seemed not entirely incongruous with the fragrance of a Concord spring.

To Louisa's delight, Mr. Redpath not only asked permission to publish her poem on John Brown in his *Echoes of Harper's Ferry*, but also sent a request for her autograph. Besides supplying the demands of her "public," the author made a riding habit for herself, discussed the plans for Anna's approaching wedding, and, ever on the alert for characters, enjoyed her sessions with the pupils of Frank Sanborn's school. Maggie Plumley would make an arch little heroine, and John Brown's daughters, Anne and Sarah, who had arrived in March, could tell many a tale about the tragedy of Harpers Ferry. Young Seymour Severance, who boarded at the Orchard House, was a splendid gymnast, and Louisa delighted in his performances as well as in the pregnant glances he bestowed upon Maggie Plumley. She would store the antics of Frank Sanborn's pupils in her mind, for one day they might provide ample material for a story, and Louisa had begun to realize that seeds early planted often came late to flower.

Rewards also came late, for on May 4, 1860, the farce that had been accepted five years before was at last produced. Though the greater portion of the audience thronged the Howard Athenaeum to see Mrs. W. H. Smith's benefit performance in *The Romance of a Poor Young Man*, Louisa came to see her own little after-sketch, entitled "Nat Bachelor's Pleasure Trip." She looked about her at the newly painted theater on Howard Street and seated herself in a private parlor box. Here was a change indeed for the frequenter of the Museum pit. She glanced a little ruefully at the playbill, which announced "a *New* Local Sketch by the Popular Authoress, Miss Louisa *Adcott*," but was satisfied that if the name was incorrectly spelled, at least it was a name and not a pseudonym.

At last the farce was acted, Miss Josephine Orton, Mr. William J. LeMoyne, and Mrs. W. H. Smith exposing the trials of a good-natured man. Louisa was not completely satisfied with the production and felt, after her experience with professional farces, that "Nat Bachelor's Pleasure Trip" was a small affair. But good Dr. Windship handed a bouquet to the playwright, and if the rafters of the Howard Athenaeum did not ring with applause, at least the sketch had been acted and the author had tasted the pleasures of a seventy-five-cent box seat.

The discouraging announcement in next day's *Transcript* to the effect that no after-sketch would follow *The Romance of a Poor Young Man* during the evening paled into insignificance when, not long after, news arrived that Theodore Parker had died in Florence. The beloved minister and friend, to whom Louisa owed so much of her education, was gone, and his place would not easily be filled.

Louisa was glad to leave the realms of tragedy for the more cheerful domain of a "romance of real life," when on the twenty-third of May, the anniversary of Mother's wedding, Anna was married to her John. Early in the morning the final touches were added to the bride's gray silk poplin, and lilies of the valley were placed in her hair. Abby arranged her blue silk net as she stood before the mirror, while Louisa, arrayed in her pepper-and-salt *barège*, wore scarlet flowers in her hair to honor the occasion. As soon as Carrie Pratt appeared on the scene, Louisa announced that the three bridesmaids in sackcloth and ashes were ready for the sacrifice. John and Anna chatted with Mr. Thoreau, Frank Sanborn, the Emersons, and Miss Peabody, while the two families looked benignly on. At eleven o'clock the couple quietly took their places in the doorway between the dining room and the parlor. Uncle Sam May performed the ceremony, assisted by Mr. Bull. Except for Uncle Sam's addressing Anna once as Amos Bronson Alcott, there was no flaw in the scene; and after Anna had emerged as Mrs. John Pratt, the guests feasted on cake and drank Mr. Bull's Concord grape wine. In the German fashion the friends danced around the pair on the lawn under the elm, and Mr. Emerson kissed the bride, an honor, Louisa thought, that would make matrimony endurable, for he was still the god of her idolatry.

There was much to distract Louisa's mind from the loss of her second sister. Harriet Tubman moved busily about in Concord, the Negress who had escaped from slavery and returned nineteen times to the South to rescue fugitives. She was in truth a Moses, one of John Brown's "men," who excited all the village with her singing of hymns and her accounts of "experience meetings." In this woman, who had rescued her brothers and sisters and her father and mother from slavery, Louisa found another character to remember until the day came when she could incorporate her into a fitting tale.

Another unforgettable figure appeared when on June 28 Mr. Hawthorne returned to Concord with his wife and three children. Mrs. Mann moved with her boys to the Sudbury Road to make room for the European arrivals, and Louisa watched the alterations that carpenter Wetherbee proceeded to make next door in the Wayside. The house in which she had grown up underwent a metamorphosis as a square tower surmounted the dwelling so that Mr. Hawthorne could imagine himself in the Via Portughese in Rome. The larches and Norway pines from England had been planted along the path from the Orchard House to the Wayside, and all day long Louisa heard the sound of hammering and sawing as boards were piled up on the lawn and shavings and sawdust filled the air.

It was interesting to have neighbors who showed stereoscopic views of Paris and Florence in exchange for the beer that Mother made from spruce sprigs, hops, and molasses. It was still more interesting to Louisa to watch Mr. Hawthorne glide by at twilight, or appear momentarily upon his hilltop, a dark, quiet figure passing slowly along in the dim light of mingled sky and branches, his tread measured, his eyes bent upon the ground, his hands clasped behind him. He was still screened in a twilight of his own creating, hatching tragedy in the Concord sunshine, walking back and forth upon the hillside, a man in whom the fires of life were banked.

Although Mr. Hawthorne was never at ease in the Orchard House, where the stove was too hot or the clock ticked too loudly, his children found no cause for such complaints when they attended the Alcott teas or dances or whist parties. The Hawthorne girls of course were not allowed to waltz, but their brother Julian gave every promise of developing quite voluntarily into a *cavaliere servente*. Louisa delighted in the tall, sturdy, handsome boy who joined in the picnics and dances of Frank Sanborn's school, where he had been enrolled. She noticed also that he evinced a tender passion for Abby, and proceeded to dilate upon the hopelessness of his attachment by inventing a rival in the shape of an imaginary English cousin. Unperturbed, Julian invited Abby upon a river excursion to watch the opening lilies, and eagerly attended the bathing parties at Walden, where, inside a tent, Louisa donned her blue flannel pantaloons and dived from the punt for a splash. At the Wayside Wednesday receptions or the nonsense-verse parties, at the Town Hall entertainments or Abby's dancing "class," Louisa stood long enough in her corner to watch the pranks of Julian and his schoolmates before she abandoned herself to the village revels.

Surely in her twenty-seven years of observation she had learned enough of life to embark upon her first novel. In August of 1860 the time seemed ripe for her to begin work on *Moods*, and for four weeks she wrote all day and planned nearly all night. Possessed by her subject, she sat before her desk, writing of death and sleepwalking and shipwreck, interweaving among the glaring threads of Sylvia's turbulent loves many a remark on goodness and godliness, books and nature, and marriage and death. From the Town Hall parties she borrowed details to plan the episode of the golden wedding, where country songs and dances, hearty good will, and honest generosity took the stage. From Mr. Emerson she quoted a remark to explain her title, "Life is a train of moods like a string of beads; and as we pass through them they prove to be many colored lenses, which paint the world their own hue, and each shows us only what lies in its own focus." From mood to mood she varied, writing of Adam, who had kindled a fire that would burn all virtue out of him unless he quenched it. The pen raced down the page to describe Ottila and Adam, the modern Samson and Delilah, who waged the old war that filled the world with evils arising from marriages based upon impulse rather than principle. But it was Sylvia who engrossed Louisa completely, Sylvia who alternated between the Alps of Warwick and the roses of Moor, Sylvia who, like Hester Prynne, lived in the shadow of grief and disappointment. The pen raced on to carry the heroine to the end of her short pilgrimage, to show that although Sylvia had not known how to live, she did know how to die. The rough draft was finished. Life might be a train of moods, but Louisa was not certain whether the moods she had chosen resembled those of life. She would put the story away for a while, satisfied that she had been enriched by a new experience.

A simpler but no less wholesome experience came to Louisa in the fall, when Concord was turned into a vast gymnasium by the villagers who donned gray tunics and tossed beanbags in the manner approved by Dr. Dio Lewis. Wands and clubs hurtled through the air after Dr. Lewis had lectured at the Town Hall and raised two iron dumbbells over his head. The new gymnastics performed to a musical accompaniment afforded to Louisa far more than the nerve stimulus and muscle training promised by the lecturer. Besides pioneering in the arm pull and shoulder push, she stored numberless amusing scenes in her mind as she watched the living windmills and inflated balloons who exercised with clubs and scepters or executed the giant's swing on the horizontal bar.

Rewards for her patient observations, however slow to come, came at last when, in October, *The Atlantic Monthly* published "A Modern Cinderella," and the proud author pocketed her seventy-five dollars, while Mother had good cause to sing "Hebron" among the pots and pans. Louisa felt free now to take time from her writing to attend the review in Boston to honor the Prince of Wales. Every balcony that overlooked the Common was crowded with spectators to watch the line of march. To the booming of cannon and the music of twenty-five full bands, His Highness Albert Edward appeared, a smooth-faced, curly-haired, quiet lad of eighteen, mounted on Black Prince. Up and down the line of troops he rode, receiving salutes, while Louisa nodded violently, waved to him as he passed, and assured herself that the prince had winked his boyish eye at her. When Pell and Trowbridge's Minstrels began to advertise a new burlesque, "The Prince of *Whales*," however, she considered that she had had enough of royalty in Boston, and applauded Father's vote in the national election for the Rail Splitter.

The winter passed quietly for Louisa, marked by no such events as had brightened the fall. After Abby had taken lessons from Johnstone in Boston, she was invited to accept a position as drawing teacher and pianist at Dr. Wilbur's Asylum in Syracuse. Louisa determined to wear sackcloth and ashes permanently, for if she could not have one sister at home, she saw no point in having sisters at all. Concord was dull without Abby, and Louisa found even her happiness over the acceptance of "Debby's Début" by *The Atlantic* a lonely delight. Between concocting oyster pies and flapjacks she dispatched Concord bulletins to Alf, Abby, and Anna, and settled down to the quiet days and nights of the slumbering town.

The time had come for Louisa to indulge in a writing fever, and, with the new year of 1861, she eagerly started a new book, "Success," in which she intended to write her own autobiography, sketching her experiences in private theatricals, glorifying her career in domestic service, and describing her trials and tribulations when she had faced the world alone. Harriet Tubman could be transformed into the courageous Negro cook, Hepsey; Mr. Thoreau might be used as a prototype for David Sterling; and Mr. Parker would reappear under the alias of Mr. Power, a portrait complete even to the flowers that he had enjoyed upon the pulpit. The pen trapped upon paper the episodes Louisa chose from her twenty-eight years of experience, and did not stop racing along the page until Mother fell ill, when the inkstand was corked up and the author was once again transformed into a nurse. The book would not suffer by the interruption, for Louisa realized that it consisted of individual episodes knit together only by Christie's character. Each chapter gave promise of turning into a complete narrative. Louisa could not forget her apprenticeship as a writer of short stories. She would be able to write her autobiography on and off whenever the subject engrossed her. Besides, there might be more stirring events to record after the author had lived a little longer.

The pen, however, seemed bent upon being dipped into ink, and when Mother rose up like a phoenix from the ashes after what she gaily called "the irrepressible conflict between sickness and the May constitution," Louisa left her spoons and basins for her papers, to remodel *Moods*. In the chill of February, while the villagers clapped their hands to their frozen ears, the author sat at her desk, a green silk cap with a red bow upon her head, an old green and red party wrap draped around her as a "glory cloak," to ponder in groves of manuscripts and drive her Pegasus with a ceaseless whip. Mother wandered in and out of the second-story room, cups of tea in her hand; Father appeared occasionally with offerings of apples and cider. But food and sleep seemed to have no bearing at all upon Sylvia's romantic problems, and Louisa had no care for the world as she delineated "the two extremes of love." At last Sylvia was softly "cradled in the heart that loved her best," and the author dropped her pen to take long walks and cold baths and recapture the sleep that would not come to her rampant mind. On the twenty-fifth of the month Anna visited the Orchard House and heard the results of Louisa's session with the muse. Father found the work entertaining and witty, enjoying particularly the chapters on "Nemesis" and "Herbs," and applauded his daughter's metaphysical discriminations. Mother pronounced *Moods* wonderful, with no reservations whatsoever; and Anna, laughing and crying in turn, boldly declared that she was proud of her sister. Whether or not the publishers would accept Louisa's first novel, she had had her reward, for her three dearest had sat till midnight listening intently, and had with deep pleasure seen the colored lenses, the string of beads, and the train of moods.

The quotation with which she had begun her book had come from Mr. Emerson. Now, when the friend in the white frame house asked the author to write another song for Father's school festival, Louisa rushed at her pen once again, exalting John Brown and Wendell Phillips to the tune of "All the Blue Bonnets Are over the Border." On sleighs or on foot the children came to the Town Hall to listen to Father's remarks, and after recess Mr. Emerson delivered his address and honored Louisa by reading her song, which was charmingly sung by the Misses Wilson, Hosmer, and Adams.

Father's triumph was completed when Master Freddy Harlow walked up to the platform to thank him for his "mild and wise counsels," and bestow upon him a copy of George Herbert's *Poems* and one of *Pilgrim's Progress* as a token of the love and respect of the children. The roof rang with cheers as Father hugged his fine books and stammered his gratitude, and when one thousand copies of his report were printed, he began to find himself the most popular and successful man in Concord. A child's primer, he had written, was still wanted, and should be some suitable story founded on American life. All the villagers applauded Father's introduction of Sunday evening meetings and gymnastics under the leadership of Dr. Lewis. Louisa had not forgotten that those same villagers had said bitter things about her father in darker days. Their malicious inventions she would not forgive, even though her own reverence for him was mingled with impatience at his unworldliness and amusement at his soarings into the infinite.

Concord settled down again after the excitement of the school exhibition. The village houses were white with snow, the drifts piled high over the fences after a March northeaster, and Louisa was impatient with a Concord where nothing more remarkable could be discussed than the delay of the Boston train or the engagement of Maggie Plumley and Seymour Severance.

The village was roused from its sleep when, in April, Fort Sumter was surrendered after a two-days' bombardment. Concord was moved to read in the papers how the Union forces had marched out from the burning fort, saluting their tattered flag with fifty guns. Concord was stirred at last when President Lincoln called for 75,000 volunteers, and Father agreed that no greater calamity could befall a people than that of deliberating long on issues imperiling liberty. Sometimes, Mr. Emerson remarked, gunpowder smelled good, for, bad as war might be, it would be safer and better than the peace that had preceded it. The war that Louisa had longed for had broken at last.

In a fashion becoming the descendants of men who had joined the Concord fight, the memorable anniversary of April 19 was celebrated. The small company, bearing the names of those who had gone to battle in 1775, mustered in the Town Hall and were formed and marched round by their lieutenant. Louisa watched while the flag was run up, listened to the salutes of the cannon, and joined in "The Star-Spangled Banner." Mr. Reynolds prayed, and the little band of soldiers, followed by all Concord, marched to the train for the relief of Washington. At the depot Louisa stood with the crowds. She waved until the cars disappeared behind Walden woods, and walked silently home, wishing that she, too, could have joined the Concord artillery.

When John Brown's daughters, Anne and Sarah, came to board at the Orchard House, they brought to Louisa more than the compulsion of setting aside her writing for more arduous housekeeping. Anne had known her father's plans at Harpers Ferry. Anne brought Harpers Ferry close to the Orchard House,

a constant reminder of why the artillery had so fittingly celebrated the anniversary of April 19. As each day passed, the war
came closer to home.

There was no doubt that the quiet village was, finally, stirred
up. The young men and boys drilled constantly; the women and
girls sewed or prepared to become nurses; the old folks settled the
fate of the nation in groves of newspapers; and the children made
the streets hideous with their own cacophonous medley of drums
and fifes. Everyone, Louisa noticed, wore a cockade in every con-
ceivable place; flags flapped overhead like particolored birds of
prey; while patriotic balmorals, cravats, handkerchiefs, and hats
perambulated daily down Main Street. "Hail Columbia" seemed
destined to take the place of the Yankee "How are yer?"

The dust of the Lexington Road was raised and would not be
settled until the war had been won. Edward Emerson's company
of Concord cadets had begun to poke each other's eyes out and
blow themselves up with gunpowder, while the East Quarter
Home Guard—consisting of one captain, one drummer, one flag
bearer, and one private—had adopted the habit of halting before
each house and giving several shrill hurrahs before they marched
away. Seeing Julian Hawthorne and Henry Wheeler drill up and
down the Lexington Road, attending meetings where the ladies
made their donations of cloth and jellies, pickles and bandages,
Louisa wondered how she could do her part. More than lint picks
were needed to win the war. She wanted to go to the front with
the men who enlisted at the courthouse, to accomplish something
more constructive than cry "On to Richmond." Since there was
no opening for her at the moment, she tried to curb her impatience by studying the report of Dr. William Home on gunshot
wounds. It was hard to sit calmly at the Orchard House when
news of Big Bethel stirred all of Boston.

It seemed inconceivable that summer should come so
serenely on, that Father should be working once more with rake
and hoe, and that the usual regatta and fireworks should be
planned to celebrate the Fourth of July. Abby returned from
Syracuse to teach at Frank Sanborn's school, and she, too, took
up her accustomed activities—drawing and boating, riding and

flirting, and enjoying whist parties—as if Sumter never had fallen. Louisa could not forget the war, not in the pages of *Amelia* or *Evelina*, or Hodson's *India* or Carlyle's *French Revolution*. Yet until the day came when a place could be found for her, she must rest content sewing blue shirts and scraping lint. Meanwhile she would learn patience by waiting, and snatch a month of peace among the mountains.

When the Willis cousins invited Louisa to Gorham, New Hampshire, she packed her new balmoral, her boots, her green-ribboned hat, her dandelion-colored gown and her gray, and boarded the train at Boston. She proceeded to take notes by the way, jotting down her observations of the dandified gentlemen, of the young ladies with full dress and weak novels, of the old men with newspapers and the ancient ladies in rusty black.

The note-taking author proceeded to record observations in her mind's eye as she sat on the piazza of Gorham's Alpine House with her cousins, or explored the country. Everything was grist for her mill, even the distressing habits of her steed, who kept his forelegs completely stationary. Louisa decided to incorporate in "Success" an account of the old woman in the meadow who mistakenly thought her the wife of Cousin Hamilton and described her own marital troubles to the fascinated listener.

Of all the journeys from Gorham, the most interesting to Louisa was the ride to Mount Washington, when the merry company of young ladies minus hoops and old ladies resembling plaid bundles piled into the mountain wagon. Cowbells tinkled, the Peabody bird cried its message from tree to tree, and the ascent began up the new carriage road between granite walls and gorges to the summit. Louisa enjoyed the remarks of the Alpiners as much as the trip itself, and promptly recorded their edifying summaries of the view from the Mount. Several old ladies hopped placidly from stone to stone like rheumatic robins, chirping as they went; geologists tapped and hammered; artists sketched and smoked; children romped; exhausted mammas dozed; fine ladies in gauze bonnets and flounced gowns looked uncomfortable; and Louisa took as many notes upon humanity as upon the view of Katahdin and Kearsarge.

During the drive down, the wagon rattled along briskly through holes and round sharp corners until part of the harness broke and Louisa triumphantly plucked off her stout green garter, briefly commanding, "Tie up the strap and come on." With Louisa Willis she retired to her room to anoint her burned nose, bandage her bruised ankle, and cogitate upon mankind among the mountains.

A rainy day gave time for the traveler to record her cogitations for Alf Whitman's benefit, promising also, "When I go back I will have a 'picter' taken for my Dolphus & as I always take very dark & hunched up you will be gratified with an image of a stout mulatto lady with a crooked nose, sleepy eyes & a tempestuous gown." Other news was less amusing to recount, for in the shocking defeat at Bull Run, five of the Concord company, Cyrus Hosmer among them, had been taken prisoner. Contemplating the tragic setback of the war, Louisa found it impossible to bask peacefully among the brooks and pines, and after her month of rest returned home. The time had not been wasted, for she had stored her mind with material for sketches from the mountains, for sketches of Americans on holiday, and in her pleasures she had not forgotten to take notes.

Concord in the fall seemed to abandon itself to a forced gaiety in which Bull Run could be forgotten. Frank Sanborn's scholars applied themselves industriously to their parties, and Louisa could not resist the smooth dancing floor and the twanging of Ball's harp. Picnics, boating excursions, and moonlight jaunts were followed by another series of plays, in which Abby assumed the role of "first walking lady" in riding habit or white muslin while Louisa continued to scold to her heart's content as "first old woman." Even Mr. Hawthorne emerged from his sky parlor to join the nonsense-verse parties and scratch off a doggerel to the Sage of Apple Slump.

Despite all the parties and plays, there was no forgetting the war in Concord. When Grant seized Paducah, the flag was run up at the town pump. When the Union Army suffered a defeat, it was lowered to half-mast. The Sanitary Commission sent out its call for blankets, quilts, wrappers, and pillows. The fast that was held to save the Union seemed to have been futile, for reverse followed reverse until Ball's Bluff became a name at which resentment flared up and mutterings were heard that the next soldier who was shot for sleeping at his post should be General McClellan. Even the peaceful *Atlantic* had turned warlike, and when Louisa wrote to Alf she announced:

> Mr. Fields says he has mss enough on hand for a dozen numbers & has to choose war stories if he can to suit the times. I will write "great guns" Hail Columbia & Concord Fight if he'll only take it for money is the staff of life & without one falls flat no matter how much genius he may carry.

Weary of the futile talk in Concord and eager to earn her share of "the staff of life," Louisa decided to accept Elizabeth Peabody's suggestion that she become a kindergarten teacher in Boston. Later on perhaps she would find a place nearer the front.

It was Mr. James T. Fields who offered Louisa his distinguished patronage, along with forty dollars to fit up her school. Despite the fact that "Love and Self-Love" as well as "A Modern Cinderella" had appeared in *The Atlantic* and he himself planned to publish "Debby's Début" when space permitted, the editor still inclined to the belief that Louisa should stick to her teaching. When Mrs. Fields invited her to spend a month at her home, Louisa decided to accept the offer, and although she disliked the thought of teaching, she determined to apply Mr. Emerson's principles of education by smuggling in as much contraband wit and fancy as possible and converting her schoolroom into a small world.

The technique that Miss Peabody wished her to follow was not uninteresting. Louisa observed the methods advanced in the new kindergarten at her old address, 20 Pinckney Street, where Miss Peabody applied her theories by introducing block building with cubes to unfold the law of symmetry, and story reading to enrich the children's moral culture. She was not at all certain that she agreed with Miss Peabody's belief that teaching kindergarten was not a craft but a religion, or that she could fulfill her conception of a kindergartner as one endowed with faith and assigned to awaken the intellect, but she would do her best.

The Reverend Charles Barnard admitted Louisa to a room in the Warren Street Chapel, where she could tell stories to her twelve pupils, experiment with prisms, and lead them in "The Cuckoos" or "The Bees." Despite the delights that Miss Peabody had promised, Louisa found that, for her, teaching kindergarten was no religion, and that she still preferred pen and ink to birch and book, for her imaginary characters seemed much easier to manage than creatures of flesh and blood.

Boston, however, offered compensations even to a schoolmarm, and Louisa enjoyed her walks, scurrying across roads where winter carriages moved on snow runners and watching the world wrap itself up in buffalo robes to brave the winter. To the tune of "John Brown's Body" she heard new words now, "The Battle Hymn of the Republic," but the city still danced the quadrille to lighter music at Papanti's and sought forgetfulness of the war in a visit to Van Amburgh's Mammoth Menagerie. Louisa joined the crowds who thronged before the performing elephant and the waltzing Shetland, and enjoyed the antics of Jocko, the monkey pony-rider. Even in Manager Frost's Moral Circus Exhibition there might be material for a story, and one day Louisa might center a narrative about that very Mammoth Menagerie.

At the home of Mrs. Fields, also, there was much to fill her mind with new thoughts, for an Arabian Nights' entertainment unfolded in the long drawing room on Charles Street, where the gay and beautiful hostess sat among her books and pictures, exchanging witticisms with Boston's notables. With audacious humor Mr. Fields, irreproachably dressed in spite of his Byronic collar, spared neither solemn respectabilities nor accredited reputations, until Louisa in her corner realized that greatness was not so impressive as she had once believed.

In April she decided to live at home and travel each day to Warren Street. Concord was in a great state of excitement over the newspaper that Ripley Bartlett was planning. When the services of "the first female writer of the age" were requested for the new enterprise, Louisa planned to write a story of local interest on the calisthenic fever that had raged in the village, and used for her characters the tyro gymnasts who made up in starch and studs what they lost in color, and the old ladies who tossed beanbags till their caps were awry. The author enjoyed particularly her delineation of August Bopp, who was, like young Severance, the leader of the class, a king of clubs, and like Dr. Solger, one of Sanborn's lecturers, a German who had come to America to seek his fortune. His "eminent" nose and blond beard and his crop of bonny brown hair graced a man of patient courage and gentle strength, and Louisa allowed Ripley Bartlett to print "The King of Clubs and the Queen of Hearts" as a serial starting in the first issue of his *Monitor.* "I get ten dollars a page for my foolish little story," she wrote to Alf, "for being very local it takes & makes the paper sell, & as money is the end & aim of my mercenary existence I scribble away." Since writing, in spite of Mr. James T. Fields, was paying better than teaching, Louisa determined to give up her work at the Warren Street Chapel.

For one reason in particular Louisa was glad to be at home in the spring. Mr. Thoreau was so ill now that his bed had been brought down to the parlor of the yellow house on Main Street, where he who had once looked upon mountains could see the villagers pass by. With the children who brought him games and flowers Louisa visited her friend, listened to the voice now sunk to a whisper, and knew that this illness would be his last. He would leave the world, he said to Father, without a regret. But Father knew that when he went hence, then Pan was dead and nature ailing throughout.

On May 9 the village schools were dismissed for Mr. Thoreau's funeral. As Anna and Louisa accompanied Father to the church, the bells tolled the forty-four years he had numbered. "The country knows not yet," Mr. Emerson said, "or in the least part, how great a son it has lost. . . . His soul was made for the noblest society; he had in a short life exhausted the capabilities of this world; wherever there is knowledge, wherever there is virtue, wherever there is beauty, he will find a home." Father read passages from Mr. Thoreau's own writings: "The ears are made to hear celestial sounds; the eyes to behold beauty not invisible." None who knew him could forget him; even his flute remembered, for it was said that a passing breeze had evoked from the instrument a plaintive note as if, in happier meadows than those that stretched to the river, the Concord Pan piped on.

Ever more restlessly Louisa helped Mother with the household chores. Nothing engrossed her except the story she wrote for *Frank Leslie's Illustrated Newspaper* in hopes of winning the one-hundred-dollar prize offered by the editor of a journal replete with alluring pictures, New York gossip, and murder trials. In "Pauline's Passion and Punishment" she rapidly sketched against a Cuban background her account of the heroine's revenge for Gilbert Redmond's infidelity, interpolating all the necessary details of forgery and brutality, capping the whole with a fitting murder. She enjoyed writing the melodramatic conversation that recalled the dialogue of the Hillside barnstormers, and allowed Pauline to answer Manuel's question, "Traitor! Shall I kill him?" with the remark that "there are fates more terrible than death, weapons more keen than poniards, more noiseless than pistols. . . . Leave Gilbert to remorse—and me." Pictures of Manuel reading Gilbert's letter or of Gilbert's despair at Pauline's final rejection would emblazon the pages of *Leslie's Illustrated Newspaper* most appropriately, and Louisa immediately dispatched her narrative to the editor, hoping that it would be a prizewinner. She explained her motives in a letter to Alf:

> I intend to illuminate the Ledger with a blood & thunder tale as they are easy to "compoze" & are better paid than moral & elaborate works of Shakespeare so dont be shocked if I send you a paper containing a picture of Indians, pirates, wolves, bears & distressed damsels in a grand tableau over a title like this "The Maniac Bride" or The Bath of Blood A Thrilling Tale of Passion.

Such stories would, of course, appear anonymously; it would not do for the author of *Flower Fables* to emerge as the creator of a "Maniac Bride" or even of "Pauline's Passion and Punishment." Nevertheless, Louisa enjoyed the ease with which she could produce a sensational story, and hoped the experience would give her practice in fancy and in language.

Writing for Frank Leslie might fill the coffers of the Alcott sinking fund, but it would in no way satisfy Louisa's desire to help the Union forces. She was fired by the sights around her, the recruiting tents on Boston Common, the music stands, and the parade ground. Every event seemed calculated to urge her on to the front; every month brought tidings that stimulated her to activity. As each day passed, the hope of victory dwindled into the fear of defeat. Sam Hoar ran away from home with Bob Higginson to join the army; Wilky James enlisted; Alf Whitman began work with his father at Falmouth, Kentucky, in the quartermaster's department. Nearly all of Frank Sanborn's scholars, who had played whist and drunk root beer in the parlor of the Orchard House, were sharing now in another game with higher stakes. Antietam succeeded the second defeat at Bull Run. Everywhere the war intruded. Sewing bees and lint picks continued, and Louisa was busy with blue flannel jackets as well as with smaller garments for the child that Anna expected. In and out of socks and shirts and mittens her needle plied, until Louisa sharply realized the truth of Mr. Emerson's remark that it was impossible to extricate oneself from the questions in which one's age was involved. She could no more keep out of politics than out of the frost.

In the breast of each, Father believed, there was a liberating angel, at whose touch the doors of the dungeon flew open and loosed the prisoner. When in November Louisa decided to apply for a place as nurse in Washington, her liberating angel released the restlessness that had for so long consumed her. Her May blood was up. It still needed more than lint picks to win a war, more than patriotic cockades or drumming and fifing.

Her nursing experience, she admitted, had not been extensive. Yet those long nights with Lizzie would never be forgotten. She had learned then to minister to sleepless hours, and the knowledge, dearly gained, could be put to other uses. Besides, Louisa considered, she fulfilled remarkably well most of the regulations that Miss Dix had proposed for nurses. She was thirty years old, of strong health, good conduct, and serious disposition. Her five feet, six inches would lend her a matronly appearance; her long chestnut hair could be demurely braided; and if the gray eyes sparkled a bit too freely, surely that would do no harm to a wounded soldier. As for dress, the black, brown, or gray of Miss Dix's circular corresponded very well with her own made-over wardrobe. In Dr. Home's report she had studied the cure of knee-joint wounds by the "long continuance of suppuration." From Florence Nightingale's *Notes on Nursing* she learned the canons of the profession. The air must be kept pure; light Whitney blankets must cover the sick; dirty carpets and papered walls infected the room. At the Armory Square, where through the aid of Hannah Stevenson she hoped to be assigned, she would be able to practice those preachments and comfort the wounded with her ministrations.

With the best of the Concord artillery she, too, had enlisted, and while the "slow coaches" of Washington lumbered along, Louisa proceeded to make her preparations for departure. On December 11 the note from Miss Stevenson arrived, summoning the nurse to fill a place, not in the Armory Square, but in the Union Hotel Hospital at Georgetown. Mrs. Hawthorne helped mark Louisa's clothes with indelible ink, and the trunk was packed with the dresses, the gray, the black, and the brown, along with her small brass inkstand and a copper teakettle. Louisa was determined to make all the soldiers jolly, and accordingly filled every empty space with all the games and copies of Dickens that she owned.

The time had come for Father to send his only son to war. After the troubled, fearful good-byes at home, Julian Hawthorne and Abby escorted Louisa to the station in the still December twilight. Perhaps, from the experiences that would befall her, she could write a finer story than any she had yet unfolded, a story that might find a place, not in *Leslie's Illustrated Newspaper*, but in *The Commonwealth* that Mr. Conway was editing. Had not Mr. Thoreau believed that wherever men have lived there was a story to be told? There in Georgetown, where men were living and dying too, she would be the storyteller and the story.

CHAPTER 7

The Union Hotel Hospital

There was time on the long journey to Washington for doubt to rise and be vanquished a thousand times. On the train to New London, on the boat to New York, on the second train from Jersey City, there was time, more than enough, to review in memory the nature of gunshot wounds, to munch gingerbread and pears from home, and to cogitate about the condition of the Union Hotel Hospital. It had been converted, Louisa knew, from the Union Tavern, but had gone through the vicissitudes of fire and change of management since George Washington had dined there. Looking out of the window, she saw at last the succession of hills rising toward the Potomac, the red lines of earthworks built for the defense of the capital, and as she watched she thought often of what the converted hotel at the corner of Bridge and Washington streets would hold for the nurse from Concord. Suddenly there loomed up on the left the unfinished white dome of the Capitol, and the Concord nurse had arrived for duty.

Near the bridge over Rock Creek, in Georgetown, Louisa was deposited at the door of the Union Hotel Hospital. She saw before her a dismal old three-story structure, a far cry from what she had heard of the Armory Square. She walked up the steps and was admitted into a building that had been cut up into a number of small rooms. Louisa glanced at the tiny windows and thought dolefully of Miss Nightingale's instructions regarding the ventilation of sick rooms. Along narrow, tortuous halls and passages she was led, her feet treading carpeted floors, her eyes confronted by paper-covered walls. What use now, she thought, were Miss Nightingale's notes on nursing when, as she was led to understand, there were no provisions for bathing, the water closets and sinks were defective, the cellars were damp, and the very woodwork was actively decaying. The air was fetid. She steeled herself to remember Harpers Ferry, to remember why she had come.

In her curtainless room with its narrow iron beds Louisa dressed by gaslight at six the next morning in her plain dark clothes, flung a red rigolette over her head, and reported for duty. Reveille came at six-thirty on the morning of December 14, and the new nurse saw the attendants and able convalescents make the beds, sweep the floors, and clean the spittoons. A quarter of an hour later, at breakfast call, the convalescents entered the dining room along with their attendants, except for those who were distributing food to the bed patients. She herself had difficulty in consuming the morning's rations, and wondered what Father would have said to the pint of coffee, the bread and butter, and the relish of meat or bacon. She downed her portion, however, and was eager to meet the staff of surgeons when they made their Sunday morning call at ten.

Louisa followed while Dr. George Winfield Stipp, surgeon-in-charge, visited each ward, the chief nurse accompanying him from bed to bed with a memorandum book in which were noted the diet, medicines, and instructions for each patient. Louisa was given so many directions, and was introduced to so many of the surgeons, that she found the morning quite confusing. She tried, first of all, to keep the names of the physicians straight in her mind. Besides Dr. Stipp, who hailed from Virginia and was now a surgeon of the United States Volunteers, there were, she learned, four acting assistant surgeons, so called because they had been civilian physicians and now served as noncommissioned officers under contract to work in the hospital.

Finally, Mrs. Ropes, the matron, acquainted Louisa with her own particular duties, taught her how to change a bottom sheet by pinning the clean one to the margin of the soiled one, informed her that the underclothes of the patients should be changed at least once a week, that bedpans must be emptied whenever used, and that the patients' hands and faces must be washed with strong brown soap. She must be prepared for duty in the linen room, or for the administration of extra diets; she must see that able convalescents made their own beds at reveille, and that there was no smoking, spitting, or swearing in the wards. If she were promoted to night duty, she would inspect the fires and lights. The army regulations allowed one nurse to every ten patients, but who could tell when such an allotment might prove impossible? A battle was raging even now, it was said, in Fredericksburg. At any rate, Miss Alcott knew her duties, and understood that her compensation would consist of one full ration and forty cents a day, to which quarters and fuel would naturally be added.

Louisa knew her duties, theoretically at least, but the morning had been a full one and she was not sorry when noon marked the dinner hour. The breakfast procedure was repeated, and over beef stew and turnips Louisa listened to the hospital talk, to stories of nurses who sang hymns and prayed violently while they stole the men's watches and money, of the Reverend Frederick Brown, the chaplain, who had approved of one estimable lady until it was found that she forced the patients to make their wills in her favor. The gossip proceeded, the malt liquor was downed, and finally the convalescents were marched back to the wards.

During the afternoon, Louisa came to know a few of her patients in Ward I. She comforted them—Hodges and Cosgrove and Ellison; it mattered not what their names were, or whether they suffered from lung wounds or pneumonia, typhoid or diphtheria; it mattered not whether they had been mustered in at New Jersey or Pennsylvania or Rhode Island; it did not even matter that among them was one Wilt, a Rebel. They were ill and suffered, and what help was hers to give, with the aid of tin basin or soap or lint, was given. The hospital itself, she thought, with its foul air and damp cellar, gave but poor comfort to the men.

Later in the day came the surgeons' evening call, but this time only those patients who required special attention were visited. At six-o'clock supper Louisa listened, over mush and molasses, not to gossip, but to more dreaded news, for there was word now that a great battle was raging to the south, and that soon the empty beds would be filled. The *Star* had carried an ominous "extra" telling of General Franklin's opposition by the enemy. Even now patients were being sent back to their home states so that there would be room for the casualties of Fredericksburg.

There was time, before tattoo and evening roll call, to read a few pages of Dickens to the ward, to play Mrs. Gamp before an audience of wounded soldiers, to look out through the tiny windowpanes and describe to the men the shoots of greenish light shed by an aurora borealis that streamed through the sky. It was a brilliant end, Louisa thought, to such a day; its token surely was a hopeful one. At taps all lights were darkened in the wards, but still the aurora climbed the skies and sent its streamers of bright hope even into the little room in Georgetown, where a Concord nurse, armed with soap and lint, had gone to war.

From reveille to taps, from brown soap to a scene from Dickens, from the making of beds to the stuffing of bedsacks, Louisa moved through the labors of the day. But the hospital routine did not continue long. At dawn on December 16 she was awakened by a sharp and ominous summons: The wounded have come! Louisa glanced out of the window and saw the carts laden with the victims of Fredericksburg, saw men with bandaged heads and faces blackened with smoke and powder totter along the street, while others led their comrades into the halls of the Union Hotel Hospital. She hastened downstairs, and knew that routine must be abandoned for hurried ministrations of lint and soap and bandages. Dr. Kennon rushed in and told how the streets of Washington looked after the desperate battle to the south, how the steamer *George Weems* had arrived on Sunday night, bearing its burden of wounded. Most of them, he said, were not dangerously injured; that was why they had been able to arrive on the first boat. The more serious cases would come later, he warned. These men had been shot at while climbing a hill; it was their heads and shoulders that were bandaged. These men could walk. Others would come who must be borne on litters. Even now, he said, the streets were filled with ambulances, and the sick were lying on sidewalks and leaning on railings. The Sanitary Commission was sending out an appeal for supplies. Under every street lamp, all Washington was talking about Fredericksburg.

They were counted out at last, the wounded who had been sent to the Union Hospital. And, in the midst of her hurried ministrations, Louisa began to know a few of the forty-five who had been assigned there. Richard Fitzgerald, the doughty Irish cavalryman with a wounded arm; Patrick Murray of Rhode Island, who suffered from an injured knee and shell concussion, each became to her more than a name on a label as she handed the sponges to Dr. Stipp and watched him drench their wounds to relieve the burning pain. And those who came later—John Suhre, the Virginia blacksmith, who stoically lay dying of a wound in the chest; Robert Bane, the jolly little nineteen-year-old sergeant from Michigan, who had lost his right arm, but planned to get a false one and shoulder a rifle again—these she knew, too, admiring their courage and helping them in their distress.

While Louisa applied poultices to promote the flow of pus or handed the saws and needles to Dr. Ottman when he tried to dislodge a Minié ball, she tried, also, to make the men forget scenes that had been written indelibly upon their memory. They could not forget, and they murmured to her, after the surgeons had left, their tales of Fredericksburg.

One remembered especially how the officers had looked at first in their bright new uniforms, their bayonets gleaming, their steeds champing, the gun carriages rattling along at the start of the battle. John Suhre told her of the little canvas city that had grown up in a night on the banks of the Rappahannock, while Richard Fitzgerald made her eyes shine with his tales of General Burnside, who shouted orders from under a slouch hat. None could forget the rain of musket balls that swept the ranks as they fastened the boats to make pontoon bridges. In their agony they saw again the shot and shell hurled through the roofs, leveling the spires of Fredericksburg, heard again the showers of whistling lead, the whiz of bullets, the roar of musketry, and the long shriek of shells and grape and shrapnel. In the morning in Ward I at the Union Hotel Hospital, they saw again the fog over Stafford Heights, and in the night, as Louisa stood by their beds, they were startled again by the flash of musketry in the darkness. The air was lurid with gun flashes, and the sound of remembered musketry mocked the silent watches of the night. These men had, like Louisa, remembered Harpers Ferry; and now to their memory and hers also was added another name, another word to catch at the throat and quicken defiance. Fredericksburg, too, would be remembered.

Yet, from time to time, she made them forget, and the men were grateful when the tall nurse in a long, straight skirt with a red rigolette flung round her head appeared before their beds with her tray of packed lint and isinglass plaster, or bore from the dispensary the tinctures and volatile oils that eased their pain. For the wounded, fresh from the field of Fredericksburg, it was no matter that the woodwork in the ancient ballroom of the Union Hotel was decaying, or that the air was fetid with gangrenous odors. It was at night, after taps, that the men especially needed reprieve from memory, and soon Louisa was placed on the night shift after Mrs. Ropes, the matron, had succumbed to illness. At midnight now she went on duty, and from then till noon made the rounds of the wards every hour, inspecting fires and lights, trimming lamps, chatting with Sergeant Bane, or trying to ease the distress of John Suhre, who was fighting now not to live, but to die.

And still the wounded came, night after night, from the banks of the Rappahannock. Almost every day in those cloudy December weeks they arrived on steamboats at the Washington wharves, the more serious cases coming now, as Dr. Kennon had warned. In their wake came brothers and mothers looking for their kin, searching the hospitals for men whose names had appeared on the casualty lists. There were over 300 patients in the Union Hotel

Hospital, which, not so long before, had been considered capable of accommodating 225.

In her own Ward I Louisa walked the rounds at night, dressing Patrick Murray's wounded knee, reading Dickens to Sergeant Bane, or soothing John Suhre, who was calmly awaiting his approaching death. Sometimes, too, she had time to keep her journal or write detailed letters to the folks in Concord, telling about Sergeant Bane's attempts to write to Dearest Jane with his left hand, or the chaplain's gloomy preaching of resignation to men who had breathed death in the air at Fredericksburg. With a sense of dramatic contrast she read the answering notes, the news of a dance at the schoolhouse or the meetings of the whist club.

Another more exciting letter arrived at the hospital, from Mr. E. G. Squier, Frank Leslie's editor and Louisa's "obedient servant," announcing that "Pauline" had been awarded the coveted one-hundred-dollar prize, and recommending that the author submit whatever she might hereafter have of the same sort for Mr. Leslie's acceptance. Although, for such rewards as this, Louisa might continue to write sensational stories, there was, as far as material was concerned, no need now to invent situations or search out exotic backgrounds to amuse her readers. Here, within the papered walls of a hotel room converted to meet the exigencies of war, here between two rows of iron beds, was material enough for letters and stories to last a lifetime. If she wished to trade on the skill she was acquiring from writing sensational tales, she might combine the blood-and-thunder technique with a hospital background. As she sat before the tiny windowpane while her patients slept, Louisa peopled the ward with contrabands and wounded Rebels, sketched in mind a doom of vengeance or murder for her plot, and planned to send the story sometime to storm the portals of *The Atlantic Monthly*. Even without benefit of blood-and-thunder there was material around her for many a story. The whining grumbler, the kind attendant, the embittered volunteer, Suhre's courage as he waited for death—all these would, Louisa was sure, find their way into print. Character, after all, might prove more significant in a story than any elaborately imagined plot.

Flame ate the candles slowly through the night. The bells of the Georgetown Seminary were long in tolling the hours away. Louisa thought often, as she waited for daylight, of the past as well as of the future, and the men and women she had known in the white village of Concord mingled in parade with those who lay about her. More than ever she thought now of Mr. Thoreau, to whom Concord had been the world. As she thought, watching beside the bed of a one-legged lad dying of wound fever, a poem sang itself in her mind, to him, the Pan who was not dead, whose flute, as some had said, still whispered music on the air, whose name was written down in violets, who could not ever die.

> *We sighing said, "Our Pan is dead;*
> *His pipe hangs mute beside the river;*
> *Around it wistful sunbeams quiver,*
> *But Music's airy voice is fled.*
> *Spring came to us in guise forlorn;*
> *The bluebird chants a requiem;*
> *The willow-blossom waits for him;—*
> *The Genius of the wood is gone."*

> *Then from the flute, untouched by hands,*
> *There came a low, harmonious breath:*
> *"For such as he there is no death;—*
> *His life the eternal life commands;*
> *Above man's aims his nature rose.*
> *The wisdom of a just content*
> *Made one small spot a continent,*
> *And turned to poetry life's prose.*

> *"Haunting the hills, the stream, the wild,*
> *Swallow and aster, lake and pine,*
> *To him grew human or divine,—*
> *Fit mates for this large-hearted child.*
> *Such homage Nature ne'er forgets,*
> *And yearly on the coverlid*
> *'Neath which her darling lieth hid*
> *Will write his name in violets.*

"To him no vain regrets belong
Whose soul, that finer instrument,
Gave to the world no poor lament,
But wood-notes ever sweet and strong.
O lonely friend! he still will be
A potent presence, though unseen,—
Steadfast, sagacious, and serene;
Seek not for him—he is with thee."

It was not strange she thought so much of death. She needed only to glance down at an iron bed nearby to see the serene eyes and grave, sweet smile of a man who was meeting death itself. John Suhre, the thirty-year-old Virginia blacksmith, seemed almost too strong to die. A Confederate ball had pierced his left lung and broken a rib, so that every struggling breath he took was a raucous gasp. Louisa might bend over him, her chestnut hair catching the light of the lamps, and smile her infectious smile, or brush his hair gently. But nearer even than the tall, bright-eyed nurse was death, the hovering ghost. Slowly, between gasps, he spoke to her about his sister or the widowed mother he had left in Virginia. Still more slowly he dictated a letter for Louisa to write to his brother. Even as he spoke, death drew closer about him, and there was nothing for the nurse to do but help him die. The brother could not answer the letter in time. For Thoreau, violets while the Concord Pan piped on; for John Suhre, the evergreen of memory.

There was a different evergreen in the hospital now, evergreen that bore a brighter hope for all mankind. Even in the narrow passageways and dank wards of the Union Hotel, the Christmas wreaths had been hung to mark, in the midst of war, the eternal hope for peace. It was different, Louisa thought, from a Christmas at Concord, where snow stayed white on the ground and the air was redolent of pine and spruce. At home the family had been invited to the Wayside for a gaily bedecked tree, and Christmas in the hospital was lonely for Louisa. Yet as she looked about her at the wounded men and the wreaths of evergreen, she realized that she could take from the scene as much as she could give to it. Surely a hospital Christmas would make a fine sketch, drawing its substance from the arrival of a holiday box and news from home. And so Louisa joined in the festivities, simple though they were, and kept her mind's eye open for impressions that would one day be turned into print on a newspaper page. When the inspiration of necessity failed her, she could always turn back to this, this dilapidated ballroom festooned with evergreen, this hospital ward crowded with the victims of Fredericksburg, this Christmas Day in 1862.

Outside the walls of the Union Hotel Hospital there was material, too, for stories of a more varied nature. On a cloudy day late in December Louisa left the hospital at last to wander about the city. It was good to breathe the fresh air of the out-of-doors and forget, for a few hours at least, the rank smell of the Union Hospital.

Along the route that crossed Rock Creek and in the city itself Louisa saw line after line of army wagons and artillery, heard the rumbling of their wheels, the clatter of galloping squads of cavalry, the measured beat of marching infantry. On every sidewalk, army blue was the color that took her eye, with the bright gold lace of officers sprinkled here and there. Here was a city at war indeed, a background against which she could write many a story. *The Commonwealth* had accepted "M.L." for publication in January, and she would dispatch to the editor any tales she might base upon her new experiences.

War might have set the predominant motif, but for all the army blue, Washington was still a city of contrasts. Louisa glanced at a wooden shack next to an old mansion that had room for slave quarters. At the same time that her eye swept the vista of the unfinished white dome or a row of stately columns she noticed the Negro huts and cabins that dotted the land. Not far from one street that trailed off into a country road she turned into Judiciary Square, elegant and fashionable with its stucco city hall. Contrast pursued her as she plowed through the muddy streets.

Even as she walked, Louisa remembered her nights at the hospital, and the names of the soldiers made a refrain in her mind that kept time to the clash of sabers and the rattling of government wagons: Eastman of New Hampshire, Shepherd of New York, Gorman of Massachusetts, Dailey of Michigan. Would she never forget the names? Would not even incorporating them in a story some day make her forget?

She walked at last into Pennsylvania Avenue, and passing Duff Green Row saw before her Capitol Hill, dreary and desolate, stretching away into a desert above the mud of the West End. On the brow of the hill was the Capitol itself, and Louisa stopped to look at Greenough's statue of Washington on the grounds. Men were working on the new white dome; everywhere she saw scaffolds, engines, and pulleys, while the noise of the workmen's hammers added another sound to the varied voices of the city. Between the White House and the Capitol there were sights to treasure for a lifetime of storytelling—Saxons and Creoles, quadroons and mulattoes, contrabands, and even a lone Indian moving toward the Capitol to offer his prayer to the Great White Father. Near the variety shows and horse bazaars Louisa saw again the gold lace of seamen or the Zouaves in their fantastic rig. And at the corner were mounted guards, sitting with drawn swords, watching the parade of ambulances and carriages and black hacks. They had not forgotten the war; nor had the men who jostled each other in the streets forgotten. Louisa heard scraps of their talk, their fear of a raid by "Jeb" Stuart's cavalry, their murmurings of the last steamer from Fredericksburg.

When she returned from her wanderings, Louisa told the wounded men what she had seen, describing for them the gold-laced officers and the Creoles of Pennsylvania Avenue. As the days passed, changes gradually took place in the wards. Patrick Murray had recently been pronounced well enough to take on the duties of a contract nurse. In a short time Sergeant Bane would be discharged from the hospital so that he might return to his home in Michigan and learn to shoulder a rifle over a false right arm. John Suhre was dead. In their places other forms lay on the iron beds; other names sang themselves in her memory—Robert Vincent, William Shoemaker, Michael Donald, Thomas Haley—making an unending refrain as she walked the familiar rounds through the wards.

The New Year dawned bright and clear after a succession of cloudy days, and Louisa listened to Dr. Kennon's accounts of the contrabands who were screaming their choruses of "Glory Hallelujah" while eggnogs were downed in every hotel along the avenue. The bellmen, the doctor said, had summoned all the Negroes to hear the Emancipation Proclamation read aloud. With the new year it seemed to Louisa that a new day was dawning for all the world.

With the new year, also, an announcement appeared in the pages of *Frank Leslie's Illustrated Newspaper* that after deliberating over the moral tendency and artistic merit of over two hundred manuscripts, the editor had decided to award the first prize to "a lady of Massachusetts" for "Pauline's Passion and Punishment." In the next number the first half of a story "of exceeding power, brilliant description, thrilling incident and unexceptionable moral" was published with appropriate illustrations, and the author delighted as much in her well-sustained anonymity as in the promise of one hundred dollars.

From time to time, on the cloudy afternoons that succeeded the first clear day of the year, Louisa rambled about near Georgetown Heights, or joined the parade of sightseers who thronged the city. It was not long, however, before she discovered that she was paying a toll for her jaunts through the mud and her midnight vigils in the damp, ill-smelling hospital. At first she dismissed her ailment as a winter cold, but even Dr. Stipp looked sharply at her when she was beset with a paroxysm of coughing and had to put down her tray of packed lint until the seizure passed. With heavier and heavier step she paced the wards, moving more and more slowly from one iron bed to the next. She had lost the energy even to write a letter home. She could not feel warm; she had forgotten, it seemed, what warmth was.

When everything became blurred before her and the blankets on the iron beds mingled vaguely with the isinglass plaster, when the fumes of volatile oils and the odor of gangrenous wounds overpowered her, she knew that she would have to yield to Dr. Stipp's command to take to her room. He prescribed calomel and called her illness pneumonia, but was not certain whether, after all, it might not prove to be typhoid. As for herself, she had no care for the name he might use to label the headache and backache, or the chill that ran through her very marrow until it alternated with fever. Mrs. Ropes, Louisa knew, was dying of pneumonia. She saw the matron's face in a blur of memory. Her own, when she dared look at a mirror, was a frightening white mask.

As the fever mounted, toward night, her mind became a confused haunt of blurred images and strange, unreal sounds. Sponges and forceps had a way of appearing suddenly before her; an organ grinder on Pennsylvania Avenue would play a plaintive tune while she stood staring at an open wound. Chaplain Brown seemed to preach hurriedly near the red towers of the Smithsonian Institution, while the colors of gangrene mingled horribly with army blue and gold lace.

Through a numbed consciousness she caught feverish glimpses of a man starting a fire in her room, or of a slight and delicate woman with a soft, musical voice. Surely from the depths of her mind she could retrieve their names, Dr. Kennon and Dorothea Dix. But then lucidity was lost, and in its place came again the delirium, the weakness, and the dry tongue. For hours at a time she lay muttering incoherent phrases until she was carried off into a long slumber from which she would awake in a panic of terror.

Once she awoke to find bending over her the long hair of a well-remembered head, the gentle, benign features of a familiar face. Father had come, then, to take her home. She looked up into his azure eyes and saw that they searched her own with a troubled, fearful, helpless look. She had not seen that look in those serene blue eyes since Lizzie died. The face blurred before her, mingled with the features of Dr. Stipp, and was lost.

Louisa herself had only the dimmest idea of the preparations for their departure. Miss Dix prepared a basket of tea, wine, medicine, and cologne for her comfort, and met her at the cars in the city. Her tongue cleaved to the roof of her mouth; the low, muttering delirium persisted. Through her mounting fever she heard the calls of farewell, saw the waving of hands, recognized momentarily the faces of Miss Thurber and Nurse Julia Kendal, who were going to help her home, and felt the rush of the train, the stop of the cars at Baltimore. After the wait at the station, the change at Philadelphia, and the long journey from New York, she arrived at last in Boston.

The night at Thomas Sewall's, the visit from Miss Stevenson, and the train trip to Concord were telescoped into moments. Una Hawthorne appeared on the cars from Boston and Louisa lay upon her shoulder all the way. At the depot she was roused momentarily by the sight of Abby's shocked face. Pursued by strange fancies, she entered the Orchard House, caught a glimpse of Mother's bewildered eyes, and sank into bed. Crazed with fear, half-dead with torment, Louisa had come home from the war, a ghost hidden in an old wrapper and a blanket, a soldier returned from her own campaign upon a field called Georgetown.

CHAPTER 8

Plots and Counterplots

At home Louisa's illness persisted. Dr. Bartlett pronounced it typhoid, but spoke hopefully. Unconsciousness gave way to delirium, which raged with the periods of fever. Louisa was haunted by hospital scenes, by memories of wounded men, by the distress of her journey and the fear that she would never get home. Strange fancies pursued her. Always the room was filled with men until she sprang out of bed to escape the horrifying visions that loomed through a glazed mist. She was harassed by an ulcerated throat and a racking cough, as well as by the fever that turned her face the color of mahogany. Through the long days and longer nights Mother and Father and Abby nursed and watched her. Gradually, the torment of chills and fever gave way to weakness. Typhoid was yielding to the less rigorous demands of convalescence.

Mrs. Hawthorne insisted that Abby take her meals at the Wayside, and Mrs. Emerson sent a housekeeper to help her neighbor with the chores. Louisa herself was sufficiently recovered now to mourn the loss of her long brown hair when she realized that, at the doctor's orders, her head had been shaved and she would have to wear a wig for a time. After she was free of fever, however, inflammatory rheumatism set in, and Louisa, pallid and hopeless, found that she could not sleep. At length, besides Dr. Bartlett, Mrs. Bliss, housekeeper and companion of Mrs. Horace Greeley, was called in. She sat at Louisa's bedside, holding her hands and "reading" her with closed eyes. After the magnetic session, Louisa rose out of bed, walked across the room alone, and even stood for a while to model a wrapper that Anna was making for her. The ache in her back and limbs disappeared, and soon she was able to go downstairs for breakfast.

It was necessary now for Louisa to begin to learn her new self, the thin, hollow-eyed face, the legs that were too weak to walk, the sore mouth, and the mind in which some of the wild fancies still clung. At length she emerged from the nightmarish domain she had inhabited, and when Paymaster Hutchins sent ten dollars for her services from December 13 to January 7, was able to smile a bit ruefully. She rallied now, and in March cleared out her piece bags and dusted her books, or embroidered "L.C." on a pincushion for the child that Anna expected, the child who must surely be named Louisa Caroline. And at last, on March 22, she left her room after the long waste of fever.

Recalling the lines she had composed during the night watch at the hospital, Louisa wrote down the verses of "Thoreau's Flute," changing only the one word "turned" to "tuned." Father found the poem among her papers and immediately read it to Mr. Hawthorne, who thought most highly of the verses. There were more exciting lines to write soon, however, lines to Anna, for on March 28 she gave birth to a baby boy, and Father returned with the great tidings that he had already imparted to everyone from Mr. Emerson to the coach driver. With one accord the family screamed for two full minutes, until Mother broke down, and Abby poured out questions, and Father repeated with satisfaction, "Anna's boy! yes, yes, Anna's boy!" Louisa thought Amos Minot Bridge Bronson May Sewall Alcott Pratt would be an appropriate name for the lad who had been added to the feminine family, and immediately dispatched the suggestion to Anna.

Louisa's nearness to death had taught her the value of life. There was so much to be done to compensate for the lost winter. Frank Leslie sent the one hundred dollars for "Pauline" and Louisa was able to pay some of her debts, but the doctor's bills remained. She was glad, therefore, when Frank Sanborn, the new editor of *The Commonwealth*, repeated Mr. Conway's suggestion that she turn her hospital letters into sketches for publication.

From the pigeonholes of her mind, where she had stored away her impressions of Georgetown, and from the letters she had sent to the Orchard House, Louisa gathered enough ideas to fill four issues of *The Commonwealth*. Before her desk in the room overlooking the Lexington Road she polished up her accounts of the doctors and attendants and soldiers, concealing their names under false initials. Again she moved in an atmosphere of brown soap and sponges and basins and bandages, chatted with Richard Fitzgerald or Robert Bane, and relived in memory the night of John Suhre's death. With one or two exceptions it was the first time, she realized, that she was relying upon truth alone, upon scenes that she had lived, upon scraps of talk that had been spoken, upon characters she had known. She herself had seen them, the willing nurse with her bandages and lint, the withered old Irishman on his cot, "overpowered by the honor of having a lady wash him," and the doctor who regarded a dilapidated body as a damaged garment and set to work on it "with the enthusiasm of an accomplished surgical seamstress." To save the faces of those who might, perchance, recognize themselves in her pictures, she omitted her information about the estimable lady who had forced the soldiers to bequeath their fortunes to her, and the nurses who had stolen watches and money from the wounded men. Save for these, she sacrificed little of the truth, and, uncertain whether her plunge into realism would prove successful, signed her letters "Tribulation Periwinkle" and dispatched them to Frank Sanborn.

On May 22 the first of the series appeared in *The Commonwealth*. The forty-dollar payment that Louisa received from the editor was nothing, however, in comparison with the letters that she later found at the post office. David Wasson wrote, expressing his extreme pleasure in her work. Henry James applauded the exquisite humanity of "Hospital Sketches" and sent a copy of *Substance and Shadow* for the edification of "Tribulation Periwinkle." To climax her joy, James Redpath and the firm of Roberts Brothers both sought permission to reprint the "Sketches" in book form. Louisa did not ponder long over the choice. Roberts Brothers, it appeared, was managed by Thomas Niles, the gentleman who long ago had acted as clerk at the Old Corner. After several years with Whittemore, Niles and Hall, he had joined the firm of Roberts Brothers, which seemed to specialize as much in the production of photograph albums as in literature. Redpath, on the other hand, had already gained a reputation as a fiery abolitionist, and Louisa subscribed not only to his beliefs but to his contract, agreeing to his offer of five cents on each of the thousand copies in the edition, while he would receive ten to pay for the cost of the book and give something to charity. Perhaps the hospital experience would pay its own expenses, and "Tribulation Periwinkle" would march to the defense of Nurse L. M. Alcott. Nurse Alcott's parents needed a defender, too, as Louisa remarked in a letter to Redpath:

> I too am sure that "he who giveth to the poor lendeth to the Lord" & on that principle devote time & earnings to the care of my father & mother, for one possesses no gift for money making & the other is now too old to work any longer for those who are happy & able to work for her.

During the summer Louisa did indeed make up in work for the time she had lost. She had but few moments to listen to Father's discussion of his work in the schools or to Mother's shouts of "Glory Hallelujah" over the papers. Abby might continue endlessly her tales of dancing and sailing, flirting and rowing at Clarks Island; Anna and John might brood over a baby who boasted a brand-new name, Freddy, along with a nose that turned straight up—Louisa lived in her inkstand and left her desk only to gather fresh ideas for her sketches. Mrs. Hawthorne had sent a copy of "Thoreau's Flute" to Mr. Fields in hopes that it would be accepted for *The Atlantic*. Between revision of the poem and a visit to Class Day, Louisa read proofs, consulted with the printers, and began to write again on *Moods*. The pen was never idle, for when she was not concocting stories, she was answering letters from

Sergeant Bane in Michigan, who had learned to write with his left hand. Frank Sanborn wanted more contributions for *The Commonwealth*, and the author brushed up the notes she had sent home from Gorham to offer as "Letters from the Mountains." "Hospital Sketches" would appear in book form soon, and Louisa found herself in a mad whirl of proofs from Washington Street. Father, looking more benign than ever, suggested that she dedicate the work to Hannah Stevenson. The Orchard House waited, breathless, for the approaching event.

On the morning of August 25, Louisa's first morning-glory opened its petals in honor of the day. In the evening her dozen free copies of *Hospital Sketches* arrived. She herself might have preferred the green covers to be darker green or drab. Perhaps the margins were not wide enough. But no such trivial disappointments could interfere with the pleasure of sending forth this book, her second-born—no flowery romances now of dewdrops or thistledown, but truth, the graphic truth—into the hands of the soldiers who had lived that truth. With delight she turned the hundred pages of the neat, green-covered work, gazed long at the title page with its initials "T.P." centered in a triangle made of a knife, a fork, and a spoon, read and reread the quotation from Sairey Gamp, "Which, naming no names, no offence could be took." Three of the author's free copies would go to soldiers, one, of course, to Sergeant Bane. Another was inscribed, with tongue in cheek, to Nurse Pratt from Nurse Periwinkle. From the twenty-five-cent paper edition that Redpath planned for army reading she would receive 10 percent. She would be glad of the money.

Louisa had not long to wait. All the Concord townsfolk were buying and reading *Hospital Sketches*, and laughing and crying over the book. One rash youth had even gone so far as to buy eight copies. The author sat back and waited for reports from more authoritative sources than the neighbors. She had always thought a few tears from a man far better than a gallon of the feminine briny, and so there was no end to her rejoicing when she heard that the American Consul at Venice had sent his compliments to "Nurse Periwinkle," after shouting with Moncure Conway over the *Sketches*. The papers seemed to vie with each other in lauding the newly discovered author. "Fluent and sparkling" with "touches of quiet humor"—high praise, this, from the *Boston Transcript*. The scenes were "graphically drawn," Louisa read in *The Waterbury American*, while *The Liberator* and the *Anti-Slavery Standard* joined forces with *The New England Farmer* and *The Wide World* in declaring *Hospital Sketches* a work of excellence. There was no doubt now that success had come, and while Louisa savored its unfamiliar, sparkling taste, she realized also the salability of scenes that were true to life. Works of blood-and-thunder based upon weird flights of her imagination would perhaps be more remunerative than *Hospital Sketches*, but truth was now a fountainhead from which the best of her stories might some day stem. If her experience at the Union Hotel Hospital had taught her nothing more than that, it had been, she knew, worth while.

For the first time in her life Louisa was writing under the compulsion not only of her own desires but of publishers' demands. When a new edition of *Hospital Sketches* was called for, Redpath asked the author for another book. After "Thoreau's Flute" had appeared in the September issue of *The Atlantic* and the author's ten-dollar payment had been received, she set to work on a fairy tale about the regeneration of three little roses, Moss, Brier, and Blush, and dispatched *The Rose Family* to James Redpath. Between realistic hospital scenes and the roses of fairyland, between domestic sketches and blood-and-thunder narratives, she alternated, glad to supply the requests of her publishers, attempting all types of stories, wondering where, in this variety of literary form, her forte would be found to lie.

The author doffed her glory cloak for the red rigolette the nurse had worn when, in September, a Concord company was scheduled to return home. The village seemed to reach a state of excitement comparable with that nineteenth of April two years before when Prescott's soldiers had marched away to war. As Louisa wandered along the Lexington Road, she saw again the flags flapping, the wreaths and star-spangled banners waving in the breeze. Now the signs were inscribed WELCOME HOME, and a drum corps consisting of eight small boys and eight large drums kept up a continual rubadub all day long. With the old rigolette round her head Louisa waited for the parade.

Amid the fluttering banners and waving handkerchiefs she waited, and thought for a moment of that other parade she had watched before she, too, had marched away to war. She had seen and felt so much in the time that had flowed between—John Suhre, Robert Bane, Dr. Kennon, Dr. Stipp, the foul-smelling, decaying ballroom of a converted hotel, illness and torment, the scars of her service. There was the gleam of gun barrels, and the little column came marching down the Boston highway. Steadily they proceeded, looking neither to right nor to left, when suddenly, just as the central file was opposite the gate where Louisa stood, the captain turned round on his heel, drew his sword from the scabbard, and shouted his command. The ranks halted, and the beating of drums and the screaming of fifes filled the air. The butts of sixty rifles thumped the ground as one. The soldiers had stopped before the Orchard House to honor one of their own. "Parade Rest." The men-at-arms relaxed, tipped back their caps, and mingled with the spectators. Louisa walked among the rank and file, a tall figure in a dark frock with a red rigolette round her head, walked and smiled and chatted, her eyes twinkling, her heart remembering other soldiers who had worn the same army blue but had not returned like these from war.

The column reformed, but before the men marched on sixty caps were held high in the air and sixty voices cheered lustily for Louisa. Then, while the Hawthornes and the neighbors waved them on their way, the little company moved on, turning the bend of the road past Moore's barn.

Louisa stood silent for a moment, looking toward the bend of the road, watching where ghosts of soldiers paced their silent way; then silently, hurriedly, she passed up the pathway to the porch and went in the house. Her heart was with them still, with all the Murrays and Fitzgeralds who might return from battlefields that bore other names than Fredericksburg, with all the Suhres who would never return. She herself was with them still, remembering, as they remembered, the snow and sleet of the battlefield, the bandaged heads, the faces blackened with powder, and the legs gashed by whistling lead. Within her also was the hope, the same that lifted the hearts of the little company marching along the Boston highway, the same that flickered and rose high in the minds of men who even now were lying on iron beds in some Union Hotel Hospital, the hope that from this slaughter and this civil war, would rise the phoenix flame of liberty.

Liberty was still no more than a hope. Louisa longed to go to Port Royal to help in its realization, to write Plantation Sketches that would make a better book than any she had written. Meantime, there was still a treasure of hospital scenes that had not yet been mined. Once again she lived with the querulous malcontent, the humane attendant, the wounded man awaiting death, and the embittered Massachusetts volunteer too early old; and converted her experiences at Georgetown into "A Hospital Christmas," "The Hospital Lamp," and "On Picket Duty."

Louisa was especially glad to be able to pay Abby's expenses between Concord and Boston, for in October she began to take anatomical drawing lessons under Dr. William Rimmer. Having won a fifty-cent prize for a picture, Abby insisted upon her own right not only to fame but to the privilege of being called "May," and Louisa bowed before her sister's decision. From vertical elements to skeleton limits, May followed the doctor's enthusiastic instructions, and Louisa in turn learned more about the zygomatic arch and the animal expression of the skull than she had ever thought possible. Perhaps Dr. Rimmer, combined with Dr. Reinhold Solger and one or two Concord villagers, would one day make an interesting foreigner in a tale of American life.

After the cider cask was set in the cellar for the winter, Louisa, too, took the train to Boston. In December the fair for the benefit of the Sanitary Commission opened in the city, and the audience flocked to the Tremont Theatre for *Scenes from Dickens*, managed by George Bartlett and dramatized by Louisa. She longed for the old Concord Amateur Dramatic Company, for the new troupe was composed of busy men and incapable women who played very poorly. The audience, however, seemed satisfied, and the six entertainments realized $2,500 for the cause.

Now that the year had drawn to its close Louisa calculated the assets not only in the Sanitary's coffers, but in the Alcott sinking fund. Her earnings amounted to nearly six hundred dollars from writing alone. Although *The Rose Family* under Redpath's imprint fared badly because it had been published too late for the holidays, demands for stories had come from Richardson of *The United States Service Magazine*, Frank Leslie, and James T. Fields. The year that had opened so hopelessly had closed in triumph for an author who had paid the family debts and found publishers for her varied output.

Louisa emerged from her manuscripts and clippings only long enough to help celebrate Freddy's first birthday, and after the sight of her nephew overpowered by his dozen gifts, retired again to her desk to write a story for Frank Leslie. The mildly exciting mystery about Italian refugees, a spy, and a woman disguised as a man was not so sensational that she wished it to appear anonymously, and, having rewarded Clyde with the love of Monica, Louisa signed her name to "Enigmas" and dispatched it to *Leslie's Illustrated Newspaper.*

Everyone shared in the triumphs of the Orchard House except the closest neighbors. Mr. Hawthorne had taken leave of his wife on the porch of the Wayside and left for New Hampshire with Franklin Pierce. A week later his body arrived in Concord. Under the pines of Sleepy Hollow he was laid, and Louisa watched as his unfinished romance was placed upon the coffin and flowers were scattered on the grave. One by one the figures of her youth were fading from sight.

The future eclipsed the past, however, when, after the dust had gathered on the manuscript of *Moods*, Mr. Aaron K. Loring agreed to issue the book provided that it was shortened. The publisher believed that there was in the manuscript the material for a great story. He particularly liked the author's conciseness in introducing characters, getting them upon the stage and into action as quickly as possible. Her *Hospital Sketches*, he noted, had endeared her name to every reader, and a new book by Miss Alcott would start with every presage of success. Mr. Loring still thought, however, that the first chapter wanted pruning, the tenth was a bit spun out, and the eleventh very cold. If the book could be reduced to 286 pages he would be pleased to publish it.

For two weeks Louisa sat at her desk, cutting ten chapters from the book, revising the relations of Warwick, Moor, and Sylvia, and attempting to delineate a life affected by the moods of her heroine. In the chapter "Dull but Necessary," she discoursed at length upon the character of Sylvia Yule. Warwick assumed the qualities of Mr. Thoreau as the author painted a man whose passions and virtues were in unison with the body they inhabited. Mr. Hawthorne also wielded his influence upon the author when she found a "Scarlet Letter" burning not only upon the bosom of Hester Prynne but within the soul of Sylvia Yule. On and on Louisa wrote or rewrote. The shipwreck scene was polished, Warwick dying as Margaret Fuller had died, and the last touches were given to the final chapter. Louisa had sacrificed many of her favorite chapters, but she believed when the revision was completed that the book had been improved and was simpler and stronger than it had been in the lengthier version.

Mr. Loring agreed with the author. With the manuscript cut down to the desired 286 pages, Louisa went to Boston to consult with the brisk though eccentric publisher in his Washington Street office. The book would be brought out immediately, the author to receive ten cents on each cloth copy as well as ten free volumes.

With *Moods* at last in the hands of the printers, Louisa emerged from her second-story retreat to share again in the life around her, and in the sharing gather fresh ideas for works that were as yet unwritten. Dr. Dio Lewis had bought a large summer hotel at Lexington, where he had recently established a school for young ladies, and Louisa observed with interest the third of the educational experiments that she had known. The Lexington seminary differed in several respects from Father's school in the

Tremont Temple and Frank Sanborn's Concord enterprise. Dr. Lewis, Louisa realized, was a crusader for more specific reforms than either of his predecessors, and with enthusiasm she watched the delicate young ladies in their gymnastic costumes with flower boxes or geologist's hammers in their hands. While the pupils followed Dr. Lewis's gospel of plain food, strong shoes, and early hours, Louisa considered that one day it might be well to champion loose belts and cooked grains in an educational narrative.

Louisa had in mind another, less placid tale, in which she decided to incorporate all the impersonations and melodramatic dialogue that she could muster from her memories of the Hillside barn. It was delightful to sit incognito behind a pen that raced along a page, weaving a long and involved story about Virginie Varens, a danseuse upon whose white flesh "two dark letters," V.V., had been tattooed above a lover's knot. Into the tale the author dropped a mysterious iron ring and drugged coffee, while she elaborated upon four violent deaths, one of which was perpetrated by a villain who fell upon his prey "with the bound of a wounded tiger." Nor was the cast of characters complete without a viscount parading as a deaf and dumb Indian servant named Jitomar and a murdered man who boasted as his champion a cousin who looked like his twin. Poison vied with pistols or daggers for "the short road to . . . revenge"; garments were dyed with blood; the heroine concluded her dark bargain, and the writer, having concluded "V.V.: or, Plots and Counterplots," decided that although she had enjoyed her flight into the darkly impossible and although the Alcott sinking fund might be enriched by her effusion, the tale itself must not appear under her own name. The author of *Hospital Sketches* could not father so "lurid" a story. The anonymous contributor would dispatch "V.V." to a sensational newspaper, while L. M. Alcott rested after her fantastic pilgrimage.

From plot to counterplot she had wandered, from a flowery fairyland to a military hospital, from the dismal swamps of the South to a homely New England village, from Sylvia's moods to V. V.'s purgatory. And to her many selves she added now another—the veiled, mysterious author stalking melodramatically behind the dainty "Flora Fairfield" and the courageous "Tribulation Periwinkle." Which of all the many selves would bring to the "lady of Massachusetts" the fame and fortune that she coveted?

To the Orchard House the author of *Moods* brought joy at least. Proudly Louisa presented her first copy to Mother along with a note in which she wrote:

> I am happy, very happy tonight, for my five years work is done, and whether it succeeds or not I shall be the richer and better for it because the labor, love, disappointment, hope and purpose that have gone into it are a useful experience that I shall not forget. Now if it makes a little money and opens the way for more I shall be satisfied, and you in some measure repaid for all the sympathy, help, and love that have done so much for me in these hard years. I hope success will sweeten me and make me what I long to become more than a great writer—a good daughter. And so God bless you, dear mother, and send us all a Happy New Year.

In its new dress the book was cherished as deeply as it had been in manuscript, and Father declared that Louisa had succeeded better in her treatment of the social problem than either Goethe or George Sand. Louisa had written, he was sure, a better book than she knew, a book that might open to her a career of wide usefulness if not of permanent fame as a novelist and a woman. Yet the author shied away from the thought of "genius" and still believed what she had once written to James Redpath:

> I'll try not to be "spoilt," & think ten or fifteen years of snubbing rather good training for an ambitious body; but people mustn't talk about "genius"—for I drove that idea away years ago & dont want it back again. The inspiration of necessity is all I've had, & it is a safer help than any other.

While she waited for the criticisms of *Moods*, Louisa dropped her pen for Mrs. Jarley's "willow wand." Long ago she had delighted in Dickens's story of Nell's wanderings and death, but more than the honesty of Kit or the scurrility of Sampson Brass, she had enjoyed the portrayal of Mrs. Jarley in *The Old Curiosity Shop*. She had dramatized the episode of the waxworks, and found that Mrs. Jarley's calm and classical exhibition could be worked into a fine monologue for an amateur theatrical troupe. Now that plays were offered in the Town Hall to raise funds for the Lyceum, or in Boston for the benefit of the New England Women's Hospital, Mrs. Jarley might once again appear in her old green dress with a large green calash on her head, clutching an umbrella and a basket and claiming the honor of presenting the finest collection of wax "statooary" in the known world. "In the words of our great national poet, George Washington," she declared, " 'Waxwork is friend of man, it refines the fancy, enlarges the sphere of reason, cultivates the soul, therefore cherish it.' "

The waxworks were cherished indeed, from the Elizabethan maid of honor who died from pricking her fingers in consequence of working on the Sabbath, to Jasper Packlemerton of atrocious memory, who destroyed all his wives by tickling the soles of their feet. Louisa's umbrella was pointed with admirable flourishes at Martha Bangs, the insane maid who poisoned fourteen families with pickled walnuts, or at Lord Byron as he appeared in the throes of composing the ninth chapter of *Childe Harold*. Lively airs were played as she allowed the audience a brief pause so that they could get out their handkerchiefs and drop a silent tear for Little Nell. Captain Kidd was displayed in the act of spilling the noble blood of Lady Boadicea FitzBattleaxe, and the proprietress of the waxworks proceeded to announce the discovery of Professor Owlsdark, the great excavator, that Shakespeare had died in Boston and been buried on "Bacon" Hill. Louisa enjoyed her performance as keenly as her audience did, and considered that Mrs. Jarley was in her way as delightful a creature as the mysterious author of "V. V."

While the anonymous contributor received periodic messages from the firm of Elliott, Thomes and Talbot, publishers of *The Dollar Monthly, The Flag of Our Union*, and ten-cent novelettes, regarding the acceptance of "V. V.," Louisa May Alcott clipped from the papers the reviews of *Moods*. Between the two selves the writer vibrated, while Father lectured on Mr. Emerson and May filled orders for pen-and-ink sketches. It was strange to read, on the one hand, a letter from Mr. Elliott, who offered an additional twenty-five dollars if "V. V." appeared in *The Flag of Our Union* under Miss Alcott's signature, and on the other, the reports of *Harper's Weekly* to the effect that *Moods* presented the conflict of passion in noble characters drawn with great delicacy and skill. After the work of Hawthorne, the reviewer could recall no American love story of equal power; and after "V. V.," James R. Elliott expressed a desire for more stories or novelettes at two dollars a column.

To the author, Washington Street had become a veritable Grub Street, for while Louisa Alcott conferred with Aaron K. Loring at number 319, her anonymous counterpart stopped at number 118 to discuss the thrilling adventures and anecdotes published by Elliott, Thomes and Talbot. Although she did not agree that *The Flag of Our Union* contained not one vulgar word or line, or that the ten-cent novelettes that issued from the Journal Building were manuals for the fireside, Louisa allowed "V. V." "By a Well Known Author" to emblazon the pages of *The Flag* throughout the month of February. Despite Mr. Emerson's objections to the "yellow-covered literature of the Sylvanus Cobb, Jr. stamp," she proceeded to supply Messrs. Elliott, Thomes and Talbot not only with poems under her own name, but with "A Marble Woman: or, The Mysterious Model," whose dramatis personae consisted of a sculptor styled Bazil Yorke, who moved in an aura of sorrow and mystery, and a benighted heroine who ate opium in her spare moments. For her second sensational contribution Louisa determined to doff her cloak of anonymity, choosing as a pseudonym the name of "A. M. Barnard." The laurels might rest upon the head of L. M. Alcott; it was "A. M. Barnard" who enriched the coffers of the Orchard House with her two dollars a column. Until the day came when fame and fortune walked hand in hand, Louisa was content to yield the former to the writer of *Moods* and the latter to the unknown author of "V. V." and "A Marble Woman."

Both the mysterious "A. M. Barnard" and the better known L. M. Alcott gave way before a joyous Louisa when news was heard that Sheridan had driven the enemy before him at Five Forks and that Lee had ordered the evacuation of Richmond. All of Boston exulted over the accounts of Appomattox. Garrison had hoisted the flag at Fort Sumter. Never again would the drums be muffled or the dirge played.

In her own life, too, Louisa exulted. *Moods*, now in its third edition, had won an encouraging reception; "V. V." had been published as a serial in *The Flag of Our Union*. Yet joy was ever short-lived, for after Father had returned from Spindle Hill, he was informed that he had not been reelected superintendent of the schools, and Louisa knew that he was deeply pained by this rebuff.

The joy not only of the Orchard House but of the nation was short-lived. Less than one triumphant week had passed after Appomattox when the appalling news of the President's assassination came. The city mourned. All cities and all villages mourned. At Concord on the nineteenth of April, the people met to tell their grief. Eloquently Mr. Emerson spoke of the ghastly blow that had befallen the nation, of the coffin that had set forward on its long march through mourning states. "The President," he said, "stood before us as a man of the people. He was thoroughly American, . . . a quite native, aboriginal man, as an acorn from the oak; . . . sound to the core."

The Concord boys returned and were greeted by the judge in the Town Hall; Sam Hoar dilated on what he had seen at the war; Booth was captured and killed in Virginia; and the maps that had been unrolled in every home gathered dust now that peace had come.

The joy and sorrow of the nation gave way in Louisa's mind to the joy and sorrow of the Orchard House. On either side of the coin happiness and sadness were stamped. It was on Lizzie's birthday that Anna's second boy was born. Even in the reviews of *Moods*, Louisa discovered that triumph mingled with defeat. In

The North American, Henry James branded the author as ignorant of human nature, but confessed that, with the exception of two or three celebrated names, he knew of no one in the country except Miss Alcott who could write a novel above the average. Her next book, she determined, would deal with facts and not ideas, those edge tools with which she had unwittingly been playing. At least James Elliott was more easily pleased than the reviewers, for after "A Marble Woman" had graced the pages of *The Flag*, the editor offered fifty dollars to "A. M. Barnard" for another sensation story.

Fame had begun to smile upon L. M. Alcott, fortune upon "A. M. Barnard," and now the third of Louisa's wishes had also been granted, for she had been invited to accompany Miss Anna Weld to Europe as a companion. William Fletcher Weld, with his fleet of barks and brigs and steamships that flew the Black Horse Flag to Hong Kong and Manila and to Cebu and Melbourne, was known, of course, in every countinghouse and wharf of Boston. Having decided that his invalid daughter, Anna, should leave her backgammon and flowers for the German baths, the master of Central Wharf had begun to look about him for a companion. Hearing that Miss Alcott had had nursing experience and wanted to travel, he proposed that she accompany Anna and her half-brother, George, who would leave the party at Liverpool. Although Louisa had doubts about her ability to manage the pretty, dark-eyed daughter of the Black Horse Flag, who was only three years younger than her companion, the thought of going up the Rhine and seeing the London home of the immortal Sairey Gamp sent doubt to the winds and the doubter to her trunk.

On the eighteenth of July Louisa left Concord for Boston, left Father and Mother saddened by her departure and disposed to blame the good fortune that took her from them. With their blessings, she boarded the Fitchburg train for a last look at Boston. The prim brick buildings with their granite steps and dark green doors would not be seen again until she had looked at grander edifices and opened doors that led to corridors undreamed of. How much there might be then to sketch for *The*

Commonwealth or the *Gazette*. Never for her the tumultuous romance of Virginie or Sylvia, but might not friendship wait for her across the sea?

The nineteenth of July gave her no time for thought or for dreams either. She must sign an oath of allegiance and her passport application before William Weld as justice of the peace, who hastily entered on the blank her thirty-two years of age, her five feet, six inches of stature. On the quay with Anna and George Weld she watched the great steam ferries plowing through the waters and the coaches lumbering down, loaded with trunks. The air was filled with the shouts of newsboys and the calls of passengers as she boarded the steamship *China*, the first screw mail packet of the Cunard line. On the morning of July 20 the single smokestack puffed mightily; Captain Hockley ascended the bridge. Louisa's heart was full now with the thought of home, but the *China* was weighing anchor for Liverpool, steaming down the harbor until Boston was a dot in the distance, and the waters widened between herself and home.

CHAPTER 9

Life in a Pension

During the nine long days of the crossing, Louisa took notes on the idiosyncrasies of a Cunarder and her traveling companions. Anna Weld liked to talk about her father and his tales of the Orient. Otherwise, Louisa did not find her charge's personality very fascinating, for though she delighted in backgammon, flowers, and watercolors, Anna Minot Weld had little in common with her more literary companion. Besides, her lack of physical strength boded not a few difficulties in crossing the Continent.

When the *China* steamed up the Mersey at dawn on July 29, Louisa harbored some misgivings about journeying on alone with Anna. She had little time for contemplation, however, for she had at last arrived at the Liverpool docks. The baggage was inspected and the trio had time for a walk along the Prince's Parade before Anna and Louisa parted from George at the Lime Street station and boarded the train for London.

During the four dull, drizzly days in the city, Louisa walked about the parks and streets and abbey as if she were the heroine of a novel instead of Anna Weld's traveling companion. The thought that she was actually abroad was still almost incredible, and the difficult voyage from Dover to Ostend did nothing to reassure her that she had finally entered the Old World. It was only at Brussels, where she wandered with Anna about the Palais du Roi or the Rue Royale that Louisa actually realized that the author of *Moods* and *Hospital Sketches* was at last in Europe. So swiftly they traveled that one image after another passed like the colors of a kaleidoscope before her eyes, until the tourists embarked upon their journey up the Rhine.

At nine o'clock on a lovely August morning, Louisa and Anna steamed away into fairyland. On the boat there was more material for a sketch or story than the author of "Letters from the Mountains" had ever found in Gorham. Louisa took copious notes on the English who sat bolt upright, the French who chattered and pranced, the Germans who smoked their meerschaums, and the Americans who stared and asked questions. Here at last was old Europe, and Louisa listened joyfully to the chorus of the ship's company who declaimed "The Castled Crag of Drachenfels" or worshiped before the Sieben Jungfrauen. At noon long tables were spread on the deck, where the Concord tourist could bask in the varied pleasures of cheese and castles, cabbage and vineyards, wine and donkeys.

At Coblenz they passed the night, and Louisa stood long on the little balcony outside her window, watching the midsummer moon that shone upon the fortress of Ehrenbreitstein, the bridge of boats, the watchtowers, and the peasant girls with gold and silver arrows in their hair. The beauty of the ancient world charmed her, and she knew that she could never forget her midsummer night's dream at Coblenz.

Before the Rhine boat reached Biebrich, Anna decided that she could endure the voyage no longer and implored to be set ashore. After a hasty conference with the captain, at sunset the two wanderers disembarked with their trunks in the village of Oestrich. As they marched upon the town, a group of peasants stared with amazement, while even the geese were bewildered by the procession of bottles, bags, shawls, and notebooks. Louisa chuckled over the natives, who tried to decipher the trunk labels until one lifted his hands and exclaimed, "Livartpool! *Ach Gott*, Livartpool!" She could not resist adding the information that they also hailed from "Amerika," at which detail the peasants with one accord removed their caps and stood with open mouths while two young Germans, reading Boston on the labels, exchanged their knowledge of Goethe for everything Louisa would tell them about Mr. Emerson. The procession continued, the band playing, the boys laughing, the donkeys braying, and the geese hissing, until at last Louisa and Anna arrived at the *gasthaus*. Had she ever doubted that she was actually in Europe, Louisa's doubt flew before the winds of language now, for when she mildly demanded a blanket she received an egg, when she implored a foot warmer she was given a cool salad, and when she ordered supper in pantomime she was overwhelmed by the appearance of towels and a flatiron. Here was Europe, ample material for a sketch called "Up the Rhine." At noon the tourists were escorted to the station while the blue-bloused peasants stared and the geese hissed their adieus.

Since Anna had planned to take the cure at Schwalbach, the pace of the travelers diminished when they arrived at the spa, and changing images no longer rushed before Louisa's eyes. Through the August and September days she had time to become familiar with the hills that rose above the valley of Schwalbach, to wander on the graveled promenades that led into the woods, or to sit for hours beneath the chestnut trees. At the home of Madame Genth they took lodgings, while Dr. Genth, author of *Der Kurort Schwalbach* and *The Iron Waters of Schwalbach*, superintended the cure. Here was still another world that differed as much from the journey up the Rhine as Gorham had differed from Georgetown, a world in which the most intense discussion concerned the relative merits of the Stahlbrunnen, the Weinbrunnen, and the Paulinenbrunnen, and the comparative taste of iron, magnesia, and carbonate of lime. Louisa observed Anna and the patients crowding the promenades near the wells and sipping the waters, and noticed that the visitors actually did take Dr. Macpherson's advice to

> *Arise betimes to pump repair,*
> *First take the waters, then the air,*
> *Most moderate be in meat and drink,*
> *And rarely, very rarely think.*

The quiet life of the spa, with its ladies feeding the swans, its coffee-drinkers, and its band, began to pall upon her. Only a carriage drive to Wiesbaden or a donkey ride to Hohenstein varied the dull monotony of the days, and Louisa plodded on in the care of her charge, studied a little French, or, gathering flowers to press for Mother in an olivewood album, planned a story in which a sheaf of wheat might be contrasted with the brilliant poppies that faded quickly.

The monotony of the fall was varied at last when, on September 20, letters arrived at the Hotel des Postes from home. With a full heart Louisa read how the family had followed her in spirit across the Atlantic in the bright, benign July days. She was touched to know how they missed her and longed for her return. Every bit of news interested her, and even the cure establishment was brighter after word from home. Anna seemed to have profited from her fidelity to the *Trinkhalle*, and when George came on the twenty-eighth, the travelers were ready to journey on the next day to Vevey, framed in enchantment by the waters of Lake Leman and the Alps of Savoy.

The Pension Victoria, Louisa discovered, boasted more than its yellow-leafed poplars or the lake that washed the terrace wall. No scenic artist of the Walpole or Concord dramatic company could have painted a lovelier background than the village of Vevey to the right with its quay and great hotel flying the flags of three nations, the gray towers of Chillon to the left, and gloomy Saint Gingolph in the shadow of the Dent du Midi. Opposite, far across the lake, rose the white Alps of Savoy, and in the pension itself there were more characters to people stories and sketches than Louisa had ever found in New England.

Every nation seemed to have sent to Vevey a representative for the delight of an author abroad, from the Russian baron who was page to the czar to an English colonel, from an Irish lady to a fat Frenchman, from a pair of Scottish sisters to a family of Rebels from South Carolina. From the first day that she seated herself with Anna at the long table in the Pension Victoria, Louisa occupied herself by taking notes, not on backgrounds now, but on characters, and although as the time passed the characters changed, she never lost her delight in observing their idiosyncrasies. The baron, she noted, was a stout and turbulent barbarian, who beguiled his time by smoking, playing billiards, and indulging in an unrequited passion for a handsome Southern girl. The family of the English colonel consisted of six pale little girls, who filed into the dining room, all dressed alike, all apparently of an age, all painfully well bred and accomplished. Every morning the six little damsels went out walking like a seminary, with six little camp stools and six little sketchbooks. The Frenchman labored under the delusion that he resembled the emperor and twirled his dyed mustache or quirked his little finger while he flirted his napkin and sipped wine. As the days passed, Louisa came to know more of the *pensionnaires*, amusing herself by observing the brisk widow who passed for a lady in all languages but English, when her native Cockney betrayed her. The pension would not have been complete without a stately, solemn, and mysterious lady who resembled Marie Antoinette, never ate in public, and was invisible throughout the day save for an occasional glimpse of a massive purple bonnet on the back terrace.

At dinner, when the baron politely asked which part of America had the happiness of being her home, Louisa saw the look of intelligence that was passed, after her reply, from her end of the table to the other, where the Southerner was seated. The Carolinian had lost five hundred slaves and proceeded to fight the Rebellion all over again by insulting Louisa daily. The English quickly gave her to understand that they were "strictly neutral," while the Scottish ladies, as timid as a pair of tabbies with a strange dog in the house, implored her to be careful of what she said, and deftly diverted any bellicose discussion with anecdotes about Sir Walter Scott. When the brisk Cockney widow emerged from the *Peerage* and Fuller's *Worthies*, however, with the revelation that Anna Weld's relatives lived in a castle and Louisa Alcott was descended from a bishop, the social and political atmosphere of the Pension Victoria changed in favor of the North.

"Life in a Pension," Louisa was sure, would make an interesting sketch for an American newspaper, but life outside the pension had its charms also. There was a calm joy in watching the barks and brigantines that floated on Lake Leman, in listening to the peal of bells from the Church of Saint Martin, in mingling with the Savoyard fishermen and mountain peasants in the market place. The Bellerive School, run by Monsieur Sillig, brought Concord into Vevey, for there, as at Frank Sanborn's academy, Louisa saw the boys on their Saturday excursions, alpenstocks in their hands and knapsacks on their backs. She was interested also in the rules of the institution, and planned to incorporate them in whatever she might write along educational lines.

Gradually, after the first novelty of cosmopolitan Vevey had worn off, Louisa began to tire of her charge's constant demands and missed the freedom she could have used to climb the mountains where the chamois roamed. The French lessons she took under the tutelage of Mademoiselle Germain did not satisfy her, and she was glad when, in November, another guest arrived at the Pension Victoria to take his place in her gallery of characters.

Ladislas Wisniewski was a charming Pole, twenty years old, who had fought in the Insurrection and been forced to leave his country. He had, apparently, suffered from exposure during the campaign, but his ill health merely increased the charm that both Louisa and Anna found in the captivating boy, whose blue and white university suit became him so well. Ladislas was the pet of all the ladies of the pension, not the least of Louisa, who harbored a weakness for courageous boys in blue. Between her own meager French and his three words of English they managed fairly well, and finally exchanged lessons, in the course of which Ladislas would slap his forehead and utter the despairing exclamation, "I am imbecile. I never can will shall to have learn this beast of English!" His music, however, was the delight of the drawing room, and Ladislas provided charming duets with the help of Madame Teihlin, who, with her cropped head and gentlemanly sack and cravat, played like a Russian Saint Cecilia. The piano vibrated, the stools creaked, the candles danced in their sockets, and everyone sat silent while four hands chased one another up and down the keys. It was not long, however, before it became apparent to Louisa that, despite the boy's interest in her role in the American Rebellion, Ladislas was far more devoted to Anna Weld than to her. On the shores of Lake Leman a little romance seemed to flower, and though it soon appeared that it might never come to fruit, Louisa observed with no lack of interest the attentions of Ladislas and the condescensions of her charge.

She felt rather old on her thirty-third birthday, and began to realize that love, with its restlessness and its sweet urgencies, might never be hers. Yet she contemplated calmly the fate of observing spinster, and knew that she had much to keep her young. In honor of the day Anna gave her a pretty painting of Chillon, and Ladislas played his sweetest airs after wishing her all good and happiness on earth and a high place in Heaven afterward. On the mild, windy, fitful day, she felt no sorrow, though she thought much of Father and his birthday and missed the little ceremony in the Orchard House.

With Ladislas and Anna she walked about Vevey and the chateau garden, gathering more flowers to press for Mother's album, or sailed on the lake and exchanged lessons not only in English and French, but in the American and Polish rebellions. It was easier for Ladislas to tell how people died in his unhappy country than to tell how they lived there. There had been no gaiety in Poland since that fateful February of 1861, when for the first time the soldiers had fired on the people of Warsaw. For his American sister-in-arms he matched Louisa's reports of Fredericksburg with stories of the Cossack march against Langiewicz, when the insurgents greeted the dragoons with scythes and pikes.

As she had found in the Union Hotel Hospital the source for sketches and tales, Louisa planned to write a story about her Polish boy, for Ladislas deserved more than a paragraph in "Life in a Pension." She would describe the thin, intelligent face, the charming manners, the military suit, and tell again the story of his part in the Polish outbreak. Alone, Ladislas would make a fine character for "My Polish Boy"; coupled with that other glorious, soaring, human boy, Alf Whitman, he might one day provide the basis of a hero for a full-length book. For a sensation paper she planned "The Baron's Gloves," centering about Sidney Power, a hero wounded in the Polish war and afflicted with an interesting cough. She would include Amy's romantic pursuit of a man with the initials "S.P." and paint the narrative not against an exotic Cuba, but against the Europe that she had come to know. The stay at Vevey had not been unfruitful, for besides her enjoyment of the young Pole's company and her interest in his attentions to Anna Weld, Louisa had gathered material for three sketches and had found a character who must delight her readers as deeply as his prototype had delighted her.

When the season was over, Anna decided to journey on to Nice with her companion. Ladislas, still wearing his blue and white military suit, accompanied his friends to Lausanne on December 6, and there, among the vineyards of the Vaudois, farewells were spoken, hands were kissed, promises made for Paris reunions, and the captivating Pole returned to Vevey, taking with him the light romance and charm which for two American tourists had transmuted winter into summer. Ladislas would not be entirely forgotten even on the journey south to Nice, even in the groves of olives and orange trees, the villas and gardens that covered hills sweeping down to the eternal summer of the Mediterranean.

After the excitement of Vevey, Anna Weld rested quietly at Nice, receiving the doctor or the consul at the pension, ever demanding more of Louisa's attentions. Each day the invalid and her companion drove along the Promenade des Anglais, passing the white bastides that made a dazzling show under the sun. With serene delight Louisa saw the mountains of the Esterel rising from the Mediterranean, and the colorful parades of red-capped fishermen, flower girls, and coral-sellers. Everywhere invalids camped under white umbrellas, leaving the market place to the sleepy mules and the brace of hens that pecked about their heels. How intensely happy she would have been in the perpetual summer of Nice, had May or her sister Anna been with her. As it was, although Christmas was beautiful outside the windows of the pension, it was a dull day within doors. Even the delights of the Promenade des Anglais paled when she shared them with a demanding invalid.

In January the travelers moved to the Rue Geoffredo, and Louisa proceeded to take notes not on life in a pension but on life in a Nice apartment. The moment they were settled, a tall, orange-colored lady in black moiré and an imposing headdress of somber crape introduced herself as Madame Rolande, proprietress of number 10 and former governess of Queen Victoria's daughters. Louisa observed immediately that nearly everything in the rooms was the gift of the Saxe-Coburg family, from ugly worsted work to chubby teapots, from inlaid portfolios to bronze Dianas. The salon displayed portraits of Victoria, Albert, the Princess Royal, and various blue-blooded infants, while in her own room Louisa found the Queen guarding her bed and the Duchess of Kent simpering at her from under a turban.

Madame Rolande, Louisa observed, fitted her regal surroundings, for occasionally she affected to forget herself and called the travelers "*Chères princesses.*" In addition to her royal background, the proprietress had the less amusing habit of listening at keyholes or reading private letters; and Julie, the maid, constantly guarded her mistresses against Madame's sly indiscretions. With Julie's help, Louisa found little difficulty in housekeeping, and soon the larder was filled with groceries from Berlandina and confectionery from Rumpelmayer's on the Rue Grimaldi.

The weeks passed quietly by, as Louisa recorded notes of La Rolande or enjoyed excursions to Cimiez and the grotto of Saint André. Along the Var the travelers saw the Mediterranean washing the base of the mountains, while hills sloped gently down to the sea.

Even the sunshine of the Riviera could not satisfy Louisa completely, and since Anna had decided to stay on indefinitely at Nice, her companion announced her determination to leave in May. There was so much to be seen abroad that she could not resign herself to more than three months longer of white umbrellas and sunshine, invalids and fashionable promenades.

154 . Louisa May Alcott

In February, Louisa found time to write a little, gathering her observations of Madame Rolande for a sketch, "A Royal Governess," and deciding to insert still another chapter in "Success," a chapter called "Companion," in which insanity, suicide, and thwarted love provided the destinies of "a mad Carrol" and a lad who frequented the gambling tables. Like Louisa, Christie sat at the bedside of her patient, while the author mingled enough melodramatic fancies with realistic observations for a sensational chapter in her autobiographical novel.

There were letters now to answer also, and Louisa read happily the good words from home, the news that Loring's statement on the sale of *Moods* credited the author with $286.90, and that Father was paying his second visit to St. Louis, where he discoursed on Hegel and Fichte.

Louisa felt her lack of freedom more than ever in March, for it was only with a wheelchair that she could tempt Anna into the woods. The mistral gave way to the enervating sirocco, and in April the tedium of constant attendance upon Anna was varied only by the Easter ceremonies at the Cathedral, or the performances of Adelaide Ristori. How her sister Anna would have enjoyed the actress's characterizations. But there were no sisters to share the pleasures of the Riviera with Louisa, and she was glad when Anna's uncle, Dr. Weld, arrived to care for the patient so that she could be freed of her onerous duties. To Mrs. Conway she wrote details of her plans to spend some time in Paris before she left for London, and also asked her to engage a room at Wimbledon for not more than one pound a week. If the queen would not admit her to Windsor, she would enjoy the babies and buttercups of Wimbledon; at any rate, she preferred a sight of Dickens to Her Majesty and the nine royal children in a row. Most of all she preferred her freedom; and, armed with letters from Rolande to her friends at court, Louisa joyfully bade farewell to Anna Weld and the Rue Geoffredo, and on May 1 departed alone for Paris.

It was a happy journey for a "Christie" freed of her charge, and happier still when Ladislas appeared at the end of it, waiting to escort Louisa to her room at Madame Dyne's on the Rue de Rivoli. Gaily he led her among the crowds thronging the Tuileries, past the fountain to the bridge over the Seine, where blue-bloused rowers plied their oars in the May sunshine. "Christie" and "Tribulation Periwinkle" were forgotten; no flights of fancy, no strange imaginings were needed now to brighten the days of the lady from Concord. The traveling companion was freed, and in her place Louisa stood, a fortnight of Paris springtime before her.

From her window early in the morning she saw the city awaken under her eyes. Ladislas called for Louisa, reminiscing about the charmed days at Vevey, inquiring about Anna Weld, and escorting her on a round of sightseeing. Of all the cities she had seen, none was more colorful or more alive than Paris; the pulsing rhythm of the streets kept time to her step as Ladislas pointed out the hack drivers in red waistcoats and glazed hats, the washerwomen beating their linen on the shore of the Seine, or the gentlemen twirling their canes and fumbling their *Figaro*s. On the Boulevard des Italiens they wandered, or from the imperial of an omnibus watched while Paris marched on parade.

Ladislas escorted her to the Tuileries Gardens for a concert by the Imperial Guard, while girls drove their hoops and boys played soldiers and nurses sat near the fountain. On the Bois de Boulogne they strolled together, exchanging tales of Nice and Warsaw. Together they rambled through the stores, looking at porcelains and perfumes, mirrors and bronzes, or shawls and sandalwood fans. In the evenings there were café concerts or performances of the Opéra Comique, theaters where the author of "Nat Bachelor's Pleasure Trip" applauded as vigorously as the claque.

Throughout the fortnight Ladislas lost none of his charm for Louisa; another boy had been added to the figures of her memory, a boy who played the piano for her in the evening or chatted gaily about the French and soberly about the Poles. He had opened for her the gates of Paris and shown her the gleaming sights of the city in May. He had opened the gates of her own passing youth and restored to her the jollity she had known in the white village of Concord. She would not forget Ladislas; he was one now with her Dolphus, with all the boys of remembrance, whose youth was perennial.

Reluctantly, on May 17, Louisa left for London to spend a fortnight at Wimbledon Common with the Conways. Mother had borrowed money so that the traveler might stay longer and see England after her work with Anna Weld, and she resolved to lose not a moment of the precious time that was left. Moncure Daniel Conway, she found, was very different from Ladislas Wisniewski, but Louisa enjoyed her friendship with him also. As Ladislas had been the perfect escort for Paris, Mr. Conway and his wife were delightful guides for Louisa in the English city.

How different it was from Paris, with its dusky lights and dark-hued brick, St. Paul's black with the city's smoke, and hosiers' and silk mercers' stores announcing their ancient pedigrees. Louisa saw now the gloved MP's with blue cravat and white linen, the bewhiskered dandies, and the damsels resembling extraordinary asparagus sticks planted in spreading dresses. The omnibuses of Paris gave way to the hansom cabs and "growlers" of London, while among the notables Mr. Conway pointed out the corrugated face of Mr. Disraeli, the urbane Monckton Milnes, and the Prince of Wales, quite changed since his visit to Boston.

Louisa was content to leave the London of sightseers and tourists when the Taylors invited her to spend the first ten days of June at Aubrey House. There she knew she would see more of the native's London, at least one aspect of it, than she could ever find by visits to the British Museum or the Crystal Palace. Mr. Conway's name, and Mr. Emerson's also, had opened for her the door of Aubrey House, the Notting Hill mansion as old as Queen Anne's time. Peter Alfred Taylor, the master of Aubrey House, was no less interesting than his domain, for as MP for Leicester he was officially connected with nearly every English movement for the promotion of freedom. He was eloquent on the subjects of personal rights, the freedom of the press, and international arbitration, and Louisa looked forward to the open evenings where P. A. T. played host, the bearded, dark-browed man who had entertained Frederick Douglass and harbored an escaped slave.

Even Mrs. Fields's home on Charles Street paled before the Aubrey House salon, where soup *à la reine* was accompanied by a discussion of the Reform Bill. A child was once again among them, taking notes not on James T. Fields or Mr. Emerson, but on Frances Cobbe, who was engaged on an edition of Theodore Parker's works, on Madame Bodichon or Elizabeth Garrett. A whole new world opened before Louisa's eyes, and she hoped that one day she, too, could take her place among these successful women of the age, such as the distinguished Mathilde Blind and the mysterious Emilie Venturi, Mazzini's faithful friend. Mazzini himself was there, pallid and diaphanous, his ardent eyes burning as he spoke of the cause for which he wore deep mourning. Louisa watched him intently, noting the black velvet waistcoat buttoned up to his throat and listening to him as he recalled the courage of another American woman, Margaret Fuller, or entered the lists of humanity to discuss the butchery of Poland. As she observed the perpetual conspirator, she planned one day to incorporate his mysterious figure in a sensational story, where a hero in the Italian revolution would play out a dramatic destiny.

Of all of London's notables, only one disappointed Louisa. She had not expected to find in Charles Dickens the handsome young man who had once visited America, but she had thought some signs of his genius would be visible. For most of his listeners at St. James's Hall he was still a magician, insinuating himself into their hearts by the disguises of his voice. But for Louisa the magic was gone, and in its place was only the foppishness of a red-faced man with false teeth and the voice of a worn-out actor. His scanty gray hair was curled; a posy brightened his buttonhole, and he himself was lost behind the glitter of diamond ring, pin, and studs. There was nothing genuine about him. At least his books remained for her delight, even though Louisa could not shake the hand that had written them. She would write a notice one day for *The Commonwealth* to give voice to her disappointment.

Louisa had seen much of London's progressive society during her visit with the Taylors, but she did not wish to trade longer on their hospitality, and so, on June 11, left Aubrey House for lodgings at Mrs. Travers' in Westbourne Grove Terrace. For the last few weeks of her journey abroad she would be free to roam about London and explore to her heart's content the Tower and gardens, the parks and haunts of the famous. She had time now to carry Madame Rolande's messages to Windsor, where she was received, not by the Queen, but by a housekeeper in black satin, lavender gloves, and blond cap, who, besides admitting her to the sights of the castle, offered the astute remark that "Rollet meant well; but she was—French."

After she had seen the London of the sightseers and the London of Aubrey House, Louisa took time to see the London of Charles Dickens. The writer himself had disappointed her, but nothing could diminish the joy she had taken in his books. When Mr. Moses Coit Tyler offered to pilot her about the city, she resolved to see at last the street where Sairey Gamp had lived. For such an excursion Mr. Tyler was a prince of guides, since the disciple of Dio Lewis was not above tapping away at Milton's chimney for a bit of the original brick, or eating gingerbread out of a bag at Smithfield. The genial Mr. Tyler was delighted to find that to Louisa St. Paul's was the place where Ralph Nickleby set his watch, and Westminster Abbey the home of the maid of honor in Mrs. Jarley's waxworks.

In a pouring rain they walked along as Major Bagstock stared down from a clubhouse window and Montague Tigg's cab dashed by on Regent Street. Surely the Micawber family passed them in a bus, doubtless accompanying the blighted Wilkins to jail, while the Tetterbys played in the mud and Bill Sikes lounged in a doorway of St. Giles. Hurrying along High Holborn, they came at last to Kingsgate Street, where the immortal nurse had collected her bottomless bandboxes and wooden pippins. The name on the door was unfortunately Pendergast instead of Sweedlepipes, and Mr. Tyler, turning to one of the Kingsgaters, asked with amiable gravity whether she could direct him to the home of Mrs. Gamp. The conversation that ensued regarding the nature of Sairey's business and the description of Sairey's figure finally evoked the answer that she lived at number 5, but the nuss' name was Britian, not Gamp.

Louisa fled precipitately with Mr. Tyler around a corner where she could enjoy a glorious laugh under an umbrella. The two Dickensians continued their pilgrimage to Saracen's Head, and although Louisa did not take "weal pie" in memory of Sam Weller or drink a modest quencher of porter to the health of Dick Swiveller, she had found the London she had dreamed of, and had gathered enough material to plan a sketch on her "Dickens Day."

Her journals and notebooks were filled, but it was too late now to answer the letters that arrived from home. It was good, nevertheless, to learn that Father had returned to Concord after his dreary days of travel and that all were anticipating Louisa's homecoming eagerly.

There was little left for Louisa to do or see in England before she embarked upon the *Africa*. One visit must still be paid, however, to Routledge regarding the English publication of *Moods*. On July 2, Messrs. George Routledge and Sons gave the author five pounds for the privilege of printing the novel, and Louisa joyfully signed the agreement before she departed. The notes she had taken must be packed, along with the gifts she had bought for her sisters, Raphael's "School of Athens" and Stirling's *Secret of Hegel* for Father, and the olivewood album for Mother. To accompany the flowers she had gathered and pressed at Schwalbach or Vevey or Nice, Louisa wrote a few lines for the European nosegay:

> *As children in the summer fields*
> *Gather each flower they see,*
> *And hurry back with eager feet*
> *To lay it on their mother's knee,*
> *So I, by ruin, lake, and lawn,*
> *Found flowers in many lands,*
> *And gladly hasten home to lay*
> *My little nose-gay in your hands.*

She had gathered more than a nosegay of flowers. The Rhine, the Mediterranean, the Alps of Savoy, and the mountains of the Esterel were not simply names to conjure with, but magic sights

160 . Louisa May Alcott

imprinted indelibly upon her mind. She had known also the
tedium of working where there was no love, and the companion's
weary hours would not be forgotten. She had found the gaiety of
youth in Ladislas, whose eternal springtime would match forever
the enchantment of Vevey. For her, Europe had painted one background after another, from the Dent du Midi to the sparkling
streets of Paris in Maytime, from the Kirchgasse of Schwalbach to
the Promenade des Anglais of Nice. London was hers also, the
London of the tourist's traveled ways, the Aubrey House salon of
London's liberals, and the rainy courts and cobblestones of Dickens. A nosegay not merely of flowers but of backgrounds was hers
for the books she would write and the stories she would imagine.
And she had found characters, too, to people her sketches, from
an Italian reformer to the *pensionnaires* of Vevey, from a royal governess to a Polish boy. All these she would stir in the crucible of
her inkstand.

Louisa had time on her voyage home to contemplate the year
that had passed, to consider how she herself had matured and
grown from the sights she had fed on. It was a long and stormy
passage, but at last on July 19 the steamer arrived at Boston, and
from the ship Louisa could see John waiting for her on the wharf.
She was forced to sleep on board, but the next day John led her,
surrounded by luggage and bubbling over with her news, to the
train. At noon she arrived at the Concord station, where Father
greeted her; and at last the traveler returned to the Orchard
House, to a reunion that was all her heart desired, for the family
would be under one roof until autumn. Anna and the babies
saluted her at the gate, May flew wildly about the lawn, and
Mother shed tears of happiness at the door. Into her arms Louisa
went; she was home at last. The ornaments and gifts were opened
and the lines read that accompanied the album of pressed flowers.
In her mother's hands Louisa laid her nosegay of remembrance.

Little Women

After the first joyous excitement of her return Louisa realized with sharp distress that although the Orchard House had not changed, the passing year had not spared her mother, who looked old and sick and tired. The time had left less of a mark upon Father, for after his election as an "auxiliary" of the St. Louis Philosophical Society he was as placid as ever, his face as serene and benignant if a little more furrowed. He was bowed, but not by age—rather by his habit of leaning forward to thrust his dreaming eyes into the secrets of the world. Louisa found Anna poorly but was delighted that she had arranged to live in Concord until the fall while John "courted" her every Saturday and Sunday when he came in from East Boston. She was blessed in her babies, in Freddy, so stout and loving, and in Johnny, a merry boy who kissed everybody. May, at least, was not altered; she was as full of plans as ever, very busy with her own affairs, attending all the parties she could. Yet the year had not passed without leaving its traces, and Louisa was glad to be once again at home, telling the family about her trials with Anna Weld and diverting all with tales of her excursions in Paris and London.

After her experiences abroad, Concord seemed to have contracted into a smaller village than even Louisa remembered. Her impression was deepened when she walked again among the loungers on the Milldam, where Asa Collier still sold watches and

Alvan Pratt repaired skates. The wooden canopy in front of Walcott and Holden's country store was, as ever, the mecca for traders' horses, and even the notices that covered the open carriage sheds appeared to have been undisturbed.

Louisa had neither the inclination nor the time to muse long about the dull and slumbering village. The family's debts had mounted since her departure, and the money Mother had borrowed to keep her in London must be repaid. The easiest way of replenishing the Alcott fund was to write sensational stories that were quickly composed and as quickly accepted. "A. M. Barnard" must again start work to pay for L. M. Alcott's travels. At the desk overlooking the Lexington Road, the mysterious author of "A Marble Woman" sketched "Behind a Mask" for the readers of *The Flag of Our Union*. On August 11, James R. Elliott accepted the story, confessed that he had found the manuscript fascinating, and wished another by September 20. After Mrs. Squier had sent two hundred dollars for two anonymous stories submitted to *Leslie's*, Louisa was able to give one hundred dollars to Cousin Sam Sewall as partial payment of her debts, and took time to add "The Abbot's Ghost: or, Maurice Treherne's Temptation" to her output for *The Flag*. She knew now that she must live for her mother, who had so long spent herself for others. It was hard to see the wrinkled face and the bowed back, the signs of relentless age upon the strong, energetic woman of old times.

Louisa could polish up her European notes for publication since, next to sensational stories, her records of travel would be the easiest to write. Once more, at the desk in the Orchard House, she sailed up the Rhine and passed ruins and castles, spent a magic night at Coblenz, and stopped off at the little village of Oestrich with Anna Weld. Just as *The Flag* had become a reliable market for the tales of "A. M. Barnard," *The Independent* was ready to accept Louisa's European jottings, and scheduled "Up the Rhine" for appearance in July.

In July, also, Louisa prepared to recapture the past in a different manner, for a dramatic entertainment was planned at the Town Hall on the eighth of the month, and the "first old woman" added still another role to her repertory, that of the tall, spare, prim-looking female of middle age known as Miss Beswick to the readers of J. T. Trowbridge's *Coupon Bonds*. George Bartlett was on hand to act as manager and play Pa Ducklow, and Annie Keyes and Jane G. Austin had joined the Concord company. James Melvin, who had lost three brothers in the war, would take the part of Reuben, the returned soldier, and for the cause of charity Louisa, with a shawl over her head, entered the Ducklow home to speak her mind to its denizens in "a pretty smart lectur'." For Reuben's benefit, Miss Beswick cleared her decks for action and retrieved the lost coupon bonds, but Louisa herself could not retrieve the joy she had once taken in private theatricals.

She was nearly thirty-five years old and felt that, after all, her achievements had been trifling. No great events appeared to be in store for her. Each slight success was a repetition of the past, "The Abbot's Ghost" simply a sequel to "V. V.," *Coupon Bonds* a successor to *The Jacobite*. She seemed to have slumbered on as Concord had.

After a rest in August at Clarks Island, Louisa returned home more fortified for work, more tolerant of the affairs of the Mill-dam. She was interested in Lucy Stone's Appeal for Woman's Right to Suffrage which Father signed, assured that woman was soon to have her place in the state with every right of the citizen. Perhaps she, too, would find her place, if not in the state at least in Boston, for in September Mr. Niles of Roberts Brothers, who had once requested permission to reprint *Hospital Sketches*, suggested that Louisa write a girls' book; and at the same time Horace Fuller invited her to act as editor of *Merry's Museum*.

At the moment, the second suggestion seemed more attractive than the first. As the successor of John N. Stearns, she would receive five hundred dollars a year for her editorial work. Mr. Fuller planned a number of improvements for *Merry's Museum* in the hope of making it not only curious and amusing but useful and instructive by facts and fancies, songs and stories taken from the wonder-book of nature. With the exception of *Flower Fables* and *The Rose Family*, Louisa had had no experience in writing for a juvenile public, and wondered how the author of "V. V." and "The

Abbot's Ghost" would adapt herself to the new enterprise. To try her hand at literature for children, she wrote a story about the German family of Hummels, who lived in an old omnibus on the flats behind the stables and subsisted on the money that little Fritz earned from selling chips. "Living in an Omnibus" appeared in October, and although it had little to do with Mr. Fuller's beautiful wonder-book called nature, it did not noticeably decrease the circulation of *Merry's Museum*. Perhaps the editorial work would extend her skill in writing and selecting material. It would at least give her a public that, with the exception of *Flower Fables*, her stories had never known. Children might prove fruitful critics, and possibly she might be able to combine her editorial responsibilities with writing for Mr. Niles. Five hundred dollars a year would be welcome at the Orchard House. Besides, Louisa would have the opportunity of living in Boston to be nearer Mr. Fuller's office on Washington Street. Washington Street had marked many a milestone in her varied literary career as "A. M. Barnard" and L. M. Alcott. Perhaps another milestone would be reached. In October, agreeing to start work as editor with the January, 1868, issue, Louisa accepted Mr. Fuller's offer, and engaged a room at 6 Hayward Place.

On October 28, Louisa rode into Boston on her load of furniture to set up housekeeping. Having immediately dubbed her abode "Gamp's Garret," she proceeded to offer "cowcumbers" and tea to any kindred spirits who might venture there. May joined her to start a drawing class and gave every promise of abandoning her wild oats and settling down into a sober teacher of the art in which she was completely engrossed. The two busiest young women in Massachusetts took time occasionally to wander about the city, and Louisa rejoiced to be back again near the surging tides of crinoline on Winter Street. Every detail might offer a hint for a story or a suggestion for background, and the prospective editor carefully eyed all the Empire bonnets and Zouave jackets in hopes that they might point a moral in stories that were still unwritten.

Before she settled down to her editorial work, there were a few sensational tales to be written that would provide Elliott,

Thomes and Talbot with ten-cent novelettes and the Alcott fund with money to pay debts. In "Gamp's Garret" the author of "V. V." uncorked her inkstand to compose a narrative about Madame Mathilde Arnheim, married to an idiot husband, and bound to him by a tie which death alone could sever. Louisa quickly followed "The Skeleton in the Closet" with *The Mysterious Key*, in which she combined her memories of Mazzini with strategic devices of false keys and feigned sleepwalking. Her hero, like his prototype, was a leader in the Italian revolution, but his efforts were directed less toward political affairs than toward the solution of Sir Richard's mysterious marriage. Since neither story was burdened by sensational accounts of murder or brutality, Louisa signed her name to each and dispatched to Messrs. Elliott, Thomes and Talbot her latest creations in the not-too-bloody and the not-too-thunderous.

It was time now for the author of *The Mysterious Key* to direct her writing to a more youthful audience, and Louisa was delighted to arrange a book for Horace Fuller before she undertook editorship of *Merry's*. "A. M. Barnard" was soon transformed into "Aunt Wee" for readers of "Morning-Glories," who would learn that spiders could be as interesting as fairy tales, and that although Mr. Thoreau had died, his companion had not forgotten how to plait a basket of rushes or enjoy the light that awakened the sleeping lilies. She would reprint "The Rose Family" and follow it with "Shadow-Children," in which young folks could learn their shortcomings from the tricks of their own shadows. The author's childhood could furnish details for "Poppy's Pranks," for it was Louisa and not "Poppy" who had been lost in Boston and had, long years ago, fallen into the Frog Pond. Once the technique had been established, the stories could be repeated with endless variations. "Aunt Wee" found that she had no difficulty in improving the minds and whetting the appetites of young people. With Miss Greene's illustrations, *Morning-Glories, and Other Stories* would make a readable book under the imprint of Horace B. Fuller, and Louisa soon began to find children's stories as simple a medium as sensational narratives. Whether they were as profitable remained to be seen.

While Mr. Fuller announced his prospectus for 1868 in the November issue of *Merry's*—promising a new cover, an enriched puzzle drawer, and an experienced and competent editor—Louisa continued her writing, leaving her inkstand only to act Mrs. Jarley for charity. The publisher followed his announcement in December with the assurance that *Merry's* would appear Enlarged, Improved, and Rejuvenated, edited by Louisa M. Alcott, the brilliant author of *Hospital Sketches*, who had hardly an equal and who had no superior as a writer for youth in the country. While Boston prepared to receive Mr. Charles Dickens, sweeping the streets, painting the State House, and stacking every bookseller's window with copies of works by the great man, Louisa prepared to act the part of the brilliant author who had no superior as a writer for youth in the country.

The lady of "Gamp's Garret," reviewing the months that had passed, was gratified to know that she had earned one thousand dollars, sent money home, paid debts, and helped May. Louisa realized that she had also gained experience in writing along varied literary lines. Since she had returned home, she had produced sensational stories, polished up her notes on Europe, and embarked upon the juvenile field. Now she knew that she would have to concentrate on the last of these, for *The Youth's Companion* offered ten dollars a story and her work as editor of *Merry's* was about to begin. Perhaps, with the new year, she would earn enough so that Uncle Sam May could stop sending fifty-dollar gifts to the Orchard House. It was a wish devoutly to be hoped that the girl who had gone out to service and worked as a lady's traveling companion would find success at last, that L. M. Alcott would emerge from her long apprenticeship in varied fields to mastery in one.

At Mr. Fuller's Washington Street office, or in "Gamp's Garret" on Hayward Place, Louisa sat surrounded by manuscripts and proofs, forcing her dream to come true. With the January 1868 issue, *Merry's Museum* appeared, as Mr. Fuller had promised, enlarged, improved, and rejuvenated, with a new editor, new contributors, new engravings, new features, and a new dress. For the first issue, "Aunt Louise" wrote two poems as well as a story, "Tilly's Christmas," accepted two serials, "Little Pearl" and "The Loggers; or, Six Months in the Forests of Maine," and selected numerous tales by "Aunt Ada" or "A. M. F. P." "Aunt Sue's" Scrap-Bag and "Aunt Sue's" Puzzle Drawer were offered replete with educational bits of information, acrostics, and rebuses; Miss Greene designed the cover as well as a few illustrations; and the publisher listed *Morning-Glories, and Other Stories* as a special premium for any person sending the name of one new subscriber along with $1.50. When Turner's Tic Douloureux or Universal Neuralgia Pill was advertised, the issue was complete except for the section known as "Merry's Monthly Chat with His Friends." The new editor decided to alter somewhat the policy of publishing subscribers' letters, in order to include what she called her "editorial." As "Cousin Tribulation" she offered for the January issue of the "Monthly Chat" an account of the manner in which Nan, Lu, Beth, and May gave up their holiday breakfast to their poor neighbors. The episode was interesting, and might one day be worked into a longer story, perhaps the story that Mr. Niles had suggested. Meanwhile, hoping that the magazine would prove as curious and amusing and as useful and instructive as Mr. Fuller had promised, Louisa sent to the public her first issue of *Merry's Museum.*

Wherever she went, whatever she did, she was pursued now by the compulsion of finding material for stories. Eating her bread and milk and baked apples in the morning, she planned a letter from "Cousin Tribulation." Making a bonnet for May or cutting out a flannel wrapper for Mother, she listed mentally the stories she would select for the February *Museum.* Even when she went to Dorchester in the evening to act Mrs. Pontifex in *Naval Engagements,* her "Kingston dear" was viewed with an eye for inclusion in a tale, and as Miss Buzzard she thought less about "Brother Benjamin" than about the possibility of introducing amateur theatricals into a story for young America. Under the constant coercion of producing copy, she must find in everything grist for her mill.

168 . Louisa May Alcott

When, on February 14, Mr. Bonner of *The New York Ledger* appeared at 6 Hayward Place offering Miss Alcott one hundred dollars for a column of advice to young ladies, Louisa felt that her industry was rewarded. Over her squash pie she sat, planning an article that would be read by all the nursemaids and cooks of the country, an article in which she lauded the "Happy Women" who, though unmarried, were yet devoted to earnest work. To the sketches of home missionary, physician, and music teacher, she could not resist the impulse of adding an account of herself as the literary member of the sisterhood. It was true that she was a happy woman, who had found a market for her wares and could spin stories with indefatigable persistence. "A. M. Barnard" had shifted easily into the less mysterious "Aunt Louise," who had found a small though appreciative public in "Dear Merrys." Surely there were other unwritten tales with which she would lure children from their play.

In May, Father, having consulted Mr. Niles of Roberts Brothers regarding publication of his own *Tablets*, inquired whether the firm would be interested in issuing a fairy book by his daughter. Mr. Niles not only rejected the idea, but repeated the suggestion he had made long since, that Louisa write a girls' story, a domestic novel, for Roberts Brothers. From his office at number 143 Washington Street he had seen vast quantities of books by "Oliver Optic" leaving the rooms of Lee and Shepard at number 149. There must be a similar market for a full-length novel that would be as popular among girls as "Oliver Optic's" narratives were among boys. If Mary Mapes Dodge had been able to write a successful book with a Dutch background called *Hans Brinker or the Silver Skates*, surely Louisa May Alcott could produce as appealing a work about young America. She had proved her ability to report her observations in *Hospital Sketches;* she had indicated her powers of appealing to juvenile readers in her editorship of *Merry's Museum.* Could not Miss Alcott combine both talents in a domestic novel that would reflect American life for the enjoyment of American youth?

Obviously, if she must write a story for girls, she must work her narrative around the only girls she had ever known well, her own sisters. If Mr. Niles had asked for a boys' story, she could have turned to the students of Frank Sanborn's school; but since "Oliver Optic" had flooded the market for boys, Louisa must remain content with a domestic novel about Hillside and the Orchard House. By this time the editor of *Merry's* had established for herself a working method whereby, after stories had simmered in her mind, they wrote themselves out upon paper. She made no alterations and no copies, for the material upon which she lavished the least time seemed the most successful. Any paper, any pen, any quiet room suited her, and at the desk overlooking the Lexington Road she had written, and could still write, from morning till night once the ideas had matured. She sat there now, finding that another story had developed without her realizing it, and that she had relived many an episode of her youth for *Merry's* and could relive more for Mr. Niles. Here was a plot at hand, a plot that she had carried in her mind for years, a plot that four sisters had lived. There was no trick in writing for juvenile readers. She must merely describe life as it actually was. There was no advantage to be gained from making young people do or say what no real young people would ever imagine. The writing itself would be simple, for she had learned enough from her experience with *Merry's* to know that she must never use a long word when a short one would do as well. Perhaps it was for this very moment that her long apprenticeship had been passed. Perhaps it was this unwritten story, this domestic novel, that would earn the fame and fortune that *Moods* had never brought. Louisa was not sure.

Father had always believed that a happy, kind, and loving family, a home where peace and gentle quiet abode, were beautiful indeed. Perhaps, if she could paint such a home and such a family, the world would also find them beautiful. Had he not said years ago that the literature of childhood was not written, that a tale embodying the simple facts and persons of the family would fill that gap? Mr. Emerson had called her the poet of children, who knew their angels. He, too, believed that the events that occurred at home were closer to people than those that were sought in senates and academies. The great facts were the near ones.

Tell men what they knew before;
Paint the prospect from their door.

The door was Hillside's. Could Louisa open it, recover those despised recollections of childhood, and find in the biography of one foolish person the miniature paraphrase of the hundred volumes of the universal history?

She had already done so. "The Sisters' Trial" had long ago pictured a year in the lives of four sisters. "A Modern Cinderella" had painted Anna and her John, Laura and Di. Her poem, "In the Garret," written for *The Flag of Our Union*, had centered about the characters of Nan, Lu, Bess, and May. "A. M. Barnard" could rest from her nightmarish labors, for Louisa Alcott had known this cast of characters. The sisters were there, waiting to be reanimated. Anna would turn into Meg, beautified of course, for there must be one beauty in the book, and after all Anna's mouth was not so large or her nose so homely as she claimed. Her John would find a place as John Brooke, for the Pratts had come from Brook Farm. For a hero she needed only to combine her memories of that very human boy, Alf Whitman, with those of the gayer whirligig, Ladislas Wisniewski, to produce—Laurie, since the one name suggested the other and Alf had made his home in Lawrence, Kansas. The Goddard donor of ancient relics would emerge as an aunt. The story would write itself, Louisa knew. By what name would her family be known? Surely not Alcott, and May was too obvious. But March would do.

Louisa took up her pen, but the Marches wrote her story. May, transmuted into Amy, afflicted once again with a nose not quite Grecian enough, struggled in laborious attempts at elegance and decided upon a bottle of cologne for Mother's—Marmee's—Christmas because it would not cost so much and she would have money left to buy pencils. Amy wrote herself into the saga of the Marches, quirking her little finger and simpering over her plate, parading her airs and graces for the amusement if not the edification of the family. Meg could indeed remember better times, and gave a soft, domestic touch to every scene she entered. Louisa would take an easier role than Jarley or Miss Buzzard, the role of herself as Jo, tall and thin and brown, with sharp gray eyes and long thick hair, with odd blunt ways and a hearty understanding of boys. Let Jo, too, write her own story and struggle once more to curb her fiery spirit. Let her love cats and apples again, and books as exciting as *The Heir of Redclyffe*. What family would not love Marmee, tall and motherly, whose gray cloak and unfashionable bonnet adorned a staunch defender of human rights? Father must be muffled, for the author realized that he would be atypical in a book on the American home. Father, with his vegetarianism, his fads, and his reforms, must be a shadow on the Hillside hearth. Laurie would inherit from Ladislas his curly black hair and big black eyes, his musical skill, and his foreign background, while Alf would endow him with high spirits and a sober kind of fascination. Another character remained, for there had been four sisters, not three, and Lizzie must reappear as Beth, glorified a little perhaps, her petty failings glossed over, until she became a cricket on the hearth who sat in corners and lived for others. Beth would be Jo's conscience.

From the moment that Louisa took up her pen, her characters touched themselves off. " 'Christmas won't be Christmas without any presents,' grumbled Jo, lying on the rug." In her choice of a gift, each sister would immediately delineate her own character. Once she had begun, the incidents also wrote themselves. The pen could not fly quickly enough to catch the remembrances. The Alcott birthday celebrations, the love of *Pilgrim's Progress* in four little girls who sped from the City of Destruction to the Celestial City, the plays in the barn—all were waiting in memory for this moment, when she who had joined in the frolics looked up from her desk to see once again four figures from the past spinning out their lives in the present. For the Hillside troupe she would take Hagar from "The Unloved Wife," Hugo from "Norna; or, The Witch's Curse," Zara from "The Captive of Castile," and miraculous potions from "Bianca," evolving a composite melodrama entitled "The Witch's Curse, an Operatic Tragedy." From the epistles penned by Father at "Concordia" there was material for

Mr. March's letters; from Mother's jottings in the children's journals there were suggestions for the room-to-room notes. The Sillig School that Louisa had seen at Vevey would provide Laurie's
background. The family post office would hold the messages of
the Marches. Louisa's literary career was Jo's now, for "The Pickwick Portfolio" had once upon a time flourished as "The Olive
Leaf," and Dr. Blimber and Mr. Snodgrass had not exercised their
influence in vain. The poor Hummels would enter the picture
from "Living in an Omnibus," and the episode of the breakfast
gift be lifted from the pages of "Merry's Monthly Chat."

The chapters were domestic, but Louisa was not sure that
they would evolve into a novel. The poverty of the Alcott family
must be glossed over and sentimentalized, to appeal to a youthful
audience and allow for the introduction of Hannah, the servant.
The style, Louisa was sure, was styleless. Good strong words that
meant something, unpolished grammar—these would create the
mannerless manner that would achieve verisimilitude. The American home was here, Louisa had no doubt. The good times, the
plays and tableaux and the sleigh rides and skating frolics, wrote
themselves naturally into the story of the Marches, while Louisa
raised her eyes from her desk only to see Amy bewailing her pickled limes or Jo pinching Meg's papered locks before the ball.
Where did fact end and fiction begin? With Amy's fall through
the ice after she had been refused permission to see "The Seven
Castles of the Diamond Lake"? With Meg's experience at Annie
Moffat's? It scarcely mattered. Fact was embedded in fiction, and
a domestic novel begun in which the local and the universal were
married, in which adolescents were clothed in flesh and blood.

Still, Louisa was not sure of her ability to spin out the tale. Mr.
Niles wanted twenty-four chapters, and she had planned only
twenty. When twelve were completed, in June, Louisa sent them
to Washington Street along with the suggestion that the book be
called "Little Women." Perhaps, if a second volume were
demanded, "Young Women" might do for the title. Louisa lived
in early memories, completing her manuscript of *Little Women* so
that she could send four hundred pages to Mr. Niles. Without the

first twelve chapters at hand she was afraid she might miss some of the threads, but the incidents seemed to spin themselves out none the less. Amy proceeded to indite her own will while Beth lay ill; Beth became indeed Jo's conscience; the *Olive Branch* blossomed forth as *The Spread Eagle*, emblazoned with "L. M. A.'s" first story, "The Rival Painters." Louisa's illness became Mr. March's; her loss of her hair was turned into an episode about the selling of her precious tresses. Father's Christmas homecoming, Mother's arrival from Washington, and the fat turkey that graced the table were details domestic enough even for Mr. Niles's demands. Jo's reactions to Meg's maturity, the desire to know what would happen "ten years hence," Laurie's insistence upon an apology from his grandfather—surely these were characteristic of adolescents.

On July 15, Louisa completed her 402 pages of *Little Women*, rang down the curtain upon what she hoped was only the first act of her domestic drama, and sent the remaining chapters to Mr. Niles. He had thought the first portion dull, and Louisa was not certain that others would not agree with him. While May designed the pictures, Louisa's strength gave out. The two and one-half months during which she had written *Little Women* had left their mark. She had traveled with three sisters from the City of Destruction, but she was not sure whether she had or ever would reach a Celestial City. But the work was done.

> *Go then, my little Book, and show to all*
> *That entertain and bid thee welcome shall,*
> *What thou dost keep close shut up in thy breast.*

For long years she had kept the loving family as a treasure locked in her heart. They were the near facts. Only Time could tell if they were the great ones. The key was turned to release the treasure now. The door to Hillside was opened, and any who would might stroll down the Lexington Road for a visit with the Marches. Had she indeed told men what they knew before, infused into her new book a new spirit?

Neither Louisa nor Mr. Niles was certain. The notes that had come from Roberts Brothers had not been too hopeful. As Louisa had known the letterhead of the firm, she began now to know the cramped and dingy quarters on Washington Street. Lewis A. Roberts still continued his manufacture of photograph albums in cloth and morocco at number 143 at the same time that he was publishing the works of Jean Ingelow, Robert Buchanan, and the Reverend W. R. Alger. Before the dingy signboard that hung opposite the Old South, Louisa stopped and climbed up the stairs. In a corner behind a green curtain she found not Mr. Roberts, but Thomas Niles, the literary representative of the firm. With deep courtesy he received the author of *Little Women* and in a quiet, scholarly manner discussed the arrangements for publishing the new domestic novel. Louisa sat opposite the slender, pale-faced, bright-eyed gentleman, finding him genial and entertaining as he encouraged her and announced that the firm would accept the story. A publisher could never tell in advance whether a book would be successful or not, and he for one could not know whether Louisa M. Alcott would ever rival "Oliver Optic." However, whether he offered three hundred dollars or one thousand dollars outright, Mr. Niles still recommended that Louisa decline the payment and retain, instead, the copyright with royalty privileges of 6.66 percent on each copy sold. Even three hundred dollars could not be scorned, for the story had taken no more than two and one-half months to write, and for her full year's work as editor of *Merry's* Louisa received only five hundred dollars. She listened, however, to the advice offered with quiet earnestness, and agreed to accept the royalty percentage. The book would appear in the fall; Miss Alcott might anticipate receiving proofs soon. Louisa emerged from behind the green curtain and walked joyously down the stairs. She looked up once again at the dingy signboard of Roberts Brothers, hoping that it would be for her a brighter symbol than any she had yet encountered upon Boston's Grub Street.

On August 26, the proofs of the whole book arrived along with Mr. Niles's word that several girls who had read the manuscript had said it was splendid. His niece, Lillie Almy, had laughed over it at Longwood till she cried. Since Lillie was a gay and vivacious twenty-year-old, unburdened by any deep literary interests, Mr. Niles considered that her opinion might well foreshadow that of other little women of America. The house of Alcott might find its fortune in the house of Roberts, for Father's *Tablets* was in the press as well as his daughter's *Little Women*. George Bartlett appeared on the Lexington Road to lavish his attentions upon Louisa and to offer his help in reading the proofs. Although she rejected the former, claiming that she had decided to settle down as a chronic old maid, she accepted the latter, and with the brown-haired, ruddy-faced amateur actor corrected the final galleys of *Little Women*. The book seemed to read better in proof than it had in manuscript. Here at least there was nothing sensational; truth and simplicity had taken the place of blood and thunder, and Louisa knew that if the work did succeed, that would be the reason.

Before the publication of her domestic novel, Louisa took time to help Jane Austin with *Cipher*, a romance upon which the author of *The Tailor Boy* and *Outpost* was now working. She was a pleasant companion for Louisa as they stood together upon the bridge, tossing chip boats into the river. Eagerly they watched to see which chips would drift ashore, and which would wreck themselves against the stone pier or remain idle and motionless in the eddy pool. Louisa had launched, and Mrs. Austin hoped to launch, a new venture, and both wondered what its fate would be as they watched the fortunes of their craft upon the Concord River. Jane Austin had children to turn to for solace if her bark should founder, but Louisa had none except loving Johnny and philosophic Freddy, and the shadow children who lived in the pages of her book. Soon they would come to life, when the curtain was raised upon the March family.

On September 1, 1868, Roberts Brothers sent to the *Publishers' Circular* a list of the books scheduled for appearance during the month. Besides a new edition of William Morris's *Earthly Paradise* and the cabinet edition of Jean Ingelow's *Poems*, the company advertised Father's *Tablets* and Louisa's *Little Women*. *Tablets* appeared, delighting the family with its shiny brown cloth binding and its gilt edges as well as with its wise and beautiful thoughts. *Little Women; Meg, Jo, Beth, and Amy. The Story of Their Lives. A Girls' Book,* by Louisa M. Alcott, promised for September 15 at the price of $1.25, was not ready, however, until the thirtieth. With the price raised to $1.50 and with three illustrations and a frontispiece by May, the book, bound in cloth and destined, according to Mr. Niles, to have a great run during the fall, made its bow to the public and to the Orchard House. Louisa looked long at the gilt oval in the center of the front cover and the gilt letters within the oval. The illustrations unfortunately seemed flat and unskillful, but the story still rang true, and Louisa impatiently waited to discover whether the world would wish the curtain rung up on a second act of her domestic drama.

She was glad that the book had appeared in time for Mother's sixty-eighth birthday. On October 8 the gifts were placed on a table in the study, and after breakfast Father escorted Mother to the big red chair, while Freddy and Johnny pranced ahead blowing their trumpets and May, Anna, and Louisa marched behind. Louisa could not help feeling that the decline had begun for her mother, that each new year would add to the change until feebleness and gentleness replaced the energy and enthusiasm of old. More than ever she must cherish the mother who had so long cherished her. More than ever she hoped that the March family would come to the defense of the Alcotts.

The welcome that the public extended to the new domestic novel was, for the most part, all that the author had wished. In *The Youth's Companion,* Roberts Brothers declared that girls who liked good stories had a rich treat in store for them. *The Nation* implied that the "agreeable little story" would have a wide appeal, for it might be read with pleasure by older people. Although things and characters were painted too much in "local colors," the March girls represented healthy types and were drawn with a certain cleverness. *The Nation's* reviewer, however, proceeded to dilate upon the poorly executed illustrations in which Miss May Alcott betrayed not only a want of anatomical knowledge but an indifference to the subtle beauty of the female figure. A week later, *The Youth's Companion* recommended the work of "Louise" M. Alcott as an exceedingly sprightly, wide-awake volume where a graphic account of a year in the lives of four sisters was depicted. The story of their adventures, according to the reviewer, was sure to interest the class of readers for whom it was designed.

On the whole, the reception, Louisa considered, was favorable. She felt capable of offering advice on writing to the poets who sent verses signed with a flourish of initials to *Merry's Museum*, and instructed one "A. W." to learn to write prose before she attempted poetry. The children at least seemed to read the tale with more excitement than the critics, for Louisa found a letter from one enthusiast who acknowledged that she had cried quarts over Beth's sickness and that neither she nor the girls in her school would ever forgive the author if she did not have Jo marry Laurie in the second part. Perhaps, after all, there would be a demand for another act of the March drama. Father, for one, was as proud of *Little Women* as he had ever been of the prototypes, and was convinced that Laurie was none other than Llewellyn Willis, while Frank Stearns discoursed upon the similarity between the hero and Julian Hawthorne. As long as people speculated, Louisa knew the book would live. Whether its life would be long was as yet uncertain.

In order to continue her editorial work in a more stimulating atmosphere than Concord, Louisa had, on October 26, taken a quiet room on Brookline Street in the new South End. Aaron Powell, editor of the *National Anti-Slavery Standard,* had asked her to send to his paper a report of Mr. Emerson's lecture on the same evening. Determined to forget for a few hours the speculations about Laurie and the possible demand for a second volume of *Little Women,* Louisa left her room for Meionaon Hall under the Tremont Temple. "Historic Notes of Life and Letters in New England" was the subject, and she heard with keen interest Mr. Emerson's remarks about Brook Farm, hung expectantly upon the words, even upon the hesitancies between words, agreeing with Father that the orator did indeed sort his keys to open the cabinet of his mind. Surely she, too, had written her own historic notes of life and letters in New England in the story of four Concord sisters.

Mr. Niles began to agree that the book might have a longer life than he had hoped. Behind the green curtain in his Washington Street office he sat, informing his new author that London had ordered an edition, and that the first two thousand copies were sold. Mr. Niles expected with some assurance to sell three or even four thousand volumes before the new year. Notices and letters had arrived indicating much interest in the four little women, and the publisher demanded a second volume for the spring.

On November 1, after Louisa had prepared *Merry's Museum*, she began work on Part Two of *Little Women*. In her quiet room on Brookline Street she sat, once again tracing the destinies of the March family in ink upon blue-lined paper. The sisters had grown three years older since the curtain had fallen upon Act One, and Meg was ready to marry her John just as Anna had done in that happy May of 1860. Once more, in her room at Brookline Street, Louisa watched her sister don her wedding gown and wear lilies of the valley in her hair. Once more the German was danced around the joyous couple and their happiness relived. May, teaching her drawing classes, developed into an Amy who made a plaster cast of her own foot or held an unfortunate fete graced by only one guest. Jo acted out Louisa's character, sending tales composed in a vortex to a *Flag of Our Union* disguised as the *Blarneystone Banner*. The criticisms that had been given to *Moods* were leveled now upon Jo's first novel, while Amy thrilled to the European voyage that had once been Louisa's, watching the riders on Rotten Row, sailing up the Rhine, and writing Frenchified letters from "Votre Amie." The blue-lined papers mounted. Each day one chapter was completed, until Jo sat in Mrs. Kirke's sky parlor, as the author had sat in Mrs. Reed's, dispatching to the *Weekly Volcano* the blood-and-thunder narratives that had emblazoned *Leslie's*.

The gossips who clamored for Jo's marriage with Laurie would be disappointed, for Louisa planned a different destiny for her heroine, a destiny in the shape of Professor Bhaer. Laurie's wheedlesome appeals and boyish love would be rejected, for in his place the author created for Jo a German professor whose traits she mined from her memories of Reinhold Solger and Dr. Rimmer. Professor Bhaer bore striking resemblances also to August Bopp, whom she had long ago delineated in "The King of Clubs." Louisa needed only to develop that sketch to paint her stout German with kind eyes and bushy beard, rusty clothes and gentle understanding.

Her technique, Louisa realized, had been composite, for she had simply amalgamated truth with some little fiction, borrowing her details from life and from her earlier stories. As each day she completed a chapter, she perceived also that her technique was still that of the short-story writer, for each portion concerned one sister, the episode of Meg's married life alternating with Amy's experiences abroad or Jo's struggles with herself at home. The Marches were good New Englanders, and yet their story seemed to Louisa to have a more universal reality than that of a single village. They were human beings also, and the episode of Meg's fifty-dollar silk appeared to her no less valid than the tale of Amy and the pickled limes. The adolescents of memory had emerged into realistic adulthood. As she launched into the future, she had given her fancy freer play, but after twelve more chapters were completed, Louisa knew that she had lived on the whole in the domain of truth. The American countryside of the mid-nineteenth century was unfolded on the blue-lined papers. Historic notes of life and letters in New England were being written at Brookline Street, as they had written themselves into the nation. The American home was here, too, the home that knew no bounds of geography, no limits of time. The latchstring was out, and soon the curtain would be raised upon the second act of her domestic drama. Then the families of the nation might open the door of Hillside to find not the Marches, but themselves waiting within. Under the roof of one New England home, they would see all the homes of America. Perhaps the tale embodying the simple facts and persons of the family was at last being completed, and the literature of childhood written.

On November 16, Louisa left the Marches to visit the Radical Club with Father at the Sargents' on Chestnut Street. Almost every extreme of liberalism would be represented in the commodious parlors at number 13, and Louisa looked forward to John Weiss's lecture on "Woman," after her concentrated work of the past two weeks. Mr. Weiss, steady as a drill sergeant at his post, beamed brightly before his audience. In shrill, penetrating tones he wittily characterized the imperfections of the present political machinery, satirizing the attempts that men had made to give a monopoly of the regulations of public affairs to the rougher half of the human family. With the style of a soldier on dress parade he gave a rose-colored picture of the future, when women would work with men in political matters.

After the clarion call he had sounded in the Chestnut Street parlors, Louisa returned to the blue-lined papers, so full of her work that she could not stop to eat or sleep. It was Beth's secret that consumed her now, Beth like Paul Dombey listening to death's whisper at the seashore, Beth to whom Jo consecrated herself as Louisa had to Lizzie. On and on she wrote, turning from Beth to Amy, who walked, as Louisa had walked, along the Promenade des Anglais, catching a glimpse of the lovely road to Villefranche and that speck out to sea called Corsica. Through Amy she relived her life in a pension, and found for Meg the household happiness that Anna had captured.

Louisa's thirty-sixth birthday was spent alone, with no presents but Father's *Tablets* to divert her from the saga of the Marches. Gradually critics were beginning to find in the first part of *Little Women* a truthful picture of American home life. The sprightly conversation had been remarked upon, and in December Louisa found recommendations of her lively story in *Godey's* and *The Lady's Friend*, while *Arthur's Illustrated Home Magazine* declared it the best Christmas story seen for a long time, originally written, and never commonplace or wearisome though it dealt with the most ordinary everyday life. If *The Ladies' Repository* objected to the lack of Christian religion in *Little Women*, declaring it no good book for the Sunday-school library, still there were enough reviewers who were beginning to find in Miss Alcott the poet of children, who knew their angels. Perhaps the new year would fulfill the uncertain promise of the old.

In December, after Louisa had launched the Christmas *Merry's*, she left Brookline Street to close up the Orchard House for the winter. Father had planned to go west; Mother had moved to Anna's home in Maplewood; and since May intended to live with Louisa in Boston, there seemed no advantage in keeping the Concord house open. Louisa was glad to turn the key on Apple Slump, and in order to indulge her sister's desire for the elegancies of modern life, engaged a room at the new Bellevue Hotel on Beacon Street.

After the burning of his seminary at Lexington, Dr. Dio Lewis had bought the seven-story residence at number 17 and opened it as a private temperance hotel. The rotund gymnast had added another story to the dwelling, and Louisa found, in addition to a Turkish bath in the basement, a passenger elevator, and an annunciator connecting with all the rooms. Although the hotel itself was a little too genteel for her taste and whisking up and down in an elevator, eating in a marble café, and sleeping on a sofa bed did not entirely appeal to her, she found the proprietor most interesting. A man of compelling personality, Dr. Lewis ranged from remarks on homeopathy and temperance to Roman baths and recommendations of Dr. Eli P. Miller's *Vital Force*. Over her lobster salad and sherbet at the Bellevue, Louisa admitted that she was witnessing yet another chapter in life and letters in Boston.

It was pleasant to live on Beacon Street near the Charles, with its red brick and the worn granite curbstones of the Hill, pleasanter still after Louisa received from Washington Street three hundred dollars as her first royalty on the sale of three thousand copies of *Little Women*. After paying her debts she was able to give two hundred dollars to Cousin Sam Sewall to invest. The Pathetic Family might emerge right side up after all, for Father was enjoying the success of his book and his Conversations, Mother was happy with Anna, and May was busy with her pupils. Although Louisa did not believe that Part Two of *Little Women* would be as popular as Part One, she determined now to complete the work for spring publication.

In the sky parlor of the Bellevue the blue-lined papers were filled again, until, among the flowers of Valrosa, Laurie learned to pluck the thornless rose that was Amy, until the pain of Lizzie's death was relived and Louisa's poem to the sister passing from her was introduced for a wider audience. In the Vevey where Louisa had wandered, Amy promised to pull always in the same boat with her Laurie. Jo, acting out her nature, had found her style at last, for something entered Jo's story that went straight to the hearts of those who read it. As Louisa had once sung to Mr. Emerson, Professor Bhaer sang to Jo, "Know'st thou the land where the citron blooms?" As Father had taught four little women the alphabet, Grandfather March instructed Demi, sharing Socratic conversations with his new pupil, not putting the thoughts into his head, but helping him unfold those already there. Under the umbrella Jo sallied forth with her professor, thinking of her poem, "In the Garret," and finding, as Louisa had found long since, that families were the most beautiful things in all the world. On the last blue-lined paper the conclusion was written.

"Yes, Jo, I think your harvest will be a good one," began Mrs. March. . . .

"Not half so good as yours, mother. Here it is, and we never can thank you enough for the patient sowing and reaping you have done,". . . .

"I hope there will be more wheat and fewer tares every year," said Amy softly.

"A large sheaf, but I know there's room in your heart for it . . ."

Devoutly Louisa hoped that the new year of 1869 would bring to the Orchard House a happy harvesting from the tears and laughter she had sowed in the book where she had found her style at last.

On the first day of the new year Louisa sent the last of her blue-lined papers to Washington Street along with several suggestions regarding the title for the sequel. "Little Women Act Second" or "Leaving the Nest. Sequel to 'Little Women' " seemed more appropriate to her than "Wedding Marches." While *Godey's* again recommended the first part as an easy and natural story, most suitable for the holidays, Louisa moved with May from her elegant sky parlor at the Bellevue to a boardinghouse on Chauncy Street, where she set up her editorial "office." She paid the toll now in headaches, cough, and weariness, for her concentrated efforts since November. Although it was impossible for her to continue to work fourteen hours a day, the compulsion to supply *Merry's Museum* with curious and instructive tidbits persisted.

As soon as one issue was prepared, there were letters to be written, reminding Alf Whitman that old Sophy had not forgotten her Dolphus.

> . . . why bless your heart I put you into my story as one of the best & dearest lads I ever knew! "Laurie" is you & my Polish boy "jintly" You are the sober half & my Ladislas (whom I met abroad) is the gay whirligig half. . . .
> All my little girlfriends are madly in love with Laurie. . . .
> . . . I can only think of you as sober Alf who used to have confidences on the couch, a la Laurie & be very fascinating without knowing it.

To her Uncle Sam May, Louisa also wrote, begging for suggestions from Grandfather May's book since she had used all the stories her uncle had given her.

> There is a constant demand for short articles & I particularly like to dip into other people's memories for incidents, anecdotes & recollections . . . do save up all the plums you get for they have the right flavor. . . .
> I am getting on very well for a "shiftless Alcott." . . . The fifth thousand [of *Little Women*] is underway I believe, & he [Roberts] says as it goes so well there is no reason why it should not run to ten thousand. It is selling in England, & though I get no copyright it helps to make "my works" known.

The sequel is in press, & I often have letters asking when it will be out. Some pretty little letters from children please me very much, for they are the best critics of such things. I dont like sequels & dont think No 2 will be as popular as No. 1, but publishers are very perverse & wont let authors have their way so my little women must grow up & be married off in a very stupid style.

... [I] scribble all I dare & in all indulge in the hope that the "Pathetic family" is coming out right side up after all.

There was little time, however, for Louisa to spend in idle hoping. Horace Fuller had mildly suggested that she write the entire magazine, and even though she did not agree to the proposal, she did find it necessary to send two sketches to the February *Merry's*. When the issue was in the press, the editor took time for a visit with the Tylers or a supper at the Parker House with Theodore Tilton. The young Apollo with the sunny locks regaled his companion with ideas on Müller Madonnas and eternal damnation, until John Dwight and Henry Denny at their tables wondered almost audibly what Louisa Alcott was doing drinking wine with a sprightly young party in a public house at ten o'clock on a Sunday night.

If Louisa enjoyed her larks with the Tylers or Mr. Tilton, she enjoyed still more the companionship of May, who was engrossed now in her art studies under William Hunt. Like Time in the primer, he stood before his class, seasoning his words with strange oaths, teaching through art the philosophy of life that showed there was no perfection, but only the half-tints of light and shadow.

There was no perfection, Louisa knew. The strolls through Boston, the suppers at the Parker House, and May's exuberances at Chauncy Street must end, and in March Louisa went home to Concord, finding that Mother had become restless at Maplewood and that Father had not been weaned from his library and rustic fences. At the Orchard House Louisa tried to rest, exulting in the knowledge that four editions of *Little Women* had been sold and that the publishers had sent her a second payment of $228. All the debts were settled now, and if the sequel found as ready a sale as the first part, Frank Leslie might no longer advertise Miss Alcott as a regular contributor to his *Illustrated Newspaper.*

In April it appeared that this would come to pass, for on the fourteenth of the month *Little Women* Part Second emerged from the press after four thousand copies had been ordered before publication. The sixth thousand of the first part was now selling, but as the weeks passed, such numbers seemed trifling compared with the sales of the completed work. By the last of the month, Louisa found herself deluged with notes of thanks and admiration from the girls of New England. Grave merchants meeting on Boston's change had begun to compare notes not on their ledgers, but on *Little Women.* The American public had for once forgotten itself, laughing and crying at the will of Louisa M. Alcott. Thirteen thousand copies had been sold, doubling in two weeks the six-months' sale of Part One. The family basked in the knowledge that Louisa had been among the first to draw her characters from New England life and scenes, but she herself took her growing repute modestly, unwilling to believe that her book had all the merit ascribed to it by the public. Still, it was breathtaking to know that the girl who had gone out to service and had modeled her story of "The Rival Prima Donnas" upon her vision of Madame Sontag, that the author who had been advised to stick to her teaching and who had hemmed pillowcases to fill the gaps in the Alcott sinking fund, had not only found her style, but her fortune with it.

Every day fresh reviews arrived to thrill the Orchard House with their contents, the *Anti-Slavery Standard* announcing that Miss Alcott could crave no richer harvest than that which was sure to come from her sowing. *The Nation* smiled upon the Marches, declaring that Miss Alcott's literary success was very like that achieved by Jo. Her book was just such a hearty, unaffected, and genial description of family life as would appeal to the majority of average readers. The general groan of dismay from the young women of the country who had discovered that Miss Alcott had forbidden the banns between Jo and Laurie was almost as loud as the hurrahs that attended the blow upon the last spike of the Union Pacific Railroad. Letter after letter arrived at the Orchard House, begging for pictures, inquiring about Laurie, acclaiming the author as elegant and splendid when she had sat on the rug and whistled in spite of Meg. The long-standing hurts were healed, the reception of the March family into the hearts of New England proving a timely restorative to one who had created that family.

While Mother cut clippings from the papers, while Father pondered upon the genius of the home and the household, and May wondered whether her sister would be as rich as Jay Cooke, reporters haunted Concord to stare at Louisa, who dodged into the woods and refused to be a lion. By the thousands the cloth copies rolled from the press into every bookseller's window and into every reader's hand. "A. M. Barnard" and "L. M. A.," the anonymous author of "Pauline's Passion," "Tribulation Periwinkle," the sewer of sheets, the Dedham housemaid, and the dreamer of dreams at Hillside had taken their places in memory. Out of them all Louisa M. Alcott, author of *Little Women*, had emerged, with fame at one hand and fortune at the other. These were sparkling new guests to entertain at the Lexington Road, for they carried in their arms riches and the fulfillment of dreams.

Roberts Brothers, knowing that fame and fortune were voracious guests who would not feed upon dreams, had demanded another book from the lion of the day, and while Louisa continued her work on *Merry's* she planned a volume to follow *Little Women*. Once she had decided to expose fashionable absurdities for the edification of her erring public, *An Old-Fashioned Girl* was quickly written. Louisa simply inverted her household portrait of *Little Women*, creating a domestic drama in reverse devoted to the Shaw home. Mrs. Shaw's velvet cloak did not cover a right motherly heart, and her home itself provided glaring examples of the follies against which Louisa determined to crusade. The wad on the top of Fanny's head, the fringe of fuzz round her forehead, the huge sashes, and the little panniers mirrored the fashions of the day, while the author proceeded to ridicule the ice cream saloon, the schools, and the orthography that placed an "ie" after a jumble of "Netties" and "Nellies" and "Sallies." Louisa professed to have forgotten her own salad days when she sent the stab of satire through the covers of "The Phantom Bride" and "Breaking a Butterfly." From one absurdity to another she ranged, from "nerves" to Grecian bends, from the giddy lives of fourteen-year-olds to the conduct of those who acted as if modesty had gone out of fashion. From the mine of memory she extracted the story of Great-Aunt Hancock, and set against the domestic drama in reverse the healthful portrait of Polly, who hailed from a home similar to the Marches', whose hearty goodwill and honest realism saved her from the fate of becoming a little prig in a goody storybook. Into the fashionable home Polly brought warmth and kindliness, and Louisa knew that if Mr. Niles wished a longer volume, she had merely to concentrate upon the career of her heroine, who would face the world as the author had done so many lives ago.

Perhaps Mr. Emerson had been right. Perhaps she was a natural source of stories, a poet of children, who knew their angels. To her the angels had been good, for the promise of the new year had been fulfilled. Like Polly, she, too, had brought comfort into the Orchard House, and glowed in the harvest after the long lean years had passed. Louisa knew that her mind was a treasure house of tales that would continue to lure children from play. Scheherazade had come from Araby to look out upon the Lexington Road, to weave a story without an end for the thousand and one nights that were yet to fall.

The Concord Scheherazade had earned her rest, and in July, Louisa left for Rivière du Loup, where her cousins, the Frothinghams, had a summer home. Octavius Brooks Frothingham raised his refined Brahman head, his intellectual brow, and scholarly eyes to find God in the Canadian precipices, and mingled his thoughts on the Fraternity Club with remarks upon birch bark and Indian canoes. Ellen forgot her translations of Auerbach and Lessing to join Louisa in drives and walks around the little village or in visits to the wigwams. Louisa, however, could not forget her obligations to Thomas Niles or Horace Fuller, and proceeded to take notes on the little brown papooses swinging in their hammocks, the plump squaws, and the red men who paddled off in their canoes to spear porpoises.

News from Washington Street pursued her even to Rivière du Loup or to Mount Desert, where she vacationed in August with May. On the first of the month Roberts Brothers announced the third thousand of Miss Alcott's newly published *Hospital Sketches and Camp and Fireside Stories*, together with the twenty-third thousand of *Little Women*, the hit of the season, orders for which continued to flow in to such an extent as to make prompt deliveries impossible. Louisa was happy in the knowledge that she had given Cousin Sam Sewall twelve hundred dollars to invest, and abandoned herself to the joys of Mount Desert. Among its cliffs and trout brooks and sheltered coves she could forget momentarily the smell of printer's ink and the incessant demands from Washington Street.

It became apparent during the autumn, as the sunny days of early October passed and the grapes and apples ripened, that Louisa had won a wide celebrity, for notices of *Little Women* had begun to pour in not merely from New England, but from all parts of the country, from every town and city where newspapers were printed. She was still unwilling to believe that there was not something unreal in the honors bestowed upon her. The spider who had woven webs of stories and had left Chauncy Street last March returned to Boston to find herself transformed into a lion. On November 1 Roberts Brothers had announced the thirtieth thousand of *Little Women* in print, and there seemed to be no end in sight for the mounting sales. Even *Camp and Fireside Stories* was receiving laudatory reviews; the old tales that had passed almost unnoticed in periodicals were acclaimed as the most graphic pictures evoked by the war. Stories that had once been rejected would find their way to print now that *Little Women* had cleared the way, and Louisa did not disdain to polish them up to meet the demands that weariness could not supply in any other way. Now when Father left for the West, he left with a brand-new trunk and gloves and cambric shirts, assured of an audience, if not for the American Plato at least for the Father of "Little Women." When Louisa moved to 43 Pinckney Street, she found herself not in a sky parlor scribbling stories, but in a city whose arms were open for the celebrity of the day.

There was time now for the author of *Little Women* to attend the Whipple Sunday evenings and see from the center of the floor Kate Field's blue silk gown or Elizabeth Peabody's hanging petticoat, to remember, as the lion hunters shook her hand, that once she had taught Mr. Whipple's child. There was time for the friends at number 43, for excursions with the Bartons or performances of *My Lady Clara* and *The Nightingale*. A lion was abroad in Boston, to whom all doors were open.

Louisa particularly enjoyed entering the doorway of number 3 Tremont Place, where the members of the New England Woman's Club sipped tea. Here Louisa took her place as one of the advanced women of the age with Caroline Severance, the president, and with the dignified Mrs. Howe, who was as much at home at 3 Tremont Place as at her own fireside. Abby May and Ednah Cheney were no more celebrated now than the author of *Little Women*, who found herself less the observer than the observed among ladies who feasted upon bread and butter and quoted Mr. Emerson while they knitted babies' stockings. Near the blooming "May" flower and the "Peabody" who chirped of kindergartens, the Alcott lion sat, hearing essays and joining in charades. At 3 Tremont Place or at Copeland's Saloon the lion could gather her lambs about her to discuss Mrs. Stowe's defense of Lady Byron or Mr. Sewall's tract on woman suffrage. The observer had moved from her corner and found a place in the sun.

From all over the country the sun shed its light upon Louisa. Father, speaking in Cleveland on New England authors, had been requested to include his daughter in his accounts of Thoreau, Margaret Fuller, Hawthorne, and Emerson. Everywhere he was introduced as the Father of Little Women and rode in a chariot of glory through the West. Louisa herself needed to wish for success no longer. The year that had passed had brought to her the fulfillment of dreams that had been dreamed for thirty-seven years. The year 1869 had surely been her *annus mirabilis*. Over three thousand copies of *Hospital Sketches* had been sold, and over thirty-eight thousand of *Little Women*. The center of all eyes, she found herself gifted with a Midas touch that turned paper to gold.

In one respect only the new year failed in its promise to Louisa, for with January she suffered from loss of voice and was forced to undergo daily cauterizations of her throat. Rheumatism of her foot and hand, together with an aching head and the inability to rest without a sleeping draft, gave signs of turning the winter of a lion into the winter of an invalid. The kindness of the good Barton neighbors brought comfort to number 43 Pinckney Street, and, despite her ailing health, Louisa forced herself to live up to the expectations of continued work from an author who was read in thousands of households and had gratified a universal desire.

With her left hand in a sling, one foot up, head aching, and no voice, Louisa spurred herself on to write the conclusion of her *Old-Fashioned Girl* for Roberts Brothers. Taking up the thread of her story "six years afterward," with tongue in cheek she continued her crusade against the absurdities of a time when doctors flourished and everyone was ill, when rats, mice, waterfalls, and switches adorned the hair of the fashionables, when the eyeglass was used as a weapon, and the fear of what people would think dominated polite society. Against such a background Polly emerged as the new but womanly woman, who earned her living by giving music lessons and was rewarded with Tom's love. Intimidated by the threats and complaints that had been showered upon her after she had refused the banns between Jo and Laurie, the author now yielded to the amiable desire of giving satisfaction by pairing off everybody she could lay her hands on. Little Maud alone escaped the marital fever, and under the guidance of one who had calmly characterized herself as a chronic old maid, became a busy, lively spinster not unlike her creator. Memory served the author again as she incorporated in her tale Mother's doctrine as a city missionary to help people help themselves, or a transformed account of the day when Margaret Fuller had paid a visit to Mr. Alcott's model children.

It had been a simple matter to complete *An Old-Fashioned Girl*, for Louisa had merely applied the style of *Little Women* to a new subject, extending her antipathy to pure English to the narrative of Tom and Polly. The author decided now to elucidate for her public the reasons for her adoption of a mannerless manner, and wrote:

> I deeply regret being obliged to shock the eyes and ears of such of my readers as have a prejudice in favor of pure English, . . . but, having rashly undertaken to write a little story about Young America, for Young America, I feel bound to depict my honored patrons as faithfully as my limited powers permit; otherwise, I must expect the crushing criticism, "Well, I dare say it's all very prim and proper, but it isn't a bit like us," and never hope to arrive at the distinction of finding the covers of "An Old-Fashioned Girl" the dirtiest in the library.

In spite of Louisa's hopes that her new book would reach such an exalted state, Mr. Niles refused her request for an increased royalty percentage. If Roberts Brothers had floated a bubble with *Little Women*, it might be more than likely to burst with the publication of *An Old-Fashioned Girl*, and the arbiter of 143 Washington Street was confident that Miss Alcott would not desert those who by their brains and their money had helped her achieve the position she held today. In the spring, however, after Father had returned from his successful visit to the West, it became apparent that Mr. Niles's fears of a bursting bubble in *An Old-Fashioned Girl* would be completely dispelled. The book with its cloth binding, gold stamping, and pictures of Tom and Polly gave every promise of becoming indeed the most eagerly thumbed volume in the library, for twelve thousand copies had been sold in advance of publication and twenty-four thousand would be needed to supply the first orders. The magic alchemy was still at work, turning to gold the papers that issued from number 43, and as she had adjusted herself to the poverty of dirty

High Street, Louisa adapted herself gradually to the riches of Pinckney Street.

The Alcott sinking fund overflowed with resources for Fechter's *Hamlet* at the Boston, or bicycles for the fad of 1870, but Louisa had no time now for such diversions. The companion who had accompanied Anna Weld to Europe's pensions in 1865 had turned the tables and was eager to make the grand tour in a fashion becoming the author of *Little Women*. May, thirsting for the art of foreign galleries, had been invited to go abroad by Alice Bartlett on condition that her celebrated sister would join the tourists, and throughout the spring Louisa rejoiced in the knowledge that May's dreams for Couture, Millet, Rousseau, and Daubigny would at last be realized. Alice Bartlett would be a fine cicerone, for the tall, brown-haired, twenty-four-year-old enthusiast spoke French and Italian, and after her recent trip abroad was familiar with the difficulties of foreign travel.

Once again Louisa made preparations for a voyage, but as she packed her black silk and her traveling suit, her dressing case, her gloves, and her veils, she could not help contemplating the change that attended a procedure so similar to that of five years before. In five short years she had indeed turned the tables upon Anna Weld, and as she rolled her flannel gown and waterproof into her shawl-strap, she contented herself with the thought that she needed only the desire to own all the percales, French chintzes, piqués, and lawns that paraded in *Godey's Lady's Book*. Now when her picture was taken by Allen of Temple Place, it was taken so that an author's stately presence, fine head, large eyes, and brown hair could be preserved for her admirers; and the sitter was invited to sign the photograph with "I am yours truly L. M. Alcott."

On March 31 the family and housemates gathered for the farewells at 43 Pinckney Street. Mother kept up bravely, nodding and smiling in a fashion true to that of Mrs. March, but Louisa saw the handkerchief go up to her eyes after it had been gaily waved. To the station Anna and the devoted admirers followed the travelers on April 1, but Louisa remembered only Father and Mother as they had gone away the day before, treasuring the memory of the single white handkerchief more than the gifts and light farewells of those who had gathered at 43 Pinckney Street. With John for escort, May and Louisa took the morning train for New York, where they planned to meet Alice Bartlett. The train boy, shouting his wares, placed *An Old-Fashioned Girl*, published that day, on the lap of its author, who, after she had murmured that she did not care for it, heard the delightful exclamation, "Bully book, ma'am! Sell a lot; better have it." When John informed the vendor whom he was addressing, Louisa thoroughly enjoyed the chuckle, stare, and astonished "No!"

In New York harbor Captain Roussau climbed the bridge of the French steamer *Lafayette*, and on April 2 the three wayfarers embarked for Brest. John was the same faithful brother waving farewell now as he had waved a welcome home four years before, but it was a different Louisa who called her good-byes from the deck of the *Lafayette*. It was a Louisa who had doffed her anonymity, who had through a long apprenticeship in diverse fields found her forte, who had indeed brought a nosegay to the Orchard House, whose flowers were perennial. Now the traveling companion of the *China* sallied forth as *the* Miss Alcott on the *Lafayette*, and Miss Weld's humble servant of the pensions would roam abroad, a lion on grand tour. Under fair omens, despite the gale of wind, the *Lafayette* weighed anchor, for it carried down the harbor and across the waters one to whom the gods had brought the fulfillment of dreams. For all her dreams surely fulfillment waited, for to the gods all things were possible.

CHAPTER 11

The Grand Tour

Between Louisa's crossing on the *China* and her voyage on the *Lafayette* not just five years alone, but a lifetime, seemed to have intervened. During the cold and rainy weather, as the ship plowed through rough seas, she could not help contrasting the attentions a traveling companion had paid to Anna Weld with those that were lavished upon a celebrity on board a French steamer. Contrast worked its magic, and nothing in Louisa's life marked the changes that had come to her so pointedly as the grand tour upon which she had embarked. Little girls, clutching their well-thumbed copies of *An Old-Fashioned Girl*, trooped into the author's cabin to pay tribute to a seasick lion wrapped up like a mummy, but nonetheless ready to receive her young public.

With Alice Bartlett and the Howes, Louisa whiled away the time by editing "The Lafayette Sherald or Voices from the Deep," in which she paid tribute to Marie, the stewardess, and plaintively asked why, if steamers were named the *Asia*, the *Russia*, and the *Scotia*, one had never been named the *Nausea*. At last the *Lafayette* lowered anchor at Brest on April 14.

As soon as the trunks were passed through the customhouse, the pleasure seekers journeyed on to Morlaix, finding themselves suddenly transported from the familiar to the unfamiliar. Louisa especially enjoyed May's raptures over every gable and turret and fountain and church, and strolling about the town abandoned herself to the delights of children in wooden shoes, girls in blue cloth caps, and boys in sheepskin jackets. They quickly made plans to study French, while the seamstress of Chauncy Street promised to do the mending for Alice, who would act as interpreter. Sitting at her window feeling the mild air of Brittany, Louisa started a letter to Mother, deciding to keep one on hand all the time in which to record her sensations for the benefit of her most appreciative public, the family. While May, surrounded by a crowd of critics in the form of Breton boys, sketched the tower of St. Melanie, Louisa looked out upon the square, planning "The Mystery of Morlaix," or wrote her impressions of storks and snails and beggars for Mother, sending her, in pen and ink, the balmy day that had introduced the travelers to Europe.

She sent home, too, a racy account of the drive from Morlaix to Dinan, when the trio were accompanied by "a fat Frenchman," who

> gabbled to A. as only a tipsy person could, quoted poetry; said he was Victor Hugo's best friend, and a child of Nature; that English ladies were all divine, but too cold,—for when he pressed A.'s hand she told him it was not allowed in England, and he was overwhelmed with remorse; bowed, sighed, rolled his eyes, and told her that he drank much ale, because it flew to his head and gave him "commercial ideas."
>
> . . . I sat, a mass of English dignity and coolness, suffering alternate agonies of anxiety and amusement, and May, who tied her head up in a bundle, looked like a wooden image.

The gaiety continued at Dinan, and Madame Coste's pension on the Place St. Louis was a fit spot in which to stay during the spring months, for the charming house overlooked a green valley where peach and plum trees bloomed, windmills turned, and a ruined castle loomed up to remind the travelers that they were still in Brittany. They immediately hired a salon with blue damask furniture and a fireplace, a small room leading out of it for Alice, and upstairs a larger room for May and Louisa with beds draped in green chintz and a sunny window opening upon the valley.

Madame Coste seemed a nobler Madame Rolande, for the tall, bewhiskered old lady embraced her new boarders, beamed upon them contentedly, and gave every sign of being happy to brood over them like a motherly hen when she was not knitting briskly or selling pigs at market.

Not as an underling now, but as the center of attraction, Louisa picked up the life in a pension that she had begun long ago, and found her fellow boarders as interesting on the Place St. Louis as they had been at the Pension Victoria. Madame Forney, a buxom widow in black moiré, appeared at the table with her handsome son Gaston and her homely daughter, whose wedding was soon to take place. They were all "desolated" that the Alcotts could not speak French, but Gaston, between bowing, scraping, and losing himself in fits of Byronic gloom, aired his little English, which May promptly undertook to improve. Madame Forney now and then plucked out her handkerchief and wept at the thought of losing her daughter, who placidly continued to gnaw bones and wipe up her gravy with bits of bread. Louisa took notes once again, knowing that an account of a French wedding would be appreciated by readers of *The Independent.*

The town of Dinan offered all the charms of Brittany in its narrow streets and overhanging gables, its carved beams and sunny promenade on the fosse. Nuns in gray gowns passed silently along. The market stalls were filled with the scent of lilacs and roses, and Louisa was transported to a strange fairyland, where ancient gateways and clock towers, pig markets and ruined ramparts mingled in a confusion of old and new. Here was a Brittany lifted out of Murray, a Brittany where the sights and smells and sounds of the present flourished side by side with the dim, storied past of Dinan.

There was time for the present as well as for the past in the long weeks near the banks of the Rance. There was time for Alice to buy a bird for the parlor, a gray bird with a red head and a lively song, that was quickly christened "Bernard du Guesclin" and called Bernie by the iconoclasts from New England. There was time to listen to his song, time such as there had never been near Washington Street. In and out of the stores they wandered, Louisa buying gloves or a white sun umbrella for May, under which she might sketch to her heart's content. There was time to dress leisurely for the evenings in the great salon, where Mademoiselle Forney played the piano and May convulsed Madame Coste's boarders by her rendition of some American "chants."

At length the trio established for themselves a routine even in Brittany, where the hours seemed undivided one from the other. It was a casual, pleasant routine, without the press of demands from Washington Street, for errands could be attended to in the cool morning before breakfast at ten, and from then till four they consulted their Murrays, wrote their journals and letters, sewed and read, or listened to the lively song of the redheaded "Bernard du Guesclin." It was a routineless routine, an enchanted life.

The routine was varied, as the days passed, by letters from Thomas Niles, who sent notes from Louisa's admiring public and the first reviews of *An Old-Fashioned Girl.* The *Transcript* had printed a sketch of Miss Alcott on the day of her departure, predicting the success of the author's new book and lauding her genius for naturalness and her gift for photographing young life, traits inspired by remembered experiences, accurate observation, and loving sympathy. Pictures of Louisa M. Alcott mounted on heavy cards were advertised everywhere. The author, sitting in her oak salon, rejoiced in the good news from home, learning that *An Old-Fashioned Girl* had reached its twenty-seventh thousand. Mr. Loring wished to share in the glory that Louisa's work reflected upon her publishers, and had, without consulting her, issued another edition of *Moods.* The sale of *Little Women* had mounted to fifty thousand, and Roberts Brothers advertised Miss Alcott's books as standard for the library, but by no means "standard" for the bookseller. The name of Louisa Alcott would not be forgotten during the author's European tour.

Values changed as Louisa wandered about the narrow streets of Dinan, until the arrival of Mademoiselle Forney's fiancé seemed almost as important as Mr. Emerson's lectures at Harvard. Jules Clomadoc, with his red face, large mustache, and tiny figure

198 . Louisa May Alcott

encased in an imposing uniform, provided no end of amusement
to the trio as he discussed their "promenade on monkeys" or their
pleasures at "the establishment of dance." Louisa noticed that the
prospective bridegroom lavished all his attentions upon Madame
Forney, merely bowing to his future wife, who contented herself
with her diamonds. Although the Americans did not attend the
wedding, they thoroughly enjoyed the preparations. The square
was filled with turnouts, but Jules's carriage was unfortunately
delayed by the breaking of a trace, and Louisa watched him fum-
ing, poking his cocked hat out of the window, exploding with
most impressive oaths, and unconsciously providing a story in
praise of spinsterdom for the New York *Independent*.

The days at Dinan provided the source for lively letters home,
and Louisa regaled the family with detailed accounts of a drive to
the mineral spring, when "The carriages were bathchairs with a
wee donkey harnessed to each . . . looking so venerable with thin
long ears and bits of feet that I felt as if I was driving my grandmother."

She described, too, a visit to a ruined château, "which we went
all over, as a part is inhabited by a farmer who keeps his hog in the
great banqueting hall, his grain in the chapel, and his hens in the
lady's chamber." Even the Dinan menus were elaborated upon for
Anna's benefit: "We have also had fun about the queer food, as we
don't like brains, liver, etc. A. does; and when we eat some mess,
not knowing what it is, and find it is sheep's tails or eels, she exults
over us, and writes poems." The *pensionnaires* apparently exulted,
too, over the illustrious visitors from America, for, as Louisa
reported to Anna:

> We have let little bits of news leak out about us, and they think
> we are dukes and duchesses in *Amérique*, and pronounce us *très
> spirituelles; très charmantes; très seductives femmes*. We laugh in pri-
> vate, and are used to having the entire company rise when we
> enter, and embrace us with ardor, listen with uplifted hands and
> shrieks of *mon Dieu! grand ciel!* etc., to all remarks, and point us
> out in public as *les dames Américaines*. Such is fame!

The Place St. Louis was almost as great a source of stories as the Lexington Road. The unloading of Madame Coste's wood, the arrival of a meek but pursy English lady in green skirt and pink calico waist with an oriole in a cage, all found their way into the journal of an author who saw the world from the windows of her oak salon. She had already obtained material at Dinan for three stories, "Pelagie's Wedding," "Little Marie of Lehon," and "The Banner of Beaumanoir," tales which would more than repay her expenses at Madame Coste's. The yellow gorse that Louisa gathered to send home to Mother gave way to roses and cherries as her notebook was filled. In May's sketchbook other figures had been drawn, Miss Kane taking her place with Madame Forney.

While May sketched Miss Kane, Louisa consulted Dr. Kane, for neither fame nor fortune nor the mild air of Brittany had entirely freed her from pain in her leg. The doctor, who had been an army surgeon in India, decided that all of Louisa's woes might be traced to the calomel that had been prescribed for her in Georgetown, and administered doses of iodine of potash, while she continued to take opium to sleep. Now when all the world lay before her, inviting her exploration, she found that she had lost some of that capacity for joy which had been hers five years ago.

On June 15 the trio left Dinan, traveling leisurely to Bex. There they settled for a month, finding in the Hotel des Bains new figures for sketchbook or journal. The Hungarian Count Szapary presented himself to the Americans as a descendant of "Semiramide" and Zenobia, and immediately entertained them with his stories. Whatever he did not know, he imagined, and Louisa enjoyed his theories about table moving or *gyromagnétisme* as well as the *magnétisme* of Count François de Szapary, while May found the prospect of a quiet little flirtation most inviting. A description of the count added a touch of color to Louisa's letter to Father, for she promptly characterized him as an "enthusiastic old man," who "imagines a good deal to suit his own pet theory." A Polish countess and her daughter enlivened the table at the Hotel des Bains, reminding Louisa of the cosmopolitan Pension Victoria. Time had brought changes, however, for the Polish countess as well as her daughter had read and enjoyed Louisa's books. It was strange to find the door of Hillside opened by a Polish woman in the far-off village of Bex.

It was strange, too, to read in the little town on the Avençon the news that France and Prussia had declared war. Here again, Louisa saw that perfection was only a word, for now when her health had improved, the Franco-Prussian War threatened the glories of her grand tour. This war she would try to escape, if escape were possible.

In the letters from Thomas Niles there was as much a refuge as in the grandeurs of the Dent du Midi, for the publisher had sent the July account of $6,212 to his celebrated author, along with the June reviews of *An Old-Fashioned Girl*. Although *The Atlantic Monthly* caviled about the bad grammar and poor writing, *Godey's* pronounced it the book of the month, *Harper's* declared it as good as *Little Women*, and *The Ladies' Repository* thought it better than its predecessor. Now, in the knowledge that $10,000 had been safely invested, Louisa was assured not only of the fame, but of the fortune of those Alcotts who could not make money. Except for John's apparently slight illness, all was well at home. The three companions were free to enjoy the delights of the Dent du Midi, unless Bismarck or Napoleon interfered with their plans.

While May gave endless accounts of her excursion up Saint Bernard, Louisa sent letters home or wrote her "Lay of a Golden Goose" to appease the editors who continued to demand sketches. On the balcony of the Hotel des Bains she sat, watching the changing aspect of the hills, writing of Mr. Fields, the "great cock-a-doodle," who from his perch had

> *Crowed daily loud and clear,*
> *Stay in the puddle, foolish bird,*
> *That is your proper sphere."* . . .

> *The owls came out and flew about,*
> *Hooting above the rest,*
> *"No useful bird was ever hatched*
> *From transcendental nest."*

The plain gray goose from the Orchard House had been an aspiring bird, and

> *At length she came unto a stream*
> *Most fertile of all* NILES,
> *Where tuneful birds might soar and sing*
> *Among the leafy isles.*

Then the goose laid golden eggs indeed. But now the literary birds across the sea must wait, for their favorite fowl looked forward to a rest at Vevey, where, not many years before, the first of her golden eggs had been hatched.

The years had brought changes to Vevey. The Pension Paradis was not so colorful as the Pension Victoria had been, for though it boasted an old Spaniard and a young Frenchman, there was no Polish boy to discuss the Insurrection or play the piano in the salon. Among the vineyards and gardens no Scottish sisters, no mustachioed Carolinian wandered; in their stead liveried servants drove the coaches of Isabella or Don Carlos. The boys of Sillig's school still walked about in the garden of Bellerive, and the author of *Little Women* looked longingly at the gate, inside of which Prince Victor-Napoléon played with the Ritter von Ofenheim as if the Franco-Prussian War had never been.

Yet there was no denying the fact of war. Mazzini had gone to Palermo, only to be arrested and imprisoned at Gaeta. The Prussians were in Strasbourg, and Paris in a state of siege. Because Germany had favored the North during the Rebellion, Louisa sympathized with the Prussian cause, though she could not help pitying the emperor, whose plans failed one by one. At best it seemed an ignoble conflict in which brutality had taken up the sword against corruption, a conflict so unlike the Polish Insurrection or the American Rebellion that Louisa wished only to escape from its encroachments.

She could drop her newspapers to visit the chalet of Monsieur Nicaud, owner of the Pension Paradis, or to study French with a governess who taught the mysteries of her language at two francs a lesson. Louisa had studied French before in Vevey; the repetition served only to remind her of the contrasts between life at the Victoria and life at the Paradis.

She, too, had changed since last she strolled along the shores of Lake Leman. The topknot that the barber had given her did not conceal her gray hair; and when she looked into the glass, she realized that she was getting fat and old. The gods had brought celebrity in place of youth, a celebrity constantly attested by the notes that Thomas Niles sent with messages from admiring young ladies. Benda, the book-and-picture dealer, had asked May if she were the Miss Alcott who wrote the popular books, for fame had followed the author of *Little Women* even to Vevey, where the gay, whirligig half of Laurie had once strolled in the garden. Mr. Niles had reported to Father that no other American author had made as much money as Louisa during the year. Over $12,000 had already been paid to her, and the newspapers had begun to report every detail of her life that the editors could discover, from her reactions to Dickens's death to the lameness of her leg. Even the great Mr. Fields, who had cautioned the author to stick to her teaching, had given up a page of *Every Saturday* to a picture of "Jo and the Professor" to "attract the pleased attention of the vast army of readers" who had been delighted with Miss Alcott's *Little Women*. *Hearth and Home* had issued an account of her life, declaring her humor, her tastes and aspirations thoroughly American, and her *Little Women* a natural picture of life in eastern Massachusetts. Louisa read with interest the description of herself as a "young lady . . . of stately presence, with a fine head, large blue eyes, brown hair," and a lively wit, who was nearer forty than thirty. *The Southern Review* had found *An Old-Fashioned Girl*, now in its thirty-second thousand, a story that every young lady should read, mark, learn, and inwardly digest, while *Little Women*, in its fifty-fourth thousand, seemed to have been transformed from the book of the day into the book of many years to come. All this had happened since Louisa had wandered about Vevey with Ladislas. Time was a strange magician, time and those gods who brought fortune and fame, and took in their place youth and the bright joy of living.

On September 3 other news arrived, of the emperor's surrender. Refugees from Paris and Strasbourg flocked into Vevey. Revolution, bloodless and impotent, seethed in Paris. Strasbourg had been bombarded. The war tightened around the refugees at Vevey until Louisa, May, and Alice decided to leave the shores of Lake Leman for Italy. If they could, they would leave the war behind them. Louisa knew that she could never leave behind the memories that Vevey had summoned up, the memories that had made the past surge into the present.

The journey to Italy, when "peak after peak of the Bernese Oberland rose behind us," was related to Mother; and Louisa included in her letter a racy report of an opera the travelers attended "in their night-gowns," for the opera house was next door to their Lugano hotel.

My Nan can imagine with what rapture I stared at the scenes going on below me, and how I longed for her as I stood there wrapped in my yellow bed-quilt, and saw gallant knights in armor warble sweetly to plump ladies in masks, or pretty peasants fly wildly from ardent lovers in red tights; also a dishevelled maid who tore her hair in a forest, while a man aloft made thunder and lightning,—and *I saw him do it!*

Milan, too, unfolded its splendors for the Americans on grand tour who watched with iconoclastic comments the gentry ride up and down in their carriages along the Corso. Here were colors for May to copy on canvas, and natives for Louisa's journals. Parma, too, had gifts for both, Correggios for May, the dust, the tatters, the emptiness of the Farnese Theater for Louisa. For the three, the priests moved about the streets of Pisa in scarlet and white, ragged urchins plunged at the holy water font, and the Arno mirrored the sepulchral shadows of the Leaning Tower and the Duomo.

They rested in Florence, hoping to forget, in the courts and the ancient houses on narrow streets, the battles that raged to the north. The sunlit valley of the Arno was shut away from the war, and Louisa raised her eyes to the Campanile or wandered about the Lungarno, buying furs for her winter in Rome.

More interesting than wood carvings or straw bonnets to the travelers were the studios of the artists. Mr. Ball received them among his marbles, and Mr. Powers invited them to see why he had left a clock factory on the banks of the Ohio to make statues on the banks of the Arno. At Mr. Hart's studio or the rooms of Miss Foley, the cameo cutter, the wanderers were welcome, for Louisa's celebrity had heralded her arrival, and *Little Women* was almost as well known in Florence as in Boston. Even Minister Marsh was eager to forget the exploits of Gambetta to exchange puns with the celebrated lady from Concord, while Mr. Hart begged to model a head of the author, and the Balls gave a party in honor of the tourists.

After her visits with the Balls and Minister Marsh, Louisa took time to drop her flowers at the grave of Theodore Parker. Standing there in the forlorn and lonely spot where his body rested, she remembered the pulpit of the Music Hall and the parlor of Exeter Place. Now she who had treasured the flowers of the Music Hall returned them to the grave of Campo Santo, where a bird sang on as though death and time and change were only dreams or the shadows of dreams.

To the three companions Rome held many promises, the promise of art to May, of friends to Alice, of rest and the source of stories to Louisa. The sudden view of St. Peter's dome and the *lucina* lit on the stairs of number 2 Piazza Barberini brought the promises nearer. In their apartment on the hill there was a balcony overlooking the piazza with its fountain of the Triton. A girl was hired to do the cooking for six dollars a month, and the tourists established themselves in their rooms during the season of dismal rains that had begun in Rome. The somber-colored fountain whispered in the silence; icicles hung from the blowing Triton. Since Louisa did not feel well, she saw her narrow Roman world at first through blue glasses, not venturing far beyond the Piazza of the Cappuccini or the Barberini Palace.

Gradually, however, the Roman world widened for the travelers as they wandered among the shops and palaces of the Corso, or explored narrow, dirty streets that led to broad squares dignified by mighty churches. Among the scholars with voluminous shovel hats surmounting their thin bodies, they walked; among prelates with snuffbox in one hand and umbrella in the other. For Louisa, these sights were as much a part of Rome as the yellow Tiber or the obelisks and domes and towers of the Eternal City. In the cobbler's stall and the *osteria*, in the old woman roasting chestnuts over her charcoal oven, she took more interest than in the seven immemorial hills of the ancient city.

The howls of the dogs, the mournful dirge of the *frati* in black, bearing their wax torches to honor the dead, and the ceaseless sound of fountains were as much a part of Rome as the city of the past that struggled to emerge from the ruins. The moon glimmered upon the ivy-covered ruins of the Coliseum, where owls hooted among the ancient stones and broken arches. Rome's past as well as its present seeped into the minds of the ladies from Boston as they wandered together from 2 Piazza Barberini over the narrow streets of the Eternal City.

May's sketchbook was filled not only with the sights of Rome, but with the models drawn in Mr. Crowninshield's studio, for she had begun to take lessons under the guidance of the young painter. Louisa added to her knowledge of Dr. Rimmer and William Hunt detailed information about the studio on the Via Margutta, where Frederic Crowninshield instructed in the art of sketching from nature. Still, she found more interest in the living model than in the drawing, in the healthy bambino than in the statue of the gladiator who had been dying in marble for so many centuries. Stories of a Turner that had been sold upside down delighted her more than Mr. Crowninshield's discussion of draperies and murals, although she found much to interest her in the room on the Via Margutta.

Louisa took time to visit another studio, not merely to look at paintings, but to sit for one. At George Healy's studio on the Via S. Nicola di Tolentino, she seated herself in a crimson brocade chair, smoothing the white lace of her black dress, giving a touch to the black ribbon round her hair. Louisa enjoyed her sittings with George Healy, who chatted of the famous subjects he had drawn, of Louis Philippe or Abraham Lincoln, as he sketched freely an outline of her face, brushing with easy strokes the brown of her hair, mixing the gray-green-blue of her eyes.

No matter how much Healy discoursed about Longfellow or the golden-haired Edith, about Guizot or Dana, he could not long refrain from talking about his children. Mary was a novelist, at present working on *A Summer's Romance*, and Louisa was generous with her suggestions about sending the manuscript to Roberts Brothers in Boston. The painting proceeded quickly, the short, sharp touches and highlights added with easy brush strokes, the olive brown of the background filled in. It was not long before the portrait was completed, and in exchange for her help to Mary Healy, Louisa received the painting on canvas whose soft tones had captured the light in her large, penetrating eyes, had set down forever the strong nose, the black dress against the crimson of the chair. It would be strange to see the portrait hanging on the walls of the Orchard House after it had left the easel of the Via S. Nicola di Tolentino, stranger still to know that she had joined the gallery of Healy's great and would live with them on canvas after she herself was dust.

There were other pleasures, too, in Rome, besides those of the Via Margutta or the Via S. Nicola di Tolentino. She enjoyed the private theatricals of the Roman Amateur Dramatic Society, rivaling the performances in the Via Frattina with her own Potato Pantomime and charades in the Piazza Barberini, or a presentation of Mrs. Jarley's waxworks on one of the seven hills. The newspapers brought welcome news also to Louisa, for her republican beliefs made her prefer a Rome guarded by its own troops to one dominated by a papal purple that covered poverty and ignorance. A new freedom seemed to blow over the city like a wholesome wind.

She herself had never known so much freedom as now, when on her thirty-eighth birthday she sat at number 2 Piazza Barberini, receiving a nosegay from Alice and a pretty sketch from May. Even the news from home added to her sense of freedom, for Roberts Brothers had announced that Miss Alcott's writings were never so popular as at this time and that the interest in them increased daily, a fact to which the sales figures testified, for *Little Women* had reached its sixtieth thousand and *An Old-Fashioned Girl* its thirty-sixth thousand. Word from the Orchard House was as comforting as that from Washington Street. John was as excellent a son-in-law as ever, and the boys as beautiful in their grandparents' eyes. Father, after working on his *Concord Days*, had started on another western tour. Louisa could stand upon her balcony and look down at the Triton without anxiety about the cares of home. All of Rome was before her, welcoming with open arms the successful author of the day.

It was strange that one word spoken, one moment passed could shatter serenity and cage the newfound freedom. The words were simply spoken. One day before Louisa's birthday John Pratt had died. There were other words, too, words of his brief sickness, of his calm directions about his affairs, and of the journey from Maplewood to Sleepy Hollow, where John had been laid. All the words returned to the one despairing fact, that a brother beyond reproach had died, that Anna, totally unprepared for his sudden death, had gone to Concord to seek and give comfort, but had found the world filled with darkness.

In her room on the Piazza Barberini Louisa sat, writing to Anna how she mourned for the brother whose quiet integrity and manly love of independence had made his thirty-seven years so precious to those who knew him. "Good-bye, my dear . . . John. . . . The world is better for your simple virtues, and those who loved you richer for the faithful heart you showed them." Her own words brought her no comfort, nor would they comfort Anna. The fact had destroyed comfort, and had, Louisa knew, made captive the freedom she had so lately found. Now she must be a father to the boys, as she had been not only a sister but a daughter and a wife and mother, too, at home. In Hillside and in the Orchard House she had embraced all relationships, finding in one household a domain wide enough in which to explore humanity. This was the nature of her love. To her family she had been, and must be more than ever now, all things, fathering her father, mothering her mother, husbanding her sister, giving them the love she had given to no man. The love was there, nonetheless, a love many-sided as it was deep, springing from one who in the crucible of her heart had melted all the relationships of home.

Out of her love she drew another book, so that John's death would not leave Anna and her children in want; and since the story would be told for John's two boys, she called it after them, *Little Men*. In her room at number 2 Piazza Barberini Louisa sat, remembering the doctrines of the Temple School and Sanborn's academy to combine them in the pedagogy of Plumfield, whose moral purpose was to give to children a home in which they could be taught courage and industry. Latin and Greek were all very well, but self-knowledge, self-help, and self-control were better.

Louisa chose her boys carefully to be ripe for the methods of Plumfield. To each she gave some fault awaiting help, to Jack his unboyish keenness and love of money, to Ned his bragging, to Nat his weakness, and to Dan his wildness. And if the sins they represented were not deadly, and if they were not transmuted into antithetical virtues, still the boys were helped to learn how to become good men, as John had been all his life a good man.

It was strange to sit on the balcony overlooking the Triton and write of Father's methods of letting the mind unfold, or of Dio Lewis's musical gymnastics. Memory was the source from which her tale was told, and Louisa plumbed her childhood for the story of her new shoes that had been told in "Poppy's Pranks," and remembered her lessons with Charles Lane to recount to her little men. Like Louisa, Demi read *The Story Without an End* and recalled playing with books to make bridges and railroads. The memory of Margaret Fuller and the model children could be used again, while the Plumfield theatricals would differ only slightly from those at Hillside.

From memory, too, she painted her characters, until Freddy and Johnny were again transmuted into Demi and Daisy, and John Pratt appeared once more as John Brooke, a man whose goodness would last when fame and money failed. Dickens exerted his influence, as Louisa alluded to Dr. Blimber and Mr. Toots's wristbands, but far more than Dickens it was Mr. Thoreau who stood near her at 2 Piazza Barberini as she wrote of Mr. Hyde, who could whistle to snakes and tickle lizards, who knew when flowers would bloom, and could tell tales of the Indians and the rocks.

The story spun itself out as Louisa raised her eyes occasionally from her paper to the fountain on the square. She had no particular plan, except to describe a few scenes in the life at Plumfield, and the episodic technique she had long since adopted was applied again in a tale that gently rambled along. Children were, after all, the best critics of stories for children, and perhaps they would receive *Little Men* with as much joy as their fathers and mothers had welcomed Mr. Alcott's teachings at the Tremont Temple. To Freddy and Johnny she would dedicate her book, the little men to whom she owed some of the best and happiest hours of her life. For their sakes the tale was told. Roses and rosemary bloomed in Rome, but Louisa wandered among the hardier blossoms of Walden woods and the Tremont Temple, gathering a nosegay from the childhood she had lost for the children who followed after her.

Christmas had come to Rome with the roses and rosemary. On every piazza the *pifferari* in their coats of coarse cloth and skins played on their bagpipes or danced the saltarello before the Madonnas in the streets. It was a strange world for Louisa to enter while her mind was filled with thoughts of John or the sound of a flute played on the Concord River.

Only three days after the cannon had boomed from St. Angelo and the great bell of St. Peter's had rung out the joy of Christmas Day, the maid had come flying in from market with the news that the Tiber had overflowed its banks and inundated the lower part of the city. Louisa left the fire of Plumfield for the flood of Rome, finding the Piazza di Spagna a Venice of rafts and boats, and the Piazza del Popolo a lake with its four stone lions above the surface still spouting water. At 2 Piazza Barberini the maid laid in stores, live fowls roosting in the kitchen with the cats, and to fortify themselves against thieves the ladies from New England prepared arms consisting of one pistol, two daggers, and a heavy umbrella.

Flood or earthquake, a royal visit or festivities lent variety to the winter in Rome. In spite of the war news, the *feste* proceeded, and the carnival played out its merry course. Louisa walked with the crowds to the Corso to watch the masqueraders turn the clerical party to ridicule, representing the new crusaders in caricature as they rode along on asses. Although the police forbade the procession, fresh caricatures appeared every day, along with the merrymakers who peppered each other with flowers and confetti. From the balcony she saw the Roman ladies toss their bouquets upon a motley crowd decked in Greek caps or Polish pelisses, while May thrilled to the red and green and blue and gold hangings draped from the windows of the Corso. Louisa shared in the gaieties until she saw the Barbary steeds play their role in the carnival, while the crowd roared on and the heavy cannon announced that the race was over. She watched until the Corso was a fiery blaze in the *Moccoli*, every window lit with tiny torches, every hand carrying its taper, until the cries of "*Senza moccolo!*" blew out the lights of the festival and the *Ave Maria* rang forth the end of the carnival.

It was difficult at times for Louisa to bridge the gap between Bess's masquerade as Cinderella at the Plumfield theatricals and the masquerade of the merrymakers on the Corso. More than anything else, letters from home served to bridge the distance between Concord and Rome, and Louisa learned with pleasure that Mr. Loring had sent $700 for *Moods* and that Roberts Brothers had remitted £25 to the author through Sampson Low of London. The sad Christmas at home had been brightened by the sympathy of good friends who had poured a drop of comfort into the bitter cup that Anna drank. The family had settled at Minot Pratt's home in Concord, and between little Johnny's illness and Mother's despondency Anna had been kept busy. Louisa knew that she would not be able to continue her grand tour much longer.

In February, when preliminary peace proposals were signed between France and Germany, she decided to return north soon with Alice and May. From London she would go home alone, leaving May to stay on in Europe for another year. She could substitute for the sketching parties on the Palatine the study of art in London. For Louisa the change would be more radical. The châteaux of France would crumble, the fountains of Rome be silenced, and the sense of freedom with which she had looked down upon the Triton from 2 Piazza Barberini irrevocably gone. In place of these the Orchard House waited for her at the end of the grand tour along a road that inevitably led not to Rome, but to a New England village called Concord.

In March, after Thiers had signed the peace proclamation at Versailles, the three companions turned their backs upon the Piazza Barberini and the narrow streets of Rome to rest for a while in Albano before journeying north. Near its lovely lake and wooded shore Louisa added a final touch to her *Little Men*, describing the golden harvest of Plumfield while cyclamen and anemones brought spring to Albano.

There were weeks also in Venice before the final journey north, weeks of a fairy pageant floating on the waters, of domes and spires piercing the skies, and of pigeons wheeling about above the Piazza San Marco. At the base of marble palaces the water flowed, below campaniles and Byzantine windows and arches of the Renaissance. At nightfall the colors were softened, the black gondolas gliding over green waters, past ancient white marble steps. To a serenade that floated up to her windows in the moonlight, Louisa slept, and awoke to find Venice a fairyland still, a midsummer night's dream she had lived in April.

Since her presence was necessary in London for the publication of *Little Men*, and since, for all the delights of Italy, she longed for home, Louisa left the magic of Venice, traveling north with May and Alice over the Brenner Pass to London. She rejoiced to be back in the city whose smoky air and grimy houses were so familiar to her, and was glad that she could now act as cicerone in a London of mud and fog, beef and beer. Hardly had the travelers settled in lodgings at Brompton Road than a grave, dark little man with fine eyes and quiet manners presented himself as Thomas Niles's brother William, who had been commissioned not only to represent Roberts Brothers in London, but to entertain the firm's most celebrated author after her grand tour.

Mr. Niles's first service was to pack the visitors into a cab and escort them to the bank for money and letters. Mr. Ford had sent a request that the author of *Little Women* contribute a serial to Mr. Beecher's *Christian Union*, for which she would receive, in addition to a circulation of at least fifty thousand, the payment of $50 a week for a story that would run a year. Perhaps Louisa might supply the weekly with notes of her travels abroad. But now the last chapter of those notes remained to be lived before it could be written.

Although William Niles was eager to do the honors of London for his celebrated companion, Louisa could not resist the temptation of showing her sister her favorite places and people. Aubrey House was open again to her, not as a guest who sat in corners, but as the woman of the age that she had dreamed to be when first she sat in the Taylors' drawing room. Despite all the transformations in the world and in those who gathered at Aubrey House, Louisa knew that none had experienced greater changes than she herself. Nowhere, save perhaps at Vevey, had she realized those changes so acutely as now, when the little-known visitor of earlier days had left her corner to emerge as a lion in silver-gray silk among the lions of Aubrey House.

Another house in London opened its doors to welcome Louisa, for Sampson Low was eager to consult with her regarding the English publication of *Little Men*. William Niles and Edward Marston, Mr. Low's partner, enjoyed many a visit from May and Louisa, with whom they chatted about foreign and American books, the importation of an edition of *Little Women*, and the technicalities of English copyright. Under the imprint of Sampson Low, *Little Men* was launched in London, and its author realized that she had come a long way since George Routledge had paid her five pounds for the privilege of issuing *Moods*.

Little else remained for her to do in the city, for she had lived the last chapter of her grand tour. The time had come for Louisa to write the finale to her notes abroad before they could be turned into a serial for *The Christian Union.* Before her departure she saw May settled in her studies with Thomas Rowbotham, and while the artist happily prated on about lines and forms, light and shade, Louisa bade her good-byes to her sister, packed her journals, her notes, and her traveling dresses, and left the city to board the *Malta.*

For May's sake she was glad that she had made the grand tour. For Louisa, also, the year had been pleasant and fruitful, in spite of the poor health that had troubled her and in spite of her anxieties about home after John's death. She had written one book and gathered sufficient material for another. She had made a triumphal entry through welcoming doors, finding that her hard-earned reputation had preceded her wherever men could read.

It was an anxious twelve-day passage, but Boston harbor appeared at the end of it, and on the afternoon of June 6 the *Malta* cast anchor near home. At the wharf there was no faithful John to meet the wanderer, but in his place Father had come with Thomas Niles, and a great red placard advertising *Little Men* had been pinned up in their carriage. Father's happiness beamed from his shining face, and Thomas Niles was exuberant with word that fifty thousand copies of Louisa's latest book had been sold in advance of its appearance. As the author's departure had been signalized by the firm's publication of *An Old-Fashioned Girl,* so the day of her return was marked by the distribution of *Little Men.*

Louisa hurried home to Concord, finding Mother feeble and considerably aged after the year of trouble. The boys were tall, bright lads devoted to their grandmother, but Anna under her apparent serenity hid a mourning heart. They had refurnished the author's room on the second floor of the Lexington Road, and Louisa, unpacking her treasures before the family, knew that she would never again go far away from the Orchard House. The year that had passed, and the years that had gone before the grand tour, had brought many riches home to Concord, but the gifts had not been freely given. Death and the ravages of time walked as the

shadows of fame and fortune, darkened even the glittering mem-
ories of Morlaix, Bex, Rome, and Venice. Not the Corso or the
Piazza Barberini was free of those shadows, but on the Lexington
Road at least Louisa could try to dispel them or hold them off by
the gift of her love. This was the nosegay she brought home to
Concord after her pilgrimage was ended.

CHAPTER 12

The Youth's Companion

To the gabled brown house on the Lexington Road the traveler had returned, to the small green parlors of Apple Slump. The wanderer had returned with her quarry of tales and the daughter had returned with her greater quarry of love. More clearly than ever Louisa observed the changes in Mother, who sat listening to stories of Rome or of London, subdued now in her soft black silk with lace at her neck and a lace cap. Father needed her no less than Mother, Father somewhat deaf, smiling blandly at his former absurdities, living as ever among his books, waiting for Pythagoras to come to Concord. The sister had returned to the Orchard House also, to an Anna who seemed to have settled down into an old woman, sober and sad, with gray hair. A husband had returned, too, to fill John's vacant place, eager to give of her strength to Anna. In the little room that had been built for the boys surely a father stood and watched and played.

The year that had passed had strengthened Louisa for the years that would follow. The family assured her that she was one of the wonders of the world, unspoiled by success, and Anna found in her the same jolly, generous, simple Louisa of old, honest, outspoken and quick, with the same warm heart and the same straightforward goodness. Although age and illness had inevitably left their mark, Louisa knew that the topsy-turvy, boyish Louy of so many lives ago had not lost her strength when she had gained the elegance and stately grace that Anna had begun to see in her. The glass told her that she was a woman now, tall in her rustling black silk, with a band of black velvet round her hair. She would never again be the robust girl of Hillside, but she was sufficiently improved in health and spirits to impart her strength to those who needed it deeply.

The glass reflected nothing of the fame that had come to her. It was still with a certain resentment and unbelieving wonder that Louisa watched unknown ladies arrive at the Orchard House in fine carriages to leave their cards with *the* Miss Alcott. The intrusions of reporters and the kindly inquisitiveness of admiring readers were less pleasing to her than the orders that flowed in for *Little Men* at the rate of one thousand a day. The statement of Roberts Brothers, that *Little Women* had reached its eightieth thousand and *An Old-Fashioned Girl* its forty-fifth thousand, was substantial proof of success. She had found her pot of gold, not at the end of a rainbow but on the summit of a pathless mountain. There she must stay, not merely finding but keeping the pot of gold so hard earned, so reluctant to be possessed. For a while, before she plunged into work again, it was comforting to know that her fame had not diminished while she had been abroad. Letters arrived at the post office from the Far West, inquiring of Miss Alcott what books should be read to build a noble character. There was testimony to her fame even in the disappointment of a child, who visited the Orchard House and mourned in sepulchral tones, "I thought you would be beautiful." To the children, Louisa responded with the warmth of her own childhood. To troublesome reporters only, she was adamant, opening the door dressed as a servant and announcing that Miss Alcott was out of town.

In the eyes of the townsfolk Louisa was unchanged by the miracle of her fame. Graciously, unobtrusively, she sat down at the Hosmer home with her knitting, or brought over her bread to be baked in a neighbor's oven as if her life had never extended beyond Main Street. Louisa walked often to the large, rambling yellow house on the Sudbury Road to visit Dr. Laura Whiting, who had come to Concord to practice medicine after her husband's death. With her she talked not of proofs from Washington Street, but of a Concord that was being transformed slowly but inevitably from the little white village of old into a suburb of Boston.

Not in Concord alone did Louisa find the past retreating, receding under the waters of the insistent present. Part of her own youth vanished when Uncle Sam May died at Syracuse. Louisa, remembering the picnics at South Scituate, the visits to Syracuse, and the help that her uncle had given the family, prayed peace to the ashes of so good a friend and realized sharply that Mother was the last of her family now.

Yet no one could live forever with the past. In October, after Louisa had engaged two girls to do the housework, she took a room in a boardinghouse at 23 Beacon Street, where black servants ushered her formally about and the aristocrats of Boston haunted her abode. There she could rest, find relief from aching bones, and enjoy the sleep that came without morphine. People, pictures, and plays would stimulate her for the next book that would keep the pot of gold filled to the brim. The city had lost none of the exhilaration that she had always found there. Where but on the Boston cars would a woman prod her knee with the point of an umbrella and ask loudly, "I say—be you Louiser Alcott?" The city had begun to know her as well as she knew the city. Here she had found her place.

Determined to enjoy the pleasures and excitements of Boston, Louisa donned her black silk dress and set forth from Beacon Street, the observed of all observers, herself an observer too. Not with the buoyant eagerness with which she had first tasted its delights, but with a calm assurance that she, too, was a part of its activities, Louisa shared in the life of the city. The agitation for woman suffrage, or the bazaar at the Music Hall to sustain *The Woman's Journal* touched her closely, for the opinions of Miss Louisa Alcott were as vital to the public as those of Julia Ward Howe or William Dean Howells.

Washington Street especially clamored for stories, opinions, and sketches by the author of *Little Men*, and with Horace Fuller,

Louisa discussed the plates of *Morning-Glories*, a book which he hoped would be revised for ten thousand children hungry for something from her pen. At the dingy old signboard of Roberts Brothers opposite the Old South, she stopped again to chat with Mr. Niles behind his green curtain. On one subject alone they clashed, on the woman's suffrage movement, for Mr. Niles refused to give books to the fair that had been planned, and Louisa was disappointed to find her publisher so reactionary.

Mr. Niles was far more interested in the scrap bag of stories that "Aunt Jo" was planning than in Louisa Alcott's opinions on opening the polls to women. Together they discussed the collection for which the young folks were already wildly clamoring. *Aunt Jo's Scrap-Bag* would include several reprints as well as three new tales. Miss Ledyard of Brooklyn would illustrate the book, in which so much interest had already been aroused. It was simple and profitable also to issue such a collection of old and new. All lives were patchwork, and *Aunt Jo's Scrap-Bag* would bring the dark and bright together in harmony. Still it was strange to realize that the hoyden "Jo March" had turned into an aunt with a scrap bag of stories.

The youngest of the "Marches" had her scrap bag, too, which she sent home in the form of letters and copies of Turner. Louisa hesitated to put an end to May's delights, but there was no doubt now that she was needed at the Orchard House to help with a mother who was becoming feeble and a sister who was still preoccupied by her sorrow. May acquiesced, leaving her Turners and the arches of Westminster, and on November 19 returned, bubbling over with tales of her merry adventures, her London lovers, and the pictures she had painted.

Louisa could at last content herself that all was well at home. The boys sat soberly at the chessboard, Johnny coolly marching up to checkmate Freddy, while Father surrounded himself with his books and manuscripts. A furnace was being installed at last so that a new climate would dispel Mother's rheumatism along with the picturesque open fires of old. Another long-cherished dream had come true, for Mother sat in her pleasant room without work or care, without the worry of poverty, and the lines that little Louy had written in her journal were lines no longer, but living truth. The pleasant, sunny chamber, the cushioned easy chair, the book laid for her reading, the vase of flowers—these were no words to remember, but mercies granted by some god of mercies.

In her own quiet, sunny room in Boston, Louisa rejoiced in dreams come true. She could take time now to attend the ball for the Grand Duke Alexis with Cousin Hamilton Willis, no longer youthful and dark-haired, but as charming an escort as ever. The young man of the hour, despite his title, might have sat for a portrait of one of "Jo's" boys, for Louisa found him a great blond lad, six feet tall, with waving, golden hair and deep blue eyes. As she joined in the dances, Louisa noticed gleefully that the duke spurned the Boston dowagers and their diamonds in favor of the pretty girls. Even the princely Alexis, however graceful and elegant, did not attract all the glories of Boston. Light was left to shine upon Louisa Alcott from admirers who thronged around to chat and dance with the stately lady from Concord, who had come to Boston from a farther country than Russia, by a route more circuitous than that of the frigate *Suetlana*.

There was time, too, before Christmas, for the Radical Club, where Louisa watched the philosophers mount their hobbyhorses and gallop away beyond time and space. Time was, as ever, the wizard of magicians, for it was strange to remember, as she looked at the tree for the boys in the parlor on the Lexington Road, that last Christmas she had been in Rome, mourning for John while *pifferari* played on their fifes and roses and rosemary bloomed. The year had been varied and good, for pain had taught her patience, and a gift taken away had been a gift given. Washington Street had dispelled the shadow of poverty from the Lexington Road, where a wizard with a Midas touch spun out her tales and filled a pot of gold.

Stories could not be written rapidly enough to supply the demands that arrived with every post. To *The Christian Register*, Louisa dispatched a sketch of "Women in Brittany" from her memories of Dinan. Mrs. Stowe forgot the wrongs that Lady

Byron had suffered to request from Louisa a serial for *The Christian Union*, while the editor of *Hearth and Home* announced to his readers that Miss Alcott was one of the brilliant popular writers engaged for the current volume.

To keep the pot of gold well filled and to supply Mrs. Stowe with a serial, Louisa relived her memories of France, expanding the notes that had been taken in Madame Coste's pension at Dinan for the delight of the readers of *The Christian Union*. There was no time now to listen to the gossip from the Concord Milldam. The characteristics of Madame Coste seemed more vivid than those of Mrs. Emerson, and May on a campstool sketching the Breton landscape more real than May on the art committee of the Agricultural Society.

After *Harper's* had reviewed *Aunt Jo's Scrap-Bag*, Louisa dispatched "Shawl Straps" to *The Christian Union*, content in the knowledge that her short stories of the winter would bring five hundred dollars to the Alcott fund. Her devices, she knew, were simple, centering upon three types of tales for her varied public. The autobiographical and travel sketches spun themselves out of memory, as the spider spun its web from its own silk. The stories designed especially for children had two aspects like the faces of a coin, the one positive, the other negative. Louisa could either tell her juvenile public what to do and how to live or what not to do and how not to live. For all her sketches the markets waited. *The Independent* would not only accept Louisa's memories of the Dinan bridegroom in "Pelagie's Wedding," but, like *The Youth's Companion*, would take juvenile and autobiographical as well as travel narratives. The literary net was wide, and all was fish that came to it. In some dim past Louisa had once been told to stick to her teaching. Now the Cooper Institute invited Miss Alcott to appear before the Lyceum; and while Thomas Niles was made a partner in Roberts Brothers, his most popular author was almost a partner of Daniel Ford, who offered in *The Youth's Companion* electric equipment, chemical cabinets, magic lanterns, and the tales of Louisa M. Alcott, which would warn against the ways of transgression and allure to those of virtue. Rejections, like youth, were affairs of blurred remembrance.

Louisa knew that she had taken her pen for a bridegroom and that the strange marriage had been successful. She had done what few in this world accomplished, lived to see her youthful wish come true. She had written a good book, she had become famous, she had traveled abroad, and she had earned riches. The resolution she had made so hopefully twenty years before was realized. The family was independent, its debts, even those that were outlawed, paid.

In September, Louisa visited Wolcott with Father and saw at last the little house on Spindle Hill where the boy Amos had dreamed the dreams he had confided many years ago to the children of the Temple School. Now she understood better the boy's longing to climb the Connecticut hills and see what lay in the world beyond. Out of her understanding she hoped to expand another tale, "The Cost of an Idea," that would explain to all lovers of stories the story of one who had built his life around a thought, a dream, a hope. Louisa had already written one chapter of that tale, her account of Fruitlands, in which she had taken a part. The poverty and the dreariness of Fruitlands were glossed over, until Louisa looked with laughing eyes upon the idiosyncrasies of the world's reformers. Here was the history of a failure, of an experiment that had been tried and found wanting. But time had healed the wounds of Fruitlands, and the wounds of Spindle Hill as well, for the boy had lived to see his *Concord Days* published, had lived to catch reflected glory from the manifold glories of a daughter who could turn even failure to success.

Still, Louisa could not work in Concord. In October, after Mr. Emerson had sailed for Liverpool with Ellen and Father's trunk had been packed for his grand tour through the West, she took a room at number 7 Allston Street in Pamelia May's quiet, old-fashioned boardinghouse. There she expanded "Shawl Straps" for publication by Roberts Brothers, adding to her memories of France those of Bex, Vevey, Rome, and London. She would refrain from giving the dimensions of any church, the population of any city, or the description of any famous place, confining herself to the personal haps and mishaps and adventures and experiences of Matilda, Lavinia, and Amanda. This had ever been her purpose, to find broad significance in the specific and the commonplace. It would be well to apply it to a book of travels, so that the outworn story of wanderers abroad might be made colorful and real. "Aunt Jo's" second *Scrap-Bag* would be no Baedeker of dry statistics, but the warm and human account of three "shawl-strappists" who had boarded the *Lafayette* for the cobblestones and sunlit courts of Europe.

Louisa forgot the flood in Rome for the fire in Boston, when on November 9 she heard the booming of bells and saw hand engines rush along the moonlit streets, helpless before flames that turned granite to powder and marble to chalk. She was awake all night, finding the sight of the ruddy dome of fire at once splendid and terrifying. Over the city's narrow, crooked streets the sheets of flame roared and cracked, eating their way through Winthrop Square toward Washington Street. Through the night Louisa watched the crowds laden with their household goods fleeing before falling walls and the rush of fire. The city was shaken with explosions of gunpowder, noisy with the hoarse shrieks of steam engines, lit by a glare that paled the light of the moon.

Work would restore the ruined buildings, extend the streets, and raise up the fallen timbers; and work would be Louisa's panacea, too, bringing forgetfulness of the sudden glare of flame and the desolation it had heralded. When once again Henry Ward Beecher sent one of the editors of *The Christian Union* with an offer of three thousand dollars for a serial by Miss Alcott, she accepted the request, dusted off the manuscript she had once called "Success," renamed it "Work," and plunged into a vortex of writing. One thousand dollars had been sent as a seal to the bargain, and Louisa was possessed by the narrative of her autobiography, transmuting herself into Christie Devon, reliving the days when she had gone out to service in Dedham and acted in the dramatic troupes of Walpole and Concord. Her life had become a tale to be told, a tale of servant and actress, companion and seam-stress, a tale of work rather than of success, for the author of *Little Women* had not forgotten her salad days.

Throughout the winter, after *Shawl-Straps* had appeared under the imprint of Roberts Brothers, she took time also to sup-ply to Daniel Ford the stories that sold now for thirty-five dollars each instead of the ten they had once brought to the editor of *Merry's Museum.* Now *The Youth's Companion* had absorbed *Merry's;* indeed, it had absorbed its editor also, for Louisa was herself a "youth's companion," weaving from her memories of Europe "The Mystery of Morlaix," embroidering the moral of kindness to animals upon the framework of "Huckleberry" and "Grandma's Team," suggesting the worth of natural, everyday English in "Mamma's Plot."

Work was less easily written than the tales for Daniel Ford. Out of the past Louisa summoned her memories of Theodore Parker, incorporating them into Mr. Power, and saw Thoreau's figure rise before her eyes to be metamorphosed into that of David Sterling. Now from her room at 7 Allston Street, a girl went forth to seek her fortune, a girl in whose mind a Boston intelligence office rose up from the ashes of yesterday, a girl who had once been ordered to blacken boots for a gentleman of Ded-ham. Again "The Demon's Daughter, or The Castle of the Sun" produced the most magnificent spectacle ever seen upon the stage, and Christie appeared, as Louisa had, in the dramatized novels of Charles Dickens. The sensational chapter devoted to the companion of a mad Carrol was reworked, for Louisa remem-bered *The Flag of Our Union* that was unfurled again in memory. Louisa remembered the war also, and her belief in the unfailing dividends paid by the Underground Railroad. All remembrance was grist for the mill of *Work.* From the farthest reaches of mem-ory Mr. Greatheart strode forth, leading the fugitives from the City of Destruction to that Celestial City that a child had long since sought. Here, in the chapters of *Work*, the episodes of Louisa's life were written, another web that a spider had woven from the silk of her own being.

On December 18 the serial made its bow in *The Christian Union*, and Louisa laid aside her pen to bask in her glories and the rest that she had surely earned. In the West, Father was welcomed now as the grandfather of Little Women, while in the East his daughter's fame was established by *The Independent*'s announcement that "Susan Coolidge" might become another "Aunt Jo." Disciples only had been lacking to make permanent Louisa's niche in literary history. Now the disciples were there, the niche hollowed out, the "youth's companion" as much a part of the country as the dome of the State House or the grasshopper that twirled above Faneuil Hall.

Beecher had advertised *Work* by declaring that Miss Alcott had found the key to the popular heart in depicting the true home life of America. Thomas Niles agreed, for Roberts Brothers paid her over two thousand dollars in royalties, while Daniel Ford increased his rates to fifty dollars a story and *The Independent* still offered one hundred dollars for a tale. As a thank offering for her success, Louisa was happy to give money to the silent poor, a class to which she herself had long belonged, the needy and respectable, the forgotten ones who were too proud to beg. When she discovered that Ladislas Wisniewski was living in Passy after he had lost everything in the Vienna *Krach*, she sent money to him also, remembering that the hero of *Little Women* had captured the hearts of young America no less than "Jo March."

Now May's wish to return to Europe could be granted, and Louisa gave the artist one thousand dollars to send her to London for another year's study. Again the trunks were packed and in Boston, on the twenty-fifth of April, Louisa bade farewell to the happy artist, who sailed the next day by tramp ship for Liverpool.

Not long after the farewell to May, Louisa joined the Concordians in arranging for another wanderer's homecoming. In the house at the fork of the roads, Father left a copy of *Concord Days* for Mr. Emerson, handbills were posted, and church bells were rung to announce the return of the town's first citizen. At the station Louisa sat with Father and the Sanborns in the procession of carriages that followed the Concord band. Down Main Street and the Lexington Road they rode, bearing the wanderer home to the triumphal arch over the street by his gate. Between rows of children singing "Home, Sweet Home" Louisa watched Mr. Emerson pass, to be welcomed by three hearty cheers from the villagers. When he could control his voice he thanked them, speaking of their common blood, "one family in Concord." Yet Louisa could not help observing the change in his appearance, the snowy, downy hair that now covered his head, the shadow that took the place of what for so many years had been purest substance.

The forgetfulness of age might overtake her also, and lest she wait too long to capture memories in words, Louisa wrote two tales a day for *The Youth's Companion* while she kept house and supervised the kitchen. Between sweeping eight rooms twice a week and ironing and scrubbing for the family, she wrote her stories for the million. All had been and would continue to be fish for the literary net, even to the new servant in the Orchard House who had read Miss Alcott's *Work* and determined to follow Christie's way of life. Louisa had not forgotten the days when she had gone out to service, and was happy now to receive in her parlor and at her table a woman who for three dollars a week brought order and neatness into the Orchard House.

Now she could be free to take Johnny to the seaside for a week and enjoy the salt air until word from home recalled her suddenly to Mother's sickroom. Dropsy of the brain threatened to destroy her reason, so that for several weeks she did not know the husband and daughter who hovered by her bedside, lavishing upon her every comfort and luxury. At last Mother slowly came back to herself, not to the self of old, but to a feeble, broken self that would never resemble the brave, energetic being of other years. Louisa's summer flowed on in quiet channels as she drove about with Mother, becoming once again part of a sleepy village.

In her own present life Louisa found little material for stories. The quiet summer deepened into autumn. Nothing but the reviews of *Work* reminded Louisa that her life extended beyond the meadows and woodlands and the lanes of Concord. *The Lake-*

side Monthly condemned the book as an immoderate apotheosis of Madam Work, pointing out to the author that slavery had been abolished and with it the necessity of cant on the subject of Negro rights. More disturbing was the remark of a *Harper's* critic to the effect that the book would not have made the author's reputation, though her reputation would make the book. Perhaps that niche that she had hollowed out for herself was too confining. Perhaps her head was crowned only with the laurels of yesterday. Yet surely in the years to come she would win fresher laurels that time would never wither. In the indolent days of early autumn, the river wound slowly along. Concord lulled her to sleep, embalmed her in its stillness.

The Orchard House at least awakened from its slumbers to celebrate Mother's seventy-third birthday. The ardor of many unquenchable Mays still shone in her face as she was escorted into the study on Father's arm, followed by Anna bearing May's portrait to represent the absent daughter. As of old, Mother read the verses that accompanied her gifts. Even the cat was not to be outdone, presenting among the pile of gruel bowls, aprons, diaries, and water carriers, a mousetrap for his lady. Louisa hovered near her mother as the family drank the toast and joined hands to dance around her big chair, singing in chorus:

> *Long may she wave, and may we all*
> *Her dear face live to see,*
> *As bright and well at seventy-four*
> *As now at seventy-three.*

From the little celebration Louisa drew another tale, "A Happy Birthday," for *The Youth's Companion*, to earn fifty dollars for carriages for Mother and let the million honor the occasion with her.

This happy birthday brought to mind other birthdays, Lizzie's celebrated in the groves of Fruitlands, Louisa's many birthdays celebrated in Boston and in Rome as well as in Concord. Somehow the past always intruded in the present, and now the golden days of Vevey were relived in memory when Louisa heard that

Ladislas had arrived in New York with a wife and two young daughters. To "Laurie," the hero of *Little Women*, rather than to his prototype, Roberts Brothers paid four hundred dollars, and Louisa laid this ghost of the past so that it would haunt the present no longer.

Ghosts were ever better laid in Boston than in Concord. In November, after Father had ventured again to the West, Louisa closed the Orchard House and took rooms for herself and the family at number 26 East Brookline Street in the South End near the Park. The boardinghouse overlooked Franklin Square, and Mother enjoyed sitting at her window watching the sparrows or entertaining the old friends who visited her. For the first time the boys were sent to school, Freddy tall, handsome, precocious, and wise beyond his ten years, the shadow to Johnny's sunshine.

As they drove about the city, Mother's reactions provided a study in contrast to Louisa's, for the Boston that boasted the Parker Fraternity Hall, the city where women discussed Elizabeth Phelps's remarks on dress-reform garments, was Mother's no longer, but Louisa's. Mother's life had gone down into the past, and with it her Boston. Granite warehouses had usurped the landmarks of her youth; her familiar haunts were gone, and she was forlorn in a city that was hers no longer.

The city was Louisa's now as ever, its bustling newness stimulating her. She awakened from the slumbers of Concord, energetically refusing Mrs. Dodge's suggestion that she provide a serial for the newly published *St. Nicholas*. Yet between the red and black covers of the magazine edited by the author of *Hans Brinker*, Louisa saw possibilities for still another market for her tales. Mrs. Dodge wished no sermonizing, no wearisome recital of facts, no rattling of dry bones. The ideal child's magazine was a pleasure ground, where soon Louisa's stories might be offered along with "Jack in the Pulpit" and "The Riddle Box."

The new year of 1874 promised to be a fruitful one for Louisa, except that Mother's illness and the remarks of the homeopathic Dr. Wesselhoeft indicated that her decline had begun. Change, that Louisa had forgotten in the excitements of work and of Boston, made itself felt again, reminding her that when she had had youth, she had had no money, and now that she had money, she had no time. When time and leisure came, she would lack the health to enjoy them. She was chained to the oar as a galley slave, but perhaps one day the ship would come into port with all sails set.

May's ship floated over smoother seas than Louisa's, for the artist was still painting her Turners in London and sketching pretty panels as potboilers, a midsummer girl upon whom the gods had smiled. Mother longed for May, her baby, and none of Louisa's devotions could check the ravages of age. Perhaps upon the sail of the ship that Louisa captained one word would be emblazoned—not fame, not success, but devotion. The daughter was transmuted into the father of the boys, into the companion of her own father, whom she consoled for Conversations that brought no pay though they attracted many listeners. Even her writing had become a form of devotion, her pen the sword that would shield the family from all foes. She herself was growing old and worn, with hardly a trace of the dashing young girl who had gone forth to seek her fortune. The price had been paid, the bargain made, and youth traded for the fortune that had come. This, too, was implied in the token on her sail, in the emblem that mirrored the life that now was hers.

In addition to the honor of having achieved disciples in her literary craft, Louisa was pleased by the fact that her work was not merely printed, but reprinted. "Aunt Jo's" third *Scrap-Bag* had been acclaimed by *Godey's* as one of the best of the holiday series. Mrs. Dodge's new juvenile magazine had more need of Louisa's contributions than the author had of *St. Nicholas* as a market for her always salable wares. Yet Louisa decided to dispatch for the March number her first tale to appear in its pages, "Roses and Forget-Me-Nots," a nosegay in which she entwined her message of kindness to the lame and the poor. *St. Nicholas* might prove a second *Youth's Companion*.

In March also, May returned from London with another portfolio of pictures, sketches of the cloisters in Westminster Abbey and copies of Turner that had evoked Ruskin's praise. Now, after a year's apprenticeship with oils and watercolors, May felt that she was at last an artist, ready to fill orders from abroad or to teach drawing. Louisa could not help observing that the bloom and brightness of her youth had gone and that in their place a certain sweetness had appeared, a strength of character that had been lacking in Amy's prototype. The midsummer girl had become a woman, reminding Mother and Louisa of the irreparable vicissitudes of time.

Still another presentiment of life's falling curtains came to Louisa when she accompanied Father and Mother to the Stone Chapel to see the tablet erected to the memory of Grandfather May. Up the broad aisle they walked together, as they had walked nearly fifty years ago to be married. After Mother had sat alone in the pew, singing softly the old hymns, she broke down, thinking of the time when her family had all gone to church together. None was left now of that family save herself. Even of Boston nothing was left that she remembered. This was not her city. She never wished to see it any more.

Louisa could not grieve long over the past. Once the magazines were supplied with Miss Alcott's spring quota, she must open up the Orchard House with May, hanging the new pictures, changing the Apple Slump of old into a home adorned with the results of the artist's revolutionary ideas. Louisa needed only a short time in Concord to know that as soon as the family was settled she must return to Boston. The most exciting news the villagers could discuss was the naming of Thoreau Street, and Louisa found that even in this development the newness was simply an attempt to commemorate the past. The generation that had led a child through the groves of Walden woods, through a library in a white frame house at the fork of the roads, was dying. The generation that had risen to take its place kept its eyes upon the past, to imitate or commemorate. Louisa was neither of the one nor of the other, though she had tasted of both.

Without regret she left the village for a room in Joy Street, where, between lauding the Elgin timepiece in "My Rococo Watch" for the *Illustrated Almanac* of the National Elgin Watch

Company, and at last sending her old story of "How I Went Out to Service" to an *Independent* that would not reject it, Louisa took time to savor Boston in the spring. The city had burgeoned forth anew with a series of lectures on dress reform, and Louisa determined to incorporate the gospel of healthful chemiloons and balmorals in a story. Boston was alive with a more modern newness than she had ever observed. An army of women were singing their temperance song under the aegis of Dio Lewis. Everywhere, Louisa found suggestions for that two-headed coin she could so skillfully turn in her tales. Miss Brackett and Mrs. Cheney espoused thoughts on the education of American girls that would one day be grist for a mill to grind out morals for the young and wrap them in Miss Alcott's sugar-coated pellets. The observer was abroad again, wandering through a Boston that was changed indeed from the city of her childhood, a Boston where the dome of the State House had been gilded, where the citizens paid homage to the future as well as to the past.

She could extend her observations now to the village of Conway, where she planned to summer with Anna and the boys. At the Atherton farm, Louisa frolicked with the children, from whom she found suggestions for her next long story, as their light infantry, composed entirely of officers, paraded in cocked hats and full regimentals. Mr. Stearns' horse, Old Sorrel, grazed in the pasture, and across the road loomed a large pine that tempted Louisa to begin the serial she had consented to write for Mrs. Dodge.

Under the pine she sat, finding that two chapters at least had worked themselves out here at Conway. In her new story there would be no rattling of dry bones such as the editor of *St. Nicholas* abhorred, but something truer, more uncompromising, than wearisome sermons. Under the shade of the old pine Louisa sat, writing a book that would turn the positive head of her coin face upmost. Uncle Alec's purpose was actually identical with the purpose of the serial itself, to show how to make healthy constitutions and convert pale-faced little ghosts into rosy, hearty girls. This was her gospel on the education of American children, a gospel that included the discarding of medicine and the use of brown bread pills instead, the substitution of new milk for strong coffee, and brown bread for hot biscuit. Louisa would exhibit a display in dress reform, unhooking Rose's tight belts and clothing her in a freedom suit, a hygienic Gabrielle. The three great remedies of sun, air, and water would be exalted, and in place of a "Blimber hot-bed," where pupils were crammed like Thanksgiving turkeys, Dr. Alec would institute gymnastics in the form of housework, less Greek and Latin, and more knowledge of the laws of health.

Occasionally Louisa found it fruitful to turn the negative head of her coin face upmost, crusading against the sensational literature to which "A. M. Barnard" had once added her tithe. An antitobacco league would join forces with an anti-earring and antislang campaign to complete the list of "Do Not's" in the decalogue of L. M. Alcott.

Once again, as she sat under the pine of the Atherton farm, Louisa remembered the model child of her own youth, transmuting Ariadne Bliss into Annabel Bliss, the prim wax doll whose example was recommended by Rose's innumerable aunts. Louisa had no need, however, to delve into the past for material. The Atherton farm was close at hand, and required only the change of a few letters to be metamorphosed into the Atkinson farm, where Fred and Jack Dove would enroll with the Snow children in a light infantry.

With broad strokes Louisa painted her dramatis personae so that they would be dominated by one distinguishing characteristic. Their traits would be adumbrated early in the book and carried through to the end—Mac's bookishness, Charlie's princeliness, and Archie's leadership. Louisa had not forgotten the simple stage directions and the broad characterizations in the plays in which she had acted, nor had she forgotten her apprenticeship in the field of short stories. Chapter by chapter, episode by episode, the serial grew.

Louisa realized that the book would be a second *Little Men*, for here, too, she was championing the new enlightenment in food, clothing, and schooling. The variation would develop from the fact that her present tale centered about the incidents of one girl's life rather than about the careers of many boys. If the serial were successful, there might be opportunity for a sequel, for Charlie's wild oats would lend color to the account of a matured and blossoming Rose. She had not attempted much in the new story beyond a few hints at Dr. Alec's experiment with her heroine, painting pictures of boy and girl life and character with as much amusement and as little preaching as possible. If the young people were able to extract an idea or a thought or two from her work, she would be satisfied. She herself was finding the actual writing a simple matter as she sat under the Atherton pine, growing stout and strong in the mountain air of New Hampshire.

Demands pursued her when she had returned to the city from the Atherton farm and taken rooms at the Bellevue again, where May might teach a drawing class and she herself might attempt to satisfy a few of the requests for stories or autographs. Between dispatching to *St. Nicholas* "The Autobiography of an Omnibus" and woefully scribbling, after the twenty-eighth application in one week,

Of all sad words the saddest are these,
To an author's ear, "An autograph please"

Louisa found that the results of the mountain air at Conway were not long lasting. Again she suffered from pain, found no sleep without morphine, and was forced to consult Dr. Hewett, whose remedies seemed less effective than those of Dr. Alec.

There was no doubt that Dr. Alec's experiment had its efficacy, for Roberts, Sampson Low, and Scribner were outbidding each other for the privilege of printing the unfinished story. While the ladies of Boston discussed the extension of suffrage advocated by *The Woman's Journal*, Louisa perceived that in Lucy Stone's newspaper she might readily find still another market for her articles. For her varied writings no market now was lacking. *The Woman's Journal* would accept articles directed to the mature women of Boston; *The Youth's Companion* and *St. Nicholas* were more eager than ever for her juvenile tales; and while Roberts and Low clamored for the right of publishing her as yet unfinished story, Louisa knew that the days of peddling her humble works were over. She had only to finish the serial to find a triple market for it.

No sooner was the manuscript of *Eight Cousins* dispatched to Mrs. Dodge's office than Louisa received an offer from Daniel Ford of seven hundred dollars for a temperance tale. The news from home freed her for the preparation of "Silver Pitchers." All was well at the Orchard House, Father happy among his Westerners, and outside of the gossip about the Beecher-Tilton scandal, 1874 had provided little excitement for the loungers on the Milldam. Although she had offered an occasional hint on the merits of cold water, Louisa had never before written a full-length story on the doctrine of temperance. She herself enjoyed a glass of cider and had not refused to drink a toast in champagne, but surely one who advocated air and sunshine for youngsters must also seize the opportunity to add water to the gospel of health and loose clothing. The Cold Water Army that Uncle Sam May had led at South Scituate had not been forgotten. The Temperance Union was planning conventions, friendly inns, and reform clubs. It was time for Louisa Alcott to add another commandment to her decalogue.

Under the emblem of "Silver Pitchers" the author would organize her own temperance league. The vice of every "Champagne Charlie" would be exorcised; the band would strike up "Drink to me only with thine eyes." The Knights of the Silver Pitcher would follow their ladies to a land where "water-ice and ice-water" took the place of more potent libations. Upon the positive face of Miss Alcott's double-headed coin, another injunction was inscribed. At the same time, Louisa could pay a debt to society and add to her many commandments one that would give variety to the crusades championed by the "youth's companion."

In February, after "Silver Pitchers" was completed, Louisa accepted the invitation issued to the friends of Woman's Higher Education to celebrate the tenth anniversary of Vassar College. On the twenty-second of the month, she seated herself in the chapel to hear Dr. Raymond discuss the natural right of woman to intellectual culture and development. After the banquet in the gymnasium, Louisa heard James Freeman Clarke's entertaining remarks, as well as the lengthy discourse of Peter Cooper. Not without a mild satisfaction, she observed that several distinguished guests were forced to depart with their papers undisturbed in their pockets, and when she herself was requested, since she would not deliver a speech, to place herself in a prominent position and revolve slowly for the benefit of her Vassar admirers, she consented.

With less willingness Louisa agreed to sign the huge pile of autograph albums that had been placed outside her door, and listened with stately courtesy to the glowing criticisms of her works imparted by Miss Cornelia Raymond and Miss Mary Botsford, who informed her that at least one "March family" had been organized at Vassar by a group who called themselves "Meg," "Jo," "Beth," and "Amy." In the stacks of books the author penciled her name, chatted with four hundred collegians, and proceeded to kiss everyone who asked her.

Louisa completed her journey with a short visit to New York before she fled from the lion hunters and returned home to a Concord preoccupied with its preparations for the Centennial. By the nineteenth of April the villagers had filled their larders, set their houses in order, and draped themselves in Centennial shawls. Louisa was awakened by a salute of one hundred guns at sunrise, and arose to see the liberty pole dressed with flags and the guests streaming toward the Fitchburg Station to start the procession. At the pavilion on the Provincial Parade the gentlemen would gather, while the ladies, Louisa among them, assembled at the Town Hall, waiting to be conducted to the Oration Tent. It was tedious to sit there quietly, catching a glimpse of the passing parade and hearing the repeated cheers, waiting to be conducted to the tent. It was even more trying to watch invited guests wander forlornly about or sit in chilly corners, meekly wondering why the hospitalities of the town seemed to be extended only to the men.

For an hour Louisa waited with the ladies until the sound of martial music so excited them that with one accord they moved down to the steps below to watch the procession, standing like a flock of feminine Casabiancas, freezing instead of burning at their posts. Under flags and streamers the pageant marched down Main Street, the United States Marine Band of Washington conspicuous in scarlet uniforms, the bay horses prancing by, drawing a barouche occupied by His Excellency, Ulysses S. Grant, president of the United States. Just as the procession had marched by the Town Hall, Louisa heard an agitated gentleman with a rosette in his buttonhole give the brief command, "Ladies, cross the Common and wait for your escort." To the Common she walked, while the granddaughter of Dr. Ripley, who had watched the fight from the Old Manse, kept up the spirits of the ladies who rallied round her little flag. Finally, when they could bear to wait no longer, they reefed their veils, kilted up their skirts, locked arms, and with one accord charged over the red bridge, up the hill, and into the tented field, disheveled but dauntless.

The great tent had been pitched for the festivities, but finding no room except on a corner of the platform, Louisa, emboldened by a smile from Senator Wilson, a nod from Representative May, and a pensive stare from Orator Curtis, inquired whether a few ladies might occupy that spot until seats could be found for them. Brusquely she was informed that the platform had been reserved for gentlemen; and even though the grandmother of Boston waited in the ranks, not a seat was offered to her or the admiring pilgrims who had come to the Mecca of the mind. On the extreme edge of an unplaned board they at last found room, and, perched there like a flock of tempest-tossed pigeons, enjoyed the privilege of reposing among the sacred boots of the Gamaliels at whose feet they sat.

At length the Reverend Grindall Reynolds opened the meeting with prayer, and Mr. Emerson rose to unveil Daniel French's bronze Minuteman and address the assemblage. From her board Louisa heard, in the bitter teeth of the April wind, James Russell Lowell's ode to a freedom

Not to be courted in play,
Not to be kept without pain. . . .

In the midst of the reading, the gods appeared to take sides with the ladies of Concord, for a Centennial breakdown caused seats to fall, tables to totter, and platforms to collapse. After Judge Hoar had bidden the guests have no fear, since Middlesex County was underneath them, he exhibited the sword carried by Isaac Davis at the North Bridge, and George Curtis arose to deliver his oration.

The festivities culminated in a ball in the Agricultural Hall, which had been heated for the occasion and lighted with gas. Louisa entered, seeing the trophies, the shields, the flags, and the rosettes of bunting looped and festooned along the cornices. Everywhere she saw the flash of bayonets or swords, while the Marine Band struck up and the deserted damsels of the morning found themselves the queens of the evening. Now ushers and marshals and escorts were not lacking for ladies who seemed to have put on the vigor of their grandmothers along with the old brocades that became them so well. Until four in the morning the dances continued, ending a celebration which in Louisa's eyes had been centered too much upon the past and too little upon the future. In Concord's desire to exalt the heroes of old, the village had forgotten the heroines of the present. In spite of Concord and its cherishing of glories that had passed, the future would evoke another protest that would in turn be heard round the world.

Louisa herself would sound a note in that protest, sending to *The Woman's Journal* her own account of "Woman's Part in the Concord Celebration," an account which would include certain items that the newspapers failed to report in their praise of the day. She would never be too preoccupied with affairs of the present to forget the necessity of sounding a clarion call for the future. In Concord itself there might be work for Louisa to do. The village had, in certain ways, struggled to come alive from its long sleep. The women suffragists had held a convention there in which Lucy Stone had declared that if she were an inhabitant of Concord, she would let her house be sold over her head before she would pay one cent of a tax levied upon women who had not been permitted to share the Centennial honors, although they had not been deprived of the privilege of paying the expenses. Mother had written to the Judge of Probate, asking for an abatement of the taxes for the year, demanding that either taxation be suspended or the exclusiveness which surrounded the ballot box broken down. A breath of new life seemed to blow over the groves and meadows of the village.

May especially throve in Concord's newness. She was a judge on the art committee of the Middlesex Agricultural Society, ready to offer an expert opinion of the waxworks, paintings, and drawings submitted at the exhibition. Louisa herself was less occupied than this sister who was sketching watercolors of Hawthorne's Tower for Mrs. Conway, planning a bust of Father, or teaching in Concord's Art Center. While May gathered her drawing materials together and planned to sketch the Bridge and Minuteman, Louisa determined to leave Concord for the Woman's Congress at Syracuse.

In October she arrived at the home of Mrs. Charles de Berard Mills, and in her gray suit and small black hat walked with her hostess to the Wieting Opera House. Maria Mitchell rose to open the meeting with a silent prayer and then addressed the assemblage, declaring that they met in the hope that by discussing plans for future work all women might be better, nobler, and happier. From all corners of the East the speakers had come to deliver their message to a world of waiting women. Louisa listened to them all, to the talks on art culture, or science in the kitchen, or the aesthetics of dress. No woman's congress would have been complete without Mrs. Howe's recitation of "The Battle Hymn," and Louisa responded to the fire and intensity of a voice that had been raised in a bloody war and was raised again in woman's bloodless revolution.

Nor, it appeared, would any woman's congress be complete without a token of respect offered to Louisa M. Alcott. No sooner had the papers announced her presence than a great commotion had begun among the young people, who insisted upon seeing her and dispatched a note to the president to invite Miss Alcott to sit upon the platform. For the Vassar girls she had consented to revolve slowly, but no amount of persuasion could induce Louisa to place herself on exhibition now. Nonetheless, at the rear of the stage she found the eager girls crowding the wings, clamoring for autographs, asking questions, and examining her through lorgnettes. One energetic woman dashed through the crowd to grasp her hand, exclaiming, "If you ever come to Oshkosh, your feet will not be allowed to touch the ground: you will be borne in the arms of the people!" Although Louisa determined never to venture to that western Mecca, she did allow Mrs. Livermore to introduce her to the congress, and graciously received the ovation that followed, as well as the honor of membership in the National Congress of the Women of the United States.

She had reached, she knew, a plateau in life, where she must pause, take account of the past, and rally her forces for the future. Roberts Brothers had published *Eight Cousins; or, The Aunt-Hill*, with the preface of an author who had promised to make amends for any shortcomings in her story in a sequel which would attempt to show the "Rose in Bloom." Before she fulfilled that promise, she would wander on to New York, spending the winter there, a lion among the lions of the metropolis. Dio Lewis had sold the Bellevue and gone to California with his wife, but Louisa recalled his interest in Eli Miller, whose work he had endorsed, and who offered at his hotel on Twenty-sixth Street a combination of single rooms, first-class board, moderate prices, and Turkish baths. There she would rest or indulge in the pleasant excitements of the city.

Although the niche she occupied was no larger than when *Little Women* had first carved it out for her, she had maintained her position in it, proving to herself as well as to the world that her success would be long-lived. In countless stories she had, as Henry James had said of Uncle Alec, ridden atilt at the shams of life. After the many years in which she had, through scores of tales and several full-length books, put to the test her Midas touch and found it still unfailing, she would savor the rewards of her labors. The seeds of her garden had been planted many lives ago by a child who had taken notes in Concord. In New York a stately lady would be ready to gather the full-blown harvest now that the season for reaping had come.

CHAPTER 13

Dr. Miller's Bath Hotel

A mong the yellow and red brick houses of West Twenty-sixth Street, where dentists and physicians flourished, Louisa walked, stopping before the Bath Hotel at number 39. Dr. Eli Peck Miller's establishment, she had been assured, was in the center of the city, near Madison Square, convenient to the horsecars and near the retail dry goods stores. For $2.50 a day she could enjoy a pleasant room, excellent table, and quiet, homelike atmosphere. In addition, at the adjoining number 41, Dr. Miller offered all the advantages of his New Hygienic Institution and Turkish Bath.

The proprietor was quick to inform his new boarder of the merits of his Turkish, electric, and Roman baths. As the author of *How to Bathe, Dyspepsia,* and *Vital Force: How Wasted and How Preserved,* Dr. Miller had qualified himself to offer to Louisa not only the practical advantages of his Hygienic Institution, but all the gratuitous advice that she could digest. Disease, he assured her, might be avoided. Suffering was simply the result of sin. Coffee, spices, pickles, tea, tobacco, and even strong milk were to be abhorred, for food exerted an undeniable influence upon the passions and vices of human beings.

At the Bath Hotel Louisa found that she received not only a diet based on Mrs. Jones's *Hygienic Cook Book,* but Dr. Miller's treatment as well. She could indulge in the sponge or towel bath, the rubbing wet sheet, the hot air or vapor bath, the electric, Russian, or Turkish bath. Kidder's Electro-Magnetic Battery, the lifting cure, and the Swedish Movement Cure were also recommended, and Louisa proceeded to take full advantage of the New Hygienic Institution by enjoying Dr. Miller's Improved Turkish Bath. From the Frigidarium to the Tepidarium she progressed, advancing to the Suditorium and Shampooing-Room, where she reclined upon a marble couch to receive the benefit of the friction glove. Dr. Miller's Turkish bath would fit Miss Alcott for the press of activity that doubtless awaited the celebrated author during her stay in the city.

At the moment, Louisa was more interested in the companionship of her fellow boarders, the agreeable Mr. Ames, who discoursed over his wholesome bread about Goethe and Hegel, or exchanged remarks about his annual pilgrimages to Concord with Louisa's impious witticisms about the sacred sandbank. The companionship of Sallie Holley was even more enjoyable to her, for the blue-eyed woman, with her bonnet demurely tied, had many a tale to tell of her life's crusade for slave women and the freedmen's school she had established for Negro children in Virginia. If all New York were as interesting as number 39 West Twenty-sixth Street, Louisa felt assured that her stay would be as varied as it might be fruitful.

From the quiet street of physicians Louisa embarked upon her journeys of exploration, leaving the signs of Dr. Freeman Bumstead and Dr. Joseph Crane for signs more colorful and more exciting. She who had seen the boulevards of Paris and of London rejoiced in the changing aspects of still another city. Each avenue, each street was for Louisa a kaleidoscope of colors all varying from one another but all brilliant. From Madison Square with its lawn and fountains to the Bowery, where Tony Pastor's opera house vied with the delights of lager beer; from Greenwich Village, where vendors hawked their baked potatoes and chimney sweeps patrolled the streets, to Union Square with its thriving colony of English sparrows, Louisa wandered, observing every changing aspect of a city of contrasts. For her the gas lamps of Broadway were lighted to glow upon carriages and wagons, carts and omnibuses, jewels, silks, satins, and laces, gentlemen in broadcloth, and beggars in squalid rags.

Louisa walked on, hearing the strolling Italian violinists, listening to the baker's boy cry his "Tea ruk," to the chimney sweep salute the early morning with his "Sweep O!" New York was loud with dramatic noises for the lady of the Concord amateur troupe. After the quiet of the village, the rumble of streetcars and lumbering stages, hacks, and carriages made exciting music. Never had Widow Pottle seen such taverns as now she passed upon her rambles. Never, in her shopping expeditions in Boston or in London or in Paris, had she seen such marble palaces as those that graced the ladies' mile.

Louisa was not allowed to wander long alone. At the Bath Hotel on Twenty-sixth Street Miss Alcott's admirers called to pay their respects. For *the* Miss Alcott, Dr. J. G. Holland gave a dinner at his Park Avenue home—the tall, large-framed ascetic eager to discourse with Louisa about his editorship of *Scribner's Monthly*, his teetotalism, and his antipathy to Walt Whitman. To all her hosts Louisa listened, amused by their beliefs if she did not entirely share them. To all their invitations she gave a ready acceptance. From the Frigidarium and Suditorium she emerged to attend ladies' day at the Lotos Club or a performance by Booth at the New Fifth Avenue Theatre. For her, John B. Gough mounted the platform to repeat his lecture on blunders. Louisa's calendar was filled with engagements that reflected the social life of all New York.

After she had heard Gough, she attended the Fraternity Club meeting to which her cousin, Octavius B. Frothingham, had invited her. At his home on Thirty-sixth Street she was received by her elegant host, who chatted on with quiet humor, his satirical, scholarly eyes flashing, his mobile mouth compressed as he cast aspersions upon woman suffrage or reminisced about Father's soliloquizing "Conversations." Mrs. Stedman was eager to talk about her husband's trip to the Caribbean, while Oliver Johnson discussed *The Christian Union*, of which he was managing editor. Louisa was pleased to meet one who had been a wheel horse in every humanitarian movement for almost half a century, and enjoyed his talk of Harriet Tubman, whom he had known in his antislavery office. No less interesting to her was the lecturer-author, Abby Sage Richardson, who had at her fingertips the history of English literature from the conquest of Britain to the death of Walter Scott, and whose manner had not diminished in queenliness since the tragedy that had attended her first husband's murder of the lover whom she had married on his deathbed. Less sensational, but no less delightful, were the confidences shared with Louisa by Mrs. Mary Mapes Dodge about the four Mapes girls, who had dramatized their childhood readings as the four March girls had done. It was with some reluctance that Louisa turned from her editor's remarks to the Fraternity Club's discussion of conformity and nonconformity, but she appreciated the lively debate, and when she herself was called upon, piped up for nonconformity and received several hearty pats on the head for her contribution. The humble Concord worm had turned indeed, to feed upon gracious admiration from every hand.

Louisa forgot the struggle between conformity and nonconformity when she saw from her window at the Bath Hotel streets alive with young people dressed as Indians, blowing tin horns and swinging watchmen's rattles to celebrate Thanksgiving. The day was perfect for a drive with Sallie Holley through Central Park, and the ladies happily mounted the hackney coach at Fifty-ninth Street to wander past the Carousel and Marble Arch and the Casino and the Maze. As Miss Holley chatted about her freedmen or her school, Louisa enjoyed the Mall and the Ramble, watching the dust rise upon the carriage road as the leaders of the bulls and bears on exchange galloped past the farmer's rockaway or the landau of the demimonde. Upon the Winter Drive planted with evergreens, the ladies of the Bath Hotel spun by, one at least rejoicing deeply in the scenic background and dramatis personae of the contrasting stage that was New York.

The stage was transformed later in the day from Central Park's Winter Drive to the home of Professor and Mrs. Botta at West Thirty-seventh Street, where Louisa had been invited for

Thanksgiving dinner. In the Botta parlors she delighted in a richer background than any she had yet seen in the city, in the cabinets filled with books, in the Venetian glass and mosaics, and in the statues and shields. Quietly, with the voice of a clouded contralto, her large, soft eyes glowing, Mrs. Botta entertained Louisa with remarks upon Ristori or Ole Bull, on her own sculpture, or Froude's essay on Spinoza which she had recently read. Here, indeed, Louisa found, as Mr. Emerson had found, the house of the expanding doors, where a Ponca chief might be entertained side by side with William Cullen Bryant or Bayard Taylor. Nor was Professor Botta less interesting than his wife, for Louisa enjoyed the conversation of the long-haired, handsome Italian who had come from Turin to teach at the University of the City of New York, and who could discourse with equal skill upon modern philosophy or the cause of the Negro.

Music followed dinner, and with it came talk of music, of Leopold Damrosch's Oratorio Society and the performance of *Les Huguenots* by Wachtel and Madame Pappenheim. When a display of pictures followed the music, Professor Botta forgot his allegiance to philosophy and Italian literature to converse with Miss Alcott about the Art Students' League. Louisa enjoyed her dish of gossip with Anne Lynch Botta, adding her own comments when the talk veered to New York's greenrooms, to John Gilbert's performance at Wallack's Theatre and Keene's appearance in *Oliver Twist*.

It was a delightful home, this house on Thirty-seventh Street, where music vied with Thanksgiving turkey for the pleasure of the guests, where conversation was a headier draught than champagne, and where Louisa found curtain after curtain raised upon the varied life of the city. Society here differed from that of London or Boston, but Louisa could take her place in it as though she had been bred upon Madison Square instead of the Lexington Road. Below the pictures and plaster casts in Mrs. Botta's home she sat, observing, taking notes, listening, and sharing in the wide gamut of conversation that opened to her door upon door in this house of the expanding doors.

From the door of the Orchard House came news that seemed tame by contrast with the sparkling talk at the Bottas'. The boys were attending school at the Wayside, where Freddy had begun Latin besides his French and singing. Anna was at Apple Slump with May, who kept house and taught once a week in Boston in addition to offering her services twice a week at Concord's Drawing School and galloping about the village on Rosa's back. Mother spent her days quietly, writing her diary, sewing, or reading, while Father eagerly discussed plans for a carriage and a barn. On the twenty-sixth Louisa wrote home so that Father would have a birthday letter from his loving "forty-three," and that all the Orchard House could share her visits to the Fraternity Club or to the Bottas', could drive with her in Central Park, and could hear John Gough on blunders.

The spontaneous eloquence of Charles Bradlaugh, teetotaler, "Iconoclast," and author of *A Plea for Atheism*, was exhibited for Louisa by a speaker who rivaled John Gough in his volcanic sincerity. The curtain rose for the celebrated author upon Joseph Proctor's *Rob Roy* at Wood's Museum, upon Clara Morris's *New Leah*, or upon George Fox's *Humpty Dumpty* at Booth's Theatre. For her the streets of the city were arrayed in somber colors as the flags were lowered to half-mast for Vice President Wilson's funeral cortege. The bustling avenues of New York were varied on Sunday by the fashionables on promenade or the churchgoers strolling past closed stores, along thoroughfares deserted by the stages.

Louisa, too, answered the peal of the church bells by joining Frothingham's congregation in the Masonic Temple on Twenty-third Street. After the fire of Parker, she found it interesting to hear the lucid expositions of one who tried to reach the heart through the brain and poured forth a stream of thoughts upon the rational faith that reads all Bibles. Listening to the words of Octavius Brooks Frothingham, she might almost believe that the age of faith was over and the age of knowledge had come.

Louisa, who delighted in dramatic contrasts, found the antithesis to the elegant Frothingham in the preaching of Henry

Whitney Bellows, brilliant and mobile as a dragonfly, and enjoyed her visit to the Church of All Souls, where the minister magnetized her along with his thronging congregation. With ringing voice he poured forth his convictions in the church of the holy zebra, the beefsteak church that contrasted so vividly with Frothingham's church of the unchurched.

From the New Hygienic Institution supervised by Dr. Miller, Louisa walked forth to find all curtains raised for her, all doors opened. For her, Mrs. Abby Sage Richardson discoursed upon Shakespeare; for her, Miss Mary L. Booth, author of a *History of the City of New York*, entertained Mrs. Stedman, Mrs. Dodge, and Mrs. Moulton at her Madison Avenue residence. For Louisa the doors of Sorosis were opened wide to welcome a famous sister into the club of New York women, where Mrs. Croly presided, honoring the literary representative from Boston.

Having seen the glitter of New York society, Louisa wished to observe the life of the underlings, and to pursue contrast to its ultimate end visited with deep interest the Newsboys' Lodging House on Duane Street. She was conducted by Mrs. O'Connor, the matron, through the dining room and kitchen, the bathrooms and schoolroom, and the laundry and gymnasium. Before her, 180 boys disported themselves while she took notes on all—on the six-year-old locking up his small shoes and ragged jacket as if they were the most precious treasures, on the thrifty lad who was putting his pennies into the savings bank, and on the children who laughed as Miss Alcott dubbed a black kitten "bootblack" and a noisy gray a "newsboy."

To Fred and Johnny, Louisa sent a full description of her visit to the Newsboys' Lodging House and, after hearing Moncure Daniel Conway's lectures, decided to plunge from the turbulence of New York life into the calm of philosophy. For a quiet December week she rested in her room at the Bath Hotel, reading Mr. Ames's copy of the second part of *Faust*. She admired Goethe anew, forgiving him his fifteen sweethearts since they had helped him unconsciously in his work. She, too, believed, as Goethe had, in the worth of experience, and took time now to muse upon the many experiences that had been hers since she had come to New York.

Still the invitations poured in, and Louisa knew that she could not for long persist in her seclusion. The invitations themselves were marked by contrast, bidding Louisa visit the theater and discuss educational affairs with Miss Brackett, or requesting her company on a tour of Randall's Island with Mrs. Abby Hopper Gibbons. To the latter she responded readily, eager to behold still another facet in that iridescent jewel that was New York.

After the bells of Trinity had rung in Christmas Day, Louisa left the Bath Hotel for Pier 22, where she took the boat to Randall's Island, finding Mr. and Mrs. Gibbons already on board. In Mrs. Gibbons especially she took a deep interest, for the little old lady in the black Quaker bonnet and plain suit had not only established the Isaac T. Hopper Home, but had faithfully carried out her self-appointed mission to spread happiness among the waifs and strays of Randall's Island. With the Georgetown nurse she could compare many a note, for Mrs. Gibbons had worked at the Patent Office Hospital in Washington during the war, and had accompanied the soldiers in open boxcars when Fredericksburg had been evacuated.

Now Louisa followed the gray-haired couple and boarded a ramshackle hack to drive to the chapel, where a boy had raced before them crying joyfully, "She's come. She's come." For more than thirty years the little poke bonnet had spent her Christmas Day at Randall's Island, and now Louisa was at her side on the platform draped in flags. After the children's songs she was amused to hear one bright lad in gray with a red band on his arm rise up to deliver a poem by Louisa M. Alcott entitled "Merry Christmas," lines which she had given to William Gill for publication in his *Horn of Plenty.*

> *Rosy feet upon the threshold,*
> *Eager faces peeping through,*
> *With the first red ray of sunshine,*
> *Chanting cherubs come in view:*

Mistletoe and gleaming holly,
Symbols of a blessed day,
In their chubby hands they carry,
Streaming all along the way.

Few enough were the symbols of the blessed day at the hospital, where the visitors drove to dispense dolls and candy among the crippled and deformed children. Hobbling on crutches, the half-blind babies groping, the sick ones beckoning, all cried for the gifts in that large brick building where Louisa found still another curtain raised, not upon a comic drama, but upon a tragedy such as the Hillside troupe had never dreamed of.

From the hospital they wandered on to the idiot house, to the hundred half-grown girls and boys ranged on either side the long hall, cheering Mrs. Gibbons as she hurried in waving her handkerchief and a handful of gay bead necklaces. The dolls were unpacked, while the blocks and ninepins were accepted with delight, and a dwarf of thirty-five received with a vacant smile a Noah's ark and a squeaking lion. Louisa watched the sights that would haunt her for a long time to come, watched the boys suck candy or stare at a toy cow, and smiled as an array of gay toys waved after the ladies bountiful.

At four, the visitors left the island, and Louisa, returning to Twenty-sixth Street, was forced to content herself with an apple for her Christmas dinner. Nonetheless, it had been a memorable day, different from any Christmas she had spent before, for the only gifts she had were those she had given away. To her family she wrote, describing the scenes that she had observed. For *The Youth's Companion* she planned another article, unlike any she had yet sent to Daniel Ford, an article that she would entitle "A New Way to Spend Christmas."

A few days later, Louisa joined Mrs. Gibbons again to behold scenes even more haunting at New York's Tombs. Every Wednesday the good Quaker devoted to that grim pile which was the city's Bridewell; and Louisa walked briskly along the Bowery to the prison, seeing the constant stream of people presenting orders and receiving passes, clinging close to the grating, or waiting patiently to be admitted. Officials came and went—clerks with books, policemen with fresh offenders, and keepers with jingling keys—until at last Mrs. Gibbons appeared with the passes and, clutching the yellow ticket marked "Visitor," Louisa followed her through the iron gate. Here was a scene more tragic than that of any hospital, a scene whose properties were bolts and bars, iron doors and grated windows, sunken walls and dampness. She walked along the narrow passage, looking up at the tiers of cells, peeping in at each whitewashed room with its occupant asleep or disconsolate, smoking or reading or pacing to and fro. A pretty girl kissed her lover between the bars. A soldierly figure in a faded blue coat sat on a bench outside his cell and returned the salute of Nurse L. M. Alcott.

From the men's prison Louisa wandered on to the women's quarters, conducted by Matron Flora Foster to an empty cell which she entered for a moment to offer a prayer for all who might later enter that narrow white tomb. Never had she been so glad to see the curtain lowered on a scene. Never had liberty seemed so sweet or sun so bright as after she had left the gloomy portal of Center Street. "A Visit to the Tombs" would provide as interesting an article for *The Youth's Companion* as her observations at Randall's Island. Meanwhile, the curtain would rise on brighter scenes as the old year of 1875 gave way to 1876.

From her window on Twenty-sixth Street Louisa could see on New Year's Day the gentlemen driving from one house to another to pay their annual respects in the drawing rooms of New York. Since she had promised to help Mrs. Croly receive, she donned her high-necked, long-sleeved black silk to journey to East Thirty-eighth Street. Louisa entered the brownstone house and was welcomed by her hostess into the long back parlor, where she was offered the large red velvet armchair reserved for guests of honor. Jane Cunningham Croly was no less delightful in the drawing room than in the president's chair at Sorosis, and Louisa was eager to hear of her editorial work on *Demorest's Magazine* and *Godey's*, of the frivolities and wrongs against which she launched the full force of her volcanic nature. From group to group she moved about, her low English voice and smile greeting each of the two hundred gentlemen who thronged the drawing room, carrying a tray with glasses of punch for Mr. Stoddard, Robert Roosevelt, or Mr. A. P. Burbank. Between the conversation about William Tweed's escape from the Ludlow Street jail or Mr. Bergh's recently incorporated Society for the Prevention of Cruelty to Children, Louisa took time to chat with little Vida Croly, who sat upon her lap and was promised a copy of *Eight Cousins*. From noon till midnight the gentlemen streamed into the room where the shades were drawn and the lights and candles glowed. Here, in the drawing room of East Thirty-eighth Street, a play unfolded with a dramatis personae of gentlemen in yellow kids and a blue-eyed hostess in evening dress. It was almost impossible for Louisa to realize that the same city that boasted salons with glimmering candles and punch bowls held also the grim pile called the Tombs and the tragic island in the East River.

After New Year's, Louisa left New York for a short visit to Philadelphia, where her cousin Joseph May was to be installed in Dr. Furness's pulpit. The dullness of the city of brotherly love was alleviated somewhat by the bustle of workmen erecting pavilions for the Centennial celebration of 1876. Besides attending the services at the Unitarian church where Uncle Sam May's son Joseph was inducted as pastor, Louisa took time to give a talk at the Germantown Academy and acknowledge the cheers of the boys as she passed up School House Lane. In the gray stone buildings of Reuben Haines's home, Wyck, she was welcomed, to see where she had once toddled as a two-year-old. Down the road, to the spot where she had been born, she walked, but the sight aroused no thrill of response in her. This was a past she knew only from Father's reminiscences; at Germantown no child had taken notes. Philadelphia was dimmer than a dream. Memory had begun in Boston.

Before Louisa returned home, she determined to hear Henry Ward Beecher preach to his congregation, to see how the man who had held slave auctions in Plymouth Church to buy the Negroes their freedom had changed after the Tilton Trial and the wages of sin, which for him had amounted to six hundred dollars a lecture. With the throngs she entered the Brooklyn church of the frolicsome transcendentalist, while the minister, arrayed in a black frock coat with a Byronic collar, mounted the platform to preach the love of Christ and the need of regeneration. There was something about this orator as he sat astride the Behemoth that was too athletic, too pugilistic, and too strenuous for a church. Louisa, remembering Theodore Parker, disliked this consecrated farmer, who appeared more like an expressman rushing for the cars than like the pastor of a Brooklyn church.

The last of the city's curtains had been raised for Miss Alcott. The latest reports from the Orchard House indicated that Father had left his readings in Wordsworth for readings in Mrs. Glover's *Science and Health*, which its author had sent him, and planned to visit the metaphysical healer in Lynn. Louisa was interested in learning more of a woman whose purpose was to cure bodily diseases by spiritual power over the minds of her patients. Perhaps such methods might be as fruitful as Dr. Eli Peck Miller's friction gloves and magnetic batteries. With all the ailing world she would search for a panacea so that she could practice her gospel of work undisturbed by the ills that flesh was heir to.

Even if work was impossible in New York, in its way the city had provided its panaceas, more effective than the Frigidarium and Suditorium of the New Hygienic Institution. On the train to Boston, on January 21, Louisa realized that she had profited deeply from her experience. She had sat in a theater, seeing curtain after curtain raised—upon a gay salon, a pulpit, a prison, or a thronging avenue. The dramatis personae of a new society had made their entrances and exits, and she, too, had left her seat to walk before the footlights of a revolving stage. For her the gentles had played out the play in a setting more brilliant than Boston, more varied than London, and more substantial than Paris. Had not Dickens said of today and yesterday that we are either going to the play or coming from it? Upon the play called New York, the curtain had fallen. But surely in the years to come other curtains would rise for the lady from Concord, before the last one fell upon a darkened stage.

🐚🐚

CHAPTER 14

The Gray Town

From Madison Square to the Lexington Road, Louisa returned. Father, looking forward to rounding out his hundredth birthday and retiring with the century, eagerly spoke to her of the new Christian Science, declaring that the attempt at reconciling science and religion and matter and mind was a significant feature of the times. Happily preparing to visit Mrs. Glover at Lynn, he had little need of his daughter. Nor did Mother depend too greatly on her presence, as she sat wrapped in her Paisley shawl, her lace cap on her head, sewing, reading her favorite Johnson, and sending her yearly barrel of comforts to the freedmen. After May had heard details of the sparkle of New York society, she, too, was content to return to her own interests, to the Saturday Club which she had recently founded in Concord, and to Rosa, on whom she rode over the countryside. The family had settled into its own channels, leaving Louisa free to work.

She had gathered material for stories from her visit to New York, and the time had come to capture thought once again in a net of words. To supply Daniel Ford with articles for *The Youth's Companion*, Louisa completed her account of Randall's Island in "A New Way to Spend Christmas," also dispatching to his offices "A Visit to the Tombs." Thomas Niles had requested a Centennial story, and at the Centennial ball at the Music Hall, Louisa gathered enough ideas to write "Independence," her tale of 'seventy-six. Together with "Silver Pitchers" and other tales, the story would make a catchpenny book for Roberts Brothers. Although *Silver Pitchers* appeared, however, it did not satisfy the requests for fresh stories that continued to flow in from Mrs. Dodge, from Thomas Niles, and from clamoring newspapers and magazines.

It was almost impossible to supply those requests in Concord. There were too many Paul Prys haunting the Lexington Road, too many schools that appeared without warning for a view of the Concord author. Louisa was not interested in the interminable gossip of the lion hunters. It had been more fruitful to sit in her room writing a letter to *The Woman's Journal* with three cheers for the girls of 1876 than to talk with their garrulous representatives. Reprints, she knew, could not satisfy demands for fresh stories, and Thomas Niles would not be content until his celebrated author wrote her promised sequel to *Eight Cousins.*

Again from the mine of memory she found the beads to string upon the thin thread of her plot. As summer ripened over the Lexington Road, Louisa left her admirers to remember, and, in remembering, to tell the tale of a "Rose in Bloom." The simple gifts that four sisters had given one another, the berries strung on grass, the acorns, cones, and feathers—these gifts Mac could present to Dulce. Like Louisa, Rose would take to house cleaning to ease her mind. Like Mother, and like Lizzie, too, Uncle Alec could catch a fever from his "poor emigrants." From May, Rose would learn the art of giving casts and easels to all eager students. From Mrs. Croly's parlors on New Year's Day Louisa gathered enough details to write of the succession of gloves and black coats that flowed in and out of the Campbell mansion.

To the beads that glittered from memory, Louisa added the beads that sparkled from the life around her, hoping that they would shine brightly for readers who might find the moral beneath the sugar coating. The bead of temperance must be strung upon her thread, Rose exacting the pledge from wild Prince Charlie on New Year's, Mac knocking the glass from Steve's hand, and Charlie finding his downfall and his death in the punch bowl. The bead of woman's rights must be inserted so that

Phebe and Rose could prove their ability to live and learn as well as to love and be loved. Philanthropy, too, was a bead to be strung upon Rose's sparkling necklace, for her creator had learned from Mother that the wisest charity was that which helped the poor to help themselves. Upon the thin thread, the "do's" and "do not's" of Louisa's decalogue shone forth.

From her characters more than her plot, Louisa spun the thread on which to string the beads. Upon Mac especially she lavished her attention—Mac who, like Father, believed that the best inspiration came from the beneficent life of a sweet and noble woman. Behind his glasses glowed a pair of understanding eyes. In his mind developed Louisa's own philosophy of life and literature: first live, then write. He would study love as well as medicine, and so be ready for his great experience when it came, winning a Rose who bloomed with her gift of living for others.

Tending Mother and watching the summer wave its asparagus plumes along the Lexington Road, Louisa wrote on, as the poles of grapevines grew up in ranks upon the hill and loads of hay went jolting along the highway between hill and meadow. From the books she had read she extracted gems for her stringing, pearls from Thoreau's *Week*, rubies from Emerson's "Self-Reliance," along with semiprecious stones from Dickens's *Nicholas Nickleby*. From her own sense of humor Louisa cut a gem in the portrayal of Aunt Myra, the capital patient who never died and never got well. Above the eastern hilltop the lights of morning glanced upon the orchard, as Louisa completed her summer book.

Not Thomas Niles alone, but the editors of the nation's magazines also, continued to send their requests for stories by Miss Alcott. The attempt to supply the perpetual demands was worthwhile, for Louisa's recompense was twofold. She would not merely receive over one thousand dollars, but enjoy the knowledge that even the English railway stalls were filled with her books. With the exception of Mother's uncertain health and the sadness that Louisa felt in seeing her feeble and broken in mind, all was well at the Orchard House. Between her pleasure in the Boston Museum of Fine Arts and her talk of the bustle or chignon, May was happier than ever, especially when she discussed the possibilities of going abroad again.

Although Mother's health seemed too precarious for her to leave the Orchard House in August, by September the family decided that May should have her well-deserved trip. She would go abroad alone, Anna remaining at Apple Slump during her absence, with Freddy and Johnny, the most remarkable boys of the Centennial year, attending school at the Wayside. Filled with courage and determination to accomplish great feats, May embarked on the *China* on September 9. Louisa watched with Father as she stood on the deck of the steamer in her long blue cloak, waving her handkerchief to them and smiling with wet eyes. The handkerchief waved until it was lost in the distance, until nothing was left of May but the ghost of a long blue cloak, nothing but the memory of a fair-haired woman bent upon high adventure.

Louisa returned to her manuscripts, taking time from *Rose in Bloom* to write a letter to Alf Whitman, whose picture had arrived in the form of an unrecognizable gentleman, reminding Louisa that she, too, had changed.

> . . . I am now as I tried to be in the play, Your fat old Sophy.

Yet there was little time to contemplate the ravages of the years. As soon as *Rose in Bloom* was ready for the press, the preface must be written with its hope that some amusement and a few helpful hints might be afforded to other roses getting ready to bloom. On the nineteenth of the month, Louisa took up her pen again to inscribe the slim journal with its marbled paper cover that she had given to Mother to use as her diary for 1876–77. Louisa watched as Mother opened the little book, dedicating the journal to May and recording upon its first page her arrival at Queenstown.

Mother's pen was seldom idle as it copied the long letters that arrived from her wandering daughter, remarks about the Scottish lady on board the *China* who had begged to see Louisa's picture, and notes about the praises of *the* Miss Alcott, whose fame reached over the seas and made a welcome for May everywhere. Mother lived vicariously now, following May with every letter that arrived.

Louisa realized that she, too, was living, more than ever before, in another, in the mother whose seventy-sixth birthday was celebrated on October 8. In Mother's room the gifts were presented after breakfast, along with the witty mottoes that Louisa had written, and good news arrived from May to fill Mother's cup of happiness to the brim. Later in the day, when Louisa attended the burial of Sophia Thoreau with Father, she could not help wondering how many years were left for Mother, how many gifts of fruit and flowers would be presented in the second-floor room after breakfast. Change and time and death would not be denied.

As *Rose in Bloom*, the fifth of Louisa's full-length juveniles, joined its predecessors on the bookshelf, its author, reaching her forty-fourth birthday, realized that she had changed indeed since she had walked to Washington Street to consult Thomas Niles about the publication of *Little Women*. The smiling mouth was firmer, the gray-blue eyes more thoughtful, and the figure far more stately than the girl of Hillside had dreamed possible. Change was the tale the mirror told.

Time, Louisa knew, was never gentle. No thread had been invented to knit together the unraveling skein of life. The old year would die and the new be born, for the pen that had flourished a Midas touch had never been granted the magic to stay time or check the flying hours.

As Freddy ushered in the year of 1877 by playing "America" on the piano, Louisa realized that the passing year had been, for her at least, beneficent. Even *The Catholic World* had praised *Silver Pitchers*, and *Harper's* had found the title story a capital temperance tale, quite different from the ordinary pattern of melodramatic misery. William Gill had printed "Merry Christmas" in his *Horn of Plenty of Home Poems and Home Pictures*, and the collection itself had been flatteringly dedicated "to all the Little Women and Little Men who have been made happy by 'Aunt Jo.' " The author of *Rose in Bloom* had reached the exalted state of finding her work issued not only in periodicals, but in the anthologies published on Washington Street.

Not Louisa only, but May, too, wore the laurels this year, for Müller of Paris had admired enthusiastically the passion and vigor of her full-length drawing of a Negro. Through her letters, Louisa continued to relive her own life abroad, following May as she walked along the Rue de Rivoli or danced with George Healy at a reception. She followed her sister closely when she read of May's meeting with Ladislas Wisniewski, who was living now in Paris with his mother, and who helped the artist in her search for bargains at the Palais Royal as he had once helped the author of *Hospital Sketches*. Louisa's past and May's present were inextricably entwined in the letters with the Paris postmark that flowed in at the post office on the Milldam.

While Mother read and reread May's notes, Louisa decided to spend a few weeks alone in Boston. It was not as *the* Miss Alcott, the "youth's companion," and the children's friend, that she returned to her room at the Bellevue, but as the ghost of the mysterious "A. M. Barnard," who was a little tired of providing moral pap for the young. The author of "V. V." and "A Marble Woman" longed to indulge again in "lurid" style and gorgeous fancies, throwing off the chain armor of propriety that had at once enslaved and liberated her. Not Louisa Alcott but "A. M. Barnard" had yielded to the delights of reading Mr. Ames's copy of *Faust* at Dr. Miller's Bath Hotel. The tale of a nineteenth-century Faust, a modern Mephistopheles, had been simmering in her mind since then. The No Name Series that Thomas Niles was sponsoring would give her an opportunity to write incognito a story dreamed by "A. M. Barnard's" ghost.

Goethe, and Hawthorne, too, had given her her theme—the motif of good contending with evil and of crime and the punishment consequent upon it. "A. M. Barnard" would give her her dramatis personae, adding to the gallery of Virginie Varens and Jitomar the pagan figure of Felix Canaris, the young Bacchus who sold his liberty and his love for fame. Against him would stand her modern Mephistopheles, Jasper Helwyze, the Sybarite who believed "in nothing invisible and divine," who sought the evil in mankind, and whose god was intellect. Olivia, the mellow beauty, and Gladys, the "white-souled," artless girl, would complete the cast of characters around whom "A. M. Barnard" could weave her anonymous tale.

In her room at the Bellevue, the contributor to *The Flag of Our Union* rose up from the past, bidding Jasper offer to Gladys hasheesh enclosed in a *bonbonnière* of tortoiseshell and silver, commanding her modern Mephistopheles to mesmerize the girl and violate the sanctity of a human soul. After the years of writing in straight, journalistic style for youthful readers, it was delightful to allow the lush words and exotic verbiage of "A. M. Barnard" to pour forth again as she wrote of

> Lustrous silks sultanas were to wear; . . . odorous woods and spices, . . . with fragrance never blown from Western hills; . . . skins mooned and barred with black upon the tawny velvet, that had lain in jungles, or glided with deathful stealthiness along the track of human feet.

Yet "A. M. Barnard" had not been quite so subtle as the anonymous author of *A Modern Mephistopheles*. Louisa's maturity would reveal itself in the admirable concealment of the denouement until the end, when Helwyze's authorship of Canaris's book was finally disclosed. A decade before, she never could have achieved the irony of the punishments that followed the crime. "A. M. Barnard" had never been endowed with sufficient wisdom to invent such penalties as these, in which Canaris lost his Gladys whom he loved too late, and Helwyze lost the intellect that had been his god.

After Anna and Mrs. Tilton had copied the manuscript so that the Paul Prys who assisted Thomas Niles would not recognize Louisa's handwriting, the author ventured to Washington Street to consult the publisher about her mysterious mission. In the corner, behind the green curtain, she sat with Thomas Niles, enjoy-

ing his remarks about the No Name writers who talked in whis-
pers of their anonymous tales, agreeing that her own volume
would appear in April as number 6 of the series.

From all but Mother and Anna, Louisa kept her secret when
she returned to the Orchard House. Bean's expressman, however,
seemed to know more than he said, for he grinned quite noticeably when he handed the author the daily parcel of proofs from
Washington Street. Mother would be proud of her daughter's latest creation, even though it differed so perceptibly from her other
books. Had she not insisted that Louisa's reputation as the best
writer for young people since Miss Edgeworth or Mrs. Barbauld
had been made for all time? Between her excitement about the
forthcoming publication of number 6 and her delight in May's letters, Mother looked forward more eagerly than she had thought
possible to the gifts that the god of 1877 would shower upon the
Orchard House.

While Father wrote to Mrs. Glover, now Mrs. Eddy, of Lynn,
and Anna quietly celebrated her birthday, Louisa discussed the
possibilities of buying the Thoreau house on Main Street for her
and the boys. The $4,000 sent from the Vermont and Eastern
Railroads must be invested; to the inheritance that Anna had
received from John, Louisa would add $2,500 so that her sister
could finally have a home of her own. Meanwhile, before number
6 appeared from the press, letters from May told that her still life
of "Fruit and Bottles" had been admitted in the Salon exhibition
at the Palais des Champs-Élysées.

In April, number 6 of the No Name Series was published.
Mother was proud of the completed volume, declaring it perfect,
wishing only that it bore Louisa's name, and assuring Father, who
did not know the title of his daughter's No Name contribution,
that it surpassed its predecessors in power and brilliancy. The
speculations of the public interested Louisa more deeply. With no
attempt to identify the writer, *The New-York Evening Post* simply
inquired, "Who is the author?" and characterized number 6 as in
some respects the best piece of work which the scheme had
brought forth. While the majority of readers attributed the book

either to Julian Hawthorne or to Harriet Prescott Spofford, Louisa waited for the periodical reviews, enjoying the excitement of her incognito.

Quietly the spring came on, Louisa keeping house and caring for Mother, who seemed, in spite of her many joys, to grow more feeble as the days passed. Early in the morning they drove together to the woods, for Mother took great comfort in her basket wagon and Louisa was happy to gather flowers for her in the fields, another nosegay of remembrance of a Concord spring. After Father's *Table-Talk* had been published, Louisa journeyed to Boston with him to complete the purchase of the Thoreau house for Anna, adding the promised $2,500 to Anna's fund to make up the $4,500 demanded for the dwelling and garden lot.

Still the gifts were showered upon the Orchard House as May slipped into June, for the letters from the wandering artist brought happy reports of her plans. With the aid of two good houseworkers, Louisa helped Anna prepare for the gift that the spring had brought to her, the new home to which she moved in July. The boys' bookcase was removed from Father's study, and May's picture, with Turner's portrait over it, was hung upon the wall beside the apostles. Yet this last of the gifts of spring had caused a deeper change than the rearrangement of a table or a bookcase. Anna took more with her than the ornaments of the Orchard House when she took the boys to Main Street. Their place was not easily filled.

Wearied from the labors of helping Anna move to the Thoreau house, Louisa was forced to rest for several weeks in July, allowing her next tale to simmer in her mind while she enjoyed the reviews of her last. *The Atlantic Monthly* had no doubt that Julian Hawthorne was the author of *A Modern Mephistopheles*. The book was a remarkable one, instinct with ability; the author had managed the variation upon Goethe's theme with much good sense. Of all the reviews, Louisa delighted most in the one issued in *Godey's*, where she read the critic's judgment that the book had been written by a young person, probably a girl, with much literary facility and fluency, who with advancing years and a larger experience might make her mark.

While a new book was sketching itself in Louisa's mind, she had less interest, however, in one that had been completed. The hero of her next serial for Mrs. Dodge would be no Jasper Helwyze, no Rose in Bloom, but a performing poodle with a tassel at the end of his tail and ruffles round his ankles. In order to get hints for the embellishment of her Sancho, Louisa visited Van Amburgh's Menagerie to gather suggestions from Hannibal, Jr., or King and Queen Lori Grandi. Gradually, the vague plot crystallized. Into the book she would pour all the sunshine that failed to glow upon the Orchard House now that Mother's illness had increased. It was possible to forget the anxieties of the present in plumbing the depths of the past. From the past "My Kingdom" could be recovered to appear once again in print. The archery fever would be substituted for the croquet and gymnastic epidemics of Concord. As Thoreau had found arrowheads by the river, Bab could discover them now. The girls of Hillside would offer suggestions for a grand theatrical combination with the potato pantomime of Chingery Wangery Chan followed by Bluebeard and a tragedy in three tableaux. May's Rosa would be transformed into Celia's Lita to teach Ben good horsemanship. In the tale all the prancing steeds and clowns and tumblers and the strong men and animals of Van Amburgh's New Great Golden Menagerie would perform their feats.

Mother's condition could momentarily be forgotten as Louisa sketched her hero, giving him a tail that quivered with excitement and a red nose that cocked up impudently, giving him eyes that gazed pensively up at a sparrow after he had bolted a tart, eyes that expressed the most deprecating "Pooh" as he observed the antics of Van Amburgh's black spaniel. Sancho would come into his own, a waltzing, parading poodle with a tassel at the end of his tail, with ruffles around his ankles, and a rapturous light in his eyes. Sancho would bring the sunshine into *Under the Lilacs* as he had brought it even into the Orchard House, where the shadow of Mother's illness lengthened as the summer passed. With a whisk of his tasseled tail he would leap from the story straight into the hearts of Mrs. Dodge's subscribers.

While Sancho performed his astounding feats on the second floor of the Orchard House, May's happy letters continued to arrive, bringing the exciting news that the artist's owl panel had been sold for fifty dollars. The early autumn seemed no less beneficent than the spring, for while Father journeyed to Connecticut, Miss Austin returned to America ready to carry out May's minute instructions in a portrait of the Alcotts.

May's suggestions, with the request that Father fluff his hair and wear clean broadcloth while he was painted, could not be carried out. Instead of returning to the Orchard House to sit for a portrait, he was called home by Mother's illness. On the seventh of September, the god of 1877 took back the gifts so generously given, when the doctor announced that Mother had reached the beginning of the end.

Inexorably the weeks passed by. Not "Aunt Jo's" magic pen nor the demands from Washington Street could bring oblivion now to Mother's suffering. The torments of dropsy and dyspepsia were Mother's to bear, Louisa's to watch. In the second-floor room death's shadow lengthened. The nurse, who arrived at the Orchard House in October, brought death closer, and the shadow lengthened over Mother's chair as she murmured, "Stay by, Louy, and help me if I suffer too much." Dr. Wesselhoeft with his homeopathic remedies could give some relief, and the year 1877 gave to the Orchard House one last gift, Mother's seventy-seventh birthday.

After her labors and her fears, Louisa herself succumbed to illness, and rose from her bed in that strange autumn month to help Mother die. Though she failed fast, Mother forbade the family to send for May and insisted that the plans for moving to Anna's house be carried out. On November 14 the gates of the Orchard House were closed, and the door of the Thoreau house on Main Street was opened. Despite the legend, it was not the ghost of Mrs. Thoreau that haunted the house, but another ghost that common sense could never lay, a specter that roamed from Louisa's casement windows to her desk, that rustled the long wine-red drapes and hovered behind the red sofa. Above the mantel on the first floor, May's portrait looked down upon that ghost; Louisa's, painted in Rome, saw it in the dining room; and in Mother's blue room the same ghost waited.

Borne upstairs in an armchair, Mother could still smile as she murmured, "This is the beginning of my ascension," but Louisa could smile no longer when she saw Mother lie in her bed, closing her Johnson and saying she would read no more. The tokens all were of farewell, the gift of a Bible to Louisa, the gesture toward May's picture. On the rainy twenty-fifth of November, at dusk, Mother fell quietly asleep in Louisa's arms.

On the twenty-seventh, Louisa walked again upon the ridge of Sleepy Hollow, watching Mother laid at sunset beside the dust that once was Lizzie. The next day the friends and relatives gathered at the mourning house on Main Street to attend the memorial service. She whom Louisa longed for was gone, as far as the barren grounds of Sleepy Hollow were from Main Street, as far as dust was from flame. From Beach Street and the Hosmer farm, from Fruitlands and Hillside, from the Orchard House and the Thoreau house she was gone. In memory only would she live, and memories fed on death but not on life. The taste of memory was bittersweet to Louisa, for she who had shared all memories would share them no longer.

Yet Louisa did not wish her back. Rather, she would be glad to follow where Mother had gone. A warmth was gone out of life; there was no motive to go on now that she who had been the source of all motive was gone. Since Mother no longer needed her, she would be ready to go after her. In the quiet days of early December, Louisa found rest in Mother's rest, comforted by the thought that she had at least lifted the burden from her last years.

Out of her sorrow and her deep love Louisa could draw no sustained book now, but a poem written in memoriam, and called "Transfiguration." There was comfort in those words for her.

Mysterious death! who in a single hour
  Life's gold can so refine,
  And by thy art divine
Change mortal weakness to immortal power! . . .

Age, pain, and sorrow dropped the veils they wore
  And showed the tender eyes
  Of angels in disguise,
Whose discipline so patiently she bore.

The past years brought their harvest rich and fair;
  While memory and love,
  Together, fondly wove
A golden garland for the silver hair.

The pattern had changed, leaving a gap in the tapestry that no woven garland could ever fill. She had set the last garland upon Mother's head, laid the last nosegay in her hands.

There was little enough on Main Street to soothe the ache of grief. Too many memories leaped forth as Louisa walked under the elms past Judge Hoar's home or the library, past the solid houses that sloped down to the river. Yet perhaps from this new milieu she would one day find the source of another Concord tale, even though there would be no Mother to read it, to declare it perfect, and to treasure the clippings that followed it. It was difficult for Louisa to contemplate her achievements, and know that Mother could share in her rejoicing no more. How proud she would have been to know that Frank Sanborn had written an account of "Miss Alcott, the Friend of Little Women and of Little Men" for the December issue of *St. Nicholas*. In the pages of Mrs. Dodge's periodical, Mother would have taken deep pleasure, for *Under the Lilacs* had begun its appearance as a serial.

During the idle January on Main Street, Father seemed restless, his anchor gone, while Anna tried patiently to take Mother's place. Father might find solace in his plans for the building of a square room on the ground floor, where he might keep the books that once had stood upon the shelves of Fruitlands, or turn the pages of his own journals until he was a boy again on Spindle Hill. In her boys Anna could live again; and May, despite the grief that overwhelmed her as she sat in her London parlor, had friends to comfort her—the Pierces and the Warners, as well as a pleasant Swiss gentleman named Ernest Nieriker, who was most tender as he played chess with the artist or read aloud to her. But for Louisa there was no solace.

Perhaps in vicarious life she could live for a while, and as she had so long lived in Mother, find happiness in May's new life. In February the post office brought word of the artist's engagement to her fellow boarder, Ernest Nieriker, who, besides being adept at chess, had a charming touch on the violin. The gallant young Swiss met every artistic demand of the painter, who found his slender figure and broad shoulders, his curly brown hair and large hazel eyes, and his handsome nose and white throat a dream fulfilled. Yet the dream was not entirely fulfilled, for Ernest was only twenty-two years old to her thirty-seven, and although he was engaged in the banking profession, his income was extremely modest. May's joy overflowed nonetheless.

In the letters with the London postmark now, Louisa lived. On March 22, May had been married in a brown silk wedding dress with a plumed hat and gloves to match. In the office of the Register, Ernest had placed upon her finger a heavy gold ring, and with a loving kiss transformed Miss May Alcott, lately of Concord, into Madame Nieriker of London and Paris. To the summer child of the Lexington Road so strangely metamorphosed into a lady of the Old World, Louisa sent one thousand dollars as her gift to add to the happiness of the new life that lay before May. That happiness was reflected in the letters that flowed in at the Concord post office, in the words of one who had for so many years longed for love and found it at last.

The excitement that had overwhelmed Bloomsbury at the report of the artist's marriage made Concord seem tamer than usual. The spring, however, brought comfort to Louisa as she drove about the village, hoping to visit May during the autumn in

her new home at Meudon and see with her the view of the winding Seine, the Trocadéro, and the gates of the Champ de Mars. In
his own way Father found forgetfulness as spring ripened, heartily
welcomed at Mrs. Eddy's class of students, and giving every evidence of rounding out his hopeful century with honor and with
peace.

Perhaps there would be peace for Louisa, also, in writing a memoir of her mother's life. In June she read with Father the letters
and diaries that carried her back to the long years of cheerless
anxiety and hopeless dependence. With tearful admiration Father
copied the pages, stricken with the knowledge of his inability to
relieve the burdens of those days of helplessness. Through her
own tears Louisa saw four sisters at the Hosmer farm, at Fruitlands, and at Hillside, a family sustained under every privation,
every wrong, and every injustice. Sweet were the compensations
that had followed, after the privations had been glorified in *Little
Women*, transmuted into gold by Louisa's Midas touch. Yet, as
Louisa read on in the diaries, and found herself admitted to her
mother's very soul, memory became too poignant to be trapped in
words. Though Thomas Niles had agreed to publish the book
and Frank Sanborn gladly offered his assistance, she could not
continue. It was too soon, the wounds too fresh, and she herself
not strong enough to complete the story of a life bound so inextricably with her own. With a full heart she decided to destroy
most of Mother's diaries, hoping that at her own death her letters
would be burned.

For Father the summer had brought solace. In July, Dr.
Hiram Jones had come from the West to indulge in discussions
of Plato and plans for a school of philosophy. Father's visions
took shape as Frank Sanborn and Mr. Emerson both agreed with
Dr. Jones that the auspicious moment had arrived for planting in
Concord's soil a seed of philosophy that would flower in the summer of 1879. Now he forgot the past for the future, dreaming of
the days when the American Plato would hold symposia and find
disciples at his feet.

Louisa had prepared to visit Meudon in September, but she abandoned her plans at the last moment, fearing to undo all the good the weary year of ease had done for her. Instead of embarking herself for Europe, she joined Daniel French in offering to Frank Elwell the funds to go abroad and enter the Beaux-Arts. Yet disappointment would not be dulled, nor discontent subdued. The time of remembering was not done yet. Diaries might be destroyed, but memory never. In October, 1878, Louisa found that she had more food for remembrance than for hope.

On the eighth of the month, instead of presenting verses with gifts piled on the table, Louisa went with Father to Sleepy Hollow with her offering of red leaves and flowers. It was a time of memorials, of anniversaries. November brought its days of remembrance also, the twenty-fifth recalling to Louisa the eventful year that had passed since Mother died, the year that had seen May married, Anna settled in her home, and Father come to honor in his old age. On his seventy-ninth birthday Father looked forward to his plans for lectures at Amherst and at Cambridge with far more confidence in the future than Louisa could summon on her forty-sixth birthday. For her the year had been less eventful than for May or for Father. *Under the Lilacs* had appeared with the imprint of Roberts Brothers, and in *A Masque of Poets*, edited by George Parsons Lathrop and issued in Thomas Niles's No Name Series, "Transfiguration" had been included. The fine edge of pleasure in work accomplished had been dulled since Mother had not shared it. The motive to take up the pen was slow to return; yet Louisa knew that without work the future would be dark indeed.

While Father prepared for his Conversation at the Young Men's Christian Union, Louisa left Main Street for Beacon Street, taking a room at the Bellevue, which had recently been refitted with Turkish and Roman baths. There she could take up her pen again, attempting to interest the readers of *The Independent* with a mild thriller, "John Marlow's Victory." Using May's romance for a thread, Louisa began an art novel also, and at the Authors' Carnival on January 22 donned once more the green dress and calash of Mrs. Jarley to present the Waxworks at the Music Hall. Mrs. Porter, who had assumed charge of "The Old Curiosity Shop," was delighted with Louisa's performance, but she herself found that a sad heart and a weary body made play hard work, that the "first old woman" of Walpole and Concord was too old now to poke her umbrella vigorously at Jasper Packlemerton or Martha Bangs. Nevertheless, the Boston days passed pleasantly enough. In her room at the Bellevue Louisa dipped into *Mary Wollstonecraft* and *Dosia*, enjoyed the works of "Henry Gréville," and at the same time took satisfaction in the rewards of L. M. Alcott, who could invest one thousand dollars for Fred's schooling after Johnny's thousand had been deposited in the bank, who could read with delight the rhapsodic review in *Harper's* of *Under the Lilacs*, which the critic claimed one of the best juveniles that had yet flowed from the author's facile pen.

Returning to Concord, Louisa still hoped to venture to Paris in the spring, for May's letters, filled with her joy in painting and in music and in love, tempted her strongly to join the happy couple. They were wise to enjoy the lovely time of their early married days. Louisa, too, could seek enjoyment, though no Ernest Nieriker was at her side and though Boston and not Paris offered its delights to her.

On February 15 she had been invited with Anna to attend a dinner of the Papyrus Club, whose members indulged not only in literary and artistic discussion but in good fellowship and libations from the punch bowl. The ladies' nights of the Papyrus Club were notable events, and Louisa gladly accepted the invitation for dinner at the Revere House. On the marble tile of the spacious hall she walked, her stately figure reflected in the mirrors as Dr. Holmes escorted her gallantly to the table. To her surprise, Louisa found herself at the right hand of the president, John Boyle O'Reilly, for she, with Mrs. Burnett, had been declared guests of honor for the evening.

Between the gallantries of the sprightly Autocrat and the vivid tales of Toastmaster O'Reilly, Louisa's cup of happiness was filled. Her cup brimmed over when the great ones of the land, assembled at Bowdoin Square to pay homage to the two ladies, rose up to toast *Little Women*, to offer libations not to the author but to the author's most cherished treasure, her work. Perhaps this was the motive that would take Mother's place, the spur to high accomplishment, to tasks yet unbegun.

Other pleasures followed the dinner of the Papyrus Club, but the news from Meudon provided the most excitement, for May expected a child in November, and Louisa ardently hoped that she could be with her then. It was strange to contemplate the prophetic history chronicled a decade ago in *Little Women*. "Amy" had her "Laurie" now; she needed only her baby to live out a tale foretold.

Louisa, too, lived out "Jo's" later life, when another group of Concord boys enjoyed her friendship, taking the place of Frank Sanborn's scholars and recapturing the past for her in a second flowering. Besides Fred and Johnny, Louisa added to the boys of memory Adams Tolman and Ellsworth Devens, inviting them to the house on Main Street for Saturday evening charades, listening to their talk of skating, of birds' nests, of Indian relics, or of butterflies, finding, as she listened, characters for a village tale.

The companionship of the boys was pleasant during the spring, for Father was consumed with his plans for the Summer School of Philosophy, and May was preoccupied with her painting of a Negress for the Paris Salon. While the artist reported her triumph in entering her second canvas at the Palais des Champs-Élysées, the American Plato discussed the opening of the Orchard House for the first session of his school, and gleamed in anticipation of the summer's fruits like Jove on smiling Olympus. Louisa was glad to escape to the quiet of her room, where she could indulge in the less esoteric preaching of kindness to the poor in "Two Little Travellers" for the less philosophical audience of Mrs. Dodge's subscribers. There was escape of a different nature in the suffrage meetings held by Louisa after the law had given women the right to vote for members of the school committee. In the parlor of the Thoreau house the ladies were instructed in the proper ways and means of casting ballots; letters were written suggesting public meetings; and in her school of suffrage Louisa tried to forget Father's School of Philosophy.

Other considerations were less easily forgotten. It was impossible to walk along the Lexington Road and pass the Orchard House standing forlorn and empty without looking up at Mother's window or at May's. No Mother looked out from the second-floor window; no golden-haired, blue-gowned May smiled down. Her window was overgrown with vines. Mother's was empty with an emptiness that even the sun of June could not fill. Yet in her carriage and her friends, in a visit to Concord's prison with Father, Louisa sought forgetfulness of the Lexington Road. To four hundred convicts guarded by armed wardens she told a hospital story, receiving in exchange material for another story, as yet unwritten. *H.M.S. Pinafore* also provided a source for a tale that would earn one hundred dollars from *St. Nicholas* by uniting the moral of industry with the pleasures of amateur theatricals. No one who had seen the operetta could fail to enjoy "Jimmy's Cruise in the 'Pinafore,' " where in spite of all temptations to belong to other nations the hero remained an "Amer-i-can."

There was little time left for writing or for escaping from the disciples of the American Plato. On July 14 the philosophers began to swarm through Main Street, while the good people of Concord exchanged jests at their expense, and the newspapers set their type to patronize the worshipers at the shrine of noble thought. The hive was ready for the clustering drones and bees who would begin their murmurings on the fifteenth. Louisa waited skeptically for the honey that would be produced in Concord's comb.

Laden with flowers, she entered the study of the Orchard House, where a bust of Plato presided over the thirty disciples seated upon chairs and a rustic settee. There was a satisfaction in seeing Father take his place as the archpriest of the symposium, a silver-haired philosopher uttering sonorous and well-rounded sentences. Among the sages, male and female, the potato-and-apple evangelist of old had come to honor, a venerable high priest surrounded at last by thirty disciples. Louisa was content in the knowledge that Father's dream had finally been realized, and was ready to dismiss from her thoughts the philosophical soarings of his disciples.

The philosophers themselves were not so easily dismissed. Throughout the summer they swarmed in Concord, marching in phalanx along the streets and sidewalks of the village, wandering to Walden or floating on the river during the cloudless summer days, mounting the coaches, filling the lodginghouses as they arrived with dusters and gripsacks, roosting on the steps of the Thoreau house like hens waiting for corn. From "the Barge," the long omnibus that conveyed them to the sessions in the Orchard House, bonnets peered forth surmounting polonaises or grenadines. From Miss Barrett's boardinghouse the philosophers streamed toward the Lexington Road, and in the boats moored at the bank philosophers contemplated the barely perceptible current of the Concord River. At Mr. Emerson's home and on the lawn of the Old Manse the disciples gathered for tea.

With a mixture of reverence and humorous criticism Louisa listened to the soarings of the Orphic philosopher who was her father, taking pride in his honor, taking pleasure in the fact that the good people of Concord had not all laughed or pitied, but had congratulated themselves upon turning their village into so lucrative a shrine. Another leaf seemed to have been added to the laurel of Concord's fame when Mrs. Elizabeth Thompson offered to contribute one thousand dollars toward the purchase of a proper site for so flourishing a school. The embattled farmers had yielded the village to the less embattled philosophers, who brought patronage to the stores on the Milldam, honor to Father, and hearty amusement to his daughter. Yet Louisa could not help wondering whether the leaf that had been added to Concord's laurels was not a decadent outgrowth that would wither and fall from the sapless stem of speculation. Concord's latest laurel seemed more gray than green.

From the Concord summer Louisa had found suggestions for enough tales to fill "Aunt Jo's" fifth *Scrap-Bag*, and while the disciples mused upon the annals of philosophy, the author contemplated the annals of a New England village, describing its Carnival of Boats in "A Jolly Fourth," and its annual fair in "Kitty's Cattle Show."

"Aunt Jo" left her *Scrap-Bag* when, on August 2, Mr. Emerson read his lecture on memory in the vestry of the Trinitarian Church. It was strange to hear the oracular phrases on memory read by an orator who needed prompting from his daughter lest he mistake a word or misplace a sheet of his manuscript. In that strong, sweet voice there was a cue to deeper thought than "Aunt Jo's" admirers could digest. There was the source for a tale more poignant than any Louisa chose to write.

In the death of young Ellsworth Devens on August 8, Louisa found a source no less poignant, but far more adaptable for a full-length story she might one day write about village life. The circle of "Aunt Jo's" boys had been broken by Elly's untimely death. Before the author wrote the record of that circle, she took time to leave Main Street for Boston with her new *Scrap-Bag*, which Roberts Brothers planned to publish. The long summer days were crowned not only with the completion of another volume and with Father's glory, but with the ecstatic letters in which May described the perfection of her married life, declaring that if she died when the baby was born, the family need not mourn, for she had had as much happiness in her short time as many had in twenty years. Louisa rejoiced in May's happiness, and after the Summer School of Philosophy had closed in triumph and the door had been shut upon the four hundredth philosopher who sought entertainment on Main Street, she rested in the quiet of Concord and consulted Mrs. Dodge about the serial for which the editor had been granted the refusal. It would be no Revolutionary tale, but a story of village life in which the death of Ellsworth Devens might play a part. Indeed, it seemed simpler to supply the editor with a book than with a picture of the author, for, as Louisa wrote to Mrs. Dodge, "A pleasant one does not exist & the picture of the forbidding woman photographers make me will carry disappointment & woe to the bosoms of the innocents who hope to

see 'Jo young & lovely with hair in two tails down her back.' "
After a week at the seaside a rejuvenated Jo could begin her work
on "Jack and Jill" with a vigor not entirely undermined by a summer of philosophy.

At the rambling Willow Cottage in Magnolia, Louisa rested, finding in the salt air, the pebbly beach, and the excursions to Nor-
mans Woe not merely exhilaration but material for her unwritten
story. Returning to Concord in September, she began the task of
writing one chapter a day to trap in a net for *St. Nicholas* the summer days at Magnolia and the winter days at Concord. A boy and
a girl in an upset sled would be discovered when the curtain was
drawn, and from then on the youthful circle of Main Street would
take the stage, reflecting a village history. Concord would be
transmuted into Harmony Village with its clubs and its skating
excursions, its Milldam stores, its hemlocks, and its river. In the
annals of a New England village the Cold Water Army would find
a place, and the May Day when bells twanged and knockers
rapped and baskets of flowers were mysteriously hung. Upon the
lively fairground cattle would low, pigs would squeal, and horses
would trot to participate in the cattle show. The yearly apple picking belonged in the village history, and the *Pinafore* epidemic that
had given a refrain to the boys. Father's school festival in the
Town Hall, where children were placed on exhibition, would be
held again in retrospect. The history would not be complete until
the Dramatic Club had offered the "Sleeping Beauty," "Scenes
from the Life of Washington," and a representation of Daniel
French's Minuteman. Like Mother, Mr. Burton would split his
gloves in his enthusiastic applause. Through the pages the quiet
life of the village would flow peacefully on. Yet Louisa feared at
times that her muse might falter, and begged Mrs. Dodge,
". . . Don't let me *prose*. If I seem to be declining and falling into
it, pull me up, and I'll try to prance as of old."

The children who lived Concord's history in Harmony would
be life studies of the children who had met on Main Street for
charades, Ellsworth Devens, barely disguised as Ed Devlin, who

was beloved not for what he did but for what he was; Frank Elwell, metamorphosed into Ralph Evans, who could paint a fireplace for *The Cricket on the Hearth*, imitate the "Member from Cranberry Centre," and combine the skill of a mechanic with the art of a sculptor. Daniel French, transformed into David German, would invite Ralph to accompany him to Rome; the tobacco-loving Sam Hoar and Fred and Johnny Pratt would walk upon a Harmony Main Street. It would be this group that Louisa would catch as they paused for a moment before pushing their boats on the ever-widening river to the sea. It was this group that would provide for the author an opportunity to offer delights for all children, the Great International Telegraph that stretched from Jack Minot's home to Jane Pecq's, the only aerial express in existence, the interroom telephone. Even though the March girls were missing from the streets of Harmony, the tale of "Jack and Jill" would be another domestic drama, not of a single family, but of a village, whose history was Concord's and whose meadows and river and sunlight were New England's.

Between the chapters of her serial there was time during September for drives or a suffrage meeting or for reading May's manual on *Studying Art Abroad*, which Roberts Brothers was glad to issue. It was strange to read May's advice on European studios or lodginghouses, to recall her description of Dinan and Morlaix while young Bostonians teetered on the seesaws of Walden and bathed in the pond where Thoreau had paddled. Perhaps this, like Father's school, was a sign of a changing Concord, which would not quite fit into the village tale that filled Louisa's mind.

The bluebirds had not changed, nor the cicadas or cornel berries of autumn. The oaks were still wine color in October, and the hickories pure gold; the crickets still shrilled by the wayside, and at Sleepy Hollow, where Louisa walked with her offering of flowers on Mother's birthday, blackberry vines trailed their red leaves, asters bloomed, and the pines sang overhead. God's acre was untouched, the only part of Concord that time had not changed or the passing years transformed.

Concord itself had slowly been transformed from the white village of her own youth into a gray town. The fairyland of Walden had been converted into a campground for spiritualists and an excursion center. To the Orchard House, where May's smiling face and Mother's had looked out from the windows, philosophers had streamed for classes in nebulous speculation. Fields once in corn and grass, where Louisa had wandered as a child, had been converted into vineyards and orchards. The woods that had crowned the hilltops had fallen to the axe. The sons and daughters of Concord had left the farmsteads for factories and trade. The metropolis had extended its boundaries, absorbing the white village of old, transmuting it into a suburb of Boston. Louisa had watched the infusion of new people, the building of new houses, and the introduction of improvements until it had become difficult to recognize the village of her childhood in the town where a state prison flourished toward the west and a School of Philosophy toward the east.

The people whom Louisa had known from childhood had changed with the town. Although Mr. Emerson still made the fall of Adam seem a false report, little save his sweet manner was left of the god of Louisa's early idolatry, who sat in his study now rereading his own works but writing no more. The villagers had left their farms to take up Concord's chief occupation, the writing of articles for *The Atlantic Monthly.* To Cummings Davis, Louisa offered a copper teakettle for his "Old Curiosity Shop," where antiques, family china, ancient furniture, and relics of the dead were placed on exhibition. Concord had grown self-conscious, self-conscious in its celebrations of past glories, in its new and lesser philosophers, who discussed the unknowable, self-conscious in its Walden picnics and its antique shop and its Tuesday Club. During the long slumber that Louisa had watched in the village, an influence had been at work, dulling the whiteness until it was gray. The whiteness she could try to recapture in her latest story; it had become historic, a motif for literature.

Louisa was weary of the gray town, Boston's self-conscious suburb. Activity might alleviate weariness, but it could not dull the disappointment with which she abandoned her long-cherished plan of visiting May. The family assured her that she was not fit to undertake a sea voyage and that she would merely add to her sister's cares, and Louisa acquiesced reluctantly. Somehow she knew that she would wish she had gone. In all her activities and all her thoughts, anxiety about May intervened, flinging itself between the writer and her work.

Louisa's keenest anxiety was exorcised when November brought the happy news that little Louisa May Nieriker had made her appearance in Paris on the eighth, bringing to the sad month of Mother's death a day for deep rejoicing. How Mother would have enjoyed the little granddaughter, the baby born to her summer child. Yet perfection had ever been a word marred by reality, by fact. The letters from Miss Plummer regarding May's failure to rally after the birth of her daughter dimmed the happiness of the moment and banished the joys of November in the dread uncertainty of the darkening winter.

Louisa lived in Paris now with May, the weight upon her heart growing heavier with every letter, her hopes struggling futilely with her fears. Even in her work she took no pleasure, in her letter that had described for *The Woman's Journal* Concord's suffrage activities and had been hopefully signed, "Yours for reforms of all kinds." She took no pleasure in "Jack and Jill," which, though still unfinished, had begun its serial appearance in the December issue of *St. Nicholas.* Concord was farther away than Paris, where May lay ill. The Nierikers were with her, but they could not take a sister's place. May should have met this trial in the Orchard House, with a mother to tend her and her sisters at her side. Surely it was a penance for all her sins that while May lay alone three thousand miles away, Louisa must sit helpless in a room on Main Street, remembering the golden-haired enthusiast who had waved farewell from the deck of the *China* more than three years before. In those three years she had fulfilled all the desires of a lifetime.

On December 31, after Anna had left for Boston and Father had walked to the post office on the Milldam hoping for a letter with a Paris postmark, Mr. Emerson appeared on Main Street with a paper in his hand. Louisa saw him look, pale and tearful, at May's portrait, and knew before he spoke the message that he bore. His voice failed, and he gave Louisa the telegram sent by Ernest Nieriker to the friend who would soften the blow. Louisa had no need to read the words. She had known that May was dead before Ernest had sent the tidings. On December 29 she had left her seven-weeks-old daughter, whom she bequeathed as her most precious legacy to Louisa. With Anna and with Father, Louisa shared the bitter sorrow that had ended all of May's brief happiness, that had divided the family. Wherever she might lie, May would always be part of the dust of Sleepy Hollow. For Louisa, words were barren and comfortless, too cold to ease the pain she bore in knowing that a sister had died in a strange land leaving behind a husband and a child whom Louisa had never seen. This dread message of the dying year was part of the grayness of Concord, part of the grayness of her own life. The summer child had slipped away with the white village where she had been born. And nothing was left but the grayness, as the old year passed into the new.

CHAPTER 15

❦

Yours for Reform

A ll that was palpable or visible, all that was possessed, seemed to drop away until nothing was left. Surely no grief had been more bitter to bear than the loss of May when life was fullest and sweetest. Of all the trials in her life Louisa had never felt any so keenly as this. To Aunt Bond she wrote on the sad New Year of 1880 to share the direful news that May was dead, gone to begin her new year with Mother in a world where she hoped there was no grief like this. From Paris letters came, with their story of May's death from cerebrospinal meningitis, telling how she had spoken now and then of "getting ready for Louy," telling of her grave in Montrouge Cemetery outside the fortifications of Paris. Ernest's sister Sophie had promised May to carry little Louisa Nieriker to Concord.

To distract her mind, Louisa tried to work on "Jack and Jill." The last chapters must be copied before the final section could be dispatched to Mrs. Dodge. In the story of Harmony Village another story intervened, the story of May, that had no happy ending, and a wave of sorrow rolled over Louisa that would not retreat before the antics of a merry flock of children. A sweeter romance had ended in Paris than any she could invent. The sad facts of life left her no heart for cheerful fiction.

With every post the letters flowed in, bringing memories of May or the Nierikers' reports that little Lulu had gone for a while to Baden with her grandmother. Still, Louisa could not make it true that May was dead. Remembering the aspirations of the summer child, Louisa drew from her heart a poem.

A child, her wayward pencil drew
On margins of her book
Garlands of flowers, dancing elves,
Bird, butterfly and brook.
Lessons undone, and play forgot
Seeking with hand and heart
The teacher whom she learned to love
Before she knew 't was Art.

A maiden, full of lofty dreams,
Slender and fair and tall
As were the goddesses she traced
Upon her chamber wall.
Still laboring with brush and tool,
Still seeking everywhere
Ideal beauty, grace and strength
In the "divine despair."

A woman, sailing forth alone,
Ambitious, brave, elate,
To mould life with a dauntless will,
To seek and conquer fate.
Rich colors on her palette glowed
Patience bloomed into power;
Endeavor earned its just reward,
Art had its happy hour.

A wife, low sitting at his feet
To paint with tender skill
The hero of her early dreams,
Artist, but woman still.
Glad now to shut the world away,
Forgetting even Rome;
Content to be the household saint
Shrined in a peaceful home.

A mother, folding in her arms
The sweet, supreme success;
Giving a life to win a life,
Dying that she might bless.
Grateful for joy unspeakable,
In that brief, blissful past;
The picture of a baby face
Her loveliest and last.

Death the stern sculptor, with a touch
No earthly power can stay,
Changes to marble in an hour
The beautiful, pale clay.
But Love the mighty master comes
Mixing his tints with tears,
Paints an immortal form to shine
Undimmed by coming years. . . .

The last page of May's brief history had been written. Her book must be closed and work repair the gap that death had torn in a changing tapestry. "Jack and Jill" was completed, the farewells paid to the children of Harmony Village, and the last sheets sent to Mrs. Dodge. Again, as after Mother's death, Louisa took no joy in her success.

With the shadows of the past lengthening upon her, Louisa put her papers in order and sent a letter to the *Transcript* giving details of the life of the late May Alcott Nieriker. In March, May's box arrived, laden with its poignant reminders of the past, the artist's Turner album, her clothes, her vases, her workbasket, and a lock of her hair in a sepia box.

An anodyne was needed for despair, since Lulu would not arrive in Concord until the autumn. Before the child came, surely the deepest forgetfulness of sorrow could be found in reform, which looked ever toward the future, seldom to the past. The time had come to recall and to practice those words with which Louisa had ended a letter to *The Woman's Journal*, signing herself "Yours for reforms of all kinds." Of all the causes for which

mankind crusaded, peace or dress reform, homeopathy or healthful food, woman suffrage seemed at the moment to offer most to
Louisa and to need her most. In a town meeting, Mr. Emerson
believed, the great secret of political science had been uncovered
and the problem solved how to give every individual his fair
weight in the government. In a town meeting the roots of society
were reached, where the rich gave counsel and the poor also.

On March 29, Louisa attended Concord's town meeting,
where, for the first time, women would cast their votes for the
school committee. She sat with Father and with the nineteen
other women who had met to exercise their newest privilege,
eager to share in the historic moment. In a private interview with
the Moderator, Father proposed that the women be allowed to
cast their ballots before the men as a token of respect, and Louisa
filed out with the ladies, dropping her vote and passing back to
her seat while the assembled gentlemen looked on in solemn
silence. Scarcely had the ladies returned to their seats when Judge
Hoar rose and proposed that the polls be closed. The motion was
carried before the laugh subsided, and the vote taken without the
ballot of a single man.

To *The Woman's Journal* Louisa sent a report of the town
meeting, recording the historic event that would widen the intellectual frontiers of the country. While the *Concord Freeman*
quoted her letter and the Milldam alternated between discussion
of Mr. Reynolds's sermon on "But" and Louisa Alcott's sermon on
woman suffrage, she herself returned to her old room at the Bellevue in April. There, perhaps, she could find more complete forgetfulness of the village Milldam, of the Main Street, and of the
Lexington Road, where a golden-haired girl who had once
walked, walked in shadow still as Concord's spring came on.

On the wide, unpaved malls of the Common, under the elms,
Louisa could stroll with none to look out of the window and say,
"There's Louisa Alcott; I wonder where she's going, what she has
on, how she does, what she is thinking about." Like woman suffrage, Boston, too, was an anodyne. In the theater there had
always been forgetfulness of self, and now in her room at the

Bellevue Louisa sat, dramatizing *Michael Strogoff*, not for the delight of the family, not for the cause of charity, or a taskmaster publisher, but simply to relive the dramatizations of earlier days. Mother would never again cry "Ankore" and clap her dress gloves to rags; May's prompting days were over; and Anna, forgetting her ambitions to shine as a prima donna, had settled into a comforting, gray-haired woman. The Bellevue was a far cry from Hillside, but yet the yellow boots tramped in memory as Louisa rewrote Jules Verne, the ghosts of happy barnstormers at her side.

Still May's face intervened, and in the hope of some day bringing her dust home, Louisa ordered a stone for her sister's grave. In the attempt to close the door upon the past, she wrote to Mrs. Dodge when she returned to Concord about the possibilities of writing "An Old-Fashioned Boy," based upon Father's journals. Meantime, there was work to be done in the village. The eleven hundred children of the North End Mission arrived in June for a happy day at Walden Pond; the Thoreau house must be cleaned and the Orchard House made ready for Mr. Harris, who had decided to rent it. Only the picture of Lulu sent by Madame Nieriker, the picture of a fat little baby in a carriage, could break the spell that work had wrought, with its reminders of May, who would never come home again. In the new rooms in the Main Street house, pleasure could still be taken, while Father reveled in his study or in the Hillside Chapel newly consecrated to philosophy.

With joy in Father's joy Louisa visited the chapel, which stood like an aspiration on the rising ground near the Orchard House. On the rustic benches beneath the trees no Mother would sit, but Dr. Hiram Jones, airily relating all corporeality to a "somewhat." Through the entrance of the chapel would pass no barnstormers of Hillside, but Dr. Hedge, plucking up drowning honor by the locks. From the Orchard House no golden-haired artist would saunter forth with sketchbook and pencil, but the new tenant, Mr. Harris of St. Louis. On the chapel platform Elizabeth Peabody might sit, forgetting the buzz of Concord flies in the louder buzz of Concord's philosophers. No *Pilgrim's Progress* would be enacted here; instead, Dr. Denton Snider would discourse on Shakespeare.

Louisa was glad to leave Father as sole monarch of this domain in which she had no part. From the newspaper reports of Concord's philosophers, from the capes and ginghams that would infest "the Barge" and the Lexington Road, from the lectures on figurative language or mysticism, she could escape, finding a refuge for the summer in York on the coast of Maine.

With Johnny and Fred, Louisa enjoyed the splendid air, the rest, the pleasant company and good table provided at the boardinghouse near the sea. Deborah, the sibyl of the town, was ready to tell fortunes to Miss Alcott, and at Eastern Point near Roaring Rock, "Old Samp" would regale any listener with tales of his fishing expeditions. The summer life was completed by the presence of Mrs. Le Brun, a loquacious visitor who pried deeply into everyone's affairs and talked endlessly about the perfect town of Concord, until Louisa freed her mind with her own more realistic point of view about the New England Mecca.

A rainy day could be filled with an examination of Frank Merrill's drawings for an illustrated edition of *Little Women*, and Louisa approved heartily of the pen-and-ink sketches. At the post office she found letters from Anna, with lively accounts of the school with its "Chinee" professors, its Julia Wards, and other gay and festive beings. Louisa was happy to have escaped from the conversations of philosophers, who had lured hundreds of eager disciples into buying tickets at Whitcomb's to enter the realms of the unknowable.

She herself preferred to speculate about the less unknowable future, which would bring Lulu to Boston in September, when Miss Nieriker would receive less philosophical guests than those who visited Father. In August, Louisa left the boardinghouse and the sea to replace Anna at home and make preparations for Lulu's arrival. Mrs. Giles had been engaged to go abroad for May's little daughter, and, provided with all the clothing that a baby might need on a sea voyage, embarked on the twenty-first of the month.

Boston on September 18, 1880, was filled with talk of the city's two hundred and fiftieth anniversary, but another anniversary was at hand, a day more significant to Louisa than that of Boston's settlement. On the nineteenth, Louisa waited on the wharf while the passengers disembarked, looking eagerly at every baby, wondering each time if this or that were hers. At length the captain appeared, in his arms a little yellow-haired, blue-eyed child in white. Next to him was Mrs. Giles, and Louisa knew the baby for her own. Behind walked a lovely, brown-eyed girl with an anxious face, who must be Ernest's sister Sophie. Able only to say Lulu's name, Louisa held out her arms to her child. While Sophie and Mrs. Giles told of the stormy passage, Louisa listened quietly, silent now that the future lay in her arms, a winning baby with shadowless blue eyes. In his diary Father recorded the event in red ink: "*She Comes!*" In her heart, Louisa recorded the event, brooding over the baby who was May's no longer, but her own.

Visitors came to see "Miss Alcott's baby," and strangers waylaid her carriage in the street. Yet, for all the love that others lavished upon her, Lulu always came to Louisa, knowing her for mother, and Louisa's heart was filled with joy. In the Orchard House she had encompassed many relationships as sister and as daughter, and as mother, too. Yet never had she known this strange relationship, that quickened the heart and enriched the days that passed, that brought to the dying years a new life for hope to feed upon.

For Lulu's sake as well as for her own, Louisa made arrangements to hire Cousin Lizzie Wells's house for the winter, while Father packed his trunks for his western tour. In the four-story red brick house on Pinckney Street, facing the south and overlooking Louisburg Square, there was room for Sophie and the boys, and Louisa was too preoccupied with the affairs of the nursery at number 81 to recall the days when four sisters had lived at number 20. Between the nursery and her desk she went, beginning again to grind the mill that would amuse other people's children.

Of far greater interest to her, however, than "Aunt Jo's" public were the activities of Louisa's very small "public," who brought more sunshine into 81 Pinckney Street than all of Harper's Young People together. Throughout the days, as winter came on, Louisa's life centered more and more closely about her baby. Far more significant than the issue of an illustrated *Little Women* from the press of Roberts Brothers was the first walk of the queen of 81 Pinckney Street, who suddenly gathered the courage to run across the room, plump down, and laugh triumphantly at her astounding feat.

Yet there were reminders that *the* Miss Alcott was still as essential to the world she lived in as to one yellow-haired toddler. When a prisoner, just released from Concord's jail, appeared at Pinckney Street to thank Louisa for a little story she had once told the convicts and to tell her of his plans for joining a geological expedition in South America, she treasured his words, knowing that one day she might use his experiences in a tale. Surely the Christmas of 1880, for all its sadness, would open a new world not only for Lulu's Aunt Wee Wee but for *the* Miss Alcott.

It was a world of Lulu's little ailments and of Mrs. Giles's outings with the baby that began for Louisa with the new year. She took time also to fill her new world with the reform activities that blew with the winds of the future, asking Mr. Niles's help in issuing a small edition of Mrs. Robinson's *Massachusetts in the Woman Suffrage Movement*, and discussing her plans for a meeting with the governor, council, and legislature. Her life itself had reflected the changing reforms of many years, as Louisa recalled in a letter to the publisher:

> I can remember when Antislavery was in just the same state that Suffrage is now, and take more pride in the very small help we Alcotts could give than in all the books I ever wrote or ever shall write.

Between two worlds her life alternated, between the world of a blond, blue-eyed baby who brooded with rapture over the delicate figures of Caldecott and Miss Greenaway, and the world of hopeful women who voted for the school committee in the spring. While Aunt Wee Wee consulted Mrs. Giles about the appearance or nonappearance of Lulu's teeth, Miss Alcott discussed Aldrich's editorship of *The Atlantic Monthly* with the literary ladies of Boston. Between the two lives, Louisa's life flowed.

When the family returned to the Thoreau house in the spring, Louisa was oppressed by the increasing dullness of Concord. Mrs. Emerson's call to pay her respects to Miss Nieriker or Ellen Emerson's reading class for the ladies of the village could not fill her life as they seemed to fill the lives of the Concordians. Nor was the dullness alleviated by Father's preparations for the third session of the School of Philosophy. After the opening meeting, Louisa could flee once again from Platonic cosmologies, faded metaphors, and evolutionary "ooze," to the more vigorating pleasures of Nonquitt, where the sands of the beach offered a stronger appeal than Concord's contemplations of the sands of time.

With the boys, she left on July 17, finding rest in the sheltered coves and wooded points of Buzzards Bay. Here in her black silk dress, with her shoulders a little bent and her cheeks somewhat thin, Louisa's eyes could sparkle as she watched the children climb the crow's nest of the *Admiral Blake* or listened under her red parasol to the cacophony of the Marion Brass Band. To Salters Point or Clark Cove she could wander, and enjoy evenings of charades and private theatricals with the nephews of the "first old woman" of Concord. On the twenty-seventh, Lulu and Mrs. Giles joined Louisa, and a pair of fat legs tramped through the long hotel piazzas, while a beloved head, surmounted by a hat tilted far back, beamed upon all the gentlemen of Nonquitt. Between hearing of the boys' exploits in boating and dancing, and supervising Lulu's warm salt bath every day, Louisa passed the time until her return to Concord.

Over the sleeping village a fresh wind blew when, on September 17, Walt Whitman paid a visit to Frank Sanborn. At the private reception in Mrs. Sanborn's back parlor, Louisa joined the neighbors with Father, once again to take notes on life and letters in America. Over her teacup she watched the poet who had sounded his barbaric yawp over the roofs of the world, the poet who, though venerable, retained a certain youthfulness and vigor bespoken by his ruff of beard and open white bosom collar. His rich, deep voice betrayed no sign of age, nor the large, shapely hands, nor the Homeric head crowned with its silver-white hair. Surely Jove had come to Concord, Jove somewhat crippled, but Jove still.

In Mrs. Sanborn's back parlor Mr. Whitman seemed to give most of his attention to Mr. Emerson, who had settled himself in his chair, peering sweetly upon the company but taking no part in the conversation. If Mr. Whitman had his own pail to milk in, Louisa had hers also, observing carefully the author of *Leaves of Grass* while Father discussed Thoreau and Margaret Fuller. It was strange to listen, when the Fortnightly Club assembled in the parlor after tea, to Frank Sanborn's reading of Thoreau's words on sphericity and Miss Fuller's letters concerning the essay. The dead presided over this meeting, the dead and the dying. Louisa only, with Mr. Whitman, looked to the future. Mr. Sanborn rustled the leaves of the past. Mr. Emerson quietly completed the arc of the perfect circle that had been his life. Only the Camden Jove held thunderbolts for the future, and the lady from Main Street dreamed not of the primitive world but of the world that was still to be.

Yet Louisa would not deny the honor due to the mighty dead. When Frank Sanborn requested that she contribute a preface for an edition of Theodore Parker's *Prayers*, she agreed, recording the account of the memorable day when she had first heard the preacher, describing the evenings at Exeter Place, and writing of her visit to his grave in Florence more than a decade ago. The pen could be dipped into ink to narrate "A Baby's Birthday" after Lulu had received two kisses and a doll's carriage for her second birthday. It was a simple matter to weave upon the framework of reform tales that would help mankind. For the soldiers' home, "My Red Cap," dispatched to *The Sword and Pen*, would exalt another Robert Bane in the shape of Joe Collins, who exchanged his blue cap for the red one of a messenger. In "A Country Christmas," a defense of wholesome literature, the sustaining, bread-and-butter books that dealt with human beings, would provide a new credo for those aspiring novelists who read *The Independent*.

In "A Country Christmas," Louisa knew that she had written her own literary credo. When the heart was left out of a work, when mind and soul grew morbid with dwelling on the metaphysical phases of life and character, the pen must be laid down. The naturalness of books must ever be their touchstone of success, and no book was successful unless it warmed and strengthened those who read it. There was an opportunity for her to practice her credo in a revision of *Moods*, which Roberts Brothers was ready to issue since Loring had transferred the copyright to the author during the summer. The morbid self-analysis and preoccupation with the metaphysical phases of life, which she had condemned in "A Country Christmas," could be erased from the new edition of her first novel. Though death had once seemed the only solution for Sylvia's perplexities, Louisa had learned in the years that had passed that happiness could be found after disappointment, that a more wholesome book would result if her heroine met a wiser but less extravagant fate. From the painted romance to the more beautiful reality Sylvia would turn now, to live, not dream, a long and happy life, unmarred by the moods that had all but wrecked her youth. Sylvia, like her creator, had learned to live by principle rather than by impulse.

Louisa left her desk when, on November 22, young Edward Bok called at Main Street in the hope that Miss Alcott would escort him to the white frame house at the fork of the roads. After they had chatted by the fire, Louisa walked with her visitor toward the Cambridge Turnpike, and they were welcomed by Ellen at the door. It was only after Edward had repeated the words of Phillips Brooks, "To have seen him, even as you may see him, is better, in a way, than not to have seen him at all," that the boy was admitted with Louisa into the study. Mr. Emerson was seated at his desk, a tall spare figure in a long black coat. Slowly, at his daughter's words, he rose with a quiet dignity, extending his hand. From his tender eyes no light of welcome shone as he silently motioned Edward to a chair beside the desk. Louisa watched while the god of her childhood's idolatry walked to the window; listened, as he stood there softly whistling, peering out as if there were no one in the room. At Edward's questioning look, she placed her finger on her lips and waited. Presently Mr. Emerson left the window and returned to his desk, bowing to the boy, maintaining his enigmatic silence. Suddenly Louisa spoke, asking whether her aged friend had read a new book by Ruskin. Mr. Emerson slowly raised his eyes to Louisa, and, bowing to her, inquired with great deliberation, "Did you speak to me, madam?" Tears sprang into her eyes, and Louisa walked to the other side of the room. Then, suddenly, out of the darkness where he wandered, the thoughts shone, and those invisible walls that had closed in upon him were razed. Louisa came forward again, her wet eyes dancing with pleasure, her face wreathed in smiles. The atmosphere of the room had changed. Mr. Emerson was once again Mr. Emerson. Then, softly, he began that ominous low whistle, looked inquiringly at Edward and Louisa, dropped his eyes to the papers on his desk. Louisa turned away. She walked back to Main Street with Edward in a silence that was unbroken until she murmured, "Phillips Brooks may be right: that it is something to have seen him even so, than not to have seen him at all. But to us it is so *sad*, so very sad. The twilight is gently closing in."

The twilight seemed far off from Mrs. Croly's glittering parlors in New York, where Louisa had been invited as guest of honor at a reception that would also welcome Oscar Wilde to the city. On the evening of January 8, she was greeted by "Jenny June" and was quickly surrounded by the lions and lion hunters who stalked New York. Mrs. Stedman and Mrs. Richardson, Kate Field and Kate Sanborn, Alexander Salvini and Mrs. Walker, the Lady Angela of *Patience*, thronged round the "youth's companion" to pay homage. For her, Clara Morris, bedecked, at Mr. Wilde's request, in white brocade satin with pearl and crystal beads, lifted her flowerlike face and gray eyes to discuss her conception of Camille or her days with Augustin Daly. At eleven o'clock the throngs who had gathered round the honored lady from Concord diminished in number to circulate round young Mr. Wilde, who entered the drawing room, his knee buckles sparkling, his diamond stud glittering in his shirt bosom, and his wide white silk tie producing the necessary contrast to the solid black in which he was arrayed. Louisa was not loath to share the honors of the evening with the mannered Oxonian who had won the Newdigate prize for English verse and at the age of twenty-seven had entered America with nothing to declare but his genius. The thick-lipped Dubliner with the long masses of dark-brown hair that fell over his broad shoulders would not exactly provide the prototype for one of "Aunt Jo's" boys, but "Aunt Jo" was nonetheless interested in the aesthete who could repeat bons mots with such exquisite perfection. In the Thirty-eighth Street drawing room they stood together, the "youth's companion" and the sensuous youth, both dressed in black, both contributors to the press of Roberts Brothers, yet divided each from each as the solid earth from the unsubstantial air. In Mrs. Croly's parlors all things were possible.

Concord, when Louisa returned, seemed more than ever content with the reflected glories of its dead forefathers and imported geniuses. Impatient with a village that expended its energies upon church fairs, tea parties, and clubs for the study of pottery, Faust, and philosophy, she sent a letter to *The Woman's Journal* condemning the town that took no active part in the great reforms of the day, and that seemed bent upon degenerating into a museum for Revolutionary relics. She at least would have no part in the Concord of tradition, but would work instead to add fresh honors to its faded laurels. Louisa could give her mind freely now to the temperance society which she helped to project in the village. Although the movement might not merit the honor of being heralded "the whirlwind of the Lord," it seemed to her a fruitful enterprise. As secretary of the society, she dispatched notices to the *Concord Freeman* and *The Woman's Journal*, writing records and letters, sending pledges, and attending meetings.

Between the society and the demands of Lulu, Louisa was occupied. For Lulu, her tales were told as spring came on in Concord, tales of "Naughty Jocko," the monkey who tickled grandpa's nose, of "Rosy's Journey" and "Cockyloo," the king of the barnyard. A storyteller had turned again to the spinning wheel. For Lulu, Scheherazade was summoned again from Araby.

Yet Concord's raw and backward spring of 1882 bore little resemblance to an Arabian April. To Mr. Emerson, Father gleefully presented a copy of his newly published *Sonnets and Canzonets*, but the friend on the Cambridge Turnpike, though pleased with the volume, was obviously suffering from the rains and chilly winds of the season. Frank Sanborn, having completed his *Thoreau*, might well begin to gather together his reminiscences of Ralph Waldo Emerson. The man who lay upon a study sofa, feverish and bewildered, would soon be consigned to the critic and biographer.

On April 27, Louisa's illustrious and beloved friend died. Concord knew its loss, and draped its streets in black. In the woods the villagers gathered maple and willow blossoms to mingle with the pine and hemlock banked around the pulpit, and Louisa made a yellow lyre of jonquils for the church. In his study by the door hung the calendar, turned as he had left it, and on the table lay the portfolio where he had put it down. The commonplace had taken on a deep significance.

On April 30, Louisa joined the neighbors and family at the white frame house at the fork of the roads to hear the services conducted by Dr. Furness, to hear Longfellow's hopeful verses read aloud:

> *There is no Death! What seems so is transition*
> *This life of mortal breath*
> *Is but a suburb of the life elysian,*
> *Whose portal we call Death.*

Louisa turned from the familiar house to join the procession to the church, where all had gathered to bid him farewell. In carriages and on foot they came, crowding the steps, filling the pews. Yet none had lost more in his death than Louisa. She filed with the throngs by the casket, to look for the last time upon his face. The Reverend Mr. Clarke had said that our souls had been fed by him, that though he had left his dust behind, his life did not die. He himself was the best argument for immortality. Yet, his death darkened; and under the pine tree on the hill above Sleepy Hollow, where the children dropped flowers and strewed twigs over the casket, not one man alone, but Concord, was interred. Mr. Emerson had found his memory now, but Concord had lost the source for remembrance, and in New England there was a blank that he alone could fill.

Louisa sat up until midnight, remembering Mr. Emerson and recalling the picnics at Walden and the explorations in the library of the white frame house at the fork of the roads. So that the children would know him, she wrote an article of "Reminiscences" for *The Youth's Companion*, telling of Concord's welcome home to its illustrious citizen and of its last farewell to him. The village had diminished since he would no more walk along its paths, and, to seek forgetfulness, Louisa turned to her pen, writing another article on "R. W. Emerson" for *Demorest's Monthly Magazine* and preparing a collection of *Proverb Stories* for Roberts Brothers.

As a sample of the effusions of one "A. M. Barnard," she would include "The Baron's Gloves" with its account of the romantic pursuit of Sidney Power, wounded in the Polish war and afflicted with an interesting cough. The shades of Amy's Laurie might rise up in that sensational story to offer to the public an example of what not to follow. From *Proverb Stories*, Louisa turned to the arrangement of "Aunt Jo's" sixth *Scrap-Bag*, in which several tales from *Morning-Glories* would be reprinted. The work of the past would come once again to the aid of the present, when the "youth's companion" wearied of piping fresh tunes for the children.

For one child Louisa seldom wearied of spinning her tales, and Lulu approved of Aunt Wee's stories as vigorously as *The Critic* commended Miss Alcott's revision of *Moods*. The baby, with her blue eyes, snowy skin, and yellow curls, brought to the Thoreau house a burst of life as she dashed about with her nurse or with Anna and Louisa. It was a large household now on Main Street, and the family of nine, including the three servants, might have engrossed Louisa's time completely had not Anna taken the burdens from her shoulders. At nineteen, the dignified Fred was so consumed with his piano, flute, or cornet, and his plans for entering a Boston banking house, that he had little time to spare for a high-spirited two-year-old. Johnny was still his father's son, less gifted perhaps and more commonplace than Fred, but filled with a nobility and sweetness that, while they might win him no laurels at Chauncy Hall, brought him the love of all who knew him. Between her household cares and her temperance activities, Louisa had little time to cogitate about the changes that had come to the Alcott home. Nevertheless, the changes were apparent, and none but Anna and Father could share her memories of four little girls who had climbed to a Celestial City in another house called Hillside.

The Celestial City rose no longer beyond the low hills of Concord. Instead, the School of Philosophy opened its doors again, and the daughter of the archpriest arranged flowers and oak branches for the occasion. Once more along the roads wandered the ideal speculators from the West, while Penny's new barge, the *Blue Plato*, rumbled by with Margaret Fullers in white muslin and Hegels in straw hats. After the disciples had studied Fichte's *Wissenschaftslehre* and Schelling's later philosophy, Louisa longed to place the three thousand miles of the continent between herself and Main Street.

Instead, after a rest at Nonquitt, she moved with John in the autumn to a Bellevue now metamorphosed into an apartment hotel. There was much to discuss as she sat at the dinner table on Beacon Street, surrounded by Boston's literary lights. If she felt herself an alien at the Hillside Chapel, here Louisa had her place in the sun. This was her dominion, where she might chuckle over the personal note in *Harper's Bazar* to the effect that Mrs. Spofford had not written *A Modern Mephistopheles*, or discuss Hawthorne's use of Father as a character in *Doctor Grimshawe's Secret*. Louisa could rest content in Father's happiness now, for with his Mystic Club and his sonnets on immortality, he had found indeed the elixir of life.

With a free mind Louisa could take up her pen at the Bellevue, beginning the tale of *Jo's Boys*, catching the thread she had dropped more than ten years ago in Rome, following her Little Men to their maturity. She returned to the dramatis personae of the past, to an Aunt Jo in a vortex and an Amy whose protégés included ambitious young painters and sculptors. Josie would take the place of her predecessor, playing the born actress not of Hillside but of Plumfield, while instead of Beth, Lulu would sit for the portrait of Bess, whose golden head would bend over her grandfather's silver one. There would be space to sound the trumpet for the "superfluous," independent spinsters, for the women whose hour had struck.

It was strange to live again with the Little Women who were little no longer, with a Jo March who had developed into a literary nursemaid providing moral pap for the young and filled with an intense dislike of official Paul Prys. Not of Jo's first scrape but of her last, Louisa wrote in her room at the Bellevue, remembering the lion hunters and autograph collectors who had haunted the groves where *the* Miss Alcott dwelt. In her tale the lady from Oshkosh and the album-laden girls of Vassar would find a place, the artists and reporters who stalked the Concord lion, that ugly duckling who had turned into a golden goose. When Thomas Niles objected to the indiscretions of describing "Jo's Last Scrape," Louisa reminded him that the success of *Little Women* had developed from precisely the same use of experience and reality, adding that in no other way could the rising generation of autograph fiends be put to shame. If "Jo's Last Scrape" were in poor taste, then all the other episodes of Jo March's life must be put to the torch, for Jo's last scrape was no less true than her first.

Louisa had little time to linger on the Plumfield Parnassus. On October 24 she was summoned home by a telegram announcing that Father had had a paralytic stroke. On his bed in the study he lay prostrate, his right side paralyzed, his mind dim and feeble, and the eyes once so wise and serene vacantly staring. Although Dr. Wesselhoeft feared that death would be a matter of days or perhaps weeks, yet the days passed and in sad eclipse Father lingered on. In the morning he was propped up in an invalid chair for an hour, holding books, trying to read them, or painfully forming letters on a sheet of paper. The Thoreau house was transformed, centering about an invalid and his nurse, centering about milk and wine jelly and bay rum, affairs unmentioned in the philosophy of Fichte or Kant. All else diminished in importance. Nothing was significant, save a word that Father was able to form as he whispered, "Up," the fruit he was able to eat, the steps he must learn to take again as a child must learn. In his chair sat the archpriest of Hillside Chapel, looking out in silence at the river and the falling leaves.

Louisa must be the mother now, not only for him, but for Lulu. Between the demands of childhood and of age she was so preoccupied that she scarcely found time to remember that on November 29, 1882, she had reached her fiftieth birthday and Father his eighty-third. It was a pathetic little celebration that honored the occasion, for Father's feast consisted of a pear and his festal robe was a wrapper on which a rose was pinned. He seemed to understand the day, although he insisted that he was twenty-three and his daughter fifteen. For Louisa it was a peculiarly sad birthday, brightened only by the remembrances of her publishers and the expressions of affection that came to her from the West as well as the East. By these, the burden of fifty years was lightened somewhat, but though, like Christiana, she might go on her way rejoicing with a cheerful heart, Louisa knew that she had turned her face toward the sunset and that the remainder of her journey would be downhill. The buoyancy was gone, and the time for dreaming. She had little interest in *The Critic*'s review of *Proverb Stories* and *Aunt Jo's Scrap-Bag*, a review that would have filled her with delight twenty years before. "Good wine needs no bush, and Miss Alcott needs no reviewer." Miss Alcott needed no praise either, for its heady draught intoxicated no more.

Boston might obliterate from her mind the sickroom on Main Street, and in order to give Anna some rest, Louisa took Lulu and a maid to the Bellevue for a month. Now she could exchange for the world of nurses and massages, wine jellies and reclining chairs, a world filled with the latest telegraph "tickings," a world humming with reports of Mrs. Eddy's school on Columbus

Avenue or Mrs. Jackson's visit to the California Mission Indians. With Lulu she walked through the familiar streets of the city, passing ladies bedecked in Indian shawls and diamond earrings, entering Notman's, where the baby sat for her picture, and buying a canary for her child. For a month she could find respite, less in her own world than in Lulu's, so brave, so new, so unexplored.

Louisa returned to Concord to cast her vote at town meeting and share the burdens of the Main Street household with Anna. Her time belonged to Father now, the poor Lear whose fine and gentle nature still glimmered through the weakness and wandering of his troubled brain, the philosopher finding less comfort in the elixir of life than in the bay rum sent by his friend Mrs. Stearns.

Quietly the summer came on in Concord. Reading a Goethe book sent by Thomas Niles and receiving Mr. Burroughs at the Thoreau house, Louisa ardently hoped that she would find the time and the strength to provide Mrs. Dodge with a story and Roberts Brothers with another set of books like *Aunt Jo's Scrap-Bag*. The School of Philosophy would not interfere with her plans this summer. Herbert Spencer might be dissected, and immortality proved without benefit of Scripture—Father would taste no fruit of the tree that he had planted in the grounds of the Orchard House.

Louisa could escape from the speculations of Concord's philosophers at the shore, where she rested with Lulu and the boys. The baby of the Thoreau house could be forgotten momentarily in the baby of Nonquitt, who boldly took her first sea bath, walking off toward Europe up to her neck and deeply afflicted that Aunt Wee would not allow her to visit the crabs at the bottom of the ocean. While the boys enjoyed the simple pleasures of the coast, Louisa was comforted by the news from Main Street, where Father seemed to be enjoying a second birth, slowly growing up from a sad infancy to a happy childhood. His mind was clear and the vacant look gone, although his speech and memory remained imperfect. Freed from her deepest cares, Louisa could give her mind to a story for Mrs. Dodge, modeling her heroine on Sophie

Nieriker and teaching once again the joys of kindness to the poor in "Sophie's Secret."

On August 10, when Anna arrived at Nonquitt, Louisa returned home to her second baby. Although she had begun a serial, "Mrs. Gay's Summer School," for *St. Nicholas,* a series of *Spinning-Wheel Stories* came tumbling into her mind, old-time tales with a thread running through all from the wheel that was introduced in the first. Out of Concord's Revolutionary relics "Tabby's Table-Cloth" was patterned, embroidered with the author's memories of a later war. From Spindle Hill another tale flowed forth, the tale of a boy who had learned his letters on the floor of a Connecticut homestead. "Eli's Education" was Father's, Eli's youth and Eli's wisdom, too. The tales could not wait to be told, but developed in the author's mind as summer gave way to autumn and autumn chilled into early winter. Even in the darkening time the spider could not leave her spinning wheel, nor the pen lose its Midas touch.

Louisa stopped writing late in November, when she moved with Lulu to Boylston Street. She could give herself again to the delights of the city, hearing Matthew Arnold lecture, listening with all of Boston to the tall Englishman who could crystallize American civilization in a phrase.

Knowing Mr. Arnold's belief that Emerson was the Marcus Aurelius of the nation, the friend of those who would live in the spirit, Louisa found it strange to read the recently published *Correspondence of Carlyle and Emerson,* with its comments on Father. Surely it had ever needed great men to understand and appreciate Father at his best. On his eighty-fourth birthday, when Louisa went home laden with gifts for the ancient child, she knew that though he lived, his life was over. He, too, must be relegated, with Emerson, with Thoreau, and with Hawthorne, to the care of editors and biographers. He had become part of that treasure of the past which historians mined for the enlightenment of those who followed. Even her own generation had been followed by another, by Johnny's. How quickly the years revolved, with youth at the heels of age, itself becoming age.

From Louisa's generation not all the great had vanished. At the Papyrus Club dinner on December 15, she saw them in all the glory of the present as they assembled in the parlors of the Revere House to meet the guest of honor, Ellen Terry. Louisa sat near her at the table, surrounded by those who had followed her father's generation, the literary great of the transient present. Their names somehow lacked the intense luster of those who had preceded them in history. Mrs. Burnett, Henry Cabot Lodge, Miss Nora Perry, and Howard Ticknor could not quite hold their own against Hawthorne and Emerson and Thoreau. Yet the dinner itself could rival any that had been offered by the mighty *Atlantic*, and Louisa thoroughly enjoyed the baked English turbot with brown sauce, in the course of which Miss Terry signed scores of menu cards with poetic couplets. Finally, the president arose, proposing the health of the company in a loving cup that was passed from guest to guest. Toasts and songs culminated in a "burlesque operatic monodrama" entitled "Titi," and Louisa rose from the table knowing that her own generation still had much to offer.

For that generation there was work still to be done. For the cause of suffrage or temperance Louisa could speak, allowing her name to appear now on the editorial heading of *The Woman's Journal*. She could attend town meeting in Concord and send a letter to *The Woman's Journal* denouncing once more the village where only eight women had appeared on time to vote for the school committee. Next time, she hoped the ladies would leave the dishes until after election. A hasty meal once a year would not harm the digestion of the lords of creation, for even in 1884 man lived not by bread only.

Even in her *Spinning-Wheel Stories*, Louisa could drop a seed of reform. The fear of what people would say could be exorcised in "Jerseys, or, The Girl's Ghost," where the "Jersey Jymnastics Club" would take up the crusade for healthful living, loose clothing, and sensible thinking. Now that the series had begun its appearance in *St. Nicholas*, Louisa continued to supply Mrs. Dodge with a monthly tale, tucking the moral in each as one might hide pills in jelly. In "The Cooking-Class" plain living could be exalted in opposition to the elegant dainties of the kitchen, while "The Hare and the Tortoise" would conclude the series with a modernization of the ancient fable. If the odds and ends in Louisa's portfolio could simultaneously provide ethical enlightenment and aesthetic pleasure, the author would be gratified, knowing that the moral she had hidden in her jelly would not be hard to swallow. From the turns of her spinning wheel she had woven a variegated fabric that would lend color to the issues of *St. Nicholas* throughout the year. Stamped in gold and black, another cloth volume by Miss Alcott could roll from the press of Roberts Brothers. Louisa's wheel drove a double spindle as it spun its threads in black and white.

In June the author left her manuscripts for documents of a different nature, for papers that gave to Mr. Harris the right of ownership in the Orchard House and its fifteen acres of woodland and orchard. Although the dwelling might be sold to him, no transaction could yield to the new owner the memories with which a quarter century had endowed the old. For Louisa, the Lexington Road was empty of all but memory, dear no longer since those who had made it dear were gone. In place of the Orchard House she bought a furnished cottage at Nonquitt, where neither the architecture nor the memories resembled in any way those of the Lexington Road.

With Lulu and John, Louisa returned to the shore on the twenty-fourth of the month, to the cottage on a sandy road some distance from the water. From the covered veranda of the light-green house she could see in the distance Buzzards Bay and a vista of woods and cranberry bogs. While Lulu was wild with the joys of her freedom, Louisa rested in the cool, quiet house. The red roofs of Nonquitt, north of the Round Hills beyond Dumpling Rock Light, still could quiet her spirit. Since she had a greater need now of rest than of money, Louisa felt no temptation to return to *Jo's Boys*, but postponed the day when she would bring to an end the saga of the Marches. What was the tale but a sequel to a sequel, whose termination would mark with a "finis" all the stories that had preceded it?

When she returned home, Louisa spent the idle days of late summer driving about the village with Father or supervising the affairs of the household. The great problem of the day, whether Lulu might eat purple grapes, must be decided. The lesser problem of the evening could be solved as the "youth's companion" spun for her child the tale of a little girl who was transformed into a mermaid and learned from her aquatic life the lesson of content. On a dolphin's back Lulu rode to the land of Nod, dreaming of Goldfin and Silvertail, of oysters and shells and fishermen.

While the baby slept her mermaid's sleep, Louisa took time to answer the letters that accumulated on her desk, reading the account of a teacher in the West about the "Conscience Book" she had borrowed from "Aunt Jo" for her pupils, and announcing to Mrs. Dodge the impossibility of a rapid completion of *Jo's Boys*. That task, with its connotations of finality for the tribe of Marches, she still postponed. Surely time itself would wait if the curtain were not rung down too soon.

Time, however, did not wait. As the years passed, the summers at Nonquitt and in Concord, the autumns in Boston revolved so quickly that they became almost indistinguishable, one from the other. Nothing differentiated the October of 1884 from the Octobers that had preceded it. The Bellevue had not changed. The city itself had not changed. Chestnut Street, where she moved in November with the boys, presented still the genial, gracious slope of other years, where a ghost might walk as the sunshine slanted through the linden leaves. Nor was the red brick dwelling at number 31, with its black marble chimney pieces and carved staircase, so different from the home of Thomas Sewall, where Louisa had found a refuge many lives ago. It was time's paradox that by its very passing yesterday could not be marked off from today.

Only the calendar distinguished the seasons, set off the memorable days from the commonplace, brought Louisa to Concord to celebrate Lulu's birthday, and put her in mind, on her own fifty-second birthday, of Mother and John and May, who had left her with the dying year. Time, Louisa knew, would wait no longer, for the night would come when she, too, could not work. While it was still day, in December, she began again to write *Jo's Boys*, sitting at her desk for two hours on three successive days, living once more with those Marches, who, though they had been poor, were a little proud of their long line of virtuous ancestors. For the enlightenment of Parnassus, Mr. March could discuss Greek comedy in the study. For the delight of Dan, Plumfield's most colorful representative, Mrs. Jo could envision a wreck in which the voyagers clung like her old friend Mr. Pillicoddy to maintop jibs and lee scuppers. For the improvement of mankind she who had signed herself "Yours for reforms of all kinds" could advocate equal opportunities for women, advance the rights of the peaceful Montana Indians, and exalt the threefold pedagogy that developed the bodies and souls as well as the minds of the young. And if the characters had not evolved beyond the stereotypes of *Little Men*, if Stuffy still deserved his name and Dolly was, always, the dandy, one at least gave signs of approaching maturity with strength of soul, the bearded Dan, to whom the author gave her heart.

The three December days took a direful toll, and Louisa, violently ill with vertigo, could not but wonder whether her night had come in which she could no longer work. For six months she was forbidden to write. *Spinning-Wheel Stories* had appeared in book form to remind the public that Louisa M. Alcott was still a weaver of tales. Instead of living in the varied world of the Marches, she must content herself with the narrow world that Christmas of 1884 had brought to Father and in some measure to herself. She who could summon up no longer the ghosts who trod the boards at Hillside must resign herself to less dramatic delights. The spinning wheel must lie idle for a time lest the spool be emptied of its silken threads.

So that she could return more rapidly to her waiting wheel, so that the ills of mind and body both might be relieved, the vertigo, the rheumatism in her right arm, and the ache at the back of her head, Louisa finally indulged in the mind cure. After all, it, too, was one of the reforms of the age, akin in some measure to hygienic dress and temperance, and though it might not prove the panacea for an ailing world, still it was fitting that she who advocated the causes of modernity should experiment with this aspect of the later newness. It was no simple matter to apply the doctrine that since man was spirit, man was not sick, but all the organs of his body in a perfectly healthy condition. Louisa's will could not easily be induced to direct and concentrate the forces which were healing agents. She found it difficult to approach the point where she realized, as the practitioner did, the omnipotence of spirit and rose supreme to the suggestions of the senses.

With the help of Mrs. Anna B. Newman, Louisa tried to rid herself of that inverted thought, that belief in the reality of disease which, according to the healer, stood in the way of her recovery. In the practitioner's office at 17 Boylston Place, they sat together in utter silence for fifteen minutes, until Louisa, her eyes closed, felt a stillness, a lightness, and seemed, as she described her sensations in a letter to Maggie Lukens, "floating away on a sea of rest. Once or twice I seemed to have no body, & to come back from another world. I felt as if I trod on air & was very happy & young for some hours."

The treatment itself was interesting. After Mrs. Newman had listened to Louisa's story, mentally denying every complaint she mentioned, she selected one for healing, and silently directed her will against the error and her patient's false belief in error. Louisa's "errors," writer's cramp and an overworked brain, were not so simply corrected. To *The Woman's Journal*, she sent an account of her experiences:

> No effect was felt except sleepiness for the first few times; then mesmeric sensations occasionally came, sunshine in the head, a sense of walking on the air, and slight trances, when it was impossible to stir for a few moments.

After the silent treatment, Mrs. Newman indulged in cheerful conversation with her patient, reminding her once again that the real man was spirit, who through his mind acted upon his body, which was the instrument whereby he met the material world. As soon as Louisa accustomed herself to the dissection of her thoughts and learned to trust in the infinite power of mind, she would be able to control all discord, to realize that there was nothing but life, but God, nothing but mind.

Louisa found it difficult so to believe. She could not enter that receptive, passive state, however faithfully she tried the experiment. Perhaps the healer was not sufficiently endowed with the essential dynamic power of thought. Perhaps Louisa had too positive a nature to receive strength from her practitioner. At any rate, she began, as she reported to *The Woman's Journal*, "to . . . doubt a theory which claimed to cure cancers, yet could not help a headache. . . . when thirty treatments left the arm no better and the head much worse, I . . . returned to the homoeopathy and massage from which I had been lured."

In its way homeopathy also was a reform of an age that, like herself, ailed and longed for respite from its ills. If she could not be active in all reforms, she could at least subscribe faithfully to *The Woman's Journal*, lending copies to her neighbors, sending the issues to hospitals, prisons, and country libraries. When pen work was allowed again, she would try to carry out her long cherished plan of a story for women told in the columns of their paper, and thus lend herself to the causes of her time.

For the present she could merely send letters to *The Woman's Journal*, a memorial account of her teacher, Sophia Foord, a description of the mind cure in which she had indulged, and a report of the Concord festival to commemorate the nineteenth of April of 1775. Mr. Fuller's dwelling on Monument Street had been converted into a Colonial household, and there a reception was held, juvenile games of a century ago revived, spinning wheels turned, and ancient china exhibited. A costumed committee did the honors, while a genuine tallyho coach carried passengers to and from the house, the station, and the battlefield. Concord, in its ailing modernity, turned neither to mind cure nor to homeopathy for the relief of its ills, but buried itself in the past, finding in the commemoration of ancient glories forgetfulness of its growing pains. Everywhere there were reminders of an age that was gone—in its cemeteries, in the moss that clung to its stone fences, and in the unkempt grass of the Old Manse. Only the trains of the Fitchburg Railroad whistled the schedule of the present as they rolled through the village. For all its whist clubs and sewing circles, its young ladies' bees, and its afternoon Bible classes, Concord was dead, and awakened only to relive the past.

For Louisa, however, the post office was alive. There she found lively reminders of the present in Roberts Brothers' statement that 175,000 copies of *Little Women* had been sold, and that over 500,000 books by Miss Alcott had rolled from the press. There, too, *The Christian Science Journal* made its appearance, with its repudiation of Louisa's remarks on the mind cure, and *The Woman's Journal*, in which "A Scientist's Patient" upheld Mrs. Eddy's beliefs.

While controversy spread among the healers, Louisa tried to forget her own ills in caring for Father, whose slow decline was painful to watch. After *The Christian Science Journal* had decided that Mrs. Newman had never studied personally under Mrs. Eddy and that Miss Alcott had been a victim of demonology, Louisa determined to become her own healing practitioner and find a "mind cure" of a different nature in writing out the tales she told Lulu. One of them, "The Candy Country," with its background of sugar snow, chocolate rocks, candied cherry twigs, and jujube streets, could be sent to *St. Nicholas*, whose subscribers would happily journey from the land of the Giant Dyspepsia to Bread land, where plain food and wholesome living made healthy bodies and happy souls. For Lulu the tiny books were tied up in little birch-bark covers and filled with tales of "How They Ran Away" to rough it in the bush, "The Fairy Box" that brought rewards for virtues and punishments for disobedience, "The Piggy Girl" who loved to be dirty and dreamed that she had turned into a pig, and "The Three Frogs," Hop the adventurous, Croak the vain, and Splash the good. In the tiny books with birch-bark covers there was a mind cure that excelled Mrs. Newman's treatment and would cause no flutter at all among the disciples of Mrs. Eddy, though Lulu's hair might stand on end and her eyes glisten under the spell of the storyteller.

These little books changed the pattern of Louisa's summer at Nonquitt, where she decided to copy them for a series entitled *Lulu's Library*. Since she dared not attempt a return to the Marches just yet, she could fill the long, lovely days in her cottage with the new enterprise that would not tax her mind, but could not fail to charm the small folks. The friendship of her new neighbors, the Crapos, also served to vary the season for Louisa. When the boys and girls planned a picnic at Round Hills, she happily agreed to chaperon them, riding along, a veritable "youth's companion," over the rough road called Featherbed Lane.

Despite the comforting reports from Main Street, Louisa knew that Father needed her, and on August 8 packed her bronze and russet gowns to return home. At home she forgot the affairs of the Milldam in the more immediate affair of *Lulu's Library*, arranging the tales that had been tied up in birch-bark covers for the more substantial ones promised by Roberts Brothers.

The new collection was simple to organize, and Louisa was able to take time from her manuscripts to look at houses in Boston, where she hoped to gather the family together for the winter. Knowing that they would soon leave the Thoreau house, Louisa started the task of sorting old letters, burning many so that curious eyes might not read them nor gossip-lovers print them, rereading her journals and adding to the early entries brief postscripts of a later year. For days she lived in the past, feeling very old as she recalled the experiences that had been hers, yet realizing even as she dwelt in the far-off times that it might be well to keep some record of her life for others to read when she, too, was gone. Such a record might be her gift to a future that would search out its roots in the past and find in the life of one New England lady the history of her times. If she had found in one household humanity depicted, perhaps in her own life those to come would find a large enough domain to reflect the annals of her country.

She herself had little time to provide such a record beyond the journals and the letters she had already written. Now the affairs of the present must engross her. In September, after she had inspected several houses and enjoyed many a lively session with the brokers, Mr. Mason of 10 Louisburg Square agreed that she might rent the dwelling for two years. On October 1 the family would move to the large, sunny, furnished house on the Square.

While Concord celebrated the two hundred and fiftieth anniversary of its incorporation, firing a salute, ringing the bells at sunrise, and parading to Main Street for exercises at the Town Hall, Louisa and Anna continued their packing. Between the trunks and the letters that demanded her attention, Louisa was too preoccupied to linger long over her farewells to the village that had known her for more than forty years. Yet, as the closets of the Thoreau house were emptied, Louisa could not but recall, as Concord itself was recalling, the old whitewashed jail and the burned courthouse, the meandering river, the sunrise over the wide Virginia meadows, the Hosmer farm, Hillside, and the Orchard House. All but the river and the sunrise had changed, and even these had been altered by time that dimmed the glory and dulled the splendor. And of the family of six who had first ventured to the village, only three were left to whisper farewells to the Lexington Road and to Sleepy Hollow. In their departure they must pull up the roots of the past, whose seeds they had planted in another life than this.

Up the granite steps with their wrought-iron rails Louisa walked, entering the red-brick house at 10 Louisburg Square. Through the white door she passed, showing to Father his upper room with a view of the garden. There he could sit comfortably by the window, near him his revolving bookcase filled with his own works. For Lulu there were a large, sunny nursery and a playhouse, and Anna and the boys were content with the broad brick house on the southern side of the Square.

The Square itself was a little island of exploration for Lulu. Aunt Wee would point out to her the weatherworn, marble statues of Aristides and Columbus within the tree-shaded oval, where all the cats of the city seemed to have taken up headquarters. To the child the sight of a cat upon Columbus soon became a familiar sight, and she never wearied of hearing the story of how a small boy had once deprived the explorer of his index finger and cast the evidence of his guilt into the Charles. Gradually she came to know all the residents of the retired island of Beacon Hill, and Lulu and Aunt Wee became familiar figures, too—a tall, stately, pale-faced lady leading by the hand a child whose radiant face presaged a happy mission.

For Lulu, Louisa rediscovered Boston. Hand in hand they walked along the streets of the city, where velvet wraps and Bernhardt capes paraded for the delight of a little girl from Concord. Bending down to give a pat to every big dog she met, Louisa escorted her young explorer to the Common, whose Frog Pond and malls offered their pleasures to Lulu as, fifty years ago, they had offered them to Lulu's Aunt Wee. On the Common a wildly exuberant little girl could scream away to her heart's content, for neither would the Brewer Fountain stop playing nor the deer cease grazing at such a display.

In caring for Lulu, Louisa could forget the indigestion and insomnia that troubled her. More effective than Vitaline or Murdock were the tales she told her child, the story of "Lu Sing" and her aunts, "Ah Wee" and "Ah Nah." Far more effective than massage or raw eggs was Louisa's interest in the young men of Louisburg Square, whom she wished to see settled in business. In Father especially, Louisa found forgetfulness of self, watching as the archpriest of Hillside Chapel played at a checkerboard or was screened during charades at number 10.

Though she could find mental quietude in the knowledge that her books had never sold better and that *Lulu's Library* would appease the children until she could work again on *Jo's Boys*, Louisa suffered from bronchial catarrh and was forced to consult Dr. Conrad Wesselhoeft. After lager beer had relieved her dyspepsia and Dr. Wesselhoeft's homeopathic doses had allayed her cough, she was able to enjoy Lulu's jolly tales of school and to rejoice with the child on her sixth birthday, celebrated by sixteen presents, including a live mouse in a revolving trap. To Father, on his eighty-sixth birthday, to the Pilgrim whose long journey toward the Celestial City was so nearly done, Louisa wrote a poem, commemorating still another milestone that the white-haired wayfarer had passed.

> Dear Pilgrim, waiting patiently,
>   The long, long journey nearly done,
> Beside the sacred stream that flows
>   Clear shining in the western sun;
> Look backward on the varied road
>   Your steadfast feet have trod,
> From youth to age, through weal and woe,
>   Climbing forever nearer God.
>
> Mountain and valley lie behind;
>   The slough is crossed, the wicket passed;
> Doubt and despair, sorrow and sin,
>   Giant and fiend, conquered at last.
> Neglect is changed to honor now;
>   The heavy cross may be laid down;
> The white head wins and wears at length
>   The prophet's, not the martyr's, crown.
>
> Greatheart and Faithful gone before,
>   Brave Christiana, Mercy sweet,
> Are Shining Ones who stand and wait
>   The weary wanderer to greet.
> Patience and Love his handmaids are,
>   And till time brings release,
> Christian may rest in that bright room
>   Whose windows open to the east.
>
> The staff set by, the sandals off,
>   Still pondering the precious scroll,
> Serene and strong, he waits the call
>   That frees and wings a happy soul.
> Then, beautiful as when it lured
>   The boy's aspiring eyes,
> Before the pilgrim's longing sight
>   Shall the Celestial City rise.

For him who had passed the Slough of Despond, the Celestial City rose near. For Louisa its shining spires seemed far off; and Boston, as the years passed, bore less and less resemblance to that pearled city of dreams. Yet there were pleasures still for her, and if the music of Madame Hopekirk, who called at Louisburg Square and played her Scottish melodies, was not a heavenly harping, "Adieu Dundee" and "Oh, Charlie Is My Darling" echoed euphoniously over Beacon Hill. Although a lecture by Madame "Henry Gréville," the stout, rosy author of *Dosia* and *Gabrielle*, might bring Louisa no nearer to Christian's goal, she enjoyed the novelist's charming account of women abroad. Tommaso Salvini, whether he played Saul or Othello, Coriolanus or Samson, would always stir her with his classic face, the grand proportions of his figure, and the vibrant, sympathetic sweetness of his voice. Louisa could not deny that Boston offered delights, even though they might not approach those of the Celestial City.

Besides, as the year ended, she could content herself with the thought that despite the ailments that had afflicted her, the hoarseness, dyspepsia, insomnia, and lack of appetite, *Lulu's Library* had appeared with the preface that offered as "Aunt Jo's" Christmas gift to her boys and girls the small blue books that had become one little listener's favorites. The idle year had not been entirely fruitless. Perhaps the one to come would see the curtain fall at last upon the Marches in the completion of *Jo's Boys*.

Louisa heartily wished, when Thomas Niles ushered in the new year with gratifying accounts of the sale of her works, that she could swamp the book room with *Jo's Boys*. Until the time came when she could again plunge into the history of the Marches, she must be satisfied with laurels already earned. The days must be filled somehow, before she returned to her manuscripts, with massages three times a week by Rhoda Lawrence, with readings in "Henry Gréville" or "H. H.," or with Fred's lively accounts of Roberts Brothers, where he was working. Yet she could not content herself long with such trivia.

Despite an attack of vertigo, Louisa mentally planned *Jo's Boys* to the end. She could wait no longer to return to the Marches, or the night would come when a return would be impossible. With Dr. Wesselhoeft's permission she began to write, at first half an hour a day, then one or two hours. Between massages by Rhoda Lawrence, Louisa worked once more upon the drama she had left so long, finding a source for the sequel in her later life, as she had once found a source for its precursors in her earlier days. Nonquitt would make a fine background for Tom's romance with Dora, provided the name were altered to Quitno. The generous and honorable Mr. Niles would serve as an excellent employer for Demi, once his name was metamorphosed to Tiber. Louisa remembered the convict who had visited her from Concord's prison, and to Dan she gave his experiences within surroundings she had seen in New York's Tombs. Like all the Marches, like all human beings who had ever struggled for light and life, Dan would climb out of the Valley of Humiliation to glimpse the Celestial City after his conflict with the Giant Despair and the fiery Apollyon. Not John Bunyan only, but Dickens, too, still sat at Louisa's side, for Demi in his love of Alice Heath was Dick Swiveller thinking of his Sophy Wackles.

The author, living once more with the Marches, was not unaware that she repeated herself. Yet if, in her attempt to recapture the glories of the past, she had stereotyped her incidents, surely enough simple domestic scenes were left to touch the hearts of her readers. At least she had made some progress on a work long postponed and often interrupted, and the day when she would complete it drew nearer. Then, perhaps, she could attempt a serial for the *St. Nicholas* of 1888, a year when she would be free for new pursuits and enterprises.

In May, 1886, the year 1888 seemed far off. Now Louisa must plan for the more immediate future, making ready for the family's return to Concord for the summer. While Anna prepared the Thoreau house for their arrival, Louisa and the boys set about closing number 10. She herself would not stay long in Concord, but would venture to Princeton, Massachusetts, for the month of June. A new ecru bonnet would complete her wardrobe; Clapp would replenish her supply of Murdock; a final massage would exhilarate her for the journey. Back at Concord, Louisa completed her arrangements for the month near Mount Wachusett, the month that would restore her buoyancy and mark, perhaps, another milestone in the progress of *Jo's Boys.*

It was pleasant to wander about in the village of Princeton, with its neat white green-shuttered houses, its little lakes, and its pines and birches. Mountain holly and chokeberry and swamp pink filled the air with the fragrance of June. Before her Louisa saw the valley pink with laurel, while behind her rose the great slope of Mount Wachusett, from which she could look down upon Fruitlands. The delightful walks twice a day, the sewing, and the reading calmed her mind. The news from Anna, who wrote that all was running smoothly at home, freed her from anxiety, and she was able to return to the Marches.

Since it was impossible for the humble historian of the March family to write a story without theatricals, Louisa gave herself up to the joys of the Plumfield plays while the sun shone over Mount Wachusett. From her experience at Georgetown she recalled details to use in one scene that depicted a ward in an army hospital, and the author of "Nat Bachelor's Pleasure Trip" and "The Rival Prima Donnas" happily abandoned lovesick girls and runaway wives to prove that there was dramatic romance in old women also. In the Owlsdark Marbles that followed Jo's play, the secretary of Concord's temperance society took care to include Hebe, who pointed the moral that the nectar of old cheered but did not inebriate. Concord's first woman voter placed among the Owlsdark Marbles the image of Minerva, whose shield bore the words, "Woman's Rights."

After her quiet stay on Princeton's hillside, Louisa returned home in time to see Anna and Lulu off for Nonquitt. At the Thoreau house she took up the thread that she had dropped at the foot of Mount Wachusett, and wove it once more upon the framework of her story. It was a double thread actually that was spun into the tale, the first a thread of memory that ran through a Plumfield where the Carnival of Boats appeared on the river, where Josie remembered, as her creator did, Miss Edgeworth's story of the three roses. With the second thread, Louisa spun her crusades, inserting a word on behalf of "superfluous" women, championing the education that was not confined to books but drew from experience. To her sewing circle Mrs. Jo would read Miss Cobbe's *Duties of Women*, Miss Brackett's *Education of American Girls*, and Mrs. Woolson's *Dress Reform* in her crusade for healthful clothing and sensible thinking. Again the author sounded her trumpet for temperance in all things. Energetically she pleaded for common sense instead of custom. The double thread had been worked through twenty chapters when Louisa took her manuscript to Roberts Brothers' new quarters at 3 Somerset Street.

In the ground-floor parlor of the yellow-front building behind his screened desk, Thomas Niles delightedly received the manuscript of Miss Alcott's new book. The first edition would consist of fifty thousand copies, since orders were already coming in quickly. And although she felt that the work was not good since there had been too many intervals between the parts, Louisa was content that her public would be happy and her promise kept. Two chapters were still needed, and back at Concord, Louisa began to write the finale to her tale, giving happy endings to her boys. Yet there was a sadness in the last appearance of the Marches upon the stage. The weary historian was strongly tempted to close her tale with an earthquake that would engulf Plumfield deeply in the bowels of the earth. Instead, having endeavored to suit her readers with many weddings, few deaths, and as much prosperity as the eternal fitness of things would permit, she would simply let the music stop, the lights die out, and the curtain fall forever on the March family.

On July 4, while the philosophers prepared to discuss Dante at the Hillside Chapel, Louisa had composed the preface to *Jo's Boys*, apologizing for its faults, accounting for the neglect of Amy and Marmee, about whom she could not write since their originals were gone. Now at last the work, written at long intervals over a period of several years, was finished, and the inkstand corked. She would dedicate the book to Dr. Conrad Wesselhoeft as a very inadequate tribute of affection and respect from his friend and patient, the author. In itself that inscription was an indication of the change that had come to her own life.

In the Alcott family there had been two weddings and four deaths, and, as with the Marches, as much prosperity as the eternal fitness of things would permit. For the Marches, the time had come for the music to stop, the lights to die out, and the curtain to fall forever. In another family, too, Louisa knew that the music echoed but faintly, and the lights were dimmed. If the curtain rose again, it must rise upon the epilogue of a drama, whose scenes had been performed, whose last act was almost over.

CHAPTER 16

🐚🐚

Dunreath Place

Louisa knew that her grist was ground and in the barn. Yet the compulsion for turning the long-worked mill continued with Mrs. Dodge's demands for a serial and Thomas Niles's request for a novel. Since the doctor had forbidden her to begin a full-length book, she considered the possibilities of writing *A Garland for Girls* as a companion piece to *Spinning-Wheel Stories*. The circle of her own life seemed to complete itself now that she who had made her bow to the public with *Flower Fables* planned to respond to a curtain call with *A Garland for Girls*.

Father, too, could taste, probably for the last time, the fruits of his garden with its metaphysical blooms, when Mrs. Julia Ward Howe lectured to the philosophers on Dante and Beatrice. Louisa entered the Hillside Chapel with Father and his nurse. He sat quietly in an armchair on the platform, while Louisa nodded to Mrs. Emerson, a slight, shy, silent figure in black, her soft white hair showing under her dark bonnet. With a rapt expression Mrs. Howe rose to speak, picturing Dante's vision of Beatrice, picturing that walk through Hell where she herself had felt the weight of leaden cloaks. Louisa felt it, too, and almost heard in the silent chapel the sound of Charon's oar.

Louisa contented herself at Concord, looking over old journals and letters, planning also to adopt John so that he could apply for the renewals of her copyrights if they expired after her death.

Death, somehow, no longer seemed an unreal shadow that lengthened over others, not herself, but assumed an almost corporeal form
with which she must reckon. Death was a fact brought closer with
each day, a blight in the garden where she had stepped, and even the
placid Concord River might echo the sound of Charon's oar.

Perhaps, in Louisburg Square, where the family returned in
September, death might be forgotten. There might be pleasure yet
in pointing out to Lulu the Masonic Temple where Father had
once taught the children, and where now in the remodeled building the company of R. H. Stearns traded in more material goods.
In her own achievements Louisa found little joy. *Jo's Boys* was
issued by Roberts Brothers with a frontispiece picture of the bas-
relief by Walton Ricketson, and the author could calculate that her
income from books alone during the year 1886 would doubtless
amount to $20,000. Rewards flowed in, but the power to enjoy
them was gone. Others now delighted in the fruits of her labors,
such as little Gracie Hill, who loved Miss Alcott very much
because she had given so much pleasure by writing those nice
books, and the reviewer of the *Tribune*, who found *Jo's Boys* a pleasant and innocent tale that would increase the author's popularity.

The fact that the author's popularity must be increased, that
the public must continue to be supplied with those nice books
that gave so much pleasure, that literary promises made to Mrs.
Dodge or the editor of *Harper's Young People* must be kept, troubled Louisa increasingly. Somehow it had been easier for her to
write a prayer than a story, asking to learn the virtues of courage
and patience instead of exalting them as morals in a sugar-coated
tale for a child to digest.

> *Courage and patience, these I ask,*
>   *Dear Lord, in this my latest strait;*
> *For hard I find my ten years' task,*
>   *Learning to suffer and to wait.*

> *Life seems so rich and grand a thing,*
>   *So full of work for heart and brain,*

316 . Louisa May Alcott

It is a cross that I can bring
No help, no offering, but pain.

The hard-earned harvest of these years
I long to generously share;
The lessons learned with bitter tears
To teach again with tender care;

To smooth the rough and thorny way
Where other feet begin to tread;
To feed some hungry soul each day
With sympathy's sustaining bread.

So beautiful such pleasures show,
I long to make them mine;
To love and labor and to know
The joy such living makes divine.

But if I may not, I will only ask
Courage and patience for my fate,
And learn, dear Lord, thy latest task,—
To suffer patiently and wait.

Louisa often felt that she could work no longer. She suffered now from a nervous prostration that prevented her even from attending to the cares of the household, and that carried in its wake a series of other ailments, such as dyspepsia and debility and insomnia and hoarseness. In despair for an appetite, she turned to Hydrastis, but no remedy could be found that would let her endure patiently the anxieties of 10 Louisburg Square, where Ellen could not learn how to tend the bell, where Julia and Mrs. Hall tried to keep the large household running smoothly under Anna's supervision, and where Father and Lulu required constant attention. No rose-colored glasses had been invented to fit upon jaundiced eyes. In the long succession of despairing weeks, only a few days glowed and still were radiant.

Louisa's fifty-fourth birthday was brightened by the lovely weather and the gifts she received—a dressing case, books, and flowers. The omens were good, for her morning verse had been, "I will lift up mine eyes unto the hills," and the hills surely meant Princeton in June. There might also be time for a visit to Concord, unless her poor health necessitated a protracted stay in Roxbury under the care of Dr. Rhoda Lawrence. Before that, she could at least spend one last Christmas Day at home, rejoicing in Fred's betrothal to Jessica Cate and trying to forget her own sadness and illness in the flowers that arrived at 10 Louisburg Square.

Such forgetfulness could not endure. Her weariness could not be mitigated without a doctor's daily care, complete rest, and freedom from anxiety. These Louisa knew she would find at Dr. Lawrence's nursing home on Dunreath Place in Roxbury. Since Dio Lewis had died, Boston offered no such retreat as that in the suburb a half-mile beyond the home of Dr. Edward Everett Hale, where the rumble of cars on the Highland Line was dulled and the sounds of the outer world muted. For some time Louisa had been interested in the career of Dr. Lawrence, who had exercised unceasingly woman's right to work. After her attendance at the Female Seminary in Charlestown, she had taught in Westboro while Louisa was sending the tales of "A. M. Barnard" to *The Flag of Our Union*. Later on she had exhibited her versatility by taking charge of the Western Union Telegraph in Jamaica Plain, and only four years ago had enrolled as a student at the Boston University School of Medicine. Now an active member of the Roxbury Homeopathic Association, Rhoda Ashley Lawrence had established at Dunreath Place a quiet retreat where medical treatment and loving attention were combined to effect the recovery of her patients. Some time ago, Louisa had consulted Samuel Sewall regarding the possibilities of raising a loan to help Rhoda Lawrence pay the first installment on a house where people weary of living might summon up their forces to live again. Dr. Wesselhoeft had offered his support for the enterprise, and Louisa herself had been strengthened by Dr. Lawrence's sympathy as well as her massages. Now the time had come when she who had applauded the undertaking for others must test its efficacy for herself.

The rambling dwelling at 10 Dunreath Place gave to Louisa a sense of security she had not known in Louisburg Square. It was for her a "Saint's Rest," where the doctor's sister, Mary Joy, played the role of housemother. In her room she could shut out the bustling world and greet the new year of 1887 with a sadness and hopelessness undisguised for the benefit of Anna or Lulu or Father. She need manifest no cheerful joy now at the announcement of Fred's engagement or at word of his promotion in Roberts Brothers to a post of responsibility. The world, with its distractions, its rejoicings, and its heedlessness of pain, could be forgotten here, where four walls offered a shelter to the sick in heart.

There was no joy for her outside that refuge, where the days careered in merry course, unmindful that she could not keep pace. There was no joy even in the reform activity that had once restored her. She could send a list of selections from her work to Anna Gordon, who was editing *The White Ribbon Birthday Book* for the Woman's Temperance Publication Association. She could dispatch to *The Young Crusader* a short tale, "What It Cost," in which her recollections of Georgetown were combined with a plea for temperance, and the story would appear as one of *The Press Leaflets*, sold in packets of one hundred for fifty cents. To the *Woman Suffrage Bazaar Journal* she could contribute "A Flower Fable" that would picture a domain ruled by gentle Queen Violet, who closed the Grapevine Hotel and opened a hospital for the sick and homeless. Such brief narratives Louisa still could write, but she who had so ardently signed herself "Yours for reforms of all kinds" found now that her ardor was gone, her tales forced. The crusader had stumbled and longed for a truce before the wars were won.

It was another world that Louisa was given in exchange for the one she had abandoned, a world that existed on two planes only, her ailments and her medications. The vertigo and headache seemed to indicate the ever-present possibility of apoplexy. The digestive difficulties might be symptoms either of her nervous disorder or of more deeply rooted disturbances, from a catarrhal condition of the stomach to ulcers, or from dyspepsia to cancer. The work that lay immediately before her was neither supplying tales for children nor righting the wrongs of a world out of joint. Her energies must be devoted to the cure of her ailments, if a cure were possible. With the concentrated devotion that she had lavished upon all her labors, Louisa turned now to the alleviation of her woes. All the remedies that had ever been advocated by the homeopaths she would try, from Clapp's triturations to Murdock's liquid food, from rhus wine to a diet of broth and gruel. Since glasses increased her headache, she gladly paid one of the ladies of Dunreath Place to read to her. Despite her determined efforts, however, she wearied of fussing over her old skeleton and longed to pack it away and start afresh with a heavenly body minus head and stomach. She wanted, occasionally, to return to the world from her refuge, to journey to Princeton in the summer with Lulu, or to visit Aunt Bond. It was a thin diet she lived on, a mixture of gruel and hope.

It was difficult for Louisa to sit serenely in her soul when she contemplated the fact that she had lost twenty-five pounds since October, and that after ten weeks of spoon-meat she was a skeleton. Though Dr. Wesselhoeft blandly ordered her to eat a plate of lobster salad, she persisted in her diet of gruel, broth, and gems, and in her hopes that she would slowly mend. It was a narrow world in which she lived, a world of baths, of readings by Dr. Lawrence, and of sewing and resting and waiting. News from the outer world drifted in to 10 Dunreath Place, with visits several times a week from Anna, who tried to cheer her with flowers, books, and reports of home. Father was comfortable, but had said, as he looked up from his paper, "Beecher has gone now; all go but me." Father, too, was waiting, for an end that seemed closer at hand than Louisa's.

Gradually the refuge to which she had turned for security became a prison that held her captive despite the books and loving notes and flowers that entered its gates. Lest she should never be able to escape, Louisa determined to try her hand once more at writing, for the flowers sent by her friends suggested stories that could be used in her *Garland for Girls*. A bouquet of scarlet poppies and a handful of green wheat reminded her of the tale that a traveling companion had planned in Schwalbach, and now in her room on Dunreath Place she sailed again up the Rhine to the spa, gathering a moral harvest along with the flowers near the ruins of Hohenstein. "Poppies and Wheat" would color her *Garland* with the contrasts in which she delighted, and "Pansies" could be offered first to *St. Nicholas*, the pansies that symbolized thoughts and that triumph of mind over body for which the author yearned.

Letters, too, must be written, a note to Mr. Carpenter describing the literary habits formed through the years by the historian of the March family:

> My methods of work are very simple. . . . My head is my study, & there I keep the various plans of stories for years sometimes, letting them grow as they will till I am ready to put them on paper.
>
> Then it is quick work, as chapters go down word for word & need no alteration. I never copy, since I find by experience that the work I spend the least time upon is best liked by critics & readers.
>
> Any paper, any pen, any place that is quiet suit me, & I used to write from morning till night without fatigue when "the steam was up."
>
> Now, however, I am paying the penalty of twenty years of over work, & can write but two hours a day, doing about twenty pages, sometimes more, though my right thumb is useless from writer's cramp.
>
> While a story is underway I live in it, see the people, more plainly than real ones, round me, hear them talk, & am much interested, surprized or provoked at their actions, for I seem to have no power to rule them, & can simply record their experiences & performances.
>
> Material for the children's tales I find in the lives of the little people about me, for no one can invent anything so droll pretty or pathetic as the sayings & doings of these small actors, . . . In the older books the events are mostly from real life, the strongest the truest & I yet hope to write a few of the novels, which have

been simmering in my brain while necessity & unexpected success have confined me to juvenile literature.

. . . I . . . find my best success in the comfort my family
enjoy, also a naughty satisfaction in proving that it was better *not*
to "stick to teaching" as advised, but to write.

To Thomas Niles Louisa wrote also, regarding his proposal for a
new edition of *A Modern Mephistopheles*, to which he wished to
append "A Whisper in the Dark," a tale too mild for "A. M.
Barnard," too "lurid" for L. M. Alcott. As a sample of "Jo
March's" necessity stories it might, however, appear in print. Stories outlined themselves in her mind as Louisa sat in her room at
Dunreath Place: "A Tragedy of To-day," which she hoped to complete during the summer; "Anna: An Episode" of Boston life; and
"The Philosopher's Wooing," based upon an incident in the
career of Mr. Thoreau.

Time and strength were needed to convert the fragmentary
sketches into completed tales. It was simpler to plan a second volume of *Lulu's Library* that would contain reprints from *Flower
Fables* along with a few newer tales. To Ellen Emerson Louisa also
dedicated this, her winter garden, and as she wrote the preface,
recalling the days when many of the stories had first been told, she
was grateful to the past that served so well the weary present. Yet,
remembering the glowworms and downy-back moles, the cowslip
hats and acorn cups of *Flower Fables*, she could not help perceiv-
ing that in the later tales nature was a delicate, dewy-eyed child no
longer, but a mother to whom the author turned for strength and
solace. In place of high adventure in a land of fairies, health and
comfort were glorified on the altar of her winter garden, those
lately apotheosized gods to whom the storyteller of Hillside had
learned to pray.

Louisa was pleased that she could supply Somerset Street with
manuscripts for the children of those children for whom she had
woven her first garland of tales. When she laid down her pen, she
could take up her needle, making garments for poor babies and
setting up a workbasket for Dr. Lawrence. She was sufficiently

strong now to drive to Louisburg Square occasionally for a visit with Father, Lulu, and Anna, or to call upon Mrs. David Reed in her Roxbury home. Her steady gain had not, however, been long-lived, and Louisa planned to consult a magnetic physician with Dr. Lawrence, giving up, for the time being, the rooms she had reserved at Princeton.

Instead of journeying to the hills in June, she paid a brief visit to Melrose, where the family had gathered for the summer. It was painful to see Father sitting serenely in his chair all day with his books, unable to talk much, but contented to be nursed and petted. It was a sad ending to watch, sadder to watch perhaps than to endure, for Father seemed fortified and sustained by a philosophy that enabled him to wait patiently for the time when he would "go up." Louisa was less patient. She had not been resigned to yielding all her cares to Anna, and now, seeing her sister's gray hair and the wrinkles fast coming upon her, she realized that one by one Anna's props had failed. Lulu only remained buoyant, a superb creature filled with life and vigor and grace, in whom were united May's complexion and hair and her father's sturdy figure and energy. Willful and tempestuous, she still offered a loving heart to all who would accept it, and had already begun to exhibit the musical talent of the Nierikers to the family. The colorful seven-year-old who darted about so boisterously with her governess marked for Louisa a dramatic contrast between the child and those who cared for her. Nothing else was dramatic at Melrose, for the curtain that had fallen swiftly upon the March family fell slowly and painfully upon their prototypes. The stage was all but empty, but still the curtain lingered.

The stage manager's name was Time, and Louisa, even as she waited for the fall of the curtain, heeded his directions. Taking a room for a week at Concord near the Thoreau house, she looked over papers once again and completed the plan for adopting her nephew, whose name was changed to John Sewall Pratt Alcott. To each of the boys she gave $25,000, and while the villagers prepared for the arrival of the philosophers, Louisa decided to spend the summer at Princeton after all in yet another search for health.

For Dr. Lawrence, who would accompany her, she engaged rooms in the farmhouse opposite Mr. Bullard's hotel, and early in July arrived at Mount Wachusett with her physician.

In her large room in the Mountain Cottage, Louisa was comfortably settled. Dr. Lawrence occupied the back room and a small one was converted into a kitchen with a tin refrigerator, pots, and pans. It was pleasant to see again the neat, green-shuttered houses of the village, to smell the fragrance of the evening primrose and the meadowsweet that flowered in July. The fine air surely would restore her as it blew over the hayfields and the gardens; and Louisa enjoyed her short walks to the library, which boasted now a copy of *Jo's Boys*, or to the region of pines and birches near Mount Wachusett. Her evening strolls were less agreeable, for the author was disturbed by the lion hunters who stalked their prey when their daylight diversions were ended.

Her days, too, were disturbed, in spite of Princeton's fine air, by pain in her limbs and lack of strength and appetite and by the vertigo and dyspepsia that discouragingly persisted. Rhoda Lawrence's companionship helped her to forget her ills for a while, and the routine of life in the mountains, with her short walks, her sewing and reading and letter writing, varied the long summer days. To Anna at Melrose, she sent notes regarding her progress, but neither the lofty flank of Mount Wachusett nor the little lakes nor the scent of meadowsweet and evening primrose diverted her from following the directions of stage manager Time, who reminded her that decisions must still be made before the drama ended.

Louisa agreed with Anna that the family would not return to the Thoreau house for several years. The lease on the house at Louisburg Square was renewed, and on July 10, in the presence of Dr. Lawrence and the witnesses who had arrived at Princeton—Otis Shepard and Helen Blanchard—Louisa signed a copy of her will that had been drawn up by Samuel Sewall. She read with satisfaction the clauses in the last testament of Louisa May Alcott, that directed Anna to give away her clothing and her library, that assigned to Lulu her ornaments and her share of the family silver. To Lulu also would be given Louisa's share of the proceeds from the sale of the Orchard House, while her rights in the Thoreau house would be Anna's. To Fred a trust fund of $10,000 would be bequeathed for the support and education of his little cousin; and to John, her adopted son, her copyrights were left in trust, the income to be divided among Anna, Fred, Lulu, and himself. The residue of the estate was left in trust for the support of the family, to Anna, who was named executrix; in witness whereof, Louisa thereunto set her hand and seal this tenth day of July in the year 1887. Surely this was the last of the stage directions that a trouper must follow.

There were distractions from pain at Mount Wachusett with the arrival of summer guests. Of them all, Louisa enjoyed most the companionship of James Murdoch and his daughters, for the aged actor and elocutionist provided spirited entertainment. With gusto he recalled for the benefit of the Georgetown nurse the readings he had given for the North during the Rebellion. His discourse ranged between grape culture and elocution, the Rush method of oratory and orthophony; and Louisa thoroughly enjoyed his robust personality, relishing his renderings of James Murdoch no less than his renderings of Shakespeare.

If ever she found a cure for her ills, it must be now at Princeton, where she was released from worry and could share, if she wished, the evenings made gay by Mr. Murdoch's conversation or a visit from John, who offered lively reports of his work as a bookkeeper in Fred's office. The family was happy at Melrose, Father comfortable, Lulu growing like a weed, and Anna reveling in her freedom from the philosophers who were searching for the unknowable in a torrid Concord.

With skill and sympathy Dr. Lawrence supervised Louisa's medications—nux vomica, aconite, or colochican. Although she could not eat anything more substantial than gluten gruel, gems, and cream, Louisa was able to sleep well and, best of all, found that she could write for an hour each day if she worked without glasses. In her room at Princeton she continued her *Garland for Girls:* "May Flowers" to champion all good charities whether organized or unorganized; "Water-Lilies" upholding sturdy courage and industry as well as the modesty that was as sweet in linsey-woolsey as in muslin. The author sent her stories to Thomas Niles, hoping that after her rest at Princeton the *Garland for Girls* would be completed.

When she returned to the nursing home in Roxbury, Louisa followed again the pattern of life that had been interrupted. It was a simple pattern, varied only by the physician's readings that suggested to the author a series of "Stories of All Nations," beginning with "Trudel's Siege" in the beleaguered city of Leyden. In the gray tapestry of Dunreath Place a few colors glittered, those of the flowers that were sent by friends and were entwined in the *Garland for Girls.* To her "May Flowers," "Water-Lilies," "Pansies," and "Poppies and Wheat," Louisa added now "Little Button-Rose," the tale of Rosy, who ended a feud. "An Ivy Spray" and "Pansies" would soon appear in *St. Nicholas,* and then the blossoms might be gathered together in her *Garland for Girls,* its preface telling how their seeds had been sown. Neither to Lulu nor to Ellen Emerson did she offer her latest harvest, but to Rhoda Lawrence, to whom the little book was affectionately inscribed by her grateful friend.

Between her pen and her needle Louisa tried to vary the pattern of Dunreath Place, leaving the flowers in her *Garland for Girls* only to shape flannel penwipers in the form of pinks or carnations. Neither pen nor needle, however, could ease the knowledge that she weighed only 136 pounds; nor did the ministrations of Dr. Milbrey Green, whom Louisa consulted in the autumn, relieve the monotony of a tapestry in which so many physicians had already stitched their medicinal abracadabras. Unlike the homeopathic Dr. Wesselhoeft, Dr. Green based his therapy upon plant remedies, believing with the botanic or eclectic practitioners that each country produced in its flora the specific remedies for its native diseases. In his office on Columbus Avenue, near Mrs. Eddy's Metaphysical College, Louisa was treated to Dr.

Green's botanic cure and his prescriptions of plain food, water, and common sense.

It was easier somehow to follow Dr. Green's advice regarding plain food and water than to resign herself after so many years of work to patient idleness. She could read and reread the verse from a little poem found under a soldier's pillow in a hospital; to apply the verse was more difficult.

> *I am no longer eager, bold, and strong,—*
> *All that is past;*
> *I am ready not to do*
> *At last—at last.*
> *My half-day's work is done,*
> *And this is all my part.*
> *I give a patient God*
> *My patient heart.*

Louisa's heart was not yet patient, though her half-day's work was done. It was hard for the hub of the family wheel to resign herself graciously to writing cheerful letters to Father and Aunt Bond. The heroine of the Orchard House, whose works had been cherished by Mother as they rolled off the press, found little pleasure in sending from a rest home a copy of *Lulu's Library* to Mother's earthly representative, Aunt Bond. She who had wandered abroad in Boston and in Paris and in London could not easily content herself with uneventful drives in the quiet suburb of Roxbury.

One drive was more eventful, for the horse ran away with the carriage and the blow Louisa received caused congestion in one side of her head. Dr. Green insisted that she see no one, except Lulu for a moment now and then, for at least one month. The cure, he announced, lay in her own hands and would result only from perfect rest even from pleasant things. By such a sacrifice Louisa hoped to hasten the time when she could return home and take her place as the hub of the family wheel. Agreeing to try the rest-and-milk cure advocated by the physician, she dwelt in a world of complete quiet, limited her diet to two quarts of milk a day, and received no visitors but Lulu. Now the refuge was indeed a prison, where in solitary confinement a harassed soul took arms in a struggle against a more harassed body. The interminable days were interrupted only by a request from Mrs. Dodge to print the story of how Marie obtained Miss Alcott's autograph, or Mr. Bok's demand for autobiographical information—an autobiography that was ending in no dramatic fall of princes, but in a sorrowful and slow decline, a rest-and-milk cure after the banquet was cleared from the tables.

There was a banquet of flowers on Louisa's fifty-fifth birthday, posies and roses that bloomed among the gifts that arrived at Dunreath Place. All the ladies in the nursing home sent pretty tokens to her room, and her little table was filled with pictures, books, bags, and cushions, a blue-and-gold rose jar, and a copy of Keats from John. In a bower of roses Louisa lay alone, her only visitor the smiling Dr. Green, who was amused at the turn his patient's quiet day had taken. Yet who could read those lines of Keats's bright star or of his nightingale, of Ruth, when, sick for home, she stood in tears amid the alien corn, of easeful death when it seemed rich to die, and not be moved? So many birthdays she remembered, with fewer gifts than this, but less, far less alone. Surely the gods would be good, restore her to life, unfold for her a calendar of brighter days.

It was certain that she was improving in all ways, walking a little and sleeping well, mending slowly but steadily. She was able to send the manuscript of "Trudel's Siege" to Mrs. Dodge, and the doctor assured the writer that her best work was yet to come. Until the time came for grander enterprises, she must content herself with happy moments snatched from the interminable hours. At least, during the difficult year that was closing, the second volume of *Lulu's Library* had been published and *A Garland for Girls* had been prepared for the press. Perhaps the halcyon years would still be hers for the half-day's work that yet was unbegun.

Louisa opened her red leather diary for 1888 to record on the rainy first of the year the progress she had made, the gratitude she felt for her mercies, and the inner peace she had found. It was less difficult now to resign herself to the rest-and-milk cure and to the homeopathic medicines from Pepsin and Company. Lulu came often to brighten her days, and besides sewing and reading, Louisa could write a little before her evening bath and massage, arranging stories for a third volume of *Lulu's Library*. In it she would include the tale she had planned long ago when she had seen the red-capped fishermen of Nice, the flower girls, and the coral-carvers. As she sat in her quiet room on Dunreath Place, she saw once again the little town of Valrosa. Before her eyes the vineyards stretched, and the alleys of lemon trees, while violets, verbena, and mignonette filled the air with their fragrance. Against the remembered background she painted the figures of Tino and Stella in the tale called "Music and Macaroni."

The past pursued her now in Roxbury, and Louisa recalled, as much for her own pleasure as for the uses of *The Youth's Companion* or Roberts Brothers, the days when a boisterous little girl had fallen into the Frog Pond and driven her hoop around the Common, when a child named Louy had been found one night by Boston's town crier or had listened raptly to *Pilgrim's Progress* and Krummacher's *Parables*. Once more the lords and ladies of Hillside trod the boards and went barnstorming. And still again a hopeful heart beat warmly under an old red shawl as Louy sat on a cartwheel in Concord, shaking her fist at fate. These treasures extracted from the mine of memory glittered no longer with life; they had been converted into "Recollections of My Childhood" for the delight of children who had never known little Louy Alcott. By so many names she had been known, names that summoned up the ghosts of the past: first Louy and then Louisa; Sophia Tetterby and Mrs. Jarley; Nurse L. M. Alcott and "Tribulation Periwinkle"; the mysterious "A. M. Barnard" and the less mysterious Louisa May Alcott; "Aunt Jo" and Aunt Wee and *the* Miss Alcott. With Louy, who had recorded in her diary an early run in the woods when the moss was velvet and the sun rose over the wide Virginia meadows, *the* Miss Alcott would have traded her fame and her fortune.

The gods did not permit such barter. The diary of 1845 could not be substituted for the red leather volume of 1888, in which *the*

Miss Alcott entered her brief observations. No run in the early morning was to be recorded now, but a variety of ills from headache to sore throat, from chest pain to weariness; no verses to Mother from her "trying daughter," but letters to an aged Father; no botany lesson in the woods, but readings in Higginson by Dr. Lawrence; no glorious sunrise over the Virginia meadows, but snowfall in Roxbury. The days that had once been too full for detailed accounting stretched interminably ahead as Louisa tried to shorten the long and weary hours.

At length the reward for her weeks of seclusion came when Dr. Green announced that his patient might drive in to see her father, who was feeble and might slip away at any moment. By yet another name the author was known as her dark carriage arrived at 10 Louisburg Square, for the small Bostonians saluted her as "Msalkot" when they ran to open the door and receive a few pennies from the tall lady who shivered in her fur wraps. For fifteen minutes Louisa sat with Anna, finding all quiet at home, hearing of Father's request that Dr. Bartol speak of him when he was gone and tell the tale of his career. A picture book was in his hands and he took a childlike delight in thumbing the pages until the representation of a wild beast frightened him and brought the tears to his eyes.

Swiftly now the days spent themselves, the past and present and future compressed together so that she scarcely knew when one ended and another began. The lovely azalea that Aunt Bond sent to Louisa became another azalea, the spray that had opened bud by bud after Mother's death. From thinking of Mother's azalea, Louisa turned to thoughts of later blossoms, those that bloomed in February for Fred's wedding. Although she could not attend the ceremony, she sat alone and blessed the pair, listening later with avid interest to Anna's account of the reception, the cutting of the bridal cake, her own black lace dress, and Lulu's pink silk. For Louisa's enjoyment the gifts were described—the marble clock from Thomas Niles, the picture from Mr. Roberts, and the solid silver guarded by a watchdog. Jessica had looked like a rose and Fred had been a complete landscape in his new suit and watered-silk vest. John had been as happy as if he had been the groom, and Lulu as sober and dignified as a matron. To her friends, Louisa sent detailed letters about the ceremony which she had seen through Anna's eyes in Dunreath Place.

Dr. Green had been well pleased with her progress: the baths brought sleep; and though she ate no solid food as yet, Louisa seemed to be gaining strength and flesh. The warm spring days would surely complete the cure that the rest-and-milk treatment had begun, and she was heartily encouraged by her improvement. Once more she could take pleasure in the visible tokens of her success, *The Critic's* laudatory review of *A Garland for Girls*, the letters that arrived from an aspiring author who asked for advice, or from a hopeful boy who sent twenty-five cents to purchase the works of L. M. Alcott. She herself had realized more than $200,000 from her books, a million copies of which had been sold.

The omens were bright. Louisa had lost twenty-three pounds in six months, but she had been promised twenty years of health if she remained at Dunreath Place for another year. Despite her weakness, she could stitch a flannel garment for a poor child, happy in the thought that before long the pen would be substituted for the needle, and the days of her seclusion ended.

Yet death was often in her thoughts as she sat in her room at Roxbury, for Father's end was at hand, she knew. Age had, as Mr. Emerson had written, set its house in order and finished its works. Father was ripe to die. When death came to her, she would be ready for it, too, wishing only for a simple service and her boys to form a guard of honor at her grave. But Louisa had no time to die; too much remained to be done; too many books must be written. For her the time had not yet come to take in sail, to hear the "no more" of that god of bounds who sets to seas a shore.

Father had heard those words long since. Conscious that it would be her last meeting on earth with him, Louisa drove in to Louisburg Square on March 1. Quickly she greeted his two nurses, undid the shawl clasp on her fur wrap, and bent her thin, wan face to his as he lay helpless and feeble. By his bedside she knelt, murmuring, "Father, here is your Louy. What are you thinking of as you lie here so happily?" He took her hand and pointed above, saying, "I am going up. Come with me." "Oh, I wish I could," she answered. Then he kissed her and bade her come soon.

To Father the farewell had been spoken, and in the carriage back to Dunreath Place Louisa bade him farewell again in her heart. Surely he would fare well, since so many who had gone before waited to greet him when his pilgrimage was ended. For him, Lizzie would still be young and May a summer child. John would take his hand again and Mother walk beside him upon ways more lovely by far than those of Concord. In the eternal summer that would soon be Father's, Louisa, too, found warmth. In his destination she had forgotten her own, forgotten the carriage where she sat, forgotten the wrap she had not put on.

She should have remembered that eternal summer was not yet hers and that March in Boston was but a false spring. Louisa soon complained of a violent headache, a dull pain, an iron weight upon her head. Dr. Green was summoned and debated with himself the possibilities of meningitis or of apoplexy while his patient sank quickly into unconsciousness, stirring only to recognize briefly the faces of John and Dr. Lawrence. For the rest, she lay unconscious—unconscious of Anna's presence or the physician's ministrations for cerebrospinal meningitis or apoplexy, unmindful of the scores of unanswered letters that lay upon her table, careless of her unfulfilled promises of stories for Mrs. Dodge. Her stories had been told, and no other leaf would be turned in the red leather diary.

She could not see the diary, nor could she smell in Dunreath Place the smilax and the violets and the roses that scented the air of 10 Louisburg Square, where Father lay in his coffin. The dawn of March 6 had come in Roxbury, and the hands of the clock pointed to half-past three in the morning. The clock ticked on, but Louisa heard it not. She had walked upon a timeless stage, where there were neither lights nor music, but only the ghosts of players upon whose moveless forms a curtain had forever fallen.

This bibliography is arranged chronologically by date of original publication. The compiler is deeply indebted to Jacob Blanck, *Bibliography of American Literature* (New Haven, 1955) I, 27–45, from which collations of books have been taken, with citations to *BAL*.

1. "Sunlight" (poem by Flora Fairfield), *Peterson's Magazine*, Vol. XX, No. 3 (September, 1851).

2. "The Rival Painters. A Tale of Rome," *Olive Branch*, Vol. XVII, No. 19 (May 8, 1852).

3. "The Masked Marriage," *Dodge's Literary Museum*, Vol. VI, No. 2 (December 18, 1852).

4. "The Rival Prima Donnas" (by Flora Fairfield), *Saturday Evening Gazette*, Series for 1854, No. 45 (November 11, 1854). Dramatized version appears as MS in Orchard House.

5. "The Flower's Lesson" (poem). In *Margaret Lyon, or, A Work for All* (Boston, Crosby, Nichols, & Co., 1854). Repr. with slight changes in *Flower Fables*. *BAL* 141.

6. "The Little Seed." In *Margaret Lyon, or, A Work for All* (Boston, Crosby, Nichols, & Co., 1854). *BAL* 141.

7. *Flower Fables*. Boston, George W. Briggs & Co., 1855. [i–ii], [1]–182 pp. *BAL* 142.

8. "A New Year's Blessing," *Saturday Evening Gazette*, Quarto Series, No. 1 (January 5, 1856).

9. "The Sisters' Trial," *Saturday Evening Gazette*, Quarto Series, No. 4 (January 26, 1856).

10. "Little Genevieve," *Saturday Evening Gazette*, Quarto Series, No. 13 (March 29, 1856).

11. "Little Paul" (poem), *Saturday Evening Gazette*, Quarto Series, No. 16 (April 19, 1856).

12. "Bertha," *Saturday Evening Gazette*, Quarto Series, Nos. 16 and 17 (April 19 and 26, 1856).

13. "Mabel's May Day," *Saturday Evening Gazette*, Quarto Series, No. 21 (May 24, 1856).

14. "Beach Bubbles" (poems), *Saturday Evening Gazette*, Quarto Series, Nos. 25, 26, 28, 30, 31, 33, and 34 (June 21, 28, July 12, 26, and August 2, 16, 23, 1856).

15. "The Mother-Moon" (poem, one of "Beach Bubbles"), *Saturday Evening Gazette*, Quarto Series, No. 34 (August 23, 1856). Repr. in *The Little Pilgrim*, Vol. V, No. 1 (January, 1858).

16. "The Lady and the Woman," *Saturday Evening Gazette*, Quarto Series, No. 40 (October 4, 1856).

17. "Ruth's Secret," *Saturday Evening Gazette*, Quarto Series, No. 49 (December 6, 1856).

18. "Songs from a Sea-Shell—The Patient Drop" (poem), *The Little Pilgrim*, Vol. V, No. 4 (April, 1858).

19. "The Rock and the Bubble" (poem), *The Little Pilgrim*, Vol. V, No. 9 (September, 1858). Repr. with slight changes in "Fancy's Friend," *Morning-Glories, and Other Stories*.

20. "Marion Earle: or, Only an Actress!" *American Union* (ca. July–September 12, 1858). Repr. in *New York Atlas* (September 12, 1858).

21. "Mark Field's Mistake," *Saturday Evening Gazette*, Vol. XLV, No. 11 (March 12, 1859).

22. "Mark Field's Success" (sequel to "Mark Field's Mistake"), *Saturday Evening Gazette*, Vol. XLV, No. 16 (April 16, 1859).

23. "With a Rose, That Bloomed on the Day of John Brown's Martyrdom" (poem), *The Liberator*, Vol. XXX, No. 3 (January 20, 1860). Repr. in James Redpath, *Echoes of Harper's Ferry* (Boston, Thayer and Eldridge, 1860). *BAL* 143.

24. "Love and Self-Love," *The Atlantic Monthly*, Vol. V, No. 29 (March, 1860).

25. "A Modern Cinderella: or, The Little Old Shoe," *The Atlantic Monthly*, Vol. VI, No. 36 (October, 1860). Repr. in *Camp and Fireside Stories*.

26. "March, march, mothers and grandmamas!" ("Song"). In *Reports of the School Committee . . . of Concord, Mass. . . . Saturday, March 16, 1861* (Concord, Benjamin Tolman, 1861). *BAL* 144.

27. "The King of Clubs and the Queen of Hearts," *The Monitor*, Vol. I, Nos. 1, 2, 3, 4, 5, 6, and 7 (April 19, 26, May 3, 10, 17, 24, and June 7, 1862). Repr. in *On Picket Duty, and Other Tales* and *Camp and Fireside Stories*.

28. "Pauline's Passion and Punishment," *Frank Leslie's Illustrated Newspaper*, Vol. XV, Nos. 379 and 380 (January 3 and 10, 1863). Repr. in Madeleine B. Stern, ed., *Behind a Mask: The Unknown Thrillers of Louisa May Alcott* (New York, William Morrow, 1975).

29. "M. L.," *The Commonwealth*, Vol. I, Nos. 21, 22, 23, 24, and 25 (January 24, 31, and February 7, 14, 22, 1863). Repr. in *The Journal of Negro History*, Vol. XIV, No. 4 (October, 1929).

30. "Hospital Sketches," *The Commonwealth*, Vol. I, Nos. 38, 39, 41, and 43 (May 22, 29, and June 12, 26, 1863). A portion repr. as "John," *Merry's Museum*, Vol. II, No. 8 (August, 1869). Repr. as *Hospital Sketches*. Boston, James Redpath, 1863. [1]–102 pp. *BAL* 145.

31. "A Whisper in the Dark," *Frank Leslie's Illustrated Newspaper*, Vol. XVI, Nos. 401 and 402 (June 6 and 13, 1863). Repr. in *A Modern Mephistopheles and A Whisper in the Dark* (Boston: Roberts Brothers, 1889); and in *Plots and Counterplots: More Unknown Thrillers of*

Louisa May Alcott, ed. Madeleine B. Stern (New York: William Morrow, 1976).

32. "Letters from the Mountains," *The Commonwealth*, Vol. I, Nos. 47, 48, 49, and 51 (July 24, 31, and August 7, 21, 1863).

33. "Debby's Début" *The Atlantic Monthly*, Vol. XII, No. 70 (August, 1863).

34. "Thoreau's Flute" (poem), *The Atlantic Monthly*, Vol. XII, No. 71 (September, 1863). Repr. in Henry W. Longfellow (ed.), *Poems of Places. America. New England. I.* (Boston, Houghton, Osgood and Company, 1879). *BAL* 190. Repr. in *Life, Letters, and Journals*, 1889; *Library of the World's Best Literature*, 1897; by E. B. Hill, Detroit, Mich., Stylus Press, 1899. *BAL* 228.

35. "A Pair of Eyes; or, Modern Magic," *Frank Leslie's Illustrated Newspaper* (October 24 and 31, 1863). Repr. in *A Double Life: Newly Discovered Thrillers of Louisa May Alcott*, ed. Madeleine B. Stern, Joel Myerson, and Daniel Shealy (Boston: Little, Brown, 1988).

36. "My Contraband; or, The Brothers," first called "The Brothers," *The Atlantic Monthly*, Vol. XII, No. 73 (November, 1863). Repr. in *Camp and Fireside Stories*.

37. *The Rose Family. A Fairy Tale*. Boston, James Redpath, 1864. [1]–47 pp. *BAL* 146.

38. "A Hospital Christmas," *The Commonwealth*, Vol. II, Nos. 19 and 20 (January 8 and 15, 1864). Repr. in *Camp and Fireside Stories*.

39. *On Picket Duty, and Other Tales*. Boston, James Redpath—New York, H. Dexter, Hamilton & Co., [1864]. [1]–96 pp. *BAL* 147.

40. "The Hospital Lamp," *The Daily Morning Drum-Beat*, Nos. III and IV (February 24 and 25, 1864). Repr. in *The Youth's Companion*, Vol. XLI, No. 27 (July 2, 1868). *BAL* 148.

41. "Night Scene in a Hospital" (from *Hospital Sketches*), *The Daily Morning Drum-Beat*, Extra No. (March 11, 1864).

42. "A Golden Wedding: and What Came of It," *The Commonwealth*, Vol. II, Nos. 35 and 36 (April 29 and May 6, 1864). Repr. with changes in *Moods*; repr. in *Good Times. By Favorite Authors* (Boston, Lothrop, [1877]).

43. "Enigmas," *Frank Leslie's Illustrated Newspaper,* Vol. XVIII, Nos. 450 and 451 (May 14 and 21, 1864). Repr. in *Frank Leslie's Ten Cent Monthly* (October, 1864) and in *Frank Leslie's Popular Monthly,* Vol. I. 4 (April, 1876).

44. "Colored Soldiers' Letters," *The Commonwealth,* Vol. II, No. 44 (July 1, 1864).

45. "Love and Loyalty," *The United States Service Magazine,* Vol. II, Nos. 1, 2, 3, 5, and 6 (July, August, September, November, and December, 1864). Repr. in *Camp and Fireside Stories.*

46. "An Hour," *The Commonwealth,* Vol. III, Nos. 13 and 14 (November 26 and December 3, 1864). Repr. in *Camp and Fireside Stories.*

47. "Mrs. Podgers' Teapot, A Christmas Story," *Saturday Evening Gazette,* Vol. L, No. 52 (December 24, 1864). Repr. in *Camp and Fireside Stories.*

48. *Moods.* Boston, Loring, 1865. [i]–[vi], [7]–297 pp. *BAL* 149.

49. "V.V.: or, Plots and Counterplots," *The Flag of Our Union,* Vol. XX, Nos. 5, 6, 7, and 8 (February 4, 11, 18, and 25, 1865). Repr. as ten-cent novelette by A. M. Barnard (Boston, Thomes & Talbot, [1865] i.e., ca. 1870). [i–ii], [7] (*sic*)–100 pp. *BAL* 165 and in *Plots and Counterplots,* ed. Madeleine B. Stern (New York: William Morrow, 1976).

50. "The Fate of the Forrests," *Frank Leslie's Illustrated Newspaper* (February 11, 18, and 25, 1865). Repr. in *A Double Life,* ed. Madeleine B. Stern, Joel Myerson, and Daniel Shealy (Boston: Little, Brown, 1988).

51. "In the Garret" (poem), *The Flag of Our Union,* Vol. XX, No. 11 (March 18, 1865). Repr. in *Little Women.*

52. "Nelly's Hospital," *Our Young Folks,* Vol. I, No. 4 (April, 1865). Repr. by U.S. Sanitary Commission, (N.p. [1865]). *BAL* 150, and in *Aunt Jo's Scrap-Bag,* III.

53. "The Sanitary Fair" (poem), *The Flag of Our Union,* Vol. XX, No. 16 (April 22, 1865).

54. "A Marble Woman: or, The Mysterious Model," *The Flag of Our Union,* Vol. XX, Nos. 20, 21, 22, and 23 (May 20, 27, and June 3,

10, 1865). (By A. M. Barnard.) Repr. in *Plots and Counterplots*, ed. Madeleine B. Stern (New York: William Morrow, 1976).

55. "A Double Tragedy. An Actor's Story," *Frank Leslie's Chimney Corner* (June 3, 1865). Repr. in *A Double Life*, ed. Madeleine B. Stern, Joel Myerson, and Daniel Shealy (Boston: Little, Brown, 1988).

56. "Ariel. A Legend of the Lighthouse," *Frank Leslie's Chimney Corner* (July 8 and 15, 1865). Repr. in *A Double Life*, ed. Madeleine B. Stern, Joel Myerson, and Daniel Shealy (Boston: Little, Brown, 1988).

57. "A Nurse's Story," *Frank Leslie's Chimney Corner* (December 2, 9, 16, 23, 30, 1865 and January 6, 1866). Repr. in *Freaks of Genius: Unknown Thrillers of Louisa May Alcott*, ed. Daniel Shealy, Madeleine B. Stern, and Joel Myerson (Westport, Conn.: Greenwood, 1991).

58. "Our Little Ghost" (poem), *The Flag of Our Union*, Vol. XXI, No. 37 (September 15, 1866). Repr. in *Merry's Museum*, Vol. I, No. 11 (November, 1868); *The Horn of Plenty of Home Poems . . .* (Boston, William F. Gill and Company, 1876) *BAL* 182; and *Sparkles for Bright Eyes* (New York, Crowell, [1879]).

59. "Behind a Mask: or, A Woman's Power," *The Flag of Our Union*, Vol. XXI, Nos. 41, 42, 43, and 44 (October 13, 20, 27, and November 3, 1866). Repr. in Madeleine B. Stern, ed., *Behind a Mask: The Unknown Thrillers of Louisa May Alcott.* (New York, William Morrow, 1975).

60. "The Freak of a Genius," *Frank Leslie's Illustrated Newspaper* (October 20, 27 and November 3, 10, 17, 1866). Repr. in *Freaks of Genius*, ed. Daniel Shealy, Madeleine B. Stern, and Joel Myerson (Westport, Conn.: Greenwood, 1991).

61. "An Autumn Song" (poem), *The Flag of Our Union*, Vol. XXI, No. 45 (November 10, 1866).

62. "The Abbot's Ghost: or, Maurice Treherne's Temptation," *The Flag of Our Union*, Vol. XXII, Nos. 1, 2, 3, and 4 (January 5, 12, 19 and 26, 1867). Repr. in Madeleine B. Stern, ed., *Behind a Mask: The Unknown Thrillers of Louisa May Alcott.* (New York, William Morrow, 1975).

63. "Hope's Debut," *Frank Leslie's Chimney Corner* (April 6, 1867). Repr. in *Louisa May Alcott: Selected Fiction*, ed. Daniel Shealy, Madeleine B. Stern, and Joel Myerson (Boston: Little, Brown, 1991).

64. "Up the Rhine," *The Independent*, Vol. XIX, No. 972 (July 18, 1867).

65. "Thrice Tempted," *Frank Leslie's Chimney Corner* (July 20, 1867). Repr. in *Louisa May Alcott: Selected Fiction*, ed. Daniel Shealy, Madeleine B. Stern, and Joel Myerson (Boston: Little, Brown, 1991).

66. Untitled Note on Dickens, *The Commonwealth*, Vol. VI, No. 3 (September 21, 1867).

67. "Living in an Omnibus. A True Story," *Merry's Museum*, Vol. LIV, No. 4 (October, 1867). Repr. in *Merry Times for Boys and Girls* (Philadelphia, Porter and Coates, [1878]); and repr. with changes as part of "The Autobiography of an Omnibus," *St. Nicholas*, Vol. I, No. 12 (October, 1874) and *Aunt Jo's Scrap-Bag*, IV.

68. "Life in a Pension," *The Independent*, Vol. XIX, No. 988 (November 7, 1867).

69. "The Skeleton in the Closet." In Perley Parker, *The Foundling*. Boston, Elliott, Thomes & Talbot, [1867]. No. 49 in *Ten Cent Novelettes* series of *Standard American Authors*. pp. [77]–99. *BAL* 151. Repr. in *Plots and Counterplots*, ed. Madeleine B. Stern (New York: William Morrow, 1976).

70. "Letter to Mr. Prang. Chromo-Lithography" (advertisement), *Boston Daily Advertiser*, Supplement, Vol. CX, No. 126 (November 23, 1867).

71. "Taming a Tartar," *Frank Leslie's Illustrated Newspaper* (November 30 and December 7, 14, and 21, 1867). Repr. in *A Modern Mephistopheles and Taming a Tartar*, ed. Madeleine B. Stern (New York: Praeger, 1987); and in *A Double Life*, ed. Madeleine B. Stern, Joel Myerson, and Daniel Shealy (Boston: Little, Brown, 1988).

72. "A Song for a Christmas Tree" (poem), *Merry's Museum*, Vol. LIV, No. 6 (December, 1867). Repr. in *Morning-Glories, and Other Sto-*

ries and *Merry Times for Boys and Girls* (Philadelphia, Porter and Coates, [1878]).

73. "What the Bells Saw and Said," *Saturday Evening Gazette*, Vol. LIII, No. 51 (December 21, 1867). Repr. in *Proverb Stories*.

74. *The Mysterious Key, and What It Opened*. Boston, Elliott, Thomes & Talbot, [1867]. No. 50 in *Ten Cent Novelettes* series of *Standard American Authors*. [5] (*sic*)–100 pp. *BAL* 152. Repr. [New York, F. M. Lupton, ca.1900]. No. 382 in *The Leisure Hour Library*. *BAL* 231. Repr. in Madeleine B. Stern, ed., *Behind a Mask: The Unknown Thrillers of Louisa May Alcott*.

75. "A Dickens Day," *The Independent*, Vol. XIX, No. 995 (December 26, 1867). Repr. with slight changes in *Shawl-Straps*.

76. *Morning-Glories, and Other Stories*. Boston, Horace B. Fuller, 1868. [i]–[iv], 5–195 pp.; blank, p. [196]; advertisements, pp. [1]–4. *BAL* 153. Copyrighted December 1867. There is also an edition bearing the imprint: New York, Carleton, 1867.

77. "Tilly's Christmas," *Merry's Museum*, Vol. I (n.s.), No. 1 (January, 1868). Repr. in *Aunt Jo's Scrap-Bag*, I; and repr. as "The Fairy Bird," in *Merry's Museum*, Vol. LXII, No. 4 (October, 1872) and *Happy Days for Boys and Girls* (Philadelphia, Porter and Coates, [1877]).

78. "Wishes" (poem), *Merry's Museum*, Vol. I, No. 1 (January, 1868).

79. "What Polly Found in Her Stocking" (poem), *Merry's Museum*, Vol. I, No. 1 (January, 1868).

80. "Grandmother's Specs," *Merry's Museum*, Vol. I, No. 1 (January, 1868). Repr. in *Sparkles for Bright Eyes*. (New York, T. Y. Crowell, [1879]). *BAL* 192. Repr. in *Meadow Blossoms* (New York, T. Y. Crowell, [1879]). *BAL* 193.

81. "Merry's Monthly Chat with His Friends," *Merry's Museum*, Vols. I and II (January, 1868–December, 1869). The "Chat" for January, 1868, contains an incident reprinted in *Little Women*.

82. "My Little Friend," *Merry's Museum*, Vol. I, No. 2 (February, 1868). Repr. as "Buzz" in *Aunt Jo's Scrap-Bag*, I, and *Sparkles for Bright Eyes* (New York, Crowell, [1879]).

83. "Where Is Bennie?" (poem), *Merry's Museum*, Vol. I, No. 2 (February, 1868).

84. "Doctor Dorn's Revenge," *Frank Leslie's Lady's Magazine* (February, 1868). Repr. in *From Jo March's Attic: Stories of Intrigue and Suspense*, ed. Madeleine B. Stern and Daniel Shealy (Boston: Northeastern University Press, 1993).

85. "My May Day among Curious Birds and Beasts," *Merry's Museum*, Vol. I, No. 3 (March, 1868). Repr. in *Will's Wonder Book, Aunt Jo's Scrap-Bag*, I, and *Sparkles for Bright Eyes* (New York, Crowell, [1879]).

86. "My Doves" (poem), *Merry's Museum*, Vol. I, No. 3 (March, 1868).

87. "Our Little Newsboy," *Merry's Museum*, Vol. I, No. 4 (April, 1868). Repr. in *The Youth's Companion*, Vol. XLI, No. 25 (June 18, 1868); *The Christian Register*, Vol. LI, No. 47 (November 23, 1872); *Aunt Jo's Scrap-Bag*, I; and *Sparkles for Bright Eyes* (New York, Crowell, [1879]). See also *BAL* 195b.

88. "Happy Women," *The New York Ledger*, Vol. XXIV, No. 7 (April 11, 1868).

89. "La Jeune; or, Actress and Woman," *Frank Leslie's Chimney Corner* (April 18, 1868). Repr. in *Freaks of Genius*, ed. Daniel Shealy, Madeleine B. Stern, and Joel Myerson (Westport, Conn.: Greenwood, 1991).

90. *Kitty's Class Day*. Boston, Loring, [1868]. [1]–12 pp. *BAL* 154. Repr. in *Louisa M. Alcott's Proverb Stories* (Boston, Loring, [1868]). *BAL* 157; repr. in *Three Proverb Stories* (Boston, Loring, [1868] i.e., after 1870). See also *BAL* 183.

91. "Will's Wonder-Book," *Merry's Museum*, Vol. I, Nos. 4, 5, 6, 7, 8, 9, 10, and 11 (April, May, June, July, August, September, October, and November, 1868). Repr. in *Will's Wonder Book* as Vol. II of *The Dirigo Series* (Boston, Horace B. Fuller, [1870]). [1]–74 pp. *BAL* 164; repr. in *Mink Curtiss; or, Life in the Backwoods* (New York, James Miller, 1876 [and 1877]; see *BAL* 185. and New York, Thomas R. Knox & Co., 1885?). Repr. as No. 1 of Clarke Juvenile Monographs, Mount Pleasant, Mich., Clarke Historical Library and Central Michigan University, 1975.

92. *Aunt Kipp.* Boston, Loring, [1868]. [1]–16 pp. *BAL* 155. Repr. *Louisa M. Alcott's Proverb Stories* and *Three Proverb Stories.* See also *BAL* 183.

93. *Psyche's Art.* Boston, Loring, [1868]. [1]–16 pp. *BAL* 156. Repr. *Louisa M. Alcott's Proverb Stories* and *Three Proverb Stories.* See also *BAL* 183.

94. "The Blue and the Gray, A Hospital Sketch," *Putnam's Magazine,* Vol. I, No. 6 (June, 1868). Repr. in *Camp and Fireside Stories.*

95. "Countess Varazoff," *Frank Leslie's Lady's Magazine* (June, 1868). Repr. in *From Jo March's Attic: Stories of Intrigue and Suspense,* ed. Madeleine B. Stern and Daniel Shealy (Boston: Northeastern University Press, 1993).

96. "The Baron's Gloves," *Frank Leslie's Chimney Corner,* Vol. VII, Nos. 160, 161, 162, and 163 (June 20, 27, and July 4, 11, 1868). Repr. in *Proverb Stories.*

97. "The Romance of a Bouquet," *Frank Leslie's Illustrated Newspaper* (June 27, 1868). Repr. in *Freaks of Genius,* ed. Daniel Shealy, Madeleine B. Stern, and Joel Myerson (Westport, Conn.: Greenwood, 1991).

98. "A Laugh and A Look," *Frank Leslie's Chimney Corner* (July 4, 1868). Repr. in *Freaks of Genius,* ed. Daniel Shealy, Madeleine B. Stern, and Joel Myerson (Westport, Conn.: Greenwood, 1991).

99. "A Royal Governess," *The Independent,* Vol. XX, No. 1023 (July 9, 1868).

100. "Fatal Follies," *Frank Leslie's Lady's Magazine* (September, 1868). Repr. in *From Jo March's Attic: Stories of Intrigue and Suspense,* ed. Madeleine B. Stern and Daniel Shealy (Boston: Northeastern University Press, 1993).

101. *Little Women or, Meg, Jo, Beth and Amy.* Boston, Roberts Brothers, 1868. [Part One]. [i]–[vi], 7–341 pp.; blank, p. [342]; advertisements paged: 3, 2, 11, 12, 8, 11. *BAL* 158.

102. "Mr. Emerson's Third Lecture," *National Anti-Slavery Standard,* Vol. XXIX, No. 26 (October 31, 1868).

103. "My Polish Boy," *The Youth's Companion*, Vol. XLI, Nos. 48 and 49 (November 26 and December 3, 1868). Repr. as part of "My Boys," *Aunt Jo's Scrap-Bag*, I.

104. "Tessa's Surprises," *Merry's Museum*, Vol. I, No. 12 (December, 1868). Repr. in *Aunt Jo's Scrap-Bag*, I.

105. "Sunshiny Sam," *Merry's Museum*, Vol. I, No. 12 (December, 1868). Repr. in *Sparkles for Bright Eyes* (New York, T. Y. Crowell, [1879]). *BAL* 192; Repr. *Water-Cresses. BAL* 194.

106. "Fate in a Fan," *Frank Leslie's Lady's Magazine* (January, 1869). Repr. in *From Jo March's Attic: Stories of Intrigue and Suspense*, ed. Madeleine B. Stern and Daniel Shealy (Boston: Northeastern University Press, 1993).

107. "Back Windows," *Merry's Museum*, Vol. II, No. 1 (January, 1869). Repr. in *Aunt Jo's Scrap-Bag*, I.

108. "Lost in a Pyramid; or, The Mummy's Curse," *The New World*, Vol. I, No. 1 (January 16, [1869]).

109. "Dan's Dinner," *Merry's Museum*, Vol. II, No. 2 (February, 1869).

110. "A Curious Call," *Merry's Museum*, Vol. II, No. 2 (February, 1869). Repr. in *Aunt Jo's Scrap-Bag*, I.

111. "Perilous Play," *Frank Leslie's Chimney Corner*, Vol. VIII, No. 194 (February 13, 1869). Repr. in *Frank Leslie's Popular Monthly*, Vol. II, No. 5 (November, 1876); and in *Plots and Counterplots*, ed. Madeleine B. Stern (New York: William Morrow, 1976).

112. "Which Wins?" *Frank Leslie's Lady's Magazine* (March, 1869). Repr. in *From Jo March's Attic: Stories of Intrigue and Suspense*, ed. Madeleine B. Stern and Daniel Shealy (Boston: Northeastern University Press, 1993).

113. "A Visit to the School-Ship," *Merry's Museum*, Vol. II, No. 3 (March, 1869).

114. "The Little Boats," *Merry's Museum*, Vol. II, No. 4 (April, 1869). Repr. as "Dandelion" in *Aunt Jo's Scrap-Bag*, I.

115. *Little Women or Meg, Jo, Beth and Amy* Part Second. Boston, Roberts Brothers, 1869. [i]–iv, 5–359 pp.; blank, p. [360]; 8 pp. advertisements. *BAL* 159.

116. "Milly's Messenger," *Merry's Museum*, Vol. II, No. 5 (May, 1869).

117. "What Fanny Heard," *The Youth's Companion*, Vol. XLII, No. 19 (May 13, 1869). Repr. in *Aunt Jo's Scrap-Bag*, III.

118. "A Little Gentleman," *Merry's Museum*, Vol. II, No. 6 (June, 1869). Repr. as "My Little Gentleman," in *Aunt Jo's Scrap-Bag*, I.

119. "Honor's Fortune," *Frank Leslie's Lady's Magazine* (June, 1869). Repr. in *From Jo March's Attic: Stories of Intrigue and Suspense*, ed. Madeleine B. Stern and Daniel Shealy (Boston: Northeastern University Press, 1993).

120. My Fourth of July," *Merry's Museum*, Vol. II, No. 7 (July, 1869).

121. "Scarlet Stockings," *Putnam's Magazine*, Vol. IV, No. 19 (July, 1869). Repr. in *Silver Pitchers*.

122. "An Old-Fashioned Girl," *Merry's Museum*, Vol. II, Nos. 7, 8, 9, 10, 11, and 12 (July, August, September, October, November, and December, 1869). Repr. as *An Old-Fashioned Girl*. Boston, Roberts Brothers, 1870. [i–iv], [1]–4, [1]–378 pp.; plus advertisements, pp. [1]–8. *BAL* 163.

123. "Madam Cluck, and Her Family," *Merry's Museum*, Vol. II, No. 8 (August, 1869). Repr. in *Aunt Jo's Scrap-Bag*, I.

124. *Hospital Sketches and Camp and Fireside Stories.* Boston, Roberts Brothers, 1869, [i–iv], i–ii, 3–379 pp. *BAL* 161.

125. "Mrs. Vane's Charade," *Frank Leslie's Chimney Corner* (August 21, 1869). Repr. in *Freaks of Genius*, ed. Daniel Shealy, Madeleine B. Stern, and Joel Myerson (Westport, Conn.: Greenwood, 1991).

126. "My Mysterious Mademoiselle," *Frank Leslie's Lady's Magazine* (September, 1869). Repr. in *From Jo March's Attic: Stories of Intrigue and Suspense*, ed. Madeleine B. Stern and Daniel Shealy (Boston: Northeastern University Press, 1993).

127. "A Marine Merry-Making," *Merry's Museum*, Vol. II, No. 10 (October, 1869). Repr. in *Aunt Jo's Scrap-Bag*, III.

128. "Becky's Christmas Dream," *Merry's Museum*, Vol. III, No. 1 (January, 1870). Repr. in *Sparkles for Bright Eyes* (New York, T. Y. Crowell, [1879]). *BAL* 192. Repr. *Water-Cresses. BAL* 194; see also *BAL* 195a.

129. "Little Things," *The Youth's Companion*, Vol. XLIII, No. 3 (January 20, 1870). Repr. as "A Genuine Little Lady" in *The Christian Register*, Vol. XLIX, No. 48 (November 26, 1870).

130. Preface to May Alcott, *Concord Sketches Consisting of Twelve Photographs from Original Drawings*. Boston, Fields, Osgood & Co., 1869. Listed Feb. 1, 1870. *BAL* 162.

131. "Betrayed by a Buckle," *Frank Leslie's Lady's Magazine* (February, 1870). Repr. in *From Jo March's Attic: Stories of Intrigue and Suspense*, ed. Madeleine B. Stern and Daniel Shealy (Boston: Northeastern University Press, 1993).

132. "La Belle Bayadère," *Frank Leslie's Lady's Magazine* (February, 1870). Repr. in *From Jo March's Attic: Stories of Intrigue and Suspense*, ed. Madeleine B. Stern and Daniel Shealy (Boston: Northeastern University Press, 1993).

133. "Uncle Smiley's Boys," *The Youth's Companion*, Vol. XLIII, Nos. 5 and 6 (February 3 and 10, 1870).

134. "Ripple" (from *Flower Fables*), *Merry's Museum*, Vol. III, No. 5 (May, 1870).

135. "Mother's Trial," *The Youth's Companion*, Vol. XLIII, No. 21 (May 26, 1870).

136. "A Sermon in the Kitchen" (from *An Old-Fashioned Girl*), *The Christian Register*, Vol. XLIX, No. 29 (July 16, 1870).

137. "The Nautilus" (poem from *Morning-Glories, and Other Stories*), *Merry's Museum*, Vol. III, No. 8 (August, 1870).

138. "Recent Exciting Scenes in Rome," *Boston Daily Evening Transcript*, Vol. 44, No. 12523 (February 3, 1871).

139. *Little Men: Life at Plumfield with Jo's Boys*. London, Sampson Low, Son, & Marston, 1871. [i–iv], [1]–332 pp. *BAL* 166. Boston, Roberts Brothers, 1871. [i–viii], [1]–376 pp. *BAL* 167.

140. *Aunt Jo's Scrap-Bag. My Boys*. Boston, Roberts Brothers, 1872. [i–viii], [1]–215 pp. *BAL* 168. [*Scrap-Bag* I].

141. "Women in Brittany," *The Christian Register*, Vol. LI, No. 1 (January 6, 1872). Repr. as part of *Shawl-Straps*.

142. "Kate's Choice," *Hearth and Home*, Vol. IV, Nos. 2 and 3 (January 13 and 20, 1872). Repr. in *Aunt Jo's Scrap-Bag*, III.

143. "Shawl Straps," *The Christian Union*, Vol. V, Nos. 12, 13, 14, and 15 (March 13, 20, 27, and April 3, 1872). Repr. in *Aunt Jo's Scrap-Bag. Shawl-Straps.*

144. "Lines to a Good Physician, from a Grateful Patient," *The Pellet. A Record of the Massachusetts Homoeopathic Hospital Fair.* No. 9 (April 15–27, 1872). *BAL* 169.

145. "Cupid and Chow-Chow," *Hearth and Home*, Vol. IV, Nos. 20 and 21 (May 18 and 25, 1872). Repr. in *Aunt Jo's Scrap-Bag*, III.

146. "Pelagie's Wedding," *The Independent*, Vol. XXIV, No. 1227 (June 6, 1872). Repr. as part of *Shawl-Straps.*

147. "The Romance of a Summer Day," *The Independent*, Vol. XXIV, No. 1239 (August 29, 1872). Repr. in *Silver Pitchers.*

148. *Address of the Republican Women of Massachusetts. To the Women of America.* Boston, September 25, 1872. Single leaf. Signed by Louisa May Alcott and others. *BAL* 170.

149. *Aunt Jo's Scrap-Bag. Shawl-Straps.* Boston, Roberts Brothers, 1872. [i]–[viii], [1]–226 pp., 6 pp. advertisements. *BAL* 171. [*Scrap-Bag* II]

150. "Grandma's Team," *The Youth's Companion*, Vol. XLV, No. 48 (November 28, 1872). Repr. in *The Christian Register*, Vol. LI, No. 52 (December 28, 1872) and *Aunt Jo's Scrap-Bag*, III.

151. "Work; or Christie's Experiment," *The Christian Union*, Vol. VI, Nos. 26 and 27, and Vol. VII, Nos. 1–25 (December 18 and 25, 1872; January 1, 8, 15, 22, 29, February 5, 12, 19, 26, March 5, 12, 19, 26, April 2, 9, 16, 23, 30, May 7, 14, 21, 28, and June 4, 11, 18, 1873). First chapter repr. as advertisement in *The Independent*, Vol. XXV, No. 1257 (January 2, 1873) and *Hearth and Home*, Vol. V, No. 3 (January 18, 1873). Repr. as *Work: A Story of Experience*. Boston, Roberts Brothers, 1873. [i–vi], [1]–443 pp. *BAL* 173.

152. "The Mystery of Morlaix," *The Youth's Companion*, Vol. XLV, No. 51 (December 19, 1872).

153. "Bonfires," *The Youth's Companion*, Vol. XLVI, No. 2 (January 9, 1873).

154. "Huckleberry," *The Youth's Companion*, Vol. XLVI, No. 3 (January 16, 1873). Repr. in *The Christian Register*, Vol. LII, No. 4 (January 25, 1873) and *Aunt Jo's Scrap-Bag*, III.

155. "Mamma's Plot," *The Youth's Companion*, Vol. XLVI, No. 6 (February 6, 1873). Repr. in *Aunt Jo's Scrap-Bag*, III.

156. *Something To Do*. London, Ward, Lock, and Tyler, [1873]. Repr. of material from *Hospital Sketches* and *Proverb Stories*. *BAL* 172.

157. "Little Boston," *The Youth's Companion*, Vol. XLVI, No. 24 (June 12, 1873). Repr. in *The Christian Register*, Vol. LII, No. 25 (June 21, 1873).

158. "Seven Black Cats," *The Youth's Companion*, Vol. XLVI, No. 31 (July 31, 1873). Repr. in *Aunt Jo's Scrap-Bag*, V.

159. "How We Saw the Shah," *The Youth's Companion*, Vol. XLVI, No. 33 (August 14, 1873). Repr. in *The Christian Register*, Vol. LII, No. 35 (August 30, 1873). The reprint is signed "May Alcott."

160. "Anna's Whim," *The Independent*, Vol. XXV, No. 1291 (August 28, 1873). Repr. in *Silver Pitchers*.

161. "Hope for Housekeepers," *Boston Transcript*, Vol. XLVI, No. 14 (November 13, 1873). Repr. as "The Servant-Girl Problem," *The Christian Register*, Vol. LII, No. 49 (December 6, 1873).

162. "Transcendental Wild Oats," *The Independent*, Vol. XXV, No. 1307 (December 18, 1873). Repr. in *The Woman's Journal*, Vol. V, No. 8 (February 21, 1874); *Silver Pitchers; Laurel Leaves. Original Poems, Stories, and Essays* (Boston, William F. Gill and Company, 1876); and *Golden Book Magazine*, Vol. XIX, No. 112 (April, 1934). See *BAL* 179.

163. *Aunt Jo's Scrap-Bag. Cupid and Chow-Chow*. Boston, Roberts Brothers, 1874. [i–viii], [1]-209 pp., blank, p. [210]; 6 pp. advertisements. *BAL* 174. [*Scrap-Bag* III].

164. "Patty's Place," *Young Folks' Journal* (private enterprise), Vol. III, Nos. 11 and 12 (January and February, 1874). Repr. in *Aunt Jo's Scrap-Bag*, IV.

165. "A Happy Birthday," *The Youth's Companion*, Vol. XLVII, No. 6 (February 5, 1874). Repr. in *The Christian Register*, Vol. LIII, No. 10 (March 7, 1874) and *Aunt Jo's Scrap-Bag*, IV.

166. "Roses and Forget-Me-Nots," *St. Nicholas*, Vol. I, No. 5 (March, 1874). Repr. in *Aunt Jo's Scrap-Bag*, IV.

167. "Lost in a London Fog," *The Youth's Companion*, Vol. XLVII, No. 15 (April 9, 1874). Repr. in *The Christian Register*, Vol. LIII, No. 23 (June 6, 1874) and *Aunt Jo's Scrap-Bag*, IV.

168. "Little Neighbors," *Hearth and Home*, Vol. VI, Nos. 15 and 16 (April 11 and 18, 1874). Repr. in *Aunt Jo's Scrap-Bag*, IV.

169. "Dolly's Bedstead," *The Youth's Companion*, Vol. XLVII, No. 18 (April 30, 1874). Repr. in *Lulu's Library*, III.

170. "What the Girls Did," *The Youth's Companion*, Vol. XLVII, No. 20 (May 14, 1874). Repr. in *The Christian Register*, Vol. LIII, No. 29 (July 18, 1874) and *Aunt Jo's Scrap-Bag*, IV.

171. "How I Went Out to Service. A Story," *The Independent*, Vol. XXVI, No. 1331 (June 4, 1874).

172. "A Little Cinderella," *The Youth's Companion*, Vol. XLVII, No. 26 (June 25, 1874).

173. "London Bridges," *The Youth's Companion*, Vol. XLVII, No. 30 (July 23, 1874).

174. "The Autobiography of an Omnibus," *St. Nicholas*, Vol. I, No. 12 (October, 1874). Repr. in *Aunt Jo's Scrap-Bag*, IV.

175. "Letter of Miss Louisa Alcott," *The Woman's Journal*, Vol. V, No. 46 (November 14, 1874).

176. "My Rococo Watch," *The National Elgin Watch Company Illustrated Almanac for 1875*. New York, The Elgin National Watch Co., [1874]. Repr. with slight changes in *Silver Pitchers*. BAL 175.

177. "Eight Cousins," *Good Things: A Picturesque Magazine for the Young of All Ages*, Vol. I (n.s.), Nos. 1, 2, 5, 7, 9, 11, 14, 17, 19, 21, 22, 24, 26, 28, 30, 32, 34, 36, 38, 40, 42, 44, 47, 49, and 52 (December 5, 12, 1874; January 2, 16, 30, February 13, March 6, 27, April 10, 24, May 1, 15, 29, June 12, 26, July 10, 24, August 7, 21, September 4, 18, October 2, 23, and November 6, 27, 1875); *St. Nicholas*, Vol. II, Nos. 3–12 (January–October, 1875). Repr. as *Eight Cousins; or, The*

Aunt-Hill. Boston, Roberts Brothers, 1875. [i–viii], [1]–290 pp., 6 pp. advertisements. *BAL* 177.

178. "Tribulation's Travels," *The Youth's Companion,* Vol. XLVIII, No. 3 (January 21, 1875).

179. "An Advertisement" (poem), *The Woman's Journal,* Vol. VI, No. 4 (January 23, 1875).

180. "Red Tulips," *The Youth's Companion,* Vol. XLVIII, No. 8 (February 25, 1875). Repr. in *The Christian Register,* Vol. LIV, No. 40 (October 2, 1875) and *Aunt Jo's Scrap-Bag,* IV. Repr. in *Frank Leslie's Chimney Corner,* Vol. XXXIX, No. 1,003 (August 16, 1884).

181. *Beginning Again. Being a Continuation of Work: a Story of Experience.* London, Sampson Low, Marston, Low, & Searle, 1875. A repr. of the second half of *Work. BAL* 176.

182. "What a Shovel Did," *The Youth's Companion,* Vol. XLVIII, No. 15 (April 15, 1875). Repr. in *Aunt Jo's Scrap-Bag,* V. Repr. in *Frank Leslie's Chimney Corner,* Vol. XXXIX, No. 1,006 (September 6, 1884).

183. "Woman's Part in the Concord Celebration," *The Woman's Journal,* Vol. VI, No. 18 (May 1, 1875). Repr. in *Saturday Evening Gazette,* Vol. LXIII, No. 19 (May 8, 1875).

184. "Silver Pitchers. A Temperance Tale," *The Youth's Companion,* Vol. XLVIII, Nos. 18–23 (May 6, 13, 20, 27, and June 3, 10, 1875). Repr. as *Silver Pitchers: and Independence, A Centennial Love Story.* Boston, Roberts Brothers, 1876. [i–iv], [1]–307 pp., plus 8 pp. advertisements. *BAL* 180.

185. "By the River," *The Independent,* Vol. XXVII, No. 1384 (June 10, 1875). Repr. in *The Woman's Journal,* Vol. VI, Nos. 25, 26, and 27 (June 19, 26, and July 3, 1875) and *Silver Pitchers.*

186. "Old Major," *The Youth's Companion,* Vol. XLVIII, No. 31 (August 5, 1875). Repr. in *The Christian Register,* Vol. LIV, No. 34 (August 21, 1875) and *Aunt Jo's Scrap-Bag,* IV.

187. "My Little School-Girl," *The Youth's Companion,* Vol. XLVIII, No. 44 (November 4, 1875). Repr. in *The Christian Register,* Vol. LV, No. 6 (February 5, 1876) and *Aunt Jo's Scrap-Bag,* V.

188. "Letty's Tramp," *The Independent,* Vol. XXVII, No. 1412 (December 23, 1875). Repr. in *The Woman's Journal,* Vol. VII, No. 5 (January 29, 1876) and *Silver Pitchers.*

189. "My Kingdom" (poem). In *The Sunny Side: a Book of Religious Songs for the Sunday School and the Home,* ed. by Charles W. Wendté and H. S. Perkins (New York, William A. Pond & Co., [1875]). *BAL* 178.

190. "Marjorie's Birthday Gifts," *St. Nicholas,* Vol. III, No. 3 (January, 1876). Repr. as "Marjorie's Three Gifts," in *Aunt Jo's Scrap-Bag,* IV.

191. "Helping Along," *St. Nicholas,* Vol. III, No. 5 (March, 1876). Repr. in part as "How One Sister Helped Her Brother," *The Christian Register,* Vol. LV, No. 24 (June 10, 1876).

192. "A New Way to Spend Christmas," *The Youth's Companion,* Vol. XLIX, No. 10 (March 9, 1876).

193. "An Evening Call," *The Youth's Companion,* Vol. XLIX, No. 15 (April 13, 1876).

194. "A Visit to the Tombs," *The Youth's Companion,* Vol. XLIX, No. 21 (May 25, 1876).

195. "Letter from Louisa M. Alcott," *The Woman's Journal,* Vol. VII, No. 29 (July 15, 1876).

196. *Rose in Bloom. A Sequel to "Eight Cousins."* Boston, Roberts Brothers, 1876. [i]–viii,[1]–375 pp. *BAL* 181.

197. "Merry Christmas" (poem). In *The Horn of Plenty of Home Poems and Home Pictures with New Poems by Miss Louisa M. Alcott . . . and Others.* Boston, William F. Gill and Company, 1876. *BAL* 182.

198. *A Modern Mephistopheles.* Boston, Roberts Brothers, 1877. [1]–290 pp., 6 pp. advertisements. (No Name Series). *BAL* 184.

199. "Clams, A Ghost Story," *The Youth's Companion,* Vol. L, No. 18 (May 3, 1877). Repr. in *Aunt Jo's Scrap-Bag,* V.

200. "The Accident" (from *An Old-Fashioned Girl*). In *Happy Days for Boys and Girls* (Philadelphia, Porter and Coates, [1877]).

201. "Polly Arrives" (from *An Old-Fashioned Girl*). In *Happy Days for Boys and Girls* (Philadelphia, Porter and Coates, [1877]).

202. "Sweet One for Polly" (from *An Old-Fashioned Girl*). In *Happy Days for Boys and Girls* (Philadelphia, Porter and Coates, [1877]).

203. "Clara's Idea," *The Youth's Companion*, Vol. L, No. 37 (September 13, 1877). Repr. as "A Bright Idea," in *Aunt Jo's Scrap-Bag*, V.

204. "Letter to N.W.C.T.U.," *Our Union*, Vol. III. No. 6 (November, 1877).

205. *Aunt Jo's Scrap-Bag. My Girls*. Boston, Roberts Brothers, 1878. [1]–229 pp.; blank p. [230]; 2 pp. advertisements. *BAL* 186. Listed Dec. 1, 1877. [*Scrap-Bag* IV].

206. "Under the Lilacs," *St. Nicholas*, Vol. V, Nos. 2-12 (December, 1877; January–October, 1878). Repr. as *Under the Lilacs*. London, Sampson Low, Marston, Searle, & Rivington, 1877 [–1878]. In parts & in one-volume edition. *BAL* 187. Boston, Roberts Brothers, 1878. [i–viii], [1]–305 pp; blank, p. [306]; 6 pp. advertisements. *BAL* 188.

207. "Mrs. Gay's Prescription," *The Woman's Journal*, Vol. IX, No. 34 (August 24, 1878).

208. "Transfiguration" (poem). In *A Masque of Poets. Including Guy Vernon, a Novelette in Verse*. [Edited by George Parsons Lathrop]. Boston, Roberts Brothers, 1878. (No Name Series). *BAL* 189. Repr. in *The Woman's Journal*, Vol. XIX, No. 10 (March 10, 1888). See also *BAL* 223.

209. "John Marlow's Victory," *The Independent*, Vol. XXX, No. 1568 (December 19, 1878).

210. "Two Little Travellers," *St. Nicholas*, Vol. VI, No. 8 (June, 1879). Repr. in *Aunt Jo's Scrap-Bag*, V.

211. "Jimmy's Cruise in the 'Pinafore,' " *St. Nicholas*, Vol. VI, No. 12 (October, 1879). Repr. in *Aunt Jo's Scrap-Bag*, V.

212. "Letter from Louisa M. Alcott," *The Woman's Journal*, Vol. X, No. 41 (October 11, 1879).

213. *Aunt Jo's Scrap-Bag. Jimmy's Cruise in the Pinafore.* Boston, Roberts Brothers, 1879. [1]–208 pp., plus 16 pp. advertisements. *BAL* 191. [*Scrap-Bag V*].

214. *Sparkles for Bright Eyes. With Contributions by Louisa M. Alcott.* New York, T. Y. Crowell, [1879]. [1]–320 pp. *BAL* 192.

215. *Meadow Blossoms. By L. M. Alcott . . . and Others.* New York, T. Y. Crowell, [1879]. *BAL* 193.

216. *Water-Cresses. By L. M. Alcott . . . and Others.* New York, T. Y. Crowell, [1879]. *BAL* 194.

217. "Jack and Jill," *St. Nicholas,* Vol. VII, Nos. 2–12 (December, 1879; January–October, 1880). Repr. as *Jack and Jill: A Village Story.* Boston, Roberts Brothers, 1880. [i–iv], [1]–325 pp.; blank p. [326]; 6 pp. advertisements. *BAL* 195.

218. "Letter from Louisa M. Alcott," *The Woman's Journal,* Vol. XI, No. 14 (April 3, 1880). Repr. in *Concord Freeman,* Vol. IV, No. 20 (April 8, 1880).

219. "How It All Happened," *Harper's Young People,* Vol. II, No. 60 (December 21, 1880). Repr. in *Aunt Jo's Scrap-Bag,* VI.

220. "Victoria. A Woman's Statue," *Demorest's Monthly Magazine,* Vol. XVII, Nos. 3, 4, and 5 (March, April, and May, 1881).

221. "An Old-Fashioned Thanksgiving," *St. Nicholas,* Vol. IX, No. 1 (November, 1881). Repr. in *Aunt Jo's Scrap-Bag,* VI, and Henry Steele Commager (ed.), *The St. Nicholas Anthology* (New York, Random House, 1948).

222. "My Red Cap," *The Sword and Pen,* Vol. I, Nos. 1, 2, 3, and 4 (December 7, 8, 9, and 10, 1881). *BAL* 197. Repr. in *Proverb Stories.*

223. "A Country Christmas," *The Independent,* Vol. XXXIII, Nos. 1724 and 1725 (December 15 and 22, 1881). Repr. in *Proverb Stories.*

224. Preface to *Prayers by Theodore Parker.* Boston, Roberts Brothers, 1882. *BAL* 198.

225. *Moods. A Novel* (revised edition). Boston, Roberts Brothers, 1882. *BAL* 199.

226. "Letter from Louisa M. Alcott," *The Woman's Journal,* Vol. XIII, No. 6 (February 11, 1882).

227. "Reminiscences of Ralph Waldo Emerson," *The Youth's Companion,* Vol. LV, No. 21 (May 25, 1882). Repr. in Moncure Daniel Conway, *Emerson at Home and Abroad* (Boston, James R. Osgood and Company, 1882). *BAL* 203. Repr. in James Parton, ed., *Some Noted Princes, Authors, and Statesmen of Our Time* (New York, Thomas Y. Crowell & Co., [1885]). *BAL* 207.

228. "W.C.T.U., of Concord," *Concord Freeman,* Vol. X, No. 26 (June 30, 1882).

229. "R. W. Emerson," *Demorest's Monthly Magazine,* Vol. XVIII, No. 9 (July, 1882).

230. "An interview with Jean Ingelow," in *Pen Pictures of Modern Authors.* New York, G. P. Putnam's Sons, 1882. *BAL* 200.

231. "Number Eleven," *The Youth's Companion,* Vol. LV, No. 33 (August 17, 1882).

232. *Proverb Stories.* Boston, Roberts Brothers, 1882. *BAL* 201.

233. *Aunt Jo's Scrap-Bag. An Old-Fashioned Thanksgiving.* Boston, Roberts Brothers, 1882. [1]-234 pp., 6 pp. advertisements. *BAL* 202. [*Scrap-Bag* VI].

234. "Grandmamma's Pearls," *St. Nicholas,* Vol. X, No. 2 (December, 1882).

235. "A Christmas Dream," *Harper's Young People,* Vol. IV, Nos. 162 and 163 (December 5 and 12, 1882). Repr. in *Lulu's Library,* I.

236. "Mr. Alcott's True Condition," *The Woman's Journal,* Vol. XIV, No. 1 (January 6, 1883).

237. "Letter from Miss Alcott," *The Woman's Journal,* Vol. XIV, No. 10 (March 10, 1883).

238. "Mrs. Gay's Hint, and How It Was Taken," (from *The Press*), *The Union Signal,* Vol. IX, No. 33 (August 30, 1883).

239. "Little Pyramus and Thisbe," *St. Nicholas,* Vol. X, Nos. 11 and 12 (September and October, 1883). Repr. as "A Hole in the Wall," in *Lulu's Library,* I.

240. "Sophie's Secret," *St. Nicholas*, Vol. XI, Nos. 1 and 2 (November and December, 1883). Repr. in *Lulu's Library*, III.

241. "Bertie's Box. A Christmas Story," *Harper's Young People*, Vol. V, No. 218 (January 1, 1884).

242. "Grandma's Story," *St. Nicholas*, Vol. XI, No. 3 (January, 1884). Repr. in *Spinning-Wheel Stories.*

243. "Address to a Robin" and extract from a letter, Dec. 28, 1869, addressed to Roberts Brothers in *Our Famous Women. An Authorized Record of the Lives and Deeds of Distinguished American Women of Our Times.* Hartford, Conn., A. D. Worthington & Co., 1884. *BAL* 204.

244. "Tabby's Table-Cloth," *St. Nicholas*, Vol. XI, No. 4 (February, 1884). Repr. in *Spinning-Wheel Stories.*

245. "Eli's Education," *St. Nicholas*, Vol. XI, No. 5 (March, 1884). Repr. in *Spinning-Wheel Stories.*

246. "Onawandah," *St. Nicholas*, Vol. XI, No. 6 (April, 1884). Repr. in *Spinning-Wheel Stories.* Repr. in Henry Steele Commager (ed.), *The Second St. Nicholas Anthology* (New York, Random House, 1950).

247. "Little Things," *St. Nicholas*, Vol. XI, No. 7 (May, 1884). Repr. in *Spinning-Wheel Stories.*

248. "Letter from Miss Louisa M. Alcott," *The Woman's Journal*, Vol. XV, No. 20 (May 17, 1884).

249. "What shall little children bring" (untitled hymn) in *The Thirty-Fifth Annual Report of the Executive Committee of the Children's Mission to the Children of the Destitute, in the City of Boston; with an Account of the Proceedings at the Annual Meeting, May 28, 1884.* Boston, Rooms of the Children's Mission, 1884. *BAL* 205.

250. "The Banner of Beaumanoir," *St. Nicholas*, Vol. XI, No. 8 (June, 1884). Repr. in *Spinning-Wheel Stories.*

251. "Jerseys, or, The Girl's Ghost," *St. Nicholas*, Vol. XI, No. 9 (July, 1884). Repr. in *Spinning-Wheel Stories.*

252. "The Little House in the Garden," *St. Nicholas*, Vol. XI, No. 10 (August, 1884). Repr. in *Spinning-Wheel Stories.*

253. "Daisy's Jewel-Box, and How She Filled It," *St. Nicholas*, Vol. XI, No. 11 (September, 1884). Repr. in *Spinning-Wheel Stories*.

254. "Corny's Catamount," *St. Nicholas*, Vol. XI, No. 12 (October, 1884). Repr. in *Spinning-Wheel Stories*.

255. "The Cooking-Class," *St. Nicholas*, Vol. XII, No. 1 (November, 1884). Repr. in *Spinning-Wheel Stories*.

256. *Spinning-Wheel Stories*. Boston, Roberts Brothers, 1884. [i–iv], [1]–276 pp., plus 8 pp. advertisements. *BAL* 206.

257. "The Hare and the Tortoise," *St. Nicholas*, Vol. XII, Nos. 2 and 3 (December, 1884, and January, 1885). Repr. in *Spinning-Wheel Stories*.

258. "In Memoriam Sophia Foord," *The Woman's Journal*, Vol. XVI, No. 15 (April 11, 1885).

259. "Miss Alcott on Mind-Cure," *The Woman's Journal*, Vol. XVI, No. 16 (April 18, 1885).

260. "Old Times at Old Concord," *The Woman's Journal*, Vol. XVI, No. 16 (April 18, 1885).

261. "Kind Words from Miss Alcott," *The Woman's Journal*, Vol. XVI, No. 20 (May 16, 1885).

262. "Baa! Baa!" *Harper's Young People*, Vol. VI, Nos. 307 and 308 (September 15 and 22, 1885). Repr. in *Lulu's Library*, I.

263. "The Candy Country," *St. Nicholas*, Vol. XIII, No. 1 (November, 1885). Repr. in *Lulu's Library*, I.

264. *Lulu's Library*. Vol. I. *A Christmas Dream*. Boston, Roberts Brothers, 1886. [1]–269 pp., advertisements, pp. [270–272]. *BAL* 210. Listed Dec. 5, 1885.

265. "To My Father on His 86th Birthday" (poem), *The Woman's Journal*, Vol. XVI, No. 50 (December 12, 1885). See also *BAL* 223.

266. "A Christmas Turkey, and How It Came," *Harper's Young People*, Vol. VII, No. 321 (December 22, 1885). Repr. in *Lulu's Library*, III.

267. "When Shall Our Young Women Marry?" *The Brooklyn Magazine*, Vol. IV, No. 1 (April, 1886).

268. "Letter on Amos Bronson Alcott," *The Brooklyn Magazine*, Vol. IV, No. 1 (April, 1886). Referred to in *The Woman's Journal*, Vol. XVII, No. 14 (April 3, 1886).

269. "The Lay of a Golden Goose" (poem), *The Woman's Journal*, Vol. XVII, No. 19 (May 8, 1886).

270. *Jo's Boys, and How They Turned Out. A Sequel to "Little Men."* Boston, Roberts Brothers, 1886. [1]–365 pp.; blank p. [366]; 2 pp. advertisements; plus 16 pp. advertisements. *BAL* 211.

271. The Blind Lark," *St. Nicholas*, Vol. XIV, No. 1 (November, 1886). Repr. in *Lulu's Library*, III.

272. "Little Lord Fauntleroy" (review), *The Book Buyer*, Vol. III, No. 11 (December, 1886).

273. "Little Robin," *Harper's Young People*, Vol. VIII, No. 371 (December 7, 1886).

274. "What It Cost," *The Young Crusader*, Vol. I, No. 6 (February 11, 1887). Also printed as No. 5 of *The Press Leaflets*.* See *BAL* 216.

275. "A Flower Fable" (from *Woman Suffrage Bazaar Journal*), *The Woman's Journal*, Vol. XVIII, No. 9 (February 26, 1887). Repr. in *The Union Signal*, Vol. XIII, No. 10 (March 10, 1887) and repr. as "Queen Aster," in *Lulu's Library*, II.

276. "A Beautiful Picture Which Louisa M. Alcott Saw on a Hot and Dusty Journey," *The Voice*, Vol. IV, No. 20 (May 19, 1887).**

277. "Early Marriages," *The Ladies' Home Journal*, Vol. IV, No. 10 (September, 1887).

278. "An Ivy Spray," *St. Nicholas*, Vol. XIV, No. 12 (October, 1887). Repr. as "An Ivy Spray and Ladies' Slippers," in *A Garland for Girls*.

* No. 2 of *The Press Leaflets* published by *The Press: A Monthly Journal devoted to the Temperance Reform* (Boston) is "Jimmy's Lecture. Written for the Young Folks. By Louisa M. Alcott." No. 4 is "A Glorious Fourth." See *BAL* 215, 214.

** *Cf.* "Merry's Monthly Chat with His Friends," *Merry's Museum* (September, 1869). "Baa! Baa!" [*Harper's Young People* (September 15 and 22, 1885)] is also similar.

279. *Lulu's Library. Vol. II. The Frost King.* Boston, Roberts Brothers, 1887. [i–ii], [1]–275 pp., 12 pp. advertisements. *BAL* 212.

280. "Pansies," *St. Nicholas*, Vol. XV, No. 1 (November, 1887). Repr. in *A Garland for Girls.*

281. "The Silver Party," *Harper's Young People*, Vol. IX, No. 421 (November 22, 1887). Repr. in *Lulu's Library*, III.

282. "The Little Red Purse," *Harper's Young People*, Vol. IX, No. 423 (December 6, 1887). Repr. in *Lulu's Library*, III.

283. Three selections in *The White Ribbon Birthday Book*, ed. by Anna A. Gordon (Chicago, Woman's Temperance Publication Association, 1887).

284. *Our Girls* [by L. M. Alcott and Others]. New York, Belford, Clarke & Co., 1887. (Contains 3 sketches by L. M. Alcott.) See *BAL* 213.

285. *A Garland for Girls.* Boston, Roberts Brothers, 1888. [i–x], [1]–258 pp., 6 pp. advertisements; plus advertisements: [i–ii], [1]–14. *BAL* 217. Listed Dec. 10, 1887.

286. "Trudel's Siege," *St. Nicholas*, Vol. XV, No. 6 (April, 1888). Repr. in *Lulu's Library*, III.

287. "Recollections of My Childhood," *The Youth's Companion*, Vol. LXI, No. 21 (May 24, 1888). Repr. in *The Woman's Journal*, Vol. XIX, No. 21 (May 26, 1888); repr. in part in *Our Dumb Animals*, Vol. XXI, No. 2 (July, 1888), and *Lulu's Library*, III.

288. *A Modern Mephistopheles and A Whisper in the Dark.* Boston, Roberts Brothers, 1889. [1]–350 pp., 2 pp. advertisements. *BAL* 219.

289. *Lulu's Library. Vol. III. Recollections.* Boston, Roberts Brothers, 1889. [3]–258 pp. *BAL* 220.

290. *Louisa May Alcott Her Life, Letters, and Journals Edited by Ednah D. Cheney.* Boston, Roberts Brothers, 1889. [i–iv], [i]–[x], [11]–404 pp., 8 pp. advertisements. *BAL* 221.

291. *Recollections of My Childhood's Days.* London, Sampson Low, 1890. *BAL* 222.

292. *Comic Tragedies Written by "Jo" and "Meg" and Acted by the "Little Women."* Boston, Roberts Brothers, 1893. [1]–317 pp., blank p. [318], 2 pp. advertisements. *BAL* 224.

293. *A Hole in the Wall.* Boston, Little, Brown, and Company, [1899]. *BAL* 225.

294. *Marjorie's Three Gifts.* Boston, Little, Brown, and Company, [1899]. *BAL* 226.

295. *May Flowers.* Boston, Little, Brown, and Company, [1899]. *BAL* 227.

296. *The Candy Country.* Boston, Little, Brown, and Company, [1900]. *BAL* 229.

297. *Poppies and Wheat.* Boston, Little, Brown, and Company, [1900]. *BAL* 230.

298. *A Christmas Dream.* Boston, Little, Brown, and Company, [1901]. *BAL* 232.

299. *Little Button Rose.* Boston, Little, Brown, and Company, [1901]. *BAL* 233.

300. *The Doll's Journey.* Boston, Little, Brown, and Company, [1902]. *BAL* 234.

301. *Pansies and Water-Lilies.* Boston, Little, Brown, and Company, [1902]. *BAL* 235.

302. "Lu Sing," *St. Nicholas,* Vol. XXX, No. 2 (December, 1902).

303. "The Eaglet in the Dove's Nest," *St. Nicholas,* Vol. XXX, No. 3 (January, 1903).

304. *Mountain-Laurel and Maidenhair.* Boston, Little, Brown, and Company. [1903]. *BAL* 236.

305. *Morning-Glories and Queen Aster.* Boston, Little, Brown, and Company, [1904]. *BAL* 237.

306. "May" (poem from "The Fairy Spring," *Lulu's Library,* II), *Woman's Home Companion,* Vol. XXXII, No. 5 (May, 1905).

307. *The Louisa Alcott Reader.* Boston, Little, Brown, and Company, 1908. *BAL* 238.

308. *A Modern Cinderella or the Little Old Shoe and Other Stories.* New York, Hurst & Company, [1908]. *BAL* 239.

309. *Bronson Alcott at Alcott House, England, and Fruitlands, New England (1842–1844)* by F. B. Sanborn. Cedar Raipds, Iowa, The Torch Press, 1908. With some material by Louisa M. Alcott. *BAL* 240.

310. *The Louisa Alcott Story Book Edited for Schools by Fanny E. Coe.* Boston, Little, Brown, and Company, 1910. *BAL* 241.

311. *Little Women Letters from the House of Alcott Selected by Jessie Bonstelle and Marian DeForest.* Boston, Little, Brown, and Company, 1914. Contains material by Louisa M. Alcott. *BAL* 242.

312. *Three Unpublished Poems.* Fruitlands Collection. N.p. [1919]. [1]–13 pp.; blank, pp. [14–15]; imprint p. [16]. *BAL* 243.

313. *The Frost King.* N.p. ca. 1925. *BAL* 244.

314. *A Long Fatal Love Chase.* New York: Random House, 1995.

No attempt has been made at a complete listing of the numerous reprints of Alcott stories that appeared after her death. The purpose of this bibliography is to record Alcott stories published and reprinted during the author's lifetime. A few of the more important recent anthologies and collections containing Alcott narratives include the following:

Elaine Showalter, ed., *Alternative Alcott* (New Brunswick: Rutgers University Press, 1988); Daniel Shealy, Madeleine B. Stern, Joel Myerson, eds., *Louisa May Alcott: Selected Fiction* (Boston: Little, Brown, 1990); *Louisa May Alcott's Fairy Tales and Fantasy Stories,* ed. by Daniel Shealy (Knoxville: University of Tennessee Press, 1992); Madeleine Stern, ed., *Behind a Mask: The Unknown Thrillers of Louisa May Alcott* (New York: William Morrow, 1995) [reprint of 1975 edition]; Madeleine B. Stern and Daniel Shealy, eds., *The Lost Stories of Louisa May Alcott* (New York: Carol Publishing Group, 1995) [originally published as *From Jo March's Attic* by Northeastern University Press]; Madeleine Stern, ed., *Louisa May Alcott Unmasked: Collected Thrillers* (Boston: Northeastern University Press, 1995); Madeleine Stern, ed., *A Marble Woman: Unknown Thrillers of Louisa May Alcott* (New York: Avon, 1995) [originally published by William Morrow as *Plots and Counterplots*]; Madeleine Stern, ed., *Modern Magic* (New York: Modern Library, 1995); Madeleine Stern, ed., *A Woman's Power: Feminist Fiction of Louisa May Alcott* (Boston: Northeastern University Press, 1996).

Among significant reprints of Alcott novels may be cited: Louisa May Alcott, *Work: A Story of Experience.* Introduction by Sarah Elbert (New York: Schocken Books, 1977); Louisa May Alcott, *A Modern Mephistopheles and Taming a Tartar* With an Introduction by Madeleine B. Stern (New York: Praeger, 1987); Louisa May Alcott, *Moods*, Edited and with an Introduction by Sarah Elbert (New Brunswick: Rutgers University Press, 1991).

In addition, the following compilations should be listed: *The Selected Letters of Louisa May Alcott*, ed. by Joel Myerson, Daniel Shealy, Madeleine Stern (Boston: Little, Brown, 1987) and *The Journals of Louisa May Alcott*, ed. by Joel Myerson, Daniel Shealy, Madeleine Stern (Boston: Little, Brown, 1989).

NOTES ON SOURCES

Most manuscript material cited in "Notes on Sources" as deposited at the Orchard House is now in the Houghton Library, Harvard University.

CHAPTER 1 *The South End*

THE BIRTHDAY FESTIVAL: K. Anthony, *Louisa May Alcott* (New York and London, 1938), 29–30; Peabody Correspondence in "Cuba Journal," *passim* (courtesy Mr. R. L. Straker and Mr. Horace Mann); E. P. Peabody to Mary T. Peabody, 1835, in "Cuba Journal" (courtesy Mr. Straker and Mr. Mann); Sandford Salyer, *Marmee: The Mother of Little Women* (Norman, 1949), 54; F. B. Sanborn and W. T. Harris, *A. B. Alcott: His Life and Philosophy* (Boston, 1893, 2 vols.), I, 203–204 (hereinafter referred to as "Sanborn and Harris"); O. Shepard (ed.), *The Journals of Bronson Alcott* (Boston, 1938), 69–70 (hereinafter referred to as *Journals of B. Alcott*).

ALCOTT'S LIFE AND OPINIONS: A. B. Alcott, *New Connecticut. An Autobiography* (Boston, 1881), *passim;* A. B. Alcott, *Table-Talk* (Boston, 1877), 15, 58; W. Alcott, "History of a Common School from 1801 to 1831," *American Annals of Education*, Vol. I, Part II, Nos. 10 and 11 (October and November 1831), 469; K. Anthony, *L. M. Alcott*, 6; R. S. Edes, *A Genealogy of the Descendants of John May* (Boston, 1878), 22; J. Flavel, *A Treatise on Keeping the Heart* (Hallowell, 1828), 147; W. L. Garrison. *The Story of His Life Told by His Children* (Boston and New York, 1894, 2 vols.), II, 27; *Germantown History consisting of Papers Read before* the Site and Relic Society of Germantown (Germantown, 1915), 19; D. McCuskey, B. Alcott, Teacher (New York, 1940), passim; Salyer, Marmee: The Mother of Little Women, 6; Sanborn and Harris, passim; O. Shepard, Connecticut Past and Present (New York and London, 1939), 235; Journals of B. Alcott, 117–19; O. Shepard, Pedlar's Progress: The Life of Bronson Alcott (Boston, 1937), passim.

THE SCENE AT HOME: L. M. Alcott to Mrs. Dall [New York], November 10, 1875 (Massachusetts Historical Society); L. M. Alcott, "Recollections of My Childhood," The Youth's Companion, Vol. LXI, No. 21 (May 24, 1888); A. B. Alcott, Table-Talk, 43; Bedford Bulletin, Vol. X, No. 5 (February 2, 1882); J. Bonstelle and M. de Forest, Little Women Letters from the House of Alcott (Boston, 1914), 188 (hereinafter referred to as "Bonstelle"); Friedrich Wilhelm Carové, The Story Without an End, tr. by Sarah Austin (London, n. d.), 9–10, 127, 129–30; M. Edgeworth, Moral Tales (New York, 1843), 6; O. S. and L. N. Fowler, Phrenology Proved, Illustrated, and Applied (New York, 1837), 39; F. A. Krummacher, Parables (London, 1858); McCuskey, B. Alcott, Teacher, 63; C. Meigs, Invincible Louisa (Boston, 1933), 34; H. Morrow, The Father of Little Women (Boston, 1927), 157; [C.] S[edgwick]., "Record of a School: Exemplifying the General Principles of Spiritual Culture," The Knickerbocker, Vol. VII, No. 2 (February, 1836), 121; Journals of B. Alcott, 74; Shepard, Pedlar's Progress, 236, 238.

ATTACKS ON ALCOTT AND DECLINE OF THE TEMPLE SCHOOL: Journals of B. Alcott, 74, 80–81, 87, 98–99; R. W. Emerson, Journals (Boston and New York, 1909–14, 10 vols.), IV, 205; McCuskey, B. Alcott, Teacher, 2; Pedlar's Progress, 191ff.; R. L. Rusk (ed.), The Letters of R. W. Emerson (New York, 1939, 6 vols.), II, 27–28, 60–63 (hereinafter referred to as "Rusk"); Sanborn and Harris, I, 21 1 ff.

CHAPTER 2 *The Hosmer Cottage*

ROUTINE OF LIFE AT THE COTTAGE: Alcott to Louisa [Concord], June 21, 1840 (Orchard House); A. B. Alcott, "Days from a Diary," The Dial, Vol. II, No. 4 (April, 1842), 426–27; K. Anthony, L. M. Alcott, 25; Bonstelle, 59–61, 85–87, 123; E. D. Cheney (ed.), Louisa May Alcott: Her Life, Letters, and Journals (Boston, 1889), 21 (hereinafter referred to as "Cheney"); The Common School Journal, Vol. III, No. 19 (October 1, 1841), 297; Meigs, Invincible Louisa, 38; Morrow, Father of Little Women,

222, 234; B. Moses, *L. M. Alcott: Dreamer and Worker* (New York and London, 1928), 16; folder, Anthony Collection (New York Public Library, courtesy Mr. Paul North Rice); E. P. Peabody, *Reminiscences of Rev. William Ellery Channing* (Boston, 1880), 414; O. Shepard, *Pedlar's Progress*, 292; *Records of a Lifelong Friendship 1807–1882. Ralph Waldo Emerson and William Henry Furness* (Boston and New York, 1910), 12; S. P. Rugg, "Louisa May Alcott, Her Father and 'Pilgrim's Progress,' " *The Christian Register*, Vol. III, No. 45 (November 10, 1932), 645; F. B. Sanborn, *Bronson Alcott at Alcott House* (Cedar Rapids, 1908), 13; F. B. Sanborn, *Recollections of Seventy Years* (Boston, 1909, 2 vols.), II, 343ff.; Sanborn and Harris, I, 309, II, 447ff.; C. Ticknor, *May Alcott* (Boston, 1928), 9, 13, 19; C. Ticknor, "The True Story of 'Amy,' " *Delineator*, Vol. CX, No. 2 (February, 1927), 31; L. H. Wood, "Beth Alcott's Playmate," *Harper's Bazar*, Vol. XLVII, No. 5 (May, 1913), 213.

THOREAU, AND EXCURSIONS WITH HIM: A. B. Alcott, *Concord Days* (Boston, 1888), 13–14, 20; G. B. Bartlett, *Concord Historic, Literary and Picturesque* (Boston, 1885), 157–58; L. Bazalgette, *Henry Thoreau, Bachelor of Nature* (New York, 1924), 61, 89; G. Bradford, *Journal* (Boston and New York, 1933), 28; W. Brewster, *Concord River* (Cambridge, 1937), 5–6; H. S. Canby, *Thoreau* (Boston, 1939), 8, 64–65, 69, 378; W. E. Channing, *Thoreau the Poet-Naturalist* (Boston, 1902), *passim*; E. Emerson, *Henry Thoreau as Remembered by a Young Friend* (Boston, 1917), *passim*; R. W. Emerson, *Lectures and Biographical Sketches* (Boston, 1887), 430–31, 438, 450; A[nnie]. F[ields]., "Mr. Emerson in the Lecture Room," *The Atlantic Monthly*, Vol. LI, No. 308 (June, 1883), 822; A. French, *Old Concord* (Boston, 1915), 101, 143; J. Hawthorne, *Memoirs* (New York, 1938), 115; N. Hawthorne, *The American Notebooks* (New Haven, 1932), 166–67; N. Hawthorne, *Mosses from an Old Manse* (Boston, 1882, 2 vols.), I, 10 ff.; G. F. Hoar, *Autobiography of Seventy Years* (New York, 1905, 2 vols.), I, 51, 70; J. Hosmer, "Henry D. Thoreau," *Concord Freeman*, May 6, 1880; A. R. Marble, *Thoreau: His Home, Friends and Books* (New York, [1902]), 74, 81, 83, 91; "Merry's Monthly Chat with His Friends," *Merry's Museum*, Vol. II, No. 3 (March, 1869), 147; O. Shepard, *Pedlar's Progress*, 298; "Reminiscences of Thoreau," *The Outlook*, Vol. LXIII, No. 14 (December 2, 1899), 818–19; H. S. Salt, *Life of H. D. Thoreau* (London, 1896), 14, 88, 92, 105; F. B. Sanborn, "A Concord Note-Book," *The Critic*, Vol. XLVIII, No. 4 (April, 1906), 340; Sanborn, *Recollections of Seventy Years*, II, 474; F. B. Sanborn, *H. D. Thoreau*

(Boston and New York, [1882]), *passim;* O. Shepard (ed.), *The Heart of Thoreau's Journals* (Boston and New York, 1927), 68, 78, 128; M. Sidney, *Old Concord* (Boston, 1893), 111; J. L. Swayne, *The Story of Concord Told by Concord Writers* (Boston, 1939), 334, 352; H. D. Thoreau, *Early Spring in Massachusetts* (Boston and New York, 1893), 273, 281; H. D. Thoreau, *Familiar Letters* (Boston and New York, 1894), 26–27; [H. D. Thoreau], "Walking," *The Atlantic Monthly,* Vol. IX, No. 56 (June, 1862), 661; H. D. Thoreau, *A Week on the Concord and Merrimack Rivers* (Boston and New York, [1893]), 6, 16, 468; H. D. Thoreau, *Writings* (Boston and New York, 1906, 20 vols.), VII, 171, 185, 261, 330, 449.

DEATH OF GRANDFATHER MAY; ALCOTT POVERTY; ALCOTT'S PREOC-CUPATIONS: A. B. Alcott, "Days from a Diary," *The Dial,* Vol. II, No. 4 (April, 1842), 410; *A Collection of Psalms and Hymns for Publick Worship* (Boston, 1799), inscribed "Abba Alcott from her father's library" (Orchard House); L. Hillyer, "Marmee," *The Parents' Magazine,* Vol. VII, No. 11 (November, 1932), 23; S. May, "Col. Joseph May," *New-England Historical and Genealogical Register,* Vol. XXVII, No. 2 (April 1873), 119; *Pedlar's Progress,* 294–96; Rusk, II, 371, 389, 393.

HAWTHORNE AND THE OLD MANSE: M. Alcott, *Concord Sketches* (Boston, 1869), 196; N. Arvin, *Hawthorne* (Boston, 1929), 108, 120; Bartlett, *Concord Historic,* 53; E. Channing, *Poems of Sixty-Five Years* (Philadelphia and Concord, 1902), 113; Channing, *Thoreau the Poet-Naturalist,* 274; M. D. Conway, *Emerson at Home and Abroad* (Boston, 1882), 256–57; [E. Dicey], "The New England States," *Macmillan's Magazine,* Vol. VI, No. 34 (August, 1862), 289; French, *Old Concord,* 89; J. Hawthorne, *Memoirs,* 20; J. Hawthorne, *Nathaniel Hawthorne and His Wife* (Boston and New York, [1884], 2 vols.), I, 49; Hawthorne, *American Notebooks,* 145–46, 154; Hawthorne, *Mosses from an Old Manse,* I, 7ff., 163; T. W. Higginson, *Short Studies of American Authors* (Boston and New York, 1888), 4; E. Hubbard (ed.), *Little Journeys to the Homes of American Authors* (New York, 1896), 205; G. P. Lathrop, *A Study of Hawthorne* (Boston, 1876), 293; R. H. Lathrop, *Memories of Hawthorne* (Boston and New York, 1897), 58; Sanborn, *Recollections of Seventy Years,* II, 518–19; F. P. Stearns, *The Life and Genius of N. Hawthorne* (Philadelphia and London, 1906), 160–61, 163; F. P. Stearns, *Sketches from Concord* (New York and London, 1895), 45–46; T. Wolfe, *Literary Shrines* (Philadelphia, 1897), 30, 32.

THE NEW ROUTINE AT THE COTTAGE: *Journals of B. Alcott*, 150, 152; D. Edgell, "B. Alcott's 'Autobiographical Index,' " *The New England Quarterly*, Vol. XIV, No. 4 (December, 1941), 711–12; D. Edgell, *The New Eden: A Study of B. Alcott's Fruitlands* (Master's essay, Wesleyan University, May 1939), 46–47; Emerson, *Journals*, VIII, 485; W. H. Harland, *Bronson Alcott's English Friends* (typescript at Fruitlands, courtesy Miss C. E. Sears); Charles Lane to Junius Alcott, Concord, November 28, 1842, and December 26, 1842 (Fruitlands); McCuskey, *B. Alcott, Teacher*, 132; O. Shepard, *Pedlar's Progress*, 344, 348, 351ff., 439; Sanborn, *B. Alcott at Alcott House*, 25ff.; Sanborn and Harris, I, 347; Wood, "Beth Alcott's Playmate," *Harper's Bazar*, Vol. XLVII, No. 5 (May, 1913), 213, 246.

SEARCH FOR CONVERTS AND NEW EDEN; PURCHASE OF WYMAN FARM: Alcott to Junius Alcott, December 26, 1842 (Fruitlands); A. B. Alcott, "Days from a Diary," *The Dial*, Vol. II, No. 4 (April, 1842), 429; Edgell, "B. Alcott's 'Autobiographical Index,' " *The New England Quarterly*, Vol. XIV, No. 4 (December, 1941), 710–12; Edgell, *New Eden*, 49, 55; Harland, *B. Alcott's English Friends;* V. F. Holden, *The Early Years of I. T. Hecker* (Washington, 1939), 157; O. Shepard, *Pedlar's Progress*, 299, 356; Sanborn, *B. Alcott at Alcott House*, 52; C. E. Sears, *Bronson Alcott's Fruitlands* (Boston and New York, 1915), 13ff.

CHAPTER 3 *The New Eden*

FRUITLANDS AND THE ROUTINE OF LIFE THERE: Alcott, *Concord Days*, 180; *Journals of B. Alcott*, 153; Alcott, *Table-Talk*, 69, 72–73; A. B. Alcott, *Tablets* (Boston, 1868), 40; V. W. Brooks, *The Flowering of New England* (New York, 1936), 275; Canby, *Thoreau*, 179; Cheney, 35; A. M. L. Clark, *The Alcotts in Harvard* (Lancaster, 1902), 15; J. F. Clarke, *Autobiography, Diary and Correspondence* (Boston and New York, 1899), 138 n. 2; Edgell, "B. Alcott's 'Autobiographical Index,' " *The New England Quarterly*, Vol. XIV, No. 4 (December 1941), 712; Edgell, *New Eden*, 59–61, 100; Emerson, *Journals*, VI, 453; "Fruitlands," *The Dial*, Vol. IV, No. 1 (July, 1843), 135–36; "Fruitlands, Famous Home of Philosophers Restored," *The Sun*, September 27, 1914 (clipping courtesy Mrs. Anna M. Stevens); Holden, *Early Years of I. T. Hecker*, 161; [G. B. Kirby], "Reminiscences of Brook Farm," *Old and New*, Vol. III, No. 4 (April, 1871), 437; C. Lane and A. B. Alcott, "The Consociate Family

Life," *The Liberator,* Vol. XIII, No. 38 (September 22, 1843), 152; Meigs, *Invincible Louisa,* 48; *The New Age, Concordium Gazette, and Temperance Advocate,* Vol. I, No. 8 (August 1, 1843), 75; "New Society," *The Liberator,* Vol. XIII, No. 29 (July 21, 1843); H. O'Brien, *Lost Utopias* (Boston, 1929), 6, 11, 18; O. Shepard, *Pedlar's Progress,* 364, 368, 371; Sanborn, *B. Alcott at Alcott House,* 56, 82; Sanborn, *H. D. Thoreau,* 137–39; Sanborn and Harris. II, 377; Sears, *B. Alcott's Fruitlands,* 17–18, 22–23, 50, 68, 87, 118; Sears, *Revised Catalogue of "Fruitlands"* (Harvard, Mass., n. d.), 3, 11; L. Swift, *Brook Farm* (New York, 1900), 64, 240; F. L. H. Willis, *Alcott Memoirs* (Boston, 1915), 33, 81.

LIZZIE'S BIRTHDAY: Edgell, "B. Alcott's 'Autobiographical Index,' " *The New England Quarterly,* Vol. XIV, No. 4 (December, 1941), 712; Edgell, *New Eden,* 63, 112–14; Sanborn, *Recollections of Seventy Years,* II, 534–37; Sears, *B. Alcott's Fruitlands,* 93–96.

GROWING TENSION AT FRUITLANDS; LANE ON FAMILY LIFE: C. L[ane]., "Brook Farm," *The Dial,* Vol. IV, No. 3 (January, 1844), 356–57; C. L[ane]., "Social Tendencies," *The Dial,* Vol. IV, Nos. 1 and 2 (July and October, 1843), 200; C. Nordhoff, *The Communistic Societies of the United States* (New York, 1875), 193; O. Shepard, *Pedlar's Progress,* 373–74; Sears, *B. Alcott's Fruitlands,* 40, 52, 121.

LOUISA'S WISH FOR A HAPPY FAMILY; MRS. ALCOTT'S BIRTHDAY: Bonstelle, 105; Cheney, 37; Sears, *B. Alcott's Fruitlands,* 108–109; Sears, *Revised Catalogue of "Fruitlands,"* 20.

THE DISCUSSION RE SEPARATION: Cheney 38–39; Edgell, "B. Alcott's 'Autobiographical Index,' " *The New England Quarterly,* Vol. XIV, No. 4 (December, 1941), 713; Edgell, *New Eden,* 71–74, 76; O. Shepard, *Pedlar's Progress,* 376, 379; Rusk, III, 230; Sears, *B. Alcott's Fruitlands,* 111, 120.

DEPARTURE OF THE ALCOTTS: *Journals of B. Alcott,* 156; Edgell, "B. Alcott's 'Autobiographical Index,' " *The New England Quarterly,* Vol. XIV, No. 4 (December, 1941), 714.

HOME IN STILL RIVER; ACTIVITIES OF ALCOTTS; BRICK ENDS: Alcott to Junius Alcott, Still River, June 15, 1844 (Fruitlands); *Journals of B. Alcott,* 156–58; Clark, *The Alcotts in Harvard,* 27; A. M. L. Clark, "How I Entertained Two Little Girls," *Wide Awake,* Vol. XIV, No. 3 (March, 1882), 151; E. D. Cheney, *Reminiscences* (Boston, 1902), 246–47; Edgell,

"B. Alcott's 'Autobiographical Index,' " *The New England Quarterly,* Vol. XIV, No. 4 (December, 1941), 714; Edgell, *New Eden,* 79–82; Meigs, *Invincible Louisa,* 71; Shepard, *Pedlar's Progress,* 380, 391; information from Mr. F. Savage.

MRS. ALCOTT'S THOUGHTS ON THE YEAR: Edgell, *New Eden,* 83.

F. L. H. WILLIS: Picture of Willis (courtesy Mrs. George M. Forbes); *The Hovey Book* (Haverhill, 1913), 261; information from Miss Mary Hovey; Willis, *Alcott Memoirs,* 13ff.

RETURN OF THE ALCOTTS TO CONCORD: Clark, *Alcotts in Harvard,* 41–42; Edgell, "B. Alcott's 'Autobiographical Index,' " *The New England Quarterly,* Vol. XIV, No. 4 (December, 1941), 714–15; Edgell, *New Eden,* 84.

CHAPTER 4 *The White Village*

HILLSIDE; THE HOUSE AND REPAIRS: *Journals of B. Alcott,* 140, 175, 177; Louisa to her mother (1845) (Houghton Library); Bartlett, *Concord Historic,* 60, 63; Brooks, *Flowering of New England,* 426; Cheney, 46; Clark, *Alcotts in Harvard,* 42; C. Gowing, *The Alcotts As I Knew Them* (Boston, 1909), 1–3 (hereinafter referred to as "Gowing"); J. Hawthorne, *Hawthorne and His Circle* (New York and London, 1903), 56–58; J. Hawthorne, *Memoirs,* 33–34; J. Hawthorne, *Nathaniel Hawthorne and His Wife,* I, 451; N. Hawthorne to "Howadji" [G. W. Curtis], Concord, July 14, 1852 (Fruitlands); Hubbard, *Little Journeys to the Homes of American Authors,* 223–24; G. P. Lathrop, *A Study of Hawthorne,* 243–44; R. H. Lathrop, *Memories of Hawthorne,* 178; L. C. Lillie, "Louisa May Alcott," *The Cosmopolitan,* Vol. V, No. 2 (April, 1888), 158–59; M. Lothrop, *The Wayside* (New York, 1940), 3, 44ff.; *Pedlar's Progress,* 391–92; Sanborn, *B. Alcott at Alcott House,* 78; Sanborn and Harris, II, 429; Stearns, *The Life and Genius of N. Hawthorne,* 439; C. Ticknor, *Classic Concord* (Boston and New York, 1926), 222; *The Voice* (Concord High School publication), November, 1932, p. 15; Willis, *Alcott Memoirs,* 25.

SOPHIA FOORD; LESSONS AND EXCURSIONS: L. M. Alcott, "In Memoriam Sophia Foord," *The Woman's Journal,* Vol. XVI, No. 15 (April 11, 1885), 117; Canby, *Thoreau,* 260–61; Channing, *Thoreau the Poet-Naturalist,* 163; Cheney, 42; Clark, *The Alcotts in Harvard,* 41–42; Emerson, *Journals,* VI, 544; Lothrop, *The Wayside,* 73; *Milton Records,*

Births, Marriages and Deaths. 1662–1843 (Boston, 1900), 26; M. Pratt, *Plants of Concord Natural and Introduced* (1878) (MS in Concord Public Library), 33, 55; Sanborn, *B. Alcott at Alcott House*, 100; A. K. Teele (ed.), *The History of Milton* (Boston, n.d.), 176, 290; Ticknor, *May Alcott*, 22.

LANE'S RETURN; THE ORDER OF DUTIES; LOUISA'S DESPAIR: *Journals of B. Alcott*, 140; Cheney, 43–44; Clark, *The Alcotts in Harvard*, 41ff.; Lothrop, *The Wayside*, 67–68; Sanborn, *B. Alcott at Alcott House*, 67–68, 93–95, 100–101; Sanborn, *Recollections of Seventy Years*, II, 340–41, 477.

LOUISA'S WALK IN THE WOODS: Cheney, 45; Sanborn, *Recollections of Seventy Years*, II, 341–42; Ticknor, *Classic Concord*, 242–43.

JOHN HOSMER'S SCHOOL; GAMES: L. M. Alcott, "Recollections of My Childhood," *The Youth's Companion*, Vol. LXI, No. 21 (May 24, 1888); *Report of the School Committee of Concord, for the Year Ending April 1st, 1845* (Concord, 1845), 5; *The Annual Report of the School Committee of Concord, for the Year April 1st, 1846* (Concord, 1846), 9; *Report of the School Committee of Concord, for the Year 1846–47* (Fitchburg, 1847), 7; *The Annual Report of the School Committee of Concord, for the Year Ending April 2d, 1849* (Charlestown, 1849), 11; *Annual Report of the School Committee of Concord, Mass. for Year 1900–1901* (Hudson, 1901), 10; G. B. Bartlett, "Concord Picnic Days," *Wide Awake*, Vol. XI, No. 3 (September, 1880), 189; Gowing, 5ff.; Lothrop, *The Wayside*, 71; information from Miss Margaret Lothrop.

LOUISA'S DIABOLIC TRAITS: *Journals of B. Alcott*, 173 and n. 26.

THE VISIT TO WALDEN: M. H. Brown, *Memories of Concord* (Boston, 1926), 96ff.; J. Burroughs, *Indoor Studies* (Boston and New York, 1900), 9; J. E. Cabot, *A Memoir of R. W. Emerson* (Boston and New York, 1887, 2 vols.), I, 283; Canby, *Thoreau*, 218; Channing, *Thoreau the Poet-Naturalist*, 7, 230, 290; W. E. Channing, *The Wanderer* (Boston, 1871), 27ff.; M. D. Conway, *Autobiography, Memories and Experiences* (Boston and New York, 1904, 2 vols.), I, 141; Conway, *Emerson at Home and Abroad*, 282ff.; H. E. Cummin, *Handbook, Concord Antiquarian Society* (Concord, 1937), 57; E. Emerson, *Henry Thoreau As Remembered by a Young Friend*, 147; Hubbard, *Little Journeys to the Homes of American Authors*, 29; Pratt, *Plants of Concord*, 5, 66; *Records of a Lifelong Friendship*, 60; Salt, *Life of H. D. Thoreau*, 68–69; H. D. Thoreau, *Walden* (New York, 1929), *passim*; H. D. Thoreau, *Works* (Boston, 1937), 681; Thoreau, *Writings*, VII, 421; Willis, *Alcott Memoirs*, 91–93.

PLAYS IN THE BARN: J. S. P. Alcott, "The 'Little Women' of Long Ago," *Good Housekeeping Magazine*, Vol. LVI, No. 2 (February, 1913), 189; *Comic Tragedies* . . . by *"Jo" and "Meg"* (Boston, 1893), *passim;* plays by Anna and Louisa Alcott in May's Waste or Day Book (Orchard House); Anthony, *L. M. Alcott*, 69; Lothrop, *The Wayside*, 49; T. Malone, *American Pilgrimage* (New York, 1942), 162; Sanborn, *Recollections of Seventy Years*, II, 474; M. B. Stern, "Louisa Alcott, Trouper," *The New England Quarterly*, Vol. XVI, No. 2 (June, 1943), 175–76.

THE DICKENS MANIA: L. M. Alcott, untitled note on Dickens, *The Commonwealth*, Vol. VI, No. 3 (September 21, 1867); C. Dickens, *Barnaby Rudge* (New York, 1931), *passim;* C. Dickens, *The Life and Adventures of Martin Chuzzlewit* (London, 1844), *passim;* C. Dickens, *The Posthumous Papers of the Pickwick Club* (London, n. d.), *passim;* Pickwick Club Members (Orchard House); Meigs, *Invincible Louisa*, 86.

EMERSON AND LOUISA: J. Albee, *Remembrances of Emerson* (New York, 1901), 29; *Journals of B. Alcott*, 198; L. M. Alcott, "Reminiscences of R. W. Emerson," in J. Parton (ed.), *Some Noted Princes, Authors, and Statesmen of Our Time* (New York, [1885]), 284–85; Bartlett, *Concord Historic*, 50; V. W. Brooks, *The Life of Emerson* (New York, 1932), 88; Brown, *Memories of Concord*, 39, 42; Cabot, *Memoir of R. W. Emerson*, II, 620; Channing, *Poems of Sixty-Five Years*, 122; Cheney, 45, 57–58; clipping at New York Public Library; A. H. Clough, *The Poems and Prose Remains* (London, 1869, 2 vols.), I, 183; Conway, *Emerson at Home and Abroad*, 217, 237; [M. D. Conway], "The Transcendentalists of Concord," *The Living Age*, 3rd Series, Vol. XXVII, No. 1063 (October 15, 1864), 108; [Dicey], "The New England States," *Macmillan's Magazine*, Vol. VI, No. 34 (August, 1862), 288; E. Emerson, *Emerson in Concord* (Boston and New York, 1889), 66, 124, 129, 167; E. Emerson, *Henry Thoreau As Remembered by a Young Friend*, 132; R. W. Emerson, *Essays* (New York, n. d.), First Series, *passim*, Second Series, 40; Emerson, *Journals*, VI, 289, VIII, 48 n. 1; R. W. Emerson, *Letters and Social Aims* (Boston, 1887), 97; R. W. Emerson, *Society and Solitude* (Boston, 1887), 204; A. F[ields]., "Mr. Emerson in the Lecture Room," *The Atlantic Monthly*, Vol. LI, No. 308 (June, 1883), 823; French, *Old Concord*, 107; J. Hawthorne, *Hawthorne and His Circle* (New York and London, 1903), 67; J. Hawthorne, "R. W. Emerson," *Harper's New Monthly Magazine*, Vol. LXV, No. 386 (July, 1882), 279; O. W. Holmes, *Ralph Waldo Emerson* (Boston, 1892), 363; M. A. de W. Howe, *Memories of a Hostess* (Boston,

1922), 89; W. D. Howells, "Impressions of Emerson," *Harper's Weekly*, Vol. XLVII, No. 2421 (May 16, 1903), 784; H. James, Sr., "Emerson," *The Atlantic Monthly*, Vol. XCIV, No. 566 (December, 1904), 745; R. H. Lathrop, *Memories of Hawthorne*, 76; E. Lazarus, "Emerson's Personality," *The Century Magazine*, Vol. XXIV, No. 3 (July, 1882), 454, 456; J. Nairn, "Emerson's Home in Concord," *Temple Bar*, Vol. CXV, No. 455 (October, 1898), 294; B. Perry, *Emerson Today* (Princeton, 1931), 23; Rusk, I, *xxxvii*; F. B. Sanborn, *Ralph Waldo Emerson* (Boston, 1901), 127; Sanborn, *Recollections of Seventy Years*, II, 573; G. W. Smalley, *Anglo-American Memories* (New York and London, 1911), 54; Stearns, *Life and Genius of Hawthorne*, 165; W. Whitman, "By Emerson's Grave," *The Critic*, Vol. II, No. 34 (May 6, 1882), 123; G. E. Woodberry, *Ralph Waldo Emerson* (New York, 1926), 82; C. J. Woodbury, *Talks with R. W. Emerson* (New York, [1890]), 126–27.

LOUISA'S SCHOOL IN THE HILLSIDE BARN: Lothrop, *The Wayside*, 76; Meigs, *Invincible Louisa*, 89; C. Meigs, "The School in the Barn," *The Elementary English Review*, Vol. IX, No. 9 (November, 1932), 227–28; Ticknor, *Classic Concord*, 207.

FLOWER FABLES: L. M. Alcott, "The Fairie Dell" (MS in Concord Public Library); L. M. Alcott, *Flower Fables* (Boston, 1855), *passim*; L. M. Alcott, "Recollections of My Childhood," *The Youth's Companion*, Vol. LXI, No. 21 (May 24, 1888); information from Miss S. R. Bartlett; Lothrop, *The Wayside*, 76.

CHAPTER 5 *Green Rooms and City Missions*

LOUISA'S HOUSEHOLD ACTIVITIES: L. M. Alcott, "Recollections of My Childhood," *The Youth's Companion*, Vol. LXI, No. 21 (May 24, 1888).

MRS. ALCOTT'S WORK AMONG THE POOR: "Miss Alcott's Mother," *The Woman's Journal*, Vol. XV, No. 38 (September 20, 1884), 303; Mrs. Alcott's Reports (Box III, Houghton Library); Hillyer, "Marmee," *The Parents' Magazine*, Vol. VII, No. 11 (November, 1932), 42.

THE SUMMER AT ATKINSON STREET: *Journals of B. Alcott*, 208; *The Boston Directory 1849/50* (Boston, 1849), 200; J. W. Chadwick, *Samuel May of Leicester* (reprinted from *New England Magazine*, April, 1899), 203, 210; Cheney, 60; O. Handlin, *Boston's Immigrants* (Cambridge, 1941), 118; "The Olive Leaf" No. 1 (Orchard House) and No. 2 (Concord Antiquarian Society); O. Shepard, *Pedlar's Progress*, 439.

FAMILY POVERTY; ALCOTT'S CHARACTER: *Journals of B. Alcott*, 217, 230–31; F. W. Brown, *Alcott and the Concord School of Philosophy* (Privately printed, 1926), 26; Emerson, *Journals*, IX, 39; Rusk, IV, 406.

LOUISA GOES OUT TO SERVICE: L. M. Alcott, "How I Went Out to Service," *The Independent*, Vol. XXVI, No. 1331 (June 4, 1874); Mrs. Alcott's Reports (Houghton Library); Cheney, 66–67; Emerson, *Essays*, First Series, 122; information from Miss Josephine Hewins of the Dedham Historical Society; Hillyer, "Marmee," *The Parents' Magazine*, Vol. VII, No. 11 (November, 1932), 24; information from Frank W. Kimball of Dedham, MA; Alvan Lamson, *A Discourse on The Life and Character of Hon. James Richardson* (Boston, 1858); M. S. Porter, "Recollections of L. M. Alcott," *The New England Magazine*, Vol. VI, No. 1 (March, 1892), 6ff.; F. Smith, *A History of Dedham, Mass.* (Dedham, 1936), 188, 226, 228; information from Dr. Arthur M. Worthington of Dedham, MA.

LOUISA'S FIRST APPEARANCE IN PRINT: Flora Fairfield, "Sunlight," *Peterson's Magazine*, Vol. XX, No. 3 (September 1851), 110. The later appearance of "The Rival Prima Donnas" under the pseudonym "Flora Fairfield" establishes the authorship of "Sunlight." The author is indebted to Mr. E. H. O'Neill of the University of Pennsylvania for aid in locating the poem.

LLEWELLYN WILLIS AND LOUISA'S FIRST PUBLISHED STORY: L. M. A., "The Rival Painters. A Tale of Rome," *Olive Branch*, Vol. XVII, No. 19 (May 8, 1852); Cheney, 68; fragment, Intelligence Office, High Street, May, 1852 (Orchard House); Willis, *Alcott Memoirs*, 24, 37–38.

MME. SONTAG'S CONCERT AT THE NEW MUSIC HALL: May Alcott's fragmentary Diary, December, 1852 (Orchard House); *Boston Daily Evening Transcript*, Vol. XXIII, Nos. 6866 and 6867 (November 20 and 22, 1852); E. Crowe, *With Thackeray in America* (London, 1893), 24; *The Life of Henriette Sontag* (New York, 1852), 6, 44, 56; J. Weiss, *Life and Correspondence of Theodore Parker* (New York, 1864, 2 vols.), I, 408.

PARKER'S DISCOURSE AT THE MUSIC HALL: ["Alcott's Conversation on New England Reformers"], *The Commonwealth*, Vol. I, No. 35 (May 1, 1863); L. M. Alcott, Preface in *Prayers by Theodore Parker* (Boston, 1882), *iii–iv;* May Alcott's fragmentary Diary, December 1852 (Orchard House); B. Brockway, *Fifty Years in Journalism* (Watertown, 1891), 125–26; J. F. Clarke, *Memorial and Biographical Sketches* (Boston and New

York, [1878]), 123; Conway, *Emerson at Home and Abroad*, 22; O. B. Frothingham, *Theodore Parker* (Boston, 1874), 334; R. A. Griffin, *Theodore Parker and the Liberal Movement in America* (Chicago, 1881), unpaged; T. W. Higginson, *Cheerful Yesterdays* (Boston and New York, 1898), 98; T. W. Higginson, *Contemporaries* (Boston and New York, 1899), 58; J. W. Howe, *Reminiscences* (Boston and New York, 1899), 244; A. D. Mayo, "A Garland for Theodore Parker," *National Anti-Slavery Standard*, Vol. XXI, No. 10 (July 21, 1860); J. T. Sargent, *Theodore Parker, The Reform Pulpit, and the Influences That Oppose It* (Boston, 1852), 14; Smalley, *Anglo-American Memories*, 39–40; C. E. Stevens, *Anthony Burns, a History* (Boston, 1856), 37; F. Tiffany, "Theodore Parker," *The New World*, Vol. IX, No. 36 (December, 1900), 698; [D. Wasson?], "Character and Historical Position of T. Parker," *The Christian Examiner*, Vol. LXXVII, No. 244 (July, 1864), 2; Weiss, *Life and Correspondence of T. Parker*, II, *491*.

LOUISA'S STORY REJECTED BY FIELDS: E. M. Bacon, *Boston. A Guide Book* (Boston, [1928]), 53; Cheney, 131; *A History of the Old Corner Bookstore* (Boston, 1903), 26; W. D. Howells, *Literary Friends and Acquaintance* (New York and London, 1902), 33, 40; "Thomas Niles—In Memoriam," *The Publishers' Weekly*, Vol. XLV, No. 23 (June 9, 1894), 859; *Park Street New and Old 1828–1923* (Boston, n. d.), 4; Woodbury, *Talks with R. W. Emerson*, 101.

"THE RIVAL PRIMA DONNAS":   Flora Fairfield, "The Rival Prima Donnas," *Saturday Evening Gazette*, Series for 1854, No. 45 (November 11, 1854); L. Harlow, *L. M. Alcott: A Souvenir* (Boston, 1888), 10; Stern, "L. Alcott, Trouper," *The New England Quarterly*, Vol. XVI, No. 2 (June, 1943), 188.

"FLOWER FABLES":   Extract from Alcott's Journal for November 17, 1854, Sanborn Papers (Houghton Library); L. M. Alcott, *Flower Fables* (Boston, 1855), dedication; Cheney, 76–77, 79; *Boston Daily Evening Transcript*, December 19, 1854; review of *Flower Fables* in *Boston Evening Transcript*, December 20, 1854; review of *Flower Fables* in *Saturday Evening Gazette*, December 23, 1854.

DRAMATIZATION OF "THE RIVAL PRIMA DONNAS":   MS of dramatized version of "The Rival Prima Donnas" (Orchard House); Cheney, 64–65; Stern, "L. Alcott, Trouper," *The New England Quarterly*, Vol. XVI, No. 2 (June, 1943), 188.

"NAT BACHELOR'S PLEASURE TRIP" AND DR. WINDSHIP'S INTEREST: Cheney, 73, 80; H. A. Clapp, *Reminiscences of a Dramatic Critic* (Boston and New York, 1902), 65; Edes, *Genealogy of the Descendants of John May*, 42; A. H. Quinn, *A History of the American Drama* (New York and London, 1923), 284; Stern, "L. Alcott, Trouper," *The New England Quarterly*, Vol. XVI, No. 2 (June, 1943), 189.

LOUISA AT THE THEATER WITH HAMILTON WILLIS: Cheney, 73, 80; M. Crawford, *Romantic Days in Old Boston* (Boston, 1910), 266, 269; *Dearborn's Reminiscences of Boston* (Boston, [1851]), 82; A. Hornblow, *A History of the Theatre in America* (Philadelphia and London, 1919, 2 vols.), II, 24; *The Log of the State Street Trust Company* (Boston, 1926), 71; *Sketches and Business Directory of Boston . . . for 1860* and *1861* (Boston, [1860]), 127, 129; *The Stranger's New Guide through Boston* (Boston, n. d.), 8; P. Willis, *Willis Records* (London, n. d.), 84; clipping *re* Mrs. John Wood in Robinson Locke Collection of Dramatic Scrapbooks, New York Public Library.

LOUISA'S STAY AT WALPOLE: *Journals of B. Alcott*, 275; lines written by Mrs. Alcott for Louisa Wells (Orchard House); G. Aldrich, *Walpole as It Was and as It Is* (Claremont, 1880), 111; *H. W. Bellows. A Biographical Sketch* (Keene, n. d.), 304; Cheney, 78, 81–83; J. Hayward, *A Gazetteer of New Hampshire* (Boston, 1849), 138; A. C. Howland, *Illustrated Catalogue of Oil Paintings* (New York, 1910), *passim*; J. M. Hunnewell, *The Ticknor Family in America* (Boston, 1919) (typescript), 101–102; T. B. Peck, *The Bellows Genealogy* (Keene, 1898), *passim*; Stern, "L. Alcott, Trouper," *The New England Quarterly*, Vol. XVI, No. 2 (June, 1943), 177ff.; B. W. Wells (ed.), *Letters of an Argonaut* (Los Angeles, n. d.), 18, 20; B. W. Wells, *Elizabeth Sewall Willis* (London, 1905), 42–43; P. Willis, *Willis Records*, 74.

THE REED HOUSEHOLD: *Boston Directory, for the Year 1856* (Boston, 1856), 280; Cheney, 85, 88; "David Reed," *D. A. B.*, XV, 445–46; "Rev. David Reed," *The Christian Register*, Vol. XLIX, No. 24 (June 11, 1870); J. L. Reed, *The Reed Genealogy* (Baltimore, [1901]), 174; information from William Howell Reed.

LOUISA AT PARKER'S SUNDAY EVENING RECEPTIONS: G. L. Austin, *The Life and Times of Wendell Phillips* (Boston, 1884), 357, 424; F. Bremer, *America of the Fifties* (New York, 1924), 47; Cheney, 79, 85–87, 90; H. S. Commager, *Theodore Parker* (Boston, 1936), 104ff.; Frothingham, *T. Parker*, 241, 248; *Garrison. The Story of His Life*, IV, 288, 322; Griffin, *T.*

Parker and the Liberal Movement, unpaged; J. Hawthorne, *Memoirs,* 242; Higginson, *Contemporaries,* 50, 266, 284, 286; J. W. Howe, *Reminiscences,* 160–62; [Wasson?], "Character and Historical Position of T. Parker," *The Christian Examiner,* Vol. LXXVII, No. 244 (July, 1864), 18, 22, 33, 36; Weiss, *Life and Correspondence of T. Parker,* II, 2–3.

CHAPTER 6 *The Orchard House*

SANBORN AND HIS SCHOOL: Abby to Alf Whitman, Concord, October 23, [1861] (Houghton Library); *Memoirs of Members of the Social Circle in Concord,* Fourth Series (Cambridge, 1909), 266,270 (hereinafter referred to as *Concord Memoirs*); Emerson, *Journals,* IX, 113 n. 2, 316; J. Hawthorne, *Memoirs,* 72–73, 77, 80, 84; *A. James. Her Brothers—Her Journal* (New York, [1934]), 4, 26–27; H. James, *Notes of a Son and Brother* (New York, 1914), 215–16, 222; B. and P. Russell (eds.), *The Amberley Papers* (London, 1937, 2 vols.), II, 66; F. B. Sanborn, *Hawthorne and His Friends* (Cedar Rapids, 1908), 13; Sanborn, *Recollections of Seventy Years,* I, 51, II, 222, 328, 337, 383, 517; V. C. Sanborn, "F. B. Sanborn," *The New England Historical and Genealogical Register,* Vol. LXXI, Whole No. 284 (October, 1917), 292; Stearns, *Sketches from Concord,* 8ff.; Swayne, *The Story of Concord,* 270; H. D. Thoreau, *Familiar Letters* (Boston and New York, 1894), 377; Thoreau, *Writings,* VI, 321 n. 1; B. E. W. Williams, *Mary C. Wheeler* (Boston, [1934]), 16.

LOUISA'S INTEREST IN BOYS: Louisa to Alf Whitman, [Concord], March 2, [1860] (Houghton Library).

CONCORD STOCK COMPANY: Abby to her father, February 4, [1858?] (Houghton Library); Abby to Alf Whitman, Boston, April 23, [1858] (Houghton Library); Louisa's Acrostic to Adolphus Tetterby, April 9, 1858 (Houghton Library); Louisa to Alf Whitman, Boston, October 27, [1858] (Houghton Library); Louisa to Alf Whitman, February 13–15, [1859] (Houghton Library); Louisa to Alf Whitman, January 6, 1869 (Houghton Library); L. M. Alcott, *Aunt Jo's Scrap-Bag,* I (Boston, 1884), 15–16; Stock Company for 1857–58 listed in back of May Alcott's fragmentary Diary for 1852 and 1854 (Orchard House); information from Miss S. R. Bartlett and Mrs. M. Whitman Chapman; E. Emerson, "When L. Alcott Was a Girl," *The Ladies' Home Journal,* Vol. XIV, No. 1 (December, 1898), 16; C. H. Farnam, *History of the Descendants of John Whitman* (New Haven, 1889), 268, 270; Stern, "L. Alcott, Trouper," *The New*

England Quarterly, Vol. XVI, No. 2 (June, 1943), 182–83; [A. Whitman], "Meg, Jo, Beth, and Amy," *The Girl's Realm*, Vol. V, No. 50 (December, 1902), 134; A. Whitman, "Miss Alcott's Letters to Her 'Laurie,' " *The Ladies' Home Journal*, Vol. XVII, No. 10 (September, 1901), 5; information from Mr. and Mrs. John Pratt Whitman.

LIZZIE'S ILLNESS, DEATH, AND FUNERAL: *Journals of B. Alcott*, 303–305, 307; Cheney, 75–76, 96–98; Emerson, *Lectures and Biographical Sketches*, 87; R. W. Emerson, *Miscellanies* (Boston, 1887), 434; Emerson, *Letters and Social Aims*, 329; H. Hoeltje, *Sheltering Tree* (Durham, 1943), 146; Morrow, *Father of Little Women*, 271–74; newspaper clipping in Ford Collection, New York Public Library; *Pedlar's Progress*, 467–68; *Smith's Homoeopathic Directory of the United States* (New York, 1857), 49; Thoreau, *Early Spring in Massachusetts*, 80, 135–36; Wood, "Beth Alcott's Playmate," *Harper's Bazar*, Vol. XLVII, No. 5 (May, 1913), 246.

ANNA'S ENGAGEMENT: *Journals of B. Alcott*, 308; L. M. Alcott's fragmentary Diary for 1858 (Houghton Library); Cheney, 98–99.

THE ORCHARD HOUSE: H. C. Ahl, *A Visit to Orchard House* (n. p., [1938]), 10; Abby to Alf Whitman, Boston, April 23, [1858] (Houghton Library); A. B. Alcott, *Concord Days*, 4ff., 43; *Journals of B. Alcott*, 301–302, 308–309; A. B. Alcott, *Tablets* (Boston, 1868), 11–12, 21; J. S. P. Alcott, "The 'Little Women' of Long Ago," *Good Housekeeping Magazine*, Vol. LVI, No. 2 (February, 1913), 188; *Appletons' Cyclopaedia of American Biography* (New York, 1900, 6 vols.), I, 41; Bartlett, "Concord Picnic Days," *Wide Awake*, Vol. XI, No. 1 (July, 1880), 66; Cheney, 99–100; S. A. Drake, *Historic Fields and Mansions of Middlesex. With Extra Illustrations* (Boston, 1874, 2 vols.), II, 376; F. T. Eaton, "An American Woman's Letter," *The Landmark*, Vol. VII, No. 12 (December, 1925), 757–58; E. Emerson, "When L. Alcott Was a Girl," *The Ladies' Home Journal*, Vol. XIV, No. 1 (December, 1898), 16; J. Hawthorne, *Memoirs*, 57; J. Hawthorne, "The Woman Who Wrote 'Little Women,' " *The Ladies' Home Journal*, Vol. XXXIX (October, 1922), 122; G. E. H. Hosmer, "L. M. Alcott: War Nurse," *The Trained Nurse and Hospital Review*, Vol. LXXXIX, No. 2 (August, 1932), 146; Howe, *Memories of a Hostess*, 74; Hubbard, *Little Journeys to the Homes of American Authors*, 224; Lathrop, *Memories of Hawthorne*, 417; *Pedlar's Progress*, 470–72; A. and W. Ricketson (eds.), *D. Ricketson and His Friends* (Boston and New York, 1902), 80, 190; Sanborn, *Hawthorne and His Friends*, 65; Sanborn and

Harris, II, 436–37; "The Spectator," *The Outlook*, Vol. CI (July 6, 1912), 552; Stearns, *Sketches from Concord*, 69ff.; Swayne, *The Story of Concord*, 146–48; H. D. Thoreau, *Letters to Various Persons* (Boston, 1865), 169; Thoreau, *Writings*, XX, 147; Ticknor, *Classic Concord*, 209–10; Woodbury, *Talks with R. W. Emerson*, 102.

Louisa and the Loverings: Louisa to Alf Whitman, Boston, October 27, [1858] (Houghton Library); Louisa to Alf Whitman, Concord, December 26, 1858 (Houghton Library); Louisa to Dear People, Boston, [October 1858] (Houghton Library).

Louisa's Letter to Alf: Louisa to Alf Whitman, Boston, April 17, [1859] (Houghton Library).

John Brown at Concord; Martyr Service; Louisa's Poem on Brown: *Journals of B. Alcott*, 315–16, 323; L. M. Alcott, "With a Rose, That Bloomed on the Day of John Brown's Martyrdom," *The Liberator*, Vol. XXX, No. 3 (January 20, 1860); G. Bradford, *Damaged Souls* (Boston and New York, 1923), 161; Channing, *Thoreau the Poet-Naturalist*, 262; Cheney, 105; "Dirge Sung at a Meeting in Concord," *The Liberator*, Vol. XXIX, No. 49 (December 9, 1859), 196; *Pedlar's Progress*, 477; J. Redpath, *Echoes of Harper's Ferry* (Boston, 1860), 437ff.; F. B. Sanborn, *Memoirs of John Brown* (Concord, 1878), 96; Sanborn, *Recollections of Seventy Years*, I, 202; H. D. Thoreau, *Miscellanies* (Boston and New York, 1893), 248, 251; Thoreau, *Writings*, XIX, 3.

Louisa's Letter to Alf: Louisa to Alf Whitman, [Concord], March 2, [1860] (Houghton Library).

Louisa's Letter to Alf: Louisa to Alf Whitman, April 5, [1860] (Houghton Library).

Performance of "Nat Bachelor": *Boston Daily Evening Transcript*, Vol. XXXI, No. 9211 (May 5, 1860); Cheney, 121; E. F. Edgett (ed.), *E. L. Davenport* (New York, 1901), 85; L. C. Moulton, "L. M. Alcott," *Our Famous Women* (Hartford, 1885), 37; playbill at Houghton Library; Stern, "L. Alcott, Trouper," *The New England Quarterly*, Vol. XVI, No. 2 (June, 1943), 190–91; J. H. Wiggin, *Personal Reminiscences of William Warren*, reprinted from *The Coming Age*, July 1900.

Anna's Wedding: *Journals of B. Alcott*, 326–27; Louisa to Alf Whitman, September 24, 1861 (Houghton Library); Cheney, 121–22,

132; J. Hawthorne, *Hawthorne and His Circle*, 70; S. J. May, MS Diary for 1860; Carrie [Pratt] to "Dolphus," Concord, June 10, [1860] (Houghton Library).

THE HAWTHORNES IN CONCORD: Abby to Alf Whitman, Concord, July 17, 1860; Alcott, *Concord Days*, 194–95; *Journals of B. Alcott*, 328; Arvin, *Hawthorne*, 266–68; Bartlett, *Concord Historic*, 64, 67–68; K. Burton, *Sorrow Built a Bridge* (London and New York, 1942), 69; M. D. Conway, *Life of N. Hawthorne* (London, [1890]), 198–99; J. Hawthorne, "A Daughter of Hawthorne," *The Atlantic Monthly*, Vol. CXLII, No. 3 (September 1928), 372, 374; J. Hawthorne, *Memoirs*, 20, 61, 63ff.; J. Hawthorne, *N. Hawthorne and His Wife*, I, 452, II, 263ff., 286; J. Hawthorne, "The Woman Who Wrote 'Little Women,'" *The Ladies' Home Journal*, Vol. XXXIX (October, 1922), 120; N. Hawthorne, *Letters to W. D. Ticknor* (Newark, 1910, 2 vols.), II, 106–107; T. W. Higginson, "Una Hawthorne," *The Outlook*, Vol. LXXVII, No. 9 (July 2, 1904), 517; Howe, *Memories of a Hostess*, 63; Howells, *Literary Friends and Acquaintance*, 51–52, 54; Lathrop, *Memories of Hawthorne*, 427–28, 430–31, 434, 447; Lillie, "L. M. Alcott," *The Cosmopolitan*, Vol. V, No. 2 (April, 1888), 161; Lothrop, *The Wayside*, 101, 130; Meigs, *Invincible Louisa*, 117; Sanborn, *Hawthorne and His Friends*, 15–16, 51; Sanborn, *H. D. Thoreau*, 189; Sanborn, *Recollections of Seventy Years*, II, 524; E. Simmons, *From Seven to Seventy* (New York and London, 1922), 14; Stearns, *The Life and Genius of Hawthorne*, 379; Stearns, *Sketches from Concord*, 66; Swayne, *The Story of Concord*, 190; Williams, *M. C. Wheeler*, 43; Wolfe, *Literary Shrines*, 65.

WRITING OF "MOODS": *Journals of B. Alcott*, 329; L. M. Alcott, *Moods* (Boston, 1865), *passim*; Cheney, 122.

"NEW GYMNASTICS" IN CONCORD: Abby to Alf Whitman, Syracuse, December 24, 1860 (Houghton Library); [L. M. Alcott], "The King of Clubs," *The Monitor*, Vol. I, Nos. 1–7 (April 19–June 7, 1862), *passim*; Cheney, 112–13; M. F. Eastman, *The Biography of Dio Lewis* (New York, 1891), 73; E. Emerson, "When L. Alcott Was a Girl," *The Ladies' Home Journal*, Vol. XIV, No. 1 (December, 1898), 16; J. Hawthorne, *Memoirs*, 138–40; [T. W. Higginson], "Gymnastics," *The Atlantic Monthly*, Vol. VII, No. 41 (March, 1861), 288–91; D. Lewis, *The New Gymnastics* (Boston, 1862), 100, 117, 165; J. Lovett, *Old Boston Boys* (Boston, 1906), 116; G. Windship, "How I Got My Strength," *The New York Ledger*, Vol. XVII, No. 51 (February 22, 1862), 8.

Louisa's Work on "Success" and "Moods": *Journals of B. Alcott,* 336–37; Louisa to James Redpath, n. d. (New York Historical Society); L. M. Alcott, *Moods, passim;* L. M. Alcott, *Work* (Boston, 1873), *passim;* Cheney, 124–26; C. Ticknor (ed.), *Dr. Holmes's Boston* (Boston and New York, 1915), 53.

School Festival; Alcott's Reputation: *Journals of B. Alcott,* 332; P. W. Brown, *Middlesex Monographs* (Cleveland, 1941), 94; Cheney, 126–27; "Merry's Monthly Chat with His Friends," *Merry's Museum,* Vol. II, No. 3 (March, 1869), 148; *Reports of the School Committee* (Concord, 1861), *passim;* Thoreau, *Letters to Various Persons,* 196.

Concord Company Leaves for Washington; War Activities in Concord: Louisa to Alf Whitman, Concord, May 19, [1861] (Houghton Library); Bartlett, *Concord Historic,* 117; H. Bridge, *Personal Recollections of N. Hawthorne* (New York, 1893), 169; Cabot, *A Memoir of R. W. Emerson,* II, 601–602; Cheney, 127; *Concord Memoirs,* Third Series, 247, Fourth Series, 53–54, 211; S. A. Drake, *History of Middlesex County* (Boston, 1880), I, 400; Emerson, *Miscellanies,* 109–10; Gowing, 68, 95; G. Reynolds, "My Memories of Concord in the Great Civil War," *A Collection of Historical and Other Papers* (Concord, 1895), 248–50, 252, 254–55; E. H. Savage, *Boston Events* (Boston, 1884), 12; M. Storey and E. W. Emerson, *E. R. Hoar* (Boston and New York, 1911), 128–29; G. Tolman, *Events of April Nineteenth* (Concord, n. d.), 4; Williams, *M. C. Wheeler,* 34; O. Wister and A. Irwin (eds.), *Worthy Women of Our First Century* (Philadelphia, 1877), 205–206.

Louisa in Gorham, N. H.: Louisa to Alf Whitman, Gorham, N. H., August 4, [1861] (Houghton Library); L. M. Alcott, "Letters from the Mountains," *The Commonwealth,* Vol. I, Nos. 47, 48, 49, and 51 (July 24–August 21, 1863); information from Mr. Frank H. Burt and the Hon. Charles A. Chandler; Cheney, 128; S. A. Drake, *The Heart of the White Mountains* (New York, 1882), 169; F. W. Kilbourne, *Chronicles of the White Mountains* (Boston and New York, [1916], 169–70; T. S. King, *The White Hills* (Boston, 1863), 327; P. Willis, *Willis Records,* 86.

Louisa's Letter to Alf: Louisa to Alf Whitman, Gorham, N. H., August 4, [1861] (Houghton Library).

Louisa's Letter to Alf: Louisa to Alf Whitman, Concord, November 12, [1861] (Houghton Library).

LOUISA TEACHES KINDERGARTEN: *Journals of B. Alcott*, 345; Louisa to Alf Whitman, [Concord], April 6, [1862] (Houghton Library); E. R. Butler, "In Memoriam Rev. Charles F. Barnard," *Forty-Ninth Annual Meeting of the . . . Warren Street Chapel* (Boston, 1885), 14–15, 23; Cheney, 130; Emerson, *Lectures and Biographical Sketches*, 154–55; J. Hawthorne, *Memoirs*, 45; Mrs. Horace Mann and Elizabeth Peabody, *Moral Culture of Infancy and Kindergarten Guide* (Boston, 1864), *passim*; E. P. Peabody, *Education in the Home, the Kindergarten, and the Primary School* (London, 1887), 15, 81, 88; *Proceedings of the Twenty-fifth Annual Meeting of the . . . Warren-street Chapel* (Boston, 1862), *passim*; *Sketches and Business Directory of Boston . . . for 1860 and 1861*, 24; L. Swift, *Literary Landmarks of Boston* (Boston and New York, 1903), 14; F. Tiffany, *C. F. Barnard* (Boston and New York, 1895), 96; L. Whiting, *Boston Days* (Boston, 1902), 182.

LOUISA'S LETTER TO ALF: Louisa to Alf Whitman, Concord, May 11, [1862] (Houghton Library).

THOREAU'S ILLNESS, DEATH, AND FUNERAL: [A. B. Alcott], "The Forester," *The Atlantic Monthly*, Vol. IX, No. 54 (April, 1862), 445; *Journals of B. Alcott*, 347–48; Louisa to Alf Whitman, Concord, May 11, [1862] (Houghton Library); W. R. Alger, *The Solitudes of Nature and of Man* (Boston, 1867), 338; Canby, *Thoreau*, 438; Channing, *Thoreau the Poet-Naturalist*, 20, 118 n. 1, 336, 340, 343; Emerson, *Lectures and Biographical Sketches*, 451–52; French, *Old Concord*, 151; Sophia Hawthorne to Mrs. A. A. Fields [c. May, 1862] (Boston Public Library); Howe, *Memories of a Hostess*, 62; R. H. Lathrop, *Memories of Hawthorne*, 431; Marble, *Thoreau: His Home, Friends and Books*, 315; "Reminiscences of Thoreau," *The Outlook*, Vol. LXIII, No. 14 (December 2, 1899), 818, 820; Rusk, V, 272 n. 35; Salt, *Life of H. D. Thoreau*, 146; Sanborn, *H. D. Thoreau*, 200, 317; F. B. Sanborn, *The Personality of Thoreau* (Boston, 1901), 66, 68–69; Thoreau; *Familiar Letters*, 36–37; "H. D. Thoreau. Emerson's Obituary," *Collectanea* (Lakeland, 1904), 5, 9.

LOUISA'S LETTER TO ALF: Louisa to Alf Whitman, Concord, June 22, [1862] (Houghton Library).

LOUISA APPLIES FOR POSITION AS NURSE AND LEAVES CONCORD: Alcott, *Tablets*, 198; Louisa to James Redpath, n. d. (New York Historical Society); Cheney, 140–41; Conway, *Autobiography, Memories and Experiences*, I, 369; J. Hawthorne, *N. Hawthorne and His Wife*, II, 326;

380 . Notes on Sources

Porter, "Recollections of L. M. Alcott," *The New England Magazine*, Vol. VI, No. 1 (March 1892), 12; Shepard (ed.), *The Heart of Thoreau's Journals*, 336.

CHAPTER 7 *The Union Hotel Hospital*

THE UNION HOTEL HOSPITAL: M. Benjamin (ed.), *Washington during War Time* (Washington, n. d.), 145; M. Leech, *Reveille in Washington* (New York and London, [1941]), 222ff.; *Frank Leslie's Illustrated Newspaper*, Vol. XII, No. 294 (July 6, 1861), 119; *The Medical and Surgical History of the War of the Rebellion* (Washington, 1870–88, 2 vols. in 3 parts each), Vol. I, Part III, 897; *Documents of the U. S. Sanitary Commission*, Vol. I, No. 23, pp. 1–3.

HOSPITAL ROUTINE AND PATIENTS: Cheney, 141, 143; information from Dr. P. M. Hamer, National Archives; *The New-York Times*, Vol. XII, No. 3509 (December 22, 1862) and Vol. XII, No. 3529 (January 15, 1863); J. J. Woodward, *The Hospital Steward's Manual* (Philadelphia, 1862), *passim*.

LOUISA'S JOURNAL AND LETTERS HOME: Abby to Alf Whitman, December 30, [1862] (Houghton Library); *Journals of B. Alcott*, 352; L. M. Alcott, *Hospital Sketches* (Boston, 1863), *passim*; Cheney, 138, 141ff.

PRIZE WON BY "PAULINE'S PASSION": E. G. Squier to L. M. Alcott [c. December 18, 1862] (Orchard House).

"THOREAU'S FLUTE": Louisa to Annie Fields, Concord, June 24, [1863] (Huntington Library); "Thoreau's Flute," *The Atlantic Monthly*, Vol. XII, No. 71 (September, 1863); Sophia Hawthorne to Annie A. Fields, June 14, 1863 (Boston Public Library); Sophia Hawthorne to Mr. Fields, June 15, 1863 (Boston Public Library); Sophia Hawthorne to Annie A. Fields, July 7, 1863 (Boston Public Library).
The version given here is unrevised. Later the fifth and eighth lines of the first stanza were changed to read respectively:

> *Spring mourns as for untimely frost;*
> *The Genius of the wood is lost.*

And the word "turned" in the last line of the second stanza was changed to "tuned."

LOUISA'S ILLNESS AND RETURN HOME: Bronson Alcott to Anna, January 30, 1863, Family Letters V (Concord Public Library; courtesy Mr. F. W. Pratt); Mrs. Alcott to her brother, 1863, Family Letters V (Concord Public Library; courtesy Mr. Pratt); *Journals of B. Alcott*, 354; pencil note by Louisa Alcott appended to a letter from John Pratt to Mother, on the back of the telegram he had received (Houghton Library); Louisa to Alf Whitman, Concord, September [1863] (Houghton Library); Cheney, 145–46, 226; S. Dunbar, *A History of Travel in America* (Indianapolis, [1915], 4 vols.), III, 1112–13; *The Encyclopedia Americana*, XXVII, 242; J. Hawthorne, "The Woman Who Wrote 'Little Women,' " *The Ladies' Home Journal*, Vol. XXXIX (October 1922), 120; Sophia Hawthorne to Annie A. Fields, February 20, 1863 (Boston Public Library); Leech, *Reveille in Washington*, 224; Meigs, *Invincible Louisa*, 158–61; Sanborn and Harris, II, 499.

CHAPTER 8 *Plots and Counterplots*

LOUISA'S ILLNESS AND EARLY DAYS AT HOME: *Journals of B. Alcott*, 354–55; Mrs. Alcott to her brother, 1863, Family Letters V (Concord Public Library; courtesy Mr. F. W. Pratt); Louisa to Alf Whitman, Concord, September, [1863] (Houghton Library); Louisa's Certificate of Service in Records of General Accounting Office, Washington, D. C.; Cheney, 146–48, 150; Sophia Hawthorne to Annie A. Fields, February 20, 1863 (Boston Public Library); Stearns, *Sketches from Concord*, 78, 81; M. B. Stern, "Louisa M. Alcott, Civil War Nurse," *Americana*, Vol. XXXVII, No. 2 (April, 1943), 319–20.

"HOSPITAL SKETCHES" PREPARED FOR PUBLICATION: L. M. Alcott, "Hospital Sketches," *The Commonwealth*, Vol. I, Nos. 38, 39, 41, and 43 (May 22–June 26, 1863); Cheney, 150; *King's Handbook of Boston*, 292–93; Sanborn, *Recollections of Seventy Years*, I, 224; Sanborn and Harris, II, 500 n. 1; Stern, "L. M. Alcott, Civil War Nurse," *Americana*, Vol. XXXVII, No. 2 (April, 1943), 321.

LOUISA'S LETTER TO REDPATH: Louisa to James Redpath, n. p., n. d. (New York Historical Society).

APPEARANCE AND RECEPTION OF "HOSPITAL SKETCHES" IN BOOK FORM: *Journals of B. Alcott*, 357; Mrs. Alcott to her brother, July 19, 1863, Family Letters V (Concord Public Library; courtesy Mr. F. W. Pratt); Louisa to James Redpath, n. d., and August 28, [1863], and

382 . Notes on Sources

September 29, [1863] (New York Historical Society); L. M. Alcott, *Hospital Sketches* (Boston, 1863), title page; criticisms of *Hospital Sketches* in Alcott Papers, Box II (Houghton Library) and Autobiographical Collections VII (1856–67) (Concord Public Library; courtesy Mr. F. W. Pratt); inscribed copy of *Hospital Sketches* for Nurse Pratt (courtesy the late Mr. Carroll A. Wilson); Cheney, 153; Stern, "L. M. Alcott, Civil War Nurse," *Americana*, Vol. XXXVII, No. 2 (April, 1943), 322–23; information from the late Mr. Carroll A. Wilson.

RETURN OF CONCORD COMPANY, SEPTEMBER, 1863:   Louisa to Alf Whitman, Concord, September, [1863] (Houghton Library); J. Hawthorne, "The Woman Who Wrote 'Little Women,' " *The Ladies' Home Journal*, Vol. XXXIX (October, 1922), 120–21; Meigs, *Invincible Louisa*, 174–75; Stern, "L. M. Alcott, Civil War Nurse," *Americana*, Vol. XXXVII, No. 2 (April, 1943), 323–25.

REVISION OF "MOODS" FOR LORING: *Journals of B. Alcott*, 366; L. M. Alcott, *Moods* (Boston, 1865); Canby, *Thoreau*, 179–80; Cheney, 160–61, 166; Clark, *The Alcotts in Harvard*, letter opp. p. 38; Emerson, *Journals*, X, 77; A. K. Loring to Louisa, n. d. (courtesy the late Mr. Carroll A. Wilson); Sanborn, *Recollections of Seventy Years*, II, 342.

"V. V.":   "V. V.: or, Plots and Counterplots," *The Flag of Our Union*, Vol. XX, Nos. 5–8 (February 4–25, 1865). The discovery and identification of Louisa Alcott's anonymous and pseudonymous works were made by Leona Rostenberg in "Some Anonymous and Pseudonymous Thrillers of L. M. Alcott," *The Papers of the Bibliographical Society of America*, Vol. XXXVII, No. 2 (April, May, and June, 1943).

LOUISA'S LETTER TO MOTHER: *Journals of B. Alcott*, 367.

LOUISA'S LETTER TO REDPATH: Louisa to James Redpath, n. p., n. d. (New York Historical Society).

MRS. JARLEY: MS copy of Mrs. Jarley made by Louisa for Alf Whitman (Houghton Library); Louisa's arrangement of Mrs. Jarley, MS (Orchard House); Louisa's Jarley costume (Orchard House); Cheney, 164–65; C. Dickens, *The Old Curiosity Shop* (New York, 1930), *passim; Mrs. Jarley's Famous Waxworks* (Chicago and New York, 1902), 7, 79; Stern, "L. Alcott, Trouper," *The New England Quarterly*, Vol. XVI, No. 2 (June, 1943), 192–93.

DEALINGS WITH ELLIOTT, THOMES AND TALBOT: "In the Garret," *The Flag of Our Union*, Vol. XX, No. 11 (March 18, 1865); "A Marble Woman," *ibid.*, Vol. XX, Nos. 20–23 (May 20–June 10, 1865); "The Sanitary Fair," *ibid.*, Vol. XX, No. 16 (April 22, 1865); "V. V.," *ibid.*, Vol. XX, Nos. 5–8 (February 4–25, 1865); *The Boston Almanac for 1864*, 52–53; E. W. Cobb, *A Memoir of Sylvanus Cobb, Jr.* (Boston, 1891), 283; Rostenberg, "Some Anonymous and Pseudonymous Thrillers of L. M. Alcott," *Papers of the Bibliographical Society of America*, Vol. XXXVII, No. 2 (April, May, and June, 1943), *passim;* G. R. Stewart, *Take Your Bible in One Hand* (San Francisco, 1939), 53.

THE WELD FAMILY: I. Anderson, *Under the Black Horse Flag* (Boston and New York, 1926), 35–36, 38, 50–51, 162; information from the late Mrs. Larz Anderson; C. F. Robinson, *Weld Collections* (Ann Arbor, 1938), 173; information from Mr. R. B. Shipley, chief, Passport Division.

LOUISA SAILS: Louisa's Passport Application and Oath of Allegiance (Passport Division); [E. Dicey], "The Outlook of the War," *Macmillan's Magazine*, Vol. VI, No. 35 (September, 1862), 408; H. A. Hill, "Boston and Liverpool Packet Lines," *The New England Magazine*, Vol. IX, No. 5 (January, 1894), 555; information from Mrs. K. D. Metcalf of the Boston Athenaeum.

CHAPTER 9 *Life in a Pension*

JOURNEY UP THE RHINE AND NIGHT AT COBLENZ: L. M. Alcott, "Up the Rhine," *The Independent*, Vol. XIX, No. 972 (July 18, 1867); Cheney, 175; G. M. Young (ed.), *Early Victorian England* (London, 1934, 2 vols.), II, 305.

SCHWALBACH: Cheney, 175; T. Fritze, *Schwalbach* (Darmstadt, 1873), *passim;* A. Genth, *The Iron Waters of Schwalbach* (Schwalbach, 1856), *passim.*

LOUISA AT VEVEY AND THE PENSION VICTORIA: L. M. Alcott, "Life in a Pension," *The Independent*, Vol. XIX, No. 988 (November 7, 1867); *Bellerive Institution Sillig 1836–1892* (Vevey, 1892), 9, 11; A. Ceresole, *Vevey: Its Environs and Climate* (Zurich, [188–?]), *passim;* Cheney, 178–79; T. Fuller, *The History of the Worthies of England* (London, 1840, 3 vols.), III, 438; [P. Girard], *Album des Photographies Officielles de la Fête des Vignerons*

(Vevey, 1927), unpaged; *A Handbook for Travellers in Switzerland* (London, 1865), 183; Carrie Pratt to Alf Whitman, Concord, December 10, [1865].

LADISLAS WISNIEWSKI; HIS RELATIONSHIP WITH LOUISA AND ANNA WELD: L. M. Alcott, "Life in a Pension," *The Independent*, Vol. XIX, No. 988 (November 7, 1867); L. M. Alcott, "My Polish Boy," *The Youth's Companion*, Vol. XLI, Nos. 48 and 49 (November 26 and December 3, 1868); Anderson, *Under the Black Horse Flag*, 162; information from the late Mrs. Larz Anderson; Cheney, 178–79; information from Mr. J. Dembinski of the Polish Information Center.

LOUISA AT NICE; MME ROLANDE: Louisa to Mrs. Conway, Nice, April 15, [1866]; L. M. Alcott, "Music and Macaroni," *Lulu's Library* (Boston, 1927, 3 vols.), III, 111; L. M. Alcott, "A Royal Governess," *The Independent*, Vol. XX, No. 1023 (July 9, 1868); *Appleton's European Guide Book* (New York, [1870]), 300; Cheney, 179–82; F. O. C. Darley, *Sketches Abroad with Pen and Pencil* (New York, 1868), 102–103; C. Dickens, *Pictures from Italy* (Leipzig, 1846), 79; *Guides Joanne. Nice, Monaco* (n. p., n. d.), 31; *Handbook for Travellers in Northern Italy* (London, 1866), 83; S. R. Hole, *Nice and Her Neighbours* (n. p., n. d.), 38, 82–83; T. Smollett, "Travels through France and Italy," *The Miscellaneous Works* (Edinburgh, 1820, 6 vols.), V, 360–61.

PARIS FORTNIGHT WITH LADISLAS: *An American Family in Paris* (New York, 1869), 12; D. W. Bartlett, *Paris: With Pen and Pencil* (New York, 1858), 155; H. W. Bellows, *The Old World in Its New Face* (New York, 1868–69, 2 vols.), I, 24–25; E. G. Buffum, *Sights and Sensations in France* (New York, 1869), 201–202, 230, 262; Cheney, 182; Darley, *Sketches Abroad*, 45; M. V. Fournel, *Ce Qu'on Voit dans les Rues de Paris* (Paris, 1859), 294–95; N. Hawthorne, *Passages from the French and Italian Note-Books* (London, 1871, 2 vols.), I, 23; E. King, *My Paris* (Boston, 1868), *passim;* J. D. McCabe, Jr., *Paris by Sunlight and Gaslight* (Philadelphia, [1869]), *passim;* H. Morford, *Paris in '67* (New York, 1867), 249; M. A. Nieriker, *Studying Art Abroad* (Boston, 1879), 43.

LOUISA AT AUBREY HOUSE; ITS RECEPTIONS AND GUESTS: Louisa to Mrs. Conway, June 5, [1866] (Columbia University); L. M. Alcott, "Reminiscences of R. W. Emerson," in Parton, *Some Noted Princes*, 287; L. M. Alcott, *Shawl-Straps* (Boston, 1891), 205–206; "Elizabeth Garrett Anderson," *D. N. B.* (1912–21), 6–7; L. G. Anderson, *E. G. Anderson*

(London, [1939]), 122, 124; [B. L. S.] Bodichon, *Objections to the Enfranchisement of Women Considered* (London, 1866), 2; Cheney, 183; "Frances Power Cobbe," *D. N. B.* (1901–11), 377–78; Conway, *Autobiography, Memories and Experiences,* I, 391, II, 57, 69; M. D. Conway, *Mazzini* (n. p., 1872), 14; F. M. Gladstone, *Aubrey House* (London, 1922), *passim;* F. J. Gould, *Chats with Pioneers of Modern Thought* (n. p., [1898]), 50; G. O. Griffith, *Mazzini: Prophet of Modern Europe* (London, 1932), 319, 327; B. King, *The Life of Mazzini* (London, n. d.), 205; Mrs. H. King, *Letters and Recollections of Mazzini* (London, 1912), 38, 54; E. W. Latimer, *England in the Nineteenth Century* (Chicago, 1895), 346; J. McCarthy, *Portraits of the Sixties* (New York and London, 1903), 228; B. P. Magliano, "Some First-Hand Recollections of Mazzini," *The Contemporary Review,* Vol. CXII, No. 122 (November, 1917), 571; *Mazzini's Letters to an English Family* (London and New York, 1922, 3 vols.), III, 118, 146; T. W. Reid, *The Life, Letters, and Friendships of R. M. Milnes* (London, 1890, 2 vols.), II, 150; P. A. Taylor, *Some Account of the Taylor Family* (London, 1875), fpiece; *M. C. Tyler, Selections from His Letters and Diaries* (New York, 1911), 27; Young, *Early Victorian England,* I, 103, 118; G. M. Young, *Victorian England* (London and New York, [1937]), 106, 114, 200.

LOUISA'S DICKENSIAN TOUR WITH M. C. TYLER: L. M. Alcott, "A Dickens Day," *The Independent,* Vol. XIX, No. 995 (December 26, 1867); Cheney, 183; II. M. Jones, *The Life of M. C. Tyler* (Ann Arbor, 1933), 68; W. Kent, *London for Dickens Lovers* (London, [1935]), 61–62; Nieriker, *Studying Art Abroad,* 33; *Tyler, Selections from His Letters and Diaries,* 24, 31–32; "Moses Coit Tyler," *D. A. B.,* XIX, 92–93.

CHAPTER 10 *Little Women*

"MERRY'S MUSEUM" CONSIDERED: S. G. Goodrich, *Recollections of a Lifetime* (New York and Auburn, 1857, 2 vols.), II, 543; "Merry's Monthly Chat with His Friends," *Merry's Museum,* Vol. LIV, No. 4 (October, 1867), 125; F. L. Mott, *A History of American Magazines, 1741–1850* (New York and London, 1930 [Vol. I]), 713 n. 1.

"MERRY'S MUSEUM" OF JANUARY, 1868: Advertisement, *The Youth's Companion,* Vol. XLI, No. 1 (January 2, 1868); *Merry's Museum,* Vol. I (n. s.), No. 1 (January, 1868), *passim;* M. B. Stern, "The First Appearance of a 'Little Women' Incident," *American Notes & Queries,* Vol. III, No. 7 (October, 1943), 99–100.

NILES RE A GIRLS' BOOK: *Boston Almanac for 1868*, 136; Cheney, 189, 198–99; "T. Niles—In Memoriam," *The Publishers' Weekly*, Vol. XLV, No. 23 (June 9, 1894), 859–60; "Roberts Brothers, Boston," *American Literary Gazette*, Vol. XVII, No. 5 (July 1, 1871), 118; information from Mrs. S. Alice Trickey and Mr. Edmund A. Whitman; J. T. Winterich, *Twenty-three Books and the Stories behind Them* (Philadelphia, 1939), 198–99.

LOUISA'S METHODS OF WORK: Louisa to Mr. Carpenter, April 1, [1887] (Houghton Library); "Methods of Work" (Orchard House); Bonstelle, 157ff.; H. Erichsen, "Methods of Authors," *The Writer*, Vol. VI, No. 6 (June, 1893), 115; Moulton, "L. M. Alcott," *Our Famous Women*, 52.

LOUISA ON JUVENILE LITERATURE: Lillie, "L. M. Alcott," *The Cosmopolitan*, Vol. V, No. 2 (April, 1888), 163; "Merry's Monthly Chat with His Friends," *Merry's Museum*, Vol. I, No. 5 (May, 1868), 208.

TRUE INCIDENTS AND CHARACTERIZATIONS IN "LITTLE WOMEN": Louisa to Alf Whitman, January 6, 1869 (Houghton Library); L. M. Alcott, *Little Women, passim;* Cheney, 193; "A Letter from Miss Alcott's Sister about 'Little Women,' " *St. Nicholas*, Vol. XXX, No. 7 (May, 1903), 631; A. A. Pratt to Julia and Alice [Lowrie], Concord, January 20, 1871; Stern, "L. Alcott, Trouper," *The New England Quarterly*, Vol. XVI, No. 2 (June, 1943), 195; information from Miss Frederika Wendté, Mr. John Pratt Whitman, and Miss K. M. Wilkinson.

ROBERTS BROTHERS AND THOMAS NILES; NILES'S OFFER FOR "LITTLE WOMEN": "L. M. ALCOTT," *The Victoria Magazine*, Vol. V, No. 36 (July, 1880), 7; E. M. Bacon, *The Book of Boston* (Boston, 1916), 56; *Boston Almanac for 1868*, 136, 207; Cheney, 199; Growoll Collection (*Publishers' Weekly*), X, 148; H. Halladay, information *re* Roberts Brothers in Notebook (*Publishers' Weekly*); information from Mr. Henry Halladay; Little, Brown and Company, *One Hundred Years of Publishing* (Boston, [1937]), 42–43; newspaper reprint in folder (Little, Brown); "T. Niles—In Memoriam," *The Publishers' Weekly*, Vol. XLV, No. 23 (June 9, 1894), 859–60; "Obituary. T. Niles," *The Publishers' Weekly*, Vol. XLV, No. 22 (June 2, 1894), 827–28; "Our Boston Book-Makers," *ibid.*, Vol. XX, No. 13 (September 24, 1881), 399–400; Anna Pratt to Alf Whitman, Concord, August 2, 1868 (Houghton Library); *Publishers and Stationers Trade List for 1868* (Philadelphia, 1868), 542–43; "Lewis A. Roberts," *The Pub-*

lishers' Weekly, Vol. LIX, No. 5 (February 2, 1901), 442; "Roberts Brothers, Boston," *American Literary Gazette*, Vol. XVII, No. 5 (July 1, 1871), 117ff.; "Roberts Brothers' Removal," *The Publishers' Weekly*, Vol. XXVII, No. 19 (May 9, 1885), 542; information from Mr. Edmund A. Whitman; percentage rate computed by author on basis of later payments to Louisa on *Little Women*.

PUBLICATION AND RECEPTION OF "LITTLE WOMEN": *Journals of B. Alcott*, 391; *American Literary Gazette*, Vol. XI, Nos. 9 and 11 (September 1 and October 1, 1868), 214, 277; *Boston Transcript*, September 30, 1868; *The Independent*, Vol. XX, No. 1034 (September 24, 1868), 6; D. L. Mann, "When the Alcott Books Were New," *The Publishers' Weekly*, Vol. CXVI, No. 13 (September 28, 1929); Moulton, "L. M. Alcott," *Our Famous Women*, 43; "New Books Published by Roberts Brothers," *The Youth's Companion*, Vol. XLI, No. 44 (October 29, 1868); D. A. Randall and J. T. Winterich, "One Hundred Good Novels," *The Publishers' Weekly*, Vol. CXXXV, No. 24 (June 17, 1939), 2183–84; review of *Little Women*, *The Nation*, Vol. VII, No. 173 (October 22, 1868), 335; *The Youth's Companion*, Vol. XLI, No. 43 (October 22, 1868); information from the late Mr. Carroll A. Wilson.

LOUISA STARTS WORK ON PART II OF "LITTLE WOMEN": Louisa to Alf Whitman, January 6, 1869 (Houghton Library); L. M. Alcott, *Little Women, passim*; information from Miss S. R. Bartlett; Cheney, 201.

NOTICES OF "LITTLE WOMEN," I: Reviews of *Little Women* in *American Literary Gazette*, Vol. XII, No. 1 (November 2, 1868), 16; *Arthur's Illustrated Home Magazine*, December, 1868, p. 375; *Godey's Lady's Book*, Vol. LXXVII, No. 462 (December, 1868), 546; *The Lady's Friend*, Vol. V, No. 12 (December, 1868), 857; *The Ladies' Repository*, Vol. XXVIII (December, 1868), 472; newspaper clipping (Box II, Houghton Library).

LOUISA'S LETTERS: Louisa to Alf Whitman, January 6, 1869 (Houghton Library); Louisa to her uncle, Boston, January 22, [1869] (Houghton Library).

PUBLICATION AND RECEPTION OF "LITTLE WOMEN," II: A. B. Alcott to Mrs. Stearns, Concord, May 19, 1869 (Fruitlands); A. B. Alcott, *Concord Days*, 83; *Journals of B. Alcott*, 396–97; *Boston Transcript*, April 14, 1869; Cheney, 207–208; T. W. Higginson, *Part of a Man's Life* (Boston and New York, 1905); 31; H. R. Hudson, "Concord Books," *Harper's*

New Monthly Magazine, Vol. LI, No. 201 (June, 1875), 27; Meigs, *Invincible Louisa*, 211; E. P. Oberholtzer, *A History of the United States Since the Civil War* (New York, 1917–37, 5 vols.), II, 477–78; V. L. Parrington, *Main Currents in American Thought* (New York, 1927–30, 3 vols.), III, 36; Reviews of *Little Women*, II, in *The Commonwealth*, Vol. VII, No. 34 (April 24, 1869), *National Anti-Slavery Standard*, Vol. XXIX, No. 52 (May 1, 1869), and *The Nation*, Vol. VIII, No. 203 (May 20, 1869); Stearns, *Sketches from Concord*, 82; C. Van Dyke, " 'Little Women' as a Play," *Harper's Bazar*, Vol. XLVI, No. 1 (January, 1912), 24.

FORTHCOMING PUBLICATION OF "AN OLD-FASHIONED GIRL"; ROBERTS'S FIGURES: *Journals of B. Alcott*, 406; *American Literary Gazette*, Vol. XIV, No. 9 (March 1, 1870), 259; J. Blanck, "Alcott's 'An Old-Fashioned Girl' A Collation," *The Publishers' Weekly*, Vol. CXXXIII, No. 8 (February 19, 1938), 967; *Boston Daily Evening Transcript*, April 2, 1870, p. 2; Cheney, 211; "Roberts Brothers' Removal," *The Publishers' Weekly*, Vol. XXVII, No. 19 (May 9, 1885), 542.

PLANS FOR EUROPEAN TOUR: *Journals of B. Alcott*, 406; Cheney, 209; Nieriker, *Studying Art Abroad*, 7.

CHAPTER 11 *The Grand Tour*

LOUISA'S LETTERS HOME: The originals of Louisa's letters on her grand tour, as well as May's, are deposited in the Concord Public Library. The citations made from them, on this and subsequent pages, appear in Cheney, 214–15, 218, 220, 223–24, 228, 239, 252–53.

MME. COSTE AND HER PENSION; LIFE IN DINAN: L. M. Alcott, "The Banner of Beaumanoir," *St. Nicholas*, Vol. XI, No. 8 (June, 1884); "Little Marie of Lehon," *Aunt Jo's Scrap-Bag*, I; "Pelagie's Wedding," *The Independent*, Vol. XXIV, No. 1227 (June 6, 1872); *Shawl-Straps, passim*; May's Sketchbook, 1870 (Orchard House); K. Baedeker, *Northern France* (Leipsic, 1889), 207–208; Cheney, 215–20, 223–24, 226; Nieriker, *Studying Art Abroad*, 62–63, 75; Ticknor, *May Alcott*, 72ff.

BEX AND ITS PEOPLE: L. M. Alcott, *Shawl-Straps*, 129–30; May Alcott to Mrs. [Edward Henry] Barton, Bex, July 29, 1870 (Berg Collection, New York Public Library); K. Baedeker, *Switzerland* (Coblenz, 1872), 201; Cheney, 239–40; Le Comte de Szapary, *Magnétisme et Magnétothérapie* (Paris, 1854), 19, 448; L. Whiting, *Kate Field* (Boston, 1899), 167–68, 278.

DETAILS ABOUT ROME: L. M. Alcott, *Shawl-Straps*, 172; Cheney, 255, 257; Darley, *Sketches Abroad*, 118, 152–53, 159; Dickens, *Pictures from Italy*, 167, 207; F. W. Fairholt, *Homes, Works, and Shrines of English Artists* (London, 1873), 182; *A Handbook of Rome and Its Environs* (London, 1871), *xii–xiii, xvii, xxii;* A. J. C. Hare, *Walks in Rome* (London, 1871, 2 vols.), I, 19, 30–31, 348; Hawthorne, *Passages from the French and Italian Note-Books*, I, 233, 236–37; G. S. Hillard, *Six Months in Italy* (Boston, 1858), 284, 287–90; W. D. Howells, *Italian Journeys* (New York, 1868), 151, 156, 158–59, 162, 171; Nieriker, *Studying Art Abroad*, 80–81, 85; C. E. Norton, *Notes of Travel and Study in Italy* (Boston, [1859]), 204; H. R. Scott, *Rome as It Is* (Philadelphia, 1875), 18, 28, 31, 90, 170, 282–83, 289; C. R. Weld, *Last Winter in Rome* (London, 1865), *passim;* F. Wey, *Rome* (New York, 1872), 4, 45.

LOUISA'S PORTRAIT PAINTED BY HEALY: Mme C. Bigot, *Life of G. P. A. Healy* (n. p., n. d.), 4; J. D. Champlin, Jr. (ed.), *Cyclopedia of Painters and Painting* (New York, 1886–87, 4 vols.), II, 219; S. R. Forbes, *Rambles in Rome* (Rome, 1872), 82; *Handbook of Rome and Its Environs, xlv;* G. P. A. Healy, *Exhibition of Paintings* (Chicago, 1913), unpaged; G. P. A. Healy, *Reminiscences of a Portrait Painter* (Chicago, 1894), 56, 125, 130, 218–19; M. Healy, *A Summer's Romance* (Boston, 1872); information from Mrs. George Johnson, Mrs. George S. Keyes, Mrs. Marie de Mare, and Mrs. B. Alcott Pratt; Stearns, *Sketches from Concord*, 86.

JOHN PRATT'S DEATH; LOUISA'S LETTER TO ANNA: Copy of portion of letter to Anna Pratt, [Rome, December, 1870] (Berg Collection); Cheney, 255; clipping *re* John Pratt (Berg Collection); Anna Pratt to [Edward Henry] Barton, Concord, December 17, 1870 (Berg Collection); Anna Pratt to Alf Whitman, Concord, January 29, 1871 (Houghton Library); Minot Pratt to his friends, Concord, November 30, 1870 (Houghton Library); *The Pratt Family* (Boston, 1889), 199.

"LITTLE MEN" AND ITS LONDON PUBLICATION BY LOW: A. B. Alcott, *Record of a School* (Boston, 1874), 3–4; L. M. Alcott, *Little Men, passim; The A B C Court Directory . . . for 1871* (London, n. d.), 91; M. F. Altstetter, "The Real Plumfield," *Peabody Journal of Education*, Vol. VI, No. 6 (May, 1929), 348; Cheney, 255–58; "Sampson Low," *D. N. B.* (Concise Dictionary to 1921), 795; E. Marston, *After Work* (London, 1904), 117, 119; *Post Office London Directory, 1870* (London, n. d.), 426, 1041, 1059, 1423.

LOUISA'S DEPARTURE AND VOYAGE HOME; NEWS OF "LITTLE MEN":
Journals of B. Alcott, 418; Cheney, 256, 258–59; information from Mrs.
K. D. Metcalf; newspaper clipping (Box II, Houghton Library); Rusk,
VI, 162; Ticknor, *May Alcott*, 100.

CHAPTER 12 *The Youth's Companion*

THE ORCHARD HOUSE AND THE FAMILY AT LOUISA'S RETURN: H. D.
Brown, *Little Miss Phoebe Gay* (Boston and New York, 1923), 29–30;
Howe, *Memories of a Hostess*, 81; R. H. Lathrop, *Memories of Hawthorne*,
416; J. R. Lowell, *Letters* (New York, 1894, 2 vols.), II, 92; Anna Pratt to
Alf Whitman, Concord, June 18, 1871 (Houghton Library); P. Saxon,
"In Memory of Louisa Alcott," *The Landmark*, Vol. VII, No. 10 (Octo-
ber, 1925), 650.

CHANGES IN LOUISA: Brown, *Little Miss Phoebe Gay*, 31; Cheney,
259; J. E. Keysor, *Sketches of American Authors* (Boston, [1895], 2 vols.),
II, 192; Anna Pratt to Alf Whitman, Concord, June 18, 1871 (Houghton
Library).

S. J. MAY'S DEATH: *Journals of B. Alcott*, 418; Cheney, 259; Samuel
May to Richard Davis Webb, July 10, 1871 (Boston Public Library); *In
Memoriam. S. J. May* (Syracuse, 1871), 36ff.; *Memoir of S. J. May*
(Boston, 1873), 295.

LOUISA AT THE BALL FOR ALEXIS: May to Mr. Niles, December 12,
1871; M. C. Ames, *Outlines of Men, Women, and Things* (New York, 1873),
63; Cheney, 261; Crawford, *Romantic Days in Old Boston*, 350; A. Fields,
Authors and Friends (Boston and New York, 1896), 53; "The Grand Duke
in Boston," *New-York Tribune*, Vol. XXXI, No. 9572 (December 9, 1871),
1; *The Log of the State Street Trust Company*, 71; I. N. Phelps Stokes, *The
Iconography of Manhattan Island* (New York, 1926, 6 vols.), V, 1947.

THE FIRE IN BOSTON: Bacon, *The Book of Boston*, 70; C. A. Bartol,
The Trial by Fire (Boston, 1872), *passim*; J. M. Bugbee, "Fires and Fire
Departments," *The North American Review*, Vol. CXVII, No. 240 (July,
1873), 116ff.; "Carleton" [C. C. Coffin], *The Story of the Great Fire*
(Boston, 1872), *passim*; *Chandler and Company's Full Account of the Great
Fire in Boston* (Boston, 1872), *passim*; Cheney, 268; Crawford, *Romantic
Days in Old Boston*, 287; M. A. deW. Howe, *Boston: The Place and the Peo-
ple* (New York and London, 1924), 364ff.; Oberholtzer, *A History of the*

United States, II, 553; H. M. Rogers, *Memories of Ninety Years* (Norwood, 1932), 168; J. Winsor (ed.), *The Memorial History of Boston* (Boston, 1882, 4 vols.), IV, 48ff.

PAYMENTS TO LOUISA; HER CHARITIES: E. W. Bok, "L. M. Alcott's Letters to Five Girls," *The Ladies' Home Journal*, Vol. XIII, No. 5 (April, 1896), 1; Cheney, 270; clipping *re* Wisniewski (Box II, Houghton Library).

MRS. ALCOTT'S BIRTHDAY: L. M. Alcott, "A Happy Birthday," *The Youth's Companion*, Vol. XLVII, No. 6 (February 5, 1874); Cheney, 265, 272.

DETAILS ABOUT WISNIEWSKI: Information from Mr. Charles B. Blanchard; Bok, "L. M. Alcott's Letters to Five Girls," *The Ladies' Home Journal*, Vol. XIII, No. 5 (April, 1896), 1; check dated October 9, 1873, from Roberts Brothers to Ladislas Wisniewski (Orchard House).

THE VACATION AT CONWAY: Information from Mrs. M. H. S. Jenney and Mrs. Herbert Payson; Anna Pratt to Alf Whitman, Conway, August 2, 1874 (Houghton Library); S. P. Rugg, "Miss Alcott in New Hampshire" (MS).

"EIGHT COUSINS":   Louisa to Mrs. Dall, [New York,] November 10, 1875 (Massachusetts Historical Society); Louisa to F. R. Stockton, Boston, January 10, 1875; L. M. Alcott, "Eight Cousins," *St. Nicholas*, Vol. II, Nos. 3–12 (January–October, 1875); Anna Pratt to Alf Whitman, Conway, August 2, 1874 (Houghton Library); S. P. Rugg, "Miss Alcott in New Hampshire" (MS).

LOUISA AT VASSAR: Anthony, *L. M. Alcott*, 205; information from Miss Mary R. Botsford; Cheney, 275; clipping (Box II, Houghton Library); "Home Matters," *The Vassar Miscellany*, Vol. IV, No. 3 (April, 1875), 469ff.; information from Miss Cornelia Raymond; J. H. Raymond, *Life and Letters* (New York, 1881), 595ff.; M. Talbot, "Glimpses of the Real L. M. Alcott," *The New England Quarterly*, Vol. XI, No. 4 (December, 1938), 734; information from Miss Joan Trumbull.

THE CONCORD CENTENNIAL AND LOUISA'S REPORT OF IT: L. M. Alcott, "Woman's Part in the Concord Celebration," *The Woman's Journal*, Vol. VI, No. 18 (May 1, 1875), *passim;* Bartlett, *Concord Historic*, 164; Cheney, 275; *Concord Memoirs*, Fourth Series, 92, 218, 339; Drake, *His-*

tory of Middlesex County, I, 402–403; Emerson, *Journals*, X, 443–44; D. H. Hurd, *History of Middlesex County* (Philadelphia, 1890, 3 vols.), II, 592; *Proceedings at the Centennial Celebration of the Concord Fight April 19, 1875* (Concord, 1876), *passim*; H. H. Robinson, *Massachusetts in the Woman Suffrage Movement* (Boston, 1881), 224ff.

THE WOMAN'S CONGRESS: L. M. Alcott, "My Girls," *Aunt Jo's Scrap-Bag*, IV, 25–26; A. S. Blackwell, *Lucy Stone* (Boston, 1930), 236; Cheney, 276–78; *Godey's Lady's Book*, Vol. XCI, No. 546 (December, 1875), 577; J. W. Howe, "Maria Mitchell," *Our Famous Women*, 458–59; Howe, *Reminiscences*, 393–94; P. M. Kendall, *Maria Mitchell* (Boston, 1896), 258–59; M. A. Livermore, *The Story of My Life* (Hartford, 1898), *xx*, 66ff., 91, 379; M. A. Livermore, "The Third Congress of Women," *The Woman's Journal*, Vol. VI, No. 43 (October 23, 1875), 340–41; H. M. Mills, "Author of 'Little Women' Lionized on Visit," *Syracuse Sunday American*, January 14, 1934; *Papers Read at the Third Congress of Women* (n. p., n. d.), *passim*; R. H. Sessions, *Sixty-Odd* (Brattleboro, [1936]), 99ff.; "The Woman's Congress," *The Woman's Journal*, Vol. VI, Nos. 43 and 44 (October 23 and 30, 1875), 338ff.

CHAPTER 13 *Dr. Miller's Bath Hotel*

THE BATH HOTEL: Cheney, 277; *Guide to New York and Vicinity* (n. p., [1873]), unpaged; *Dio Lewis's Nuggets*, Vol. I, No. 1 (August, 1885), inside back cover; information from Dr. Archibald Malloch; [E. P. Miller], *The Bible Standard of Social Purity* (n. p., n. d.), 7, 14; E. P. Miller, *A Father's Advice* (New York, 1875), *passim*; E. P. Miller, *How to Bathe* (New York, 1878), *passim*; E. P. Miller, *The Improved Turkish Bath* (New York, 1870), *passim*; E. P. Miller, *Vital Force* (New York, 1872), *passim*; C. E. Prescott (ed.), *The Hotel Guests' Guide to the City of New York* (New York, 1872), 26; *Wilson's Business Directory of New York City*, XXVIII (1875).

LOUISA AT FRATERNITY CLUB: Cheney, 278–79; O. B. Frothingham, *Recollections and Impressions* (New York and London, 1891), 51–52, 128–29; "O. B. Frothingham," *D. A. B.*, VII, 44; W. H. Lyon, *F. H. Hedge* (Brookline, 1906), 19; E. C. Stedman, *O. B. Frothingham and The New Faith* (New York, 1876), 9; *Trow's New York City Directory for the Year Ending May 1, 1876*; Whiting, *Boston Days*, 278; Whiting, *K. Field*, 168; *Woman Suffrage Unnatural and Inexpedient* (Boston, 1894), 7.

THE BOTTAS: A. C. L. Botta, *Hand-Book of Universal Literature* (Boston, 1875), *passim*; A. C. L. Botta, *Memoirs* (New York, 1894), *passim*;

A. C. L. Botta, *Poems* (New York, 1881), *passim;* "A. C. L. Botta," *D. A. B.,* II, 470; V. Botta, "Historical Sketch of Modern Philosophy in Italy," in F. Ueberweg, *History of Philosophy* (New York, 1903, 2 vols.), II, 461; "V. Botta," *D. A. B.,* II, 470; Cheney, 277, 279; R. Odell, *H. H. Jackson* (New York and London, 1939), 157; E. A. Poe, *The Literati* (Boston, 1884), 566; K. Sanborn, *Memories and Anecdotes* (New York and London, 1915), 81; *Trow's New York City Directory for the Year Ending May 1, 1876;* D. Wecter, *The Saga of American Society* (New York, 1937), 322.

LOUISA HEARS FROTHINGHAM AND BELLOWS: S. C. Beane, *H. W. Bellows* (Concord, N. H., 1882), 9; *Henry Whitney Bellows . . . from . . . "The Bellows Genealogy,"* by T. B. Peck (Keene, n. d.), 291, 304; J. W. Chadwick, *H. W. Bellows* (New York, 1882), 12; Cheney, 279; O. B. Frothingham, *Knowledge and Faith* (New York, 1876), 4; Frothingham, *Recollections and Impressions,* 76–77, 127–28; Lyon, *F. H. Hedge,* 19; M. H. Smith, *Sunshine and Shadow in New York* (Hartford, 1868), 336–37; Stedman, *O. B. Frothingham,* 10ff., 23, 47.

LOUISA AT NEWSBOYS' LODGING HOUSE; HER LETTER TO HER NEPHEWS: C. L. Brace, *Short Sermons to News Boys* (New York, 1866), *passim;* Cheney, 281–84; J. D. McCabe, Jr., *Lights and Shadows of New York Life* (Philadelphia, [1872]), 741; *Trow's New York City Directory for the Year Ending May 1, 1876.*

LOUISA'S VISIT TO RANDALL'S ISLAND WITH MR. AND MRS. GIBBONS: L. M. Alcott, "Merry Christmas," in *The Horn of Plenty of Home Poems* (Boston, 1876); L. M. Alcott, "A New Way to Spend Christmas," *The Youth's Companion,* Vol. XLIX, No. 10 (March 9, 1876); Cheney, 284–88; L. M. Child, *Isaac T. Hopper* (New York, [1881]), *v, vii;* "Christian Festival," *New-York Daily Tribune,* Vol. XXXV, No. 10839 (December 27, 1875); *Fifty-first Annual Report of the . . . Society for the Reformation of Juvenile Delinquents. (1875)* (New York, 1876), 48; "J. S. Gibbons," *D. A. B.,* VII, 242; *House of Refuge By-Laws, Rules and Regulations* (Philadelphia, 1876), 27; McCabe, *Lights and Shadows of New York Life,* 647; *McLaughlin's New York Guide* (New York, [1875]), 111; A. M. Powell, *Personal Reminiscences* (New York, 1899), 240–41; "Reforming the Young," *New York Times,* November 11, 1883, p. 8; L. G. Runkle, "A. H. Gibbons," *Our Famous Women, passim; Trow's New York City Directory for the Year Ending May 1, 1875.*

LOUISA'S VISIT TO THE TOMBS AND HER ARTICLE ABOUT IT: L. M. Alcott, "A Visit to the Tombs," *The Youth's Companion,* Vol. XLIX, No. 21

(May 25, 1876); Cheney, 277, 288; "A. H. Gibbons," *D. A. B.*, VII, 238; McCabe, *Lights and Shadows of New York Life*, 232ff.; Powell, *Personal Reminiscences*, 241; Runkle, "A. H. Gibbons," *Our Famous Women*, 319; C. Sutton, *The New York Tombs* (New York, 1874), 51, 663.

NEW YEAR'S AT MRS. CROLY'S: Anthony, *L. M. Alcott*, 210ff.; Cheney, 294; *Memories of J. C. Croly* (New York and London, 1904), *passim*; McCabe, *Lights and Shadows of New York Life*, 573; P. Sainsbury, *Cushman Chronicles* (New York, 1932), 48; information from Mrs. Vida Croly Sidney; Smith, *Sunshine and Shadow in New York*, 40; Stokes, *The Iconography of Manhattan Island*, V, 1959; *Trow's New York City Directory for the Year Ending May 1, 1876*; D. Van Pelt, *Leslie's History of the Greater New York* (New York, n. d.), I, 439, 480; E. I. Zeisloft, *The New Metropolis* (New York, [1899]), 356.

LOUISA'S VISIT TO PHILADELPHIA: Cheney, 295; Edes, *Genealogy of the Descendants of John May*, 23; *Germantown History*, 19, 331; Meigs, *Invincible Louisa*, 228–29; E. Strahan (ed.), *A Century After* (Philadelphia, 1875), *passim*; W. R. Winn, *Centennial Guide Book to Philadelphia* (Philadelphia, [1876]), 31, 34, 43.

LOUISA HEARS BEECHER: A. B. Alcott, *Concord Days*, 269; ["Alcott's Conversation on New England Reformers,"] *The Commonwealth*, Vol. I, No. 38 (May 22, 1863); H. W. Beecher, *Patriotic Addresses* (New York, 1889), 56; Bremer, *America of the Fifties*, 88; Cheney, 295; Emerson, *Journals*, IX, 570; P. Hibben, *H. W. Beecher* (New York, [1927]), 325; Howells, *Literary Friends and Acquaintance*, 99; McCabe, *Lights and Shadows of New York Life*, 655, 657; Smith, *Sunshine and Shadow in New York*, 87ff.; E. Terry, *Memoirs* (New York, 1932), 223; C. Ticknor, *Hawthorne and His Publisher* (Boston and New York, 1913), 25; Zeisloft, *The New Metropolis*, 88.

CHAPTER 14 *The Gray Town*

LOUISA'S RETURN TO THE ORCHARD HOUSE; FAMILY ACTIVITIES: *Journals of B. Alcott*, 465–67; A. B. Alcott, *Table-Talk*, 108; Bartlett, *Concord Historic*, 133; E. S. Bates and J. V. Dittemore, *Mary Baker Eddy* (New York, 1932), 167–68; V. W. Brooks, *New England: Indian Summer* (New York, 1940), 335; Hillyer, "Marmee," *The Parents' Magazine*, Vol. VII, No. 11 (November, 1932), 42–43; L. P. Powell, *Mary Baker Eddy* (New York, 1930), 133; Sears, *Revised Catalogue of "Fruitlands,"* 15; Ticknor, *May Alcott*, 128, 209, 243, 255.

"ROSE IN BLOOM" WRITTEN: *Journals of B. Alcott*, 468–69; L. M. Alcott, *Rose in Bloom*, *passim*; Cheney, 289, 295; Anna Pratt to Alf Whitman, Concord, September 12, 1876 (Houghton Library); F. B. S[anborn]., "Miss Alcott, the Friend of Little Women and of Little Men," *St. Nicholas*, Vol. V, No. 2 (December, 1877), 131.

LOUISA'S LETTER TO ALF: Louisa to Alf Whitman, [Concord? September 12, 1876?] (Houghton Library).

MRS. ALCOTT'S DIARY 1876–77; Details about May: Abby May Alcott's last Diary 1876–77 (Orchard House); Ticknor, *May Alcott*, 124ff.

"ROSE IN BLOOM" PUBLISHED; LOUISA'S BIRTHDAY; HER APPEARANCE: Cheney, 289, 296; Lillie, "L. M. Alcott," *The Cosmopolitan*, Vol. V, No. 2 (April, 1888), 163; S[anborn]., "Miss Alcott, the Friend of Little Women," *St. Nicholas*, Vol. V, No. 2 (December, 1877), 131.

LOUISA'S INTEREST IN THE "LURID"; INFLUENCE OF "FAUST"; "A MODERN MEPHISTOPHELES" WRITTEN: L. M. Alcott, *A Modern Mephistopheles*, *passim*; Cheney, 296; L. C. Pickett, *Across My Path* (New York, 1916), 107.

PURCHASE OF THOREAU HOUSE: Abby May Alcott's last Diary (Orchard House); *Journals of B. Alcott*, 474, 477; Louisa's Will; Cheney, 289, 297; Ticknor, *May Alcott*, 177.

REVIEWS OF "A MODERN MEPHISTOPHELES": In *The Atlantic Monthly*, Vol. XL, No. 237 (July, 1877), 109; and *Godey's Lady's Book*, Vol. XCV, No. 565 (July, 1877), 86.

"UNDER THE LILACS"; MOTHER'S ILLNESS: Abby May Alcott's last Diary (Orchard House); *Journals of B. Alcott*, 473; L. M. Alcott, *Under the Lilacs*, *passim*; H. Barnum, *Illustrated and Descriptive History of the Animals . . . in Van Amburgh and Company's . . . Menagerie* (New York, 1869), *passim*; Cheney, 289, 298–99, 301–302; Hoeltje, *Sheltering Tree*, 189.

FAMILY MOVES TO THOREAU HOUSE: *Journals of B. Alcott*, 473; May to Mrs. Conway, December 23, 1877 (Columbia University); information from Dr. M. May Allen; Cheney, 299; Bessie Holyoke to Una, Syracuse, August 8, 1878 (University of Pennsylvania); information from Mrs. B. Alcott Pratt; Sanborn, *The Personality of Thoreau*, 10; A Story-Teller, "A Concord Ghost Story," *Time and the Hour*, Vol. II, No. 5 (July 11, 1896), 14ff.

396 . *Notes on Sources*

MRS. ALCOTT'S DEATH AND BURIAL; THE MEMORIAL SERVICE: *Journals of B. Alcott*, 473, 480; Louisa to May, November 25, [1877] in Abby May Alcott's last Diary (Orchard House); May to Mrs. Conway, December 23, 1877 (Columbia University); Cheney, 300; Hillyer, "Marmee," *The Parents' Magazine*, Vol. VII, No. 11 (November, 1932), 43; Ticknor, *May Alcott*, 249.

MAY AND ERNEST NIERIKER; MAY'S MARRIAGE: A. B. Alcott to Dear Brother, Concord, May 1, 1879; Louisa to Dear Girls, Concord, June 23, [1878]; "L. M. Alcott Centenary Year," *The Publishers' Weekly*, Vol. CXXII, No. 1 (July 2, 1932), 25; Cheney, 308, 315; *Dictionnaire Historique & Biographique de la Suisse* (Neuchâtel, 1921–33, 7 vols.), V, 148; Gowing, 129; Ticknor, *May Alcott*, 259–60, 262, 284–85.

LOUISA AND THE MEMOIR OF MRS. ALCOTT: *Journals of B. Alcott*, 482–83, 490–91; Louisa to Dear Girls, Concord, June 23, [1878]; Louisa's addition to her copy of H. Martineau on privacy of letters, July, 1878 (Orchard House); Cheney, 316; S. May to Louisa, June 24, 1878 (Box III, Houghton Library); Sanborn, *Recollections of Seventy Years*, II, 471; Ticknor, *May Alcott*, 274–76.

PAPYRUS CLUB DINNER: [G. F. Babbitt], *Papyrus Primer* (Boston, 1882), *passim; Boston England and Boston New England* (Boston, 1930), 19–20; V. Burnett, *The Romantick Lady* (New York and London, 1927), 77, 79, 90, 92ff.; Cheney, 318; Crawford, *Romantic Days in Old Boston*, 403; W. H. Rideing, *Many Celebrities and a Few Others* (London, 1912), 185, 187; Rogers, *Memories of Ninety Years*, 180, 186, 196; J. A. Rooney, "Reminiscences of Early Days," *The Catholic World*, Vol. CI, No. 601 (April, 1915), 96; "Whitman on His Contemporaries," *The American Mercury*, Vol. II, No. 7 (July, 1924), 332.

OPENING OF SCHOOL OF PHILOSOPHY; PHILOSOPHERS IN CONCORD AND LOUISA'S ATTITUDE TOWARD THEM: *Journals of B. Alcott*, 496, 498; C. A. Bartol, *A. B. Alcott* (Boston, 1888), 5, 8; H. A. Beers, *Four Americans* (New Haven, 1919), 61, 64, 68, 69; Brown, *Alcott and the Concord School of Philosophy*, 4, 7, 9, 11; Brown, *Memories of Concord*, 82; Cheney, 314, 320–21; *Godey's Lady's Book*, Vol. C, No. 600 (June, 1880), 571–73; J. Hawthorne and L. Lemmon, *American Literature* (Boston, 1891), 145; C. E. Norton, *Letters* (Boston and New York, 1913, 2 vols.), II, 113; *Pedlar's Progress*, 507; Porter, "Recollections of L. M. Alcott," *The New England Magazine*, Vol. VI, No. 1 (March, 1892), 15; Sanborn, *Recollec-*

tions of Seventy Years, II, 504; A. Warren, "The Concord School of Philosophy," *The New England Quarterly,* Vol. II, No. 2 (April, 1929), 203.

LOUISA'S LETTERS TO MRS. DODGE: Louisa to Mrs. Dodge, August 17, n. y. (Carroll Wilson Collection); Cheney, 303.

LOUISA RETURNS TO CONCORD; "JACK AND JILL": L. M. Alcott, "Jack and Jill," *St. Nicholas,* Vol. VII, Nos. 2–12 (December, 1879–October, 1880); Cheney, 321; J. Hawthorne, *Memoirs,* 73; Swayne, *The Story of Concord,* 308.

CHANGES OF CONCORD; ITS GRAYNESS: Bartlett, *Concord Historic,* 120–21; Beers, *Four Americans,* 76; Brooks, *New England: Indian Summer,* 335; *Concord Memoirs,* Fourth Series, 108–109; E. P. Conklin, *Middlesex County and Its People* (New York, 1927, 4 vols.), II, 560; Emerson, *Journals,* X, 475–76; M. M. Engel, *I Remember the Emersons* (Los Angeles, 1941), 4, 11; A. French, *Historic Concord* (Concord, 1942), 39; Hurd, *History of Middlesex County,* II, 589; *A. James. Her Brothers,* 74; Lowell, *Letters,* II, 175; *Pedlar's Progress,* 492; Pickett, *Across My Path,* 107; H. N. Powers, "A Day with Emerson," *Lippincott's Magazine,* Vol. IV, No. 29 (November, 1882), 480; Anna Pratt to Alf Whitman, Concord, May 2, [1882] (Houghton Library); Ticknor, *Classic Concord,* 222–23; G. Tolman, *Catalogue of a Portion of the . . . Concord Antiquarian Society* (Concord, 1911), 17.

LOUISA'S THOUGHTS AND FEARS ABOUT MAY; MAY'S DEATH: *Journals of B. Alcott,* 514; Louisa to the *Transcript* (Houghton Library); Cheney, 304, 311–12, 323–24.

CHAPTER 15 *Yours for Reform*

LOUISA'S GRIEF; NEWS OF MAY: Louisa to Mrs. Stearns, February 21, 1881 (Fruitlands); Louisa to the *Transcript* (Houghton Library); *Journals of B. Alcott,* 515–16; Cheney, 311–13, 325–28; Ellen D. Conway to Louisa, Bedford Park, January 29, 1880 (Box III, Houghton Library); J. Hawthorne, "The Woman Who Wrote 'Little Women,' " *The Ladies' Home Journal,* Vol. XXXIX (October, 1922), 124; Rose Peckham to Louisa (Box III, Houghton Library); Porter, "Recollections of L. M. Alcott," *The New England Magazine,* Vol. VI, No. 1 (March, 1892), 17; Ticknor, *May Alcott,* 308–309; Marston Watson to Louisa, Hillside, January 2, 1880 (Box I, Houghton Library).

CONCORD TOWN MEETING AND LOUISA'S REPORT OF IT: "Letter from L. M. Alcott," *The Woman's Journal,* Vol. XI, No. 14 (April 3, 1880), 105; Cheney, 327; R. W. Emerson, *The Town Meeting* (Old South Leaflets, First Series, Number 4 [1883]), 2; Gowing, 28; Swayne, *The Story of Concord,* 160 n. 1.

LOUISA DRAMATIZES "MICHAEL STROGOFF": Louisa to Laura Hosmer, April 22; Cheney, 330, 335; L. C. Holloway, *Adelaide Neilson* (New York, 1885), 49; Stern, "L. Alcott, Trouper," *The New England Quarterly,* Vol. XVI, No. 2 (June, 1943), 197.

LOUISA AT YORK; MERRILL'S ILLUSTRATIONS FOR "LITTLE WOMEN": Louisa to Laura Hosmer, July 14; Louisa to Laura Hosmer, July 31; Louisa's comments on Frank Merrill's illustrations; "L. M. Alcott," *The Victoria Magazine,* Vol. V, No. 36 (July, 1880), 11; Cheney, 330, 334, 336; S. D. Clark, "A Summer at York," *Harper's New Monthly Magazine,* Vol. LXV, No. 388 (September, 1882); Frank Merrill to Mrs. Dorothy K. Brintnall, Dorchester, February 6, 1933.

LOUISA'S LETTER TO NILES: Cheney, 342.

LOUISA'S LIFE AT NONQUITT: *Journals of B. Alcott,* 525; Louisa to Laura Hosmer, August 3; information from Mr. T. P. Carter; J. Hawthorne, "The Woman Who Wrote 'Little Women,' " *The Ladies' Home Journal,* Vol. XXXIX (October, 1922), 124; E. F. Kimball, "On the Shores of Buzzards Bay," *The New England Magazine,* Vol. VII, No. 1 (September, 1892); Moses, *L. M. Alcott,* 309–10; *Rand McNally Commercial Atlas* (1943), 191; A. A. Ryder, *Lands of Sippican on Buzzards Bay* (New Bedford, 1934), 277.

WHITMAN'S VISIT TO CONCORD: *Journals of B. Alcott,* 522, 527–28; N. Arvin, *Whitman* (New York, 1938), 40; Higginson, *Contemporaries,* 72–73; E. Holloway, *Whitman* (New York and London, 1926), 5, 163, 299–300; Howells, *Literary Friends and Acquaintance,* 74; F. B. Sanborn, *The Life of H. D. Thoreau* (Boston and New York, 1917), 199, 310; F. B. Sanborn, "Reminiscent of Whitman," *The Conservator,* Vol. VIII, No. 3 (May, 1897), 39; "Whitman on His Contemporaries," *The American Mercury,* July, 1924, p. 329; W. Whitman, *Democratic Vistas* (London, 1888), 22, 30; W. Whitman, "How I Still Get Around and Take Notes," *The Critic,* Vol. I, No. 24 (December 3, 1881), 330; W. Whitman, *Leaves of Grass* (New York, 1928), 262–63; W. Whitman, *Specimen Days in America* (London, [1906]), 299–300; Wolfe, *Literary Shrines,* 203.

VISIT TO EMERSON WITH EDWARD BOK: E. Bok, *The Americanization of Edward Bok* (New York, 1922), 53 ff.; Brown, *Memories of Concord*, 45; Holmes, *R. W. Emerson*, 343–44.

MRS. CROLY'S RECEPTION: H. C. Brown, *Brownstone Fronts and Saratoga Trunks* (New York, 1935), 261; Mrs. Croly, "Clara Morris," *Demorest's Monthly Magazine*, Vol. XXII, No. 9 (July, 1886), 581–83; A. Gardiner, "Oscar in Buncoland," *The Colophon*, Part 12 (1932), 19–20; L. Lewis and H. J. Smith, *Oscar Wilde Discovers America* (New York, [1936]), *passim;* "Clara Morris," *D. A. B.*, XIII, 204; "A Reception in Miss Alcott's Honor," *New-York Daily Tribune*, Vol. XLI, No. 12839 (January 9, 1882), 5; J. M. Rogers, "Henry Watterson," *The Booklovers Magazine*, Vol. V, No. 3 (March, 1905), 306; "Hon. Robert B. Roosevelt," *The New York Society of . . . Founders and Patriots of America*, No. 15 (May 14, 1906), 50–51; "R. B. Roosevelt," *D. A. B.*, XVI, 135; H. Watterson, *The Compromises of Life* (New York, 1903), *vi;* H. Watterson, *"Marse Henry"* (New York, 1919, 2 vols.), I, 15–16; "H. Watterson," *D. A. B.*, XIX, 555; O. Wilde, *Impressions of America* (Sunderland, 1906), 11, 39–40.

LOUISA AND THE CONCORD TEMPERANCE SOCIETY: Cheney, 332, 343–44; C. W. Ferguson, *Fifty Million Brothers* (New York and Toronto, [1937]), 61.

EMERSON'S FUNERAL AND LOUISA'S REACTIONS: L. M. Alcott, "R. W. Emerson," *Demorest's Monthly Magazine*, Vol. XVIII, No. 9 (July, 1882); L. M. Alcott, "Reminiscences of R. W. Emerson" in Parton, *Some Noted Princes*, 288; C. Barrus, *The Life and Letters of John Burroughs* (Boston and New York, 1925, 2 vols.), I, 239; C. A. Bartol, *R. W. Emerson* (Boston, 1882), 14; G. B. Bartlett, *Concord Historic*, 52–53; T. Beer, *The Mauve Decade* (London, 1926), 17, 266; Bok, "L. M. Alcott's Letters to Five Girls," *The Ladies' Home Journal*, Vol. XIII, No. 5 (April, 1896), 2; Brown, *Memories of Concord*, 44; J. Burroughs, "Emerson's Burial Day," *The Critic*, Vol. II, No. 34 (May 6, 1882); Cheney, 345; Conway, *Emerson at Home and Abroad*, 8–9; Cummin, *Handbook Concord Antiquarian Society*, 61; Edward W. Emerson to Mr. Cook, Concord, April 28, 1882 (Fruitlands); Emerson, *Emerson in Concord*, 196; "The Funeral of Emerson," *Harper's Weekly*, Vol. XXVI, No. 1325 (May 13, 1882), 292; Holmes, *R. W. Emerson*, 350ff.; J. Hawthorne, "R. W. Emerson," *Harper's New Monthly Magazine*, Vol. LXV, No. 386 (July, 1882), 278, 281; H. James, *Partial Portraits* (London, 1899), 23; Whiting, *Boston Days*, 185ff.; Wolfe, *Literary Shrines*, 27.

LOUISA ON NILES'S OBJECTION TO "JO'S LAST SCRAPE": Louisa to Niles, n. d. (courtesy the late Mr. Arthur Pforzheimer).

ALCOTT'S ILLNESS AND LOUISA'S RETURN TO CONCORD; THE HOUSE-HOLD: *Journals of B. Alcott*, 531; Louisa to Mrs. Stearns, November 4 (Fruitlands); Louisa to Mrs. Stearns, Sunday and November 7 (Fruitlands); Cheney, 352; *Pedlar's Progress*, 514; Porter, "Recollections of L. M. Alcott," *The New England Magazine*, Vol. VI, No. 1 (March, 1892), 4; Anna Pratt to Alf Whitman, Concord, Monday eve., 188— (Houghton Library).

LOUISA'S FIFTIETH BIRTHDAY: Louisa to Mrs. Stearns, December 5 (Fruitlands); Moulton, "L. M. Alcott," *Our Famous Women*, 49.

PAPYRUS CLUB DINNER IN HONOR OF ELLEN TERRY: J. Hatton, *Henry Irving's Impressions of America* (London, 1884), 185ff.; B. Stoker, *Personal Reminiscences of Henry Irving* (London, 1907), 362; "Ellen Terry," *D. N. B.* (1922–30), 829.

LOUISA'S INTEREST IN REFORM: Louisa to Laura Hosmer, February 18; *The Woman's Journal*, Vol. XV, No. 8—Vol. XIX, No. 9 (February 23, 1884–March 3, 1888).

ORCHARD HOUSE SOLD; LOUISA AT NONQUITT: Louisa to Samuel E. Sewall, September 1 (Massachusetts Historical Society); information from Mr. T. P. Carter; Cheney, 347, 355; Kimball, "On the Shores of Buzzards Bay," *The New England Magazine*, Vol. VI, No. 6 (September, 1892), 3, 9; Sanborn, *Recollections of Seventy Years*, II, 486–87; information from Miss K. M. Wilkinson.

LOUISA'S MIND-CURE TREATMENTS: Louisa to Laura Hosmer, Friday, and Saturday A.M.; Louisa to Maggie [Lukens], March 15, [1885]; "Miss Alcott on Mind-Cure," *The Woman's Journal*, Vol. XVI, No. 16 (April 18, 1885), 121; *The Boston Almanac . . . for 1885*, 439; M. B. G. Eddy, *Historical Sketch of Christian Science Mind-Healing* (Boston, 1890), 22; F. Lord, *Christian Science Healing* (Chicago, 1888), 221, 225–26; L. M. Marston, *Essentials of Mental Healing* (Boston, 1886), 87–89, 108; Mrs. A. B. Newman, *Trust in the Infinite* (Boston, 1886), 6, 14; J. A. Root, *Healing Power of Mind* (Peoria, 1886), 149, 152–53.

CONCORD FESTIVAL; CONCORD'S PREOCCUPATION WITH THE PAST: L. M. A[lcott]., "Old Times at Old Concord," *The Woman's Journal*, Vol.

XVI, No. 16 (April 18, 1885); Bartlett, *Concord Historic,* 134; Whitman, "How I Still Get Around and Take Notes," *The Critic,* Vol. I, No. 24 (December 3, 1881), 331.

LOUISA CONSIDERS A RECORD OF HER LIFE: Cheney, 357; Sanborn, *Recollections of Seventy Years,* II, 341.

LOUISA AT 10 Louisburg Square: Louisa to Laura Hosmer, Friday eve.; E. M. Bacon, *Literary Pilgrimages in New England* (New York and Boston, 1902), 264; A. Chamberlain, *Beacon Hill* (Boston and New York, 1925), 196, 200; Cheney, 357; Gowing, 76; information from Mr. Jerome C. Hunsaker; *Pedlar's Progress,* 514; W. H. Rideing, "The Homes of Some New England Authors," *The Chautauquan,* Vol. VIII, No. 2 (November, 1887), 82; R. Shackleton, *The Book of Boston* (Philadelphia, 1916), 24–26, 47; M. F. Sweetser and M. King, *An Alphabetical Guide to Boston* (Boston, [1883]), 107; Swift, *Literary Landmarks of Boston,* 12; H. W. Winkley, "Annals of Louisburg Square," *Proceedings of the Bostonian Society,* January 19, 1926.

LIFE AT PRINCETON: Louisa to Laura Hosmer, Thursday eve.; *Annual Reports of . . . Princeton, for the Year Ending February 13, 1887* (Worcester, 1887), 26; F. E. Blake, *History of the Town of Princeton* (Princeton, Mass., 1915, 2 vols.), I, 383, II, 51; Cheney, 358, 372; P. T. Gilbert, *Princeton, Mass.* (Gardner, n. d.), 3, 8; Miss C. E. Sears to Little, Brown, September 23, 1933.

LOUISA'S WORK ON "Jo's BOYS":   Louisa to Laura Hosmer, July 15; Louisa to Thomas Niles, n. d. (courtesy the late Mr. Carroll A. Wilson); L. M. Alcott, *Jo's Boys, passim;* Cheney, 358–59, 372–73, 376; Growoll Collection (*Publishers' Weekly*), X, 148.

CHAPTER 16 *Dunreath Place*

"Jo's BOYS" PUBLISHED; LOUISA'S INCOME AND REPUTATION: Louisa to Mr. Carpenter, April 1, [1887] (Houghton Library); Cheney, 348; Gracie Hill to Louisa, October, 1886 (Box III, Houghton Library); Anna Pratt to Alf Whitman, Melrose, July, [1887] (Houghton Library).

LOUISA'S AILMENTS AND HOUSEHOLD CARES: Louisa to Laura Hosmer, November 30; Cheney, 367; Lillie, "L. M. Alcott," *The Cosmopolitan,* Vol. V, No. 2 (April, 1888), 164; Anna Pratt to Alf Whitman, Melrose, July, [1887] (Houghton Library).

RHODA LAWRENCE AND HER NURSING HOME: Louisa to Miss Mary Joy, n. d. (Fruitlands); Louisa to Mr. Sewall, September 28, [1875?] (Massachusetts Historical Society); Anthony, *L. M. Alcott*, 277–78; information from Miss K. Anthony; *The Boston Directory for the Year Commencing July 1, 1887*, 719, 1473; Cheney, 367; information from Miss A. A. Dunne, town clerk of Westboro, Mass.; Anna Pratt to Alf Whitman, Melrose, July, [1887], and Boston, February 17, [1889?] (Houghton Library); *Seventeenth Annual Report of the Massachusetts Homoeopathic Hospital* (Boston, 1887), 48; information from Mr. Arthur Sullivan, Suffolk County Probate Court, and Dr. Burnham S. Walker, Boston University School of Medicine.

LOUISA'S PHYSICAL AND MENTAL CONDITION: Louisa to Laura Hosmer, Sunday, February 20, and Sunday, March 6; Louisa to My Two Dear Annas, n. d. (Houghton Library); Louisa to Rhoda Lawrence, February 1 (Fruitlands); Cheney, 378; diagnosis of Louisa's illness by Dr. William M. Siskind on the basis of her letters to Laura Hosmer; *Celebration of the Two Hundred and Fiftieth Anniversary of the Settlement of Boston* (Boston, 1880), 140; *King's Handbook of Boston* (1883), 346; Anna Pratt to Alf Whitman, Boston, February 17, [1889?] (Houghton Library); *The Pearl Almanac* (New York, [1869]), 108; I. T. Talbot, *The Common Sense of Homoeopathy* (Boston, 1862), 8.

LOUISA'S LETTER TO CARPENTER: Louisa to Mr. Carpenter, April 1, [1887] (Houghton Library); Bonstelle, 157ff.

LOUISA'S ACTIVITIES AND VISIT TO MELROSE: Louisa to Laura Hosmer, June 1; Cheney, 367, 369; Anna Pratt to Alf Whitman, Melrose, July, [1887] (Houghton Library); information from William Howell Reed.

LOUISA AT CONCORD; SHE ADOPTS JOHN AND GIVES MONEY TO NEPHEWS: Louisa to Laura Hosmer, Thursday A.M.; Bonstelle, 197; Cheney 367–68; Anna Pratt to Alf Whitman, Melrose, July, [1887] (Houghton Library).

LOUISA AT PRINCETON: Louisa to Laura Hosmer, Monday A.M., Monday P.M., Tuesday P.M., Thursday A.M., and Mountain Cottage, July 3; Louisa to Mr. Niles, August 7 (Fruitlands); *Annual Reports of . . . Princeton, for the Year Ending February 13, 1887*, Appendix 2, p. 2; Blake, *History of the Town of Princeton*, I, 386–87; Cheney, 368; Gilbert,

Princeton, Mass., 3; Anna Pratt to Alf Whitman, Melrose, July, [1887] (Houghton Library).

DECISIONS CONCERNING THOREAU HOUSE AND LOUISBURG SQUARE; LOUISA'S WILL: Louisa to Laura Hosmer, Tuesday P.M.; Louisa's will (Register of Probate, Middlesex County, Mass.); Anna Pratt to Alf Whitman, Melrose, July, [1887] (Houghton Library); information from the late Mr. Carroll A. Wilson.

LOUISA'S CONDITION; LOUISA AND DR. MILBREY GREEN: Louisa's Diary for 1888 (Orchard House); Louisa to her father, October 13 (Houghton Library); *The Boston Almanac for 1887*, 103, 435; "Death of Miss Alcott," (clipping of March 7, 1888, New York Public Library); *Index-Catalogue of the Library of the Surgeon-General's Office* (Washington, 1884), Series I, Vol. V, 597; *Medical Directory of Greater Boston* (Boston, 1906), 103; information from Miss Genevieve Miller of Johns Hopkins University.

LOUISA'S REST-AND-MILK CURE; HER ROUTINE OF LIFE: Louisa's Diary for 1888 (Orchard House); Louisa to Laura Hosmer, December 1 and January 13; Louisa to John, n. d. (American Antiquarian Society); Porter, "Recollections of L. M. Alcott," *The New England Magazine*, Vol. VI, No. 1 (March, 1892), 17.

FRED'S WEDDING; LOUISA'S PROGRESS AND SUCCESS: Louisa's Diary for 1888 (Orchard House); Louisa to Laura Hosmer, February 8, 1888, and February 12; Bonstelle, 196; Cheney, 369–70, 385–86, 397–98, 402–403; "Death of Miss Alcott," *The Ladies' Home Journal*, Vol. V, No. 6 (May, 1888), 3; Anna Pratt to Alf Whitman, Boston, February 17, [1889?] (Houghton Library); review of *A Garland for Girls, The Critic*, Vol. XII, No. 215 (February 11, 1888), 67.

LOUISA'S THOUGHTS OF DEATH: Letter from Louisa (Massachusetts Historical Society); Cheney, 371–72; R. W. Emerson, *Poems* (Boston, 1887), 216; Emerson, *Society and Solitude*, 309; Porter, "Recollections of L. M. Alcott," *The New England Magazine*, Vol. VI, No. 1 (March, 1892), 14.

LOUISA'S LAST VISIT TO ALCOTT: Louisa to Laura Hosmer, February 12; Louisa's Diary for 1888 (Orchard House); "L. M. Alcott," *Boston Transcript*, March 6, 1888; Cheney, 370; "Death of Miss Alcott," *The Ladies' Home Journal*, Vol. V, No. 6 (May, 1888), 3; Porter, "Recollections of L. M. Alcott," *The New England Magazine*, Vol. VI, No. 1 (March, 1892), 17, 19; Anna Pratt to Alf Whitman, Boston, February 17, [1889?] (Houghton Library).

LOUISA'S LAST ILLNESS AND DEATH: Copy of Louisa's Death Record (Registry Department of Boston); "L. M. Alcott," *Boston Transcript*, March 6, 1888; Louisa's Diary for 1888 (Orchard House); "L. M. Alcott," *The Evening Post*, Vol. LXXXVII (March 6, 1888), 1; Cheney, 370–71; "Death of Miss Alcott," *The Ladies' Home Journal*, Vol. V, No. 6 (May, 1888), 3; "Father and Daughter. Last Tributes," *Boston Post*, March 7, 1888; A. Howard, *Mary Mapes Dodge of St. Nicholas* (New York, 1943), 182; Porter, "Recollections of L. M. Alcott," *The New England Magazine*, Vol. VI, No. 1 (March, 1892), 19; Anna Pratt to Laura Hosmer, [March 6, 1888]; Anna Pratt to Alf Whitman, Boston, February 17, [1889?] (Houghton Library).

INDEX

N indicates a reference to Notes on Sources, B indicates the Bibliography.

Alcott House, Ham Common, Surrey,
England: 24
Alcox [Alcott], Anna Bronson: 5, 78
Alcox [Alcott], Joseph Chatfield: 5
Aldrich, Thomas Bailey: 286
Alexis, Grand Duke of Russia: 219, N 390
Alger, William Rounseville: 174
Allen, E. L.: 192
Almy, Lillie: 175
Amateur Dramatic Company, Walpole,
N.H.: 73–74, 78, 81, 148, 222
*American Literary Gazette and Publishers'
Circular:* 175–76
Anderson, Elizabeth Garrett: 157
Appomattox, Va.: 142f
Apthorp, Robert E.: 67
Armory Square Hospital, Washington,
D.C.: 112, 114–15
Arnold, Matthew: 297
Arthur's Illustrated Home Magazine: 180
Art Students' League, N.Y.: 244
Atherton, Danforth: 230ff
Atlantic Monthly, The: 89, 92ff, 100f, 107,
120, 131, 133, 200, 260, 275, 286,
298
Aubrey House, Kensington, London:
156f, 160, 212, N 384–5
Auerbach, Berthold: 187
"Aunt Jo" (L. M. Alcott): 218, 224, 256,
262, 271–72, 284, 290, 292, 300,
309, 328
"Aunt Louise" (L. M. Alcott): 167f
"Aunt Sue's Puzzle Drawer," *Merry's
Museum:* 167
"Aunt Sue's Scrap-Bag," *Merry's
Museum:* 167
"Aunt Wee" (L. M. Alcott): 165
Austin, Jane Goodwin: 163, 175; *Cipher,*
175; *Outpost,* 175; *The Tailor Boy,* 175

Ball, Thomas: 204
Bane, Robert: 118ff, 124, 130, 132, 134,
287
Barbauld, Anna Letitia: 17, 259
"Barnard, A. M." (pseudonym of L. M.
Alcott): 141f, 162, 164f, 168, 170,
186, 231, 257f, 292, 317, 321, 328
Barnard, Charles Francis: 108
Barrett, Emma: 271
Barron, Nancy: 18
Barrow, Julia: 75f

Barry, Thomas: 75, 76f, 85
Bartlett, Alice: 192ff, 203f, 206, 210f
Bartlett, George B.: 80, 81f, 87, 135,
163, 175
Bartlett, Josiah: 85, 128
Bartlett, Samuel Ripley: 109
Bartol, Cyrus Augustus: 329
Bath Hotel, N.Y.: 238f, 242f, 246f, 257,
N 392
Beach, Meribah: 3, 9–10
Beecher, Henry Ward: 212, 222, 224,
250–51, 319, N 394
Beecher-Tilton scandal: 233
Bellerive School, Vevey: 150, 201; *see also*
Sillig School
Bellevue Hotel, Boston: 181–83, 232,
238, 257f, 267–68, 281f, 293–95, 300
Bellows, Henry Whitney: 75, 245–46,
N 393
Bergh, Henry: 250
Bex, Switzerland: 199, 214, 221, N 388
Biebrich, Germany: 146
Bigot, Mary Healy: 206; *A Summer's
Romance,* 206
Blanchard, Helen: 323
Blind, Mathilde: 157
Bliss, Ariadne: 9, 231
Blitz, Antonio: 3f, 17
Bodichon, Barbara Leigh Smith: 157
Bok, Edward: 288f, 327, N 399
Bond, Louisa Greenwood: 278, 319,
326, 329
Bonner, Robert: 168
Booth, Edwin T.: 60, 77, 242
Booth, John Wilkes: 142
Booth, Junius Brutus: 60
Booth, Mary L.: 246; *History of the City
of New York,* 246
Boston, Mass.: 14, 19, 28, 37, 39, 57ff,
65, 68f, 72–73, 74f, 77f, 80, 85, 87,
89ff, 100f, 104f, 107f, 127, 135f,
137, 140ff, 143f, 147, 156, 160,
163ff, 174, 181, 184f, 188f, 204ff,
213, 217f, 219, 223, 226ff, 232f,
235, 242, 244ff, 250f, 257, 260,
267–68, 272, 275ff, 281, 283f, 286,
293f, 295, 297, 300, 305, 307, 309,
317, 321, 326, 328, 331; fire in, 222,
N 390–91; 250th anniversary, 284
Boston Daily Evening Transcript: 70, 96,
133, 197, 280

MADELEINE B. STERN is partner in the New York rare-book firm of Leona Rostenberg & Madeleine Stern. She is also the author of numerous biographies and books on feminism and publishing history, among them *The Life of Margaret Fuller* and *Purple Passages: The Life of Mrs. Frank Leslie*. She has edited or co-edited six volumes of Alcott's sensation fiction. With Leona Rostenberg, she has authored five books, including *Old & Rare: Early Years in the Book Business*. Madeleine Stern and Leona Rostenberg are currently writing their joint biography.

ABOUT THE TYPE

The text of this book was set in Janson, a misnamed typeface
designed in about 1690 by Nicholas Kis, a Hungarian in Amster-
dam. In 1919 the matrices became the property of the Stempel
Foudry in Frankfurt. It is an old-style book face of excellent clar-
ity and sharpness. Janson serifs are concave and splayed; the contrast between thick and thin strokes is marked.